Foundation Photoshop

Colin Smith
Al Ward
Vicki Loader
Marilène Oliver
Sham Bhangal

friendsof
DESIGNER TO DESIGNER™

Foundation Photoshop 6

© 2001 friends of ED

Trademark Acknowledgements

Published by friends of ED

30 Lincoln Road, Olton, Birmingham.
B27 6PA. UK.
Printed in USA

ISBN 1-903450-66-7

Foundation Photoshop 6

Credits

Authors
Colin Smith
Al Ward
Vicki Loader
Marilène Oliver
Sham Bhangal

Content Architect
Julia Gilbert

Editors
Luke Harvey
Libby Hayward
Adam Juniper
Dan Squier

Graphic Editors
Chantal Hepworth
Deb Murray
David Spurgeon

Technical Reviewers
Jan Badger
Rowan Dodds
John Flanagan
Denis E. Graham
Bill Perry
Martin White

Index
Simon Collins

Cover Design
Katy Freer

Author Agent
Sophie Edwards

Project Administrators
Jennifer Harvey
Thomas Stiff

Proof Readers
Julie Closs
Simon Collins
Joanna Farmer
Jim Hannah
Luke Harvey
Libby Hayward
Mel Jehs
Matthew Knight
Keith Small
Thomas Stiff

Book Concept
Simon Gurney

Production Manager
Tom Bartlett

Team Leader
Joanna Farmer

Colin Smith

Colin Smith is an award winning Graphic Designer who has caused a stir in the design community with his stunning photorealistic illustrations composed entirely in Photoshop. He is also founder of the popular PhotoshopCAFE web resource for Photoshop users and web designers. His images have been featured on the National Association Of Photoshop Professionals web site. He has won numerous design contests and awards, including the Guru Award at the 2001 Photoshop World Convention in LA. Colin's work has been recognized by Photoshop User, Mac Design, Dynamic Graphics, and WWW Internet Life magazines. Colin is listed in the International Who's Who of Professional Management, and is is an active member of the National Association Of Photoshop Professionals (NAPP). He also moderates the forum for the web portal Planet Photoshop.

Al Ward

A certified Photoshop Addict and Webmaster of Action FX Photoshop Resources (www.actionfx.com) hails from Missoula, Montana. A former submariner in the U.S. Navy, Al now spends his time creating add-on software for Photoshop and writing on graphics related topics. Al has been a contributor to Photoshop User Magazine, a contributing writer for 'Inside Photoshop 6' from New Riders Publishing, and writes for several Photoshop related web sites.

In his time off he enjoys his church, his family, fishing the great Northwestern United States, and scouring the Web for Photoshop related topics.

Vicki Loader   www.vickiloader.com

Vicki is passionate about sunshine and sea, the moon, Cava, champagne cocktails, foreign movies, music, tapas bars, and technology. Working as a freelance trainer for more years than she is willing to admit, Vicki is currently living in the UK, where in an attempt to finance these passions, she provides training either directly to private companies or through a select number of high-profile London-based training concerns. In her limited spare time, she struggles to maintain a web site which functions as an ongoing training site by providing trainees with links to training resources.

Marilène Oliver MA RCA   http://www.marilène.co.uk

Born in Essex, England in 1977. Studied Fine Art Printmaking and Photomedia at Central Saint Martins School of Art and Design, London before going on to do an MA in Fine Art Printmaking at the Royal College of Art, London.

She is now working as fine artist, her work seeks to address how new technologies such as medical imaging and electronic communication systems are affecting the intimate and sensual body. She has exhibited with Beaux Arts gallery, London and is currently working towards a number of exhibitions including a solo show of her sculptural works that reconstruct digitally preserved bodies such as the Virtual Human and the Virtual Mummy.

Sham Bhangal

Sham Bhangal originally started out as an engineer, specializing in industrial computer based display and control systems. His spare time was partly taken up by freelance web design, something that slowly took up more and more of his time until the engineering had to go. He is now also writing for friends of ED, something that is taking more and more time away from web design...funny how life repeats itself! Sham lives in Devon, England, with his partner Karen.

Foundation Photoshop 6

3 ## Selection   75

4 **Paths** **133**

5 **Basic Layers** **185**

6   Color and Printing   255

7   Graphic Elements for the Web   291

8 Image Correction 333

Welcome

Welcome to Foundation Photoshop 6

Photoshop is a powerful instrument in any designer's toolkit, whether they're preparing images for print or for the Web. It allows you to manipulate photographic images without spending hours in a darkroom or getting your hands dirty with chemicals. It speeds up the process of resizing, cropping, and color correction. And, as you will discover in this book, it can even automate these processes, streamlining the most boring aspects of production work.

Using Photoshop's impressive array of painting tools, you can also create images from scratch, and it allows you to generate great effects and textures that add depth to your work. Photoshop's little brother, ImageReady, will allow you to optimize images for the Web, and to create effective rollovers and animations.

The aim of this book

This book will teach you Photoshop from the very beginning, to a level at which you'll feel comfortable creating and manipulating a wide variety of artwork for print, for the Web, and for use with other applications (for example Flash and Director). Accompanied by professional designers, you will take a journey through the essential tools and techniques that Photoshop and ImageReady have to offer, and learn a few of their secrets along the way.

Each chapter contains step-by-step practical examples for you to work through, and there's a real world case study that runs in instalments from Chapters 3 to 11. In the case study you'll learn how to build a fully functioning web site along with printed advertisements.

If you've used earlier versions of Photoshop then you'll discover the added features of this latest version, which has introduced improved vector support, expanded web tools (including a Slice tool), editable text layers, a context-sensitive options bar, a new layer interface, and annotations.

▶

PCs and Macs

This book is for both PC and Mac users. We've stuck with each author's chosen system and also provided instructions for the alternative system.

Just as a quick reference, here are the main differences:

PC	Mac
Right-click	CTRL-click
CTRL	COMMAND
ALT	OPTION

What you'll need to know

No prior knowledge of Photoshop is required, but if you *are* familiar with older versions, or you want to refresh your knowledge, then you'll certainly find this book useful too.

You *will* need to be comfortable with either the Windows or Mac operating systems and know how to create folders, rename files, etc. You will also need a basic knowledge of using the Internet.

Conventions

We've tried to keep this book as clear and easy to follow as possible, so we've only used a few layout styles:

- When you come across an important word or phrase, it will be in **bold** type.

- We'll use a different font to emphasize phrases that appear on the screen, code and filenames.

- Menu commands are written in the form Menu > Sub-menu > Sub-menu.

- Keyboard shortcuts appear like this: select the Magic Wand tool (w)

- When there's some information we think is really important, we'll highlight it like this:

> *This is very important stuff - don't skip it!*

Worked exercises are laid out like this:

Exercise heading

1. Open the file `start.psd`

2. Do something

3. Save your file as `finish.psd`

and so on.

Files for download

You will need to download the source files required to complete the exercises from our web site: www.friendsofed.com, or you can use similar images of your own.

Support

If you have any questions about the book or about friends of ED, check out our web site www.friendsofed.com. There's a range of contact details there, or you can use feedback@friendsofed.com.

There's a host of other features on the site: interviews with top designers, samples from our other books, and a message board where you can post your questions, discussions and answers, or just take a back seat and look at what other designers are talking about. If you have any comments or problems, please write to us - we'd love to hear from you.

1 Introducing Photoshop

In this chapter we will cover:

- *A brief history of Photoshop*

- *How to get started*

- *The basic Photoshop interface*

- *Managing palette windows*

- *Navigating images*

- *Using the Navigator palette*

- *Saving options*

The history of Photoshop

Photoshop has come a long way, rising from relatively humble beginnings, to become the industry-standard graphics-editing package. Along the way the program has evolved, responding to the needs of the print and design communities, perhaps this is what makes it such an intuitive tool. In this chapter, we will look at the basics needed to get to grips with Photoshop 6, and introduce you to its interface. First, though, we'll consider the evolution of the program, and see what makes it an essential tool for all designers, photographers, and artists.

Photoshop grew out of a collaboration between two brothers, Thomas and John Knoll. In 1987, Thomas was working on a programming project to get black and white bitmap monitors to display grayscale images. John was working at the Industrial Light and Magic movie company, experimenting with computers to create special effects for films. Learning of each other's work, they decided to work together to develop a program that could manipulate bitmap images on the computer.

After two years of modifying the program, Photoshop 0.87 was released as an accompanying CD for Barneyscan scanners under the name of Barneyscan XP. At this stage, Photoshop was able to read and write various file formats, process image routines (which later became filter plug-ins), create selections, adjust tones, color balance, hue/saturation, and offered the capability to paint. Soon after, Adobe bought the right to license and distribute Photoshop, and version 1.0 was released in early 1990.

Since then there have been numerous newer, bigger, and better versions of Photoshop, which have been propelled by the demands of desktop publishing, commercial printing, and the World Wide Web. Let's run through the major changes now:

- In June 1991, Photoshop 2 brought with it a rasterizer for vector based images, support for CMYK color, duotones, and a pen tool for creating paths. This meant that users could handle their own color separations, which soon revolutionised desktop publishing, and the printing industries.

- Photoshop 2.5, released in November 1992, was the first Windows version. It also introduced palettes.
- 1993 saw version 3. and the advent of layers.

- A new Adobe standard interface was introduced with version 4 in 1996, along with grids and guides and the free transform feature.

- Version 5 and the History palette arrived in 1998.

- By 1999, the increasing presence of the World Wide Web encouraged Adobe to expand its web capabilities, and Photoshop 5.5 was released, with an integrated program, ImageReady, which allowed users to prepare and save images for the Web.

- The latest version, Photoshop 6, brings with it increased vector support, new web tools, a context-sensitive options bar, a new layer interface and annotations.

Workflows and context

As we have seen, Photoshop has evolved to cater for a variety of users, but most significantly for the needs of desktop publishers and web designers. Aside from these two main areas, Photoshop is also used to prepare images for Interactive multimedia such as CD ROMs, animations, and 3D design. It is where the ingredients for any digital artwork or design work are prepared. Sometimes it is used for seemingly non-digital work; recently in my own work as an artist, I have used Photoshop to prepare images to be screen printed on to sheets of clear acrylic, which were then assembled as a sculpture.

The flow chart shows the most common uses of Photoshop. Everything above the center line represents ways of importing images into the program, and everything below shows the destination of the final work. This should give you some idea of the program's versatility. You are probably keen to get on with some practical work. So let's go!

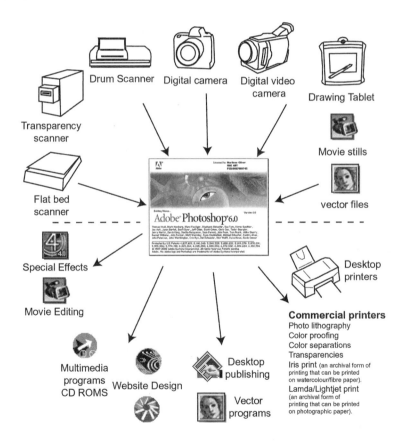

Drum Scanner Digital camera Digital video camera

Drawing Tablet

Transparency scanner

Movie stills

Flat bed scanner

vector files

Adobe Photoshop 6.0

Special Effects

Desktop printers

Movie Editing

Commercial printers
Photo lithography
Color proofing
Color separations
Transparencies
Iris print (an archival form of printing that can be printed on watercolour/fibre paper).
Lamda/Lightjet print (an archival form of printing that can be printed on photographic paper).

Multimedia programs CD ROMS

Website Design

Desktop publishing

Vector programs

Getting started

To start working in Photoshop we first need an image to work with. As the flow chart shows, there are many ways of sourcing images to use in Photoshop. It is possible, however, to create one from scratch, by starting with a fresh document that contains no image, and then creating one using the various brushes and paint tools explained in Chapter 2. Let's break ourselves in gently, by learning how to open a file.

Opening a new document

1. Move your cursor over File to the right of the menu bar, at the top of the program window. Click once and the File menu will appear. At the top of the menu you will see New. You will notice that next to New on the File menu there is COMMAND +N (Mac OS) or CTRL + N (Windows). This is a shortcut that saves having to go through the File menu to open a new file. You can also press CTRL and double-click to open a new file in Windows. As we proceed through this book, you will become more familiar with these shortcuts.

2. The New window will be launched. As you can see, there are many options.

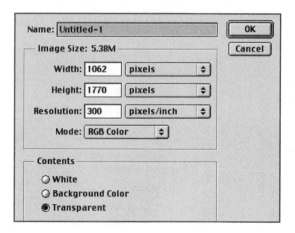

3. First you must select the size you want. Do this by keying your desired sizes in to the boxes next to Width and Height. If you click on the bar to the right of these boxes (Mac users: keep the mouse down) you will see some options of units.

✔ **pixels**
inches
cm
points
picas

    The units that are most commonly used are pixels, inches and centimetres Pixel is short for picture element. It is a square of color that works with many other squares of different colors to make an image. For now we will work with what we know, so let us make a document that will fit on an A4 portrait sheet. Key in 7 inches into the Width box and 10 inches into the Height box.

4. The next option is Resolution or dpi (dots per inch). This is how much information or how many pixels are contained in one square inch of your image. The higher the resolution/dpi, the bigger the file size. You may need a high resolution if you wanted to make a high quality print from your file or enlarge it at a later stage. For commercial printing the average resolution is 300dpi. If you are working for the Web, the resolution doesn't need to be very high as the image will only be seen on screen and monitors can't display more than 72dpi. Web work, therefore, should always be at 72dpi. For now, so that we can work quickly, we will work at 200dpi, so key in 200 next to Resolution.

5. Now let's look at the Mode options. This decides whether your image will be in color or black and white. The black and white options are Bitmap and Grayscale. The Bitmap option produces an image made up only of black and white. Grayscale however, as the name suggests, is made up of shades of grays ranging from black to white. The color options are RGB (images made up of red, green and blue), CMYK (images made up of cyan, magenta, yellow and black, and traditionally used for print work), and Lab Color.

> RGB *are additive colors, as they combine to produce white. This mode is used to display color on monitors.* CMYK *are subtractive colors used for four-color printing. When deciding which color option to use, it is important to think of your output. If you are making images for the Web, select* RGB, *as some browsers don't support* CMYK *images. If you are getting something commercially printed, check how the printer prefers your image before you start work, as to change mode at the end will affect how the colors look.*

6. Choose RGB.

Finally, under the Contents section you can change the color of the document, rather like a painter choosing the color of their canvas. You can either select white, a background color that you would already have selected, or transparent. If you choose transparent it will open a document with a gray and white check. This is not part of your image but signifies that an area is transparent. If you decide that you do not like the check, it is possible to change it later, by going into the Preferences menu. (Edit > Preferences > Transparency & Gamut.

7. Before clicking OK, it is possible to give the document a name. If you don't do this, the document will be called Untitled until you do decide to call it something. Let's call this Tabula Rasa by typing this in to the name box at the top of the window. Now that all the options have been selected, click on the OK button or press return on your keyboard.

8. You should now have a lovely Tabula Rasa (clean slate), to work on!

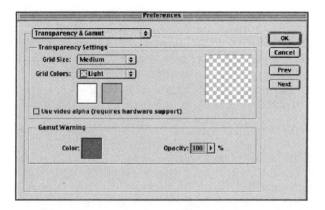

Before continuing with our document, we shall first learn how to open some other images that may have been sourced in ways shown in the flow chart. Scanned images or captured digital photos can be directly imported into Photoshop 6 by going to the File menu and then Import. If you have scanning or capturing software on your machine it will be listed in the Import submenu. In the example on the next page, the scanner is an Agfa ScanWise, which you can see at the top of the Import submenu.

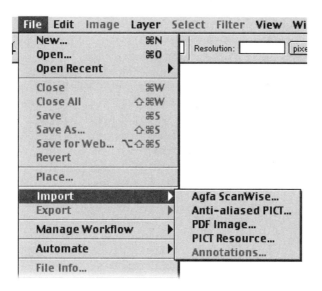

Most scanning software gives scanning options. These include scale, mode, and resolution. They usually offer screen options too, and it is good to be aware of the significance of this. Images from magazines and books will have been printed with a 'screen' on them that will show up and look ugly when scanned into Photoshop. Many scanning packages offer a de-screen mode that gets rid of this pattern for you. It is worth taking time to learn about your scanning software if you plan to scan printed images. Indeed, you will need to practise scanning various images to get the effects you want, as there are many options to choose from when scanning in different media. Experiment a little to see the cool effects you can create.

Opening a file

1. Go to File and in the menu below New you will see Open (COMMAND+ O/ CTRL + O). Click on this.

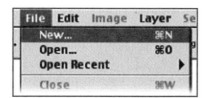

2. The Open window will be launched. Navigate to find the image you want to open. In our example, we have opened shrine.psd, which can be downloaded from the friends of ED web site at www.friendsofed. com/code.html

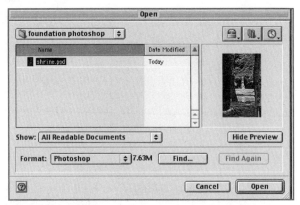

Yet again this window has many options. You can ask the window to display just certain file types, to show a thumbnail of the image you have selected, and to open the image in different ways using the Format options. The Find button is a useful tool for browsing for a document.

This is an example of how the Open window options will appear on a Mac. Naturally, it will appear slightly differently for Windows users. The main options are the same, you can select the file formats to be displayed in the Files of Type field, and you can choose whether to see thumbnails of the images by going to the View Menu icon, in the top right hand corner. To select different ways of opening the document you need to go to File > Open As…

3. We want to open this image as a Photoshop document so highlight shrine.psd and click on Open or press ENTER/RETURN.

   You should now see shrine.psd open on your screen.

Opening an EPS, PDF or Illustrator file

A **vector** image is an image made up of mathematical points that come together to make lines and shapes. A **bitmap** however is a grid of blocks of information, like little dots; these are known as pixels. Photoshop is a bitmap program, so for Photoshop to open an image created in a vector program (such as Illustrator), it has to convert it to a grid and calculate where the lines/shapes go on the grid. This process is called **rasterizing**.

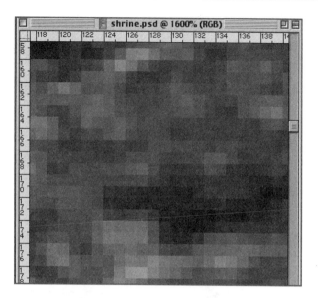

For these next few steps, you will need to either use an Illustrator (.ai) file of your own, or download the homebutton.ai file from the friends of ED web site.

1. Go to File and Open (COMMAND O/CTRL O) homebutton.ai. Click Open.

2. A new pop-up window will appear. Again it allows you to decide the size, resolution and mode of the image. The image provided for you is one that is destined to become a button for a web site, so make the width 100 pixels and height 100 pixels, and opt for a resolution of 72dpi. Make the mode RGB.

3. You will see two other boxes at the bottom of the window. The first asks if you want the image to be Anti-aliased. **Anti-aliasing** helps prevent the jagged edges that often appear when rasterizing an image. If you have a low resolution, these jagged edges may still appear, as there aren't enough pixels to make the line look smooth. The second box, Constrain Proportions keeps the proportions of width and height the same as they were in the original program. Check both of these boxes.

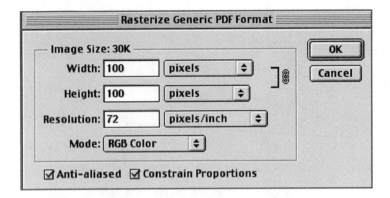

4. Click OK and Photoshop will now rasterize the file.

Just as an experiment, try opening the file without checking the Anti-aliased box, and you will notice that when you zoom in to the image the edges are rather more jagged.

The image on the left is the homebutton.ai with anti-aliasing, the image on the right shows the same image with no anti-aliasing.

Basic interface

Photoshop's interface consists of a menu bar, a Toolbox, an Options bar and a number of floating palettes. Photoshop 6 has introduced some changes to the interface that has made it more manageable and less cluttered. If you have a small monitor, however, it can easily get overcrowded. Many designers and artists like to use two monitors: one for the image and one for all the floating palettes. To set up your computer to display on multiple monitors you need two video cards; make sure that your system can support them. To find out more about using multiple monitors visit:

MAC OS   http://www.lowendmac.com/macdan/2k1025cl.html
WINDOWS   http://support.microsoft.com/directory/article.asp?ID=KB;EN-US;Q238886

The Toolbox

The **Toolbox** is the long window on the left hand side of the screen. If you can't see it on your desktop go to Window > Show Tools. To choose a tool, click on the icon or use the shortcuts, shown below next to their respective tools. For example, to select the Paintbrush tool, press SHIFT + B. To select the Rectangular Marquee tool, press SHIFT + M.

If you are ever unsure of what a tool does or what its shortcut is, let the mouse hover over the icon and a box will appear with a tool description.

You will notice that some of the icons have a little arrow in the bottom right corner. This signifies that when the icon is held down, you can access more related tools.

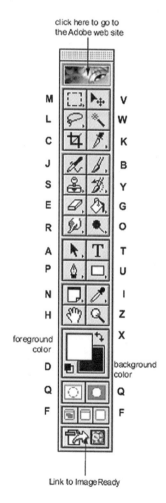

click here to go to the Adobe web site

foreground color

background color

Link to ImageReady

To access these related tools, click and hold on the tool button until a menu, like the ones here, pops up. If it all seems a little complex at the moment, don't worry. The rest of the book will introduce all of the tools one at a time, so you will have time to get to know them.

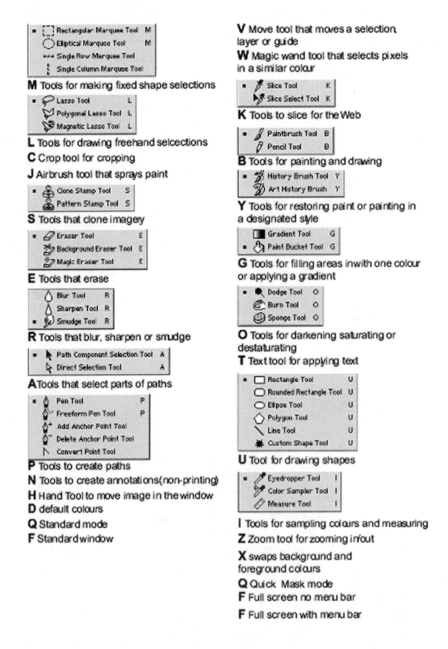

M Tools for making fixed shape selections

L Tools for drawing freehand selections

C Crop tool for cropping

J Airbrush tool that sprays paint

S Tools that clone imagery

E Tools that erase

R Tools that blur, sharpen or smudge

A Tools that select parts of paths

P Tools to create paths

N Tools to create annotations (non-printing)

H Hand Tool to move image in the window

D default colours

Q Standard mode

F Standard window

V Move tool that moves a selection, layer or guide

W Magic wand tool that selects pixels in a similar colour

K Tools to slice for the Web

B Tools for painting and drawing

Y Tools for restoring paint or painting in a designated style

G Tools for filling areas in with one colour or applying a gradient

O Tools for darkening saturating or destaturating

T Text tool for applying text

U Tool for drawing shapes

I Tools for sampling colours and measuring

Z Zoom tool for zooming in/out

X swaps background and foreground colours

Q Quick Mask mode

F Full screen no menu bar

F Full screen with menu bar

The Options bar

Each of the tools can be modified using the Options bar that is at the top of your screen under the menu bar. If you cannot see the Options bar, go to Window > Show Options. Select some of the different tools in the toolbox to see how the Options bar changes. Each tool has a number of different settings, in the Options bar for the Paintbrush for example, you can select the size and look of your brush, the Mode of the brush and its Opacity.

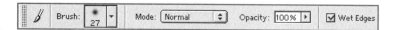

Click on a few of the tools yourself and notice how the tool options bar changes.

The image window

The image window tells us a lot about the image it contains: the name of the file, the mode, the size, the view percentage, Scratch sizes, Efficiency, Timing, the current tool, and even how it fits onto a sheet of paper (to see this information click on the triangle at the bottom left of the image window). Try opening up different files to see how the Image window changes depending on the image it contains.

Palettes

Photoshop 6 has twelve different palettes in the form of floating windows that allow you to work easily with navigation, colors and patterns (known as swatches/styles), the history of your commands and actions, layers, channels, paths, and text. To help with screen space, Photoshop organizes the palettes into default groups but the palettes can be separated and regrouped to suit you. To open the palettes, go to Window and you will see a list of palettes. To open or close all the palettes, press TAB on your keyboard (if you want to open or close all of the palettes except the toolbox press SHIFT+TAB). Many of the palettes have extra options that can be accessed through the little arrow in the top right of the palette window. Some of the palettes can also be resized by dragging the bottom right hand corner. Again, don't worry that you don't know what each palette does. Just practice moving them around and get a feel for them. You'll find out their function as you work through the book.

The Info palette

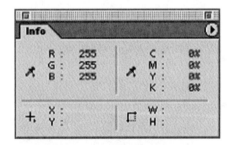

The Color palette

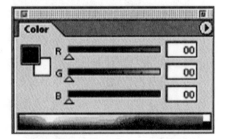

The History palette

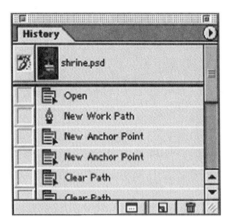

Managing the palettes

Through the Window menu, open a few of the different palettes. Depending on how the palettes were organized last time they were open they will either be grouped or separated. Try separating a group of palettes by pressing down on the name of the palette (in the top left hand corner) and dragging it away from the group.

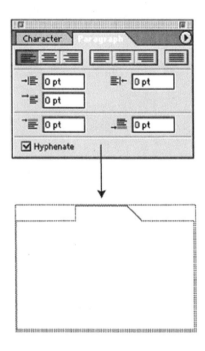

Similarly, if the palettes are separated try grouping them by dragging one palette onto another. To make a palette in a group active, click on its name tab.

1. Open the Styles palette. Drag the bottom right hand corner in or out to resize the window. Make the palette shrink or expand by clicking its minimize/maximize button in the top right hand corner.

2. Click on the arrow in the top right hand corner that signifies more options for the palette. Select Large Thumbnail and then Text Only to see how the palette changes.

3. Close the Styles palette by clicking the close button in the top left hand corner of the palette.

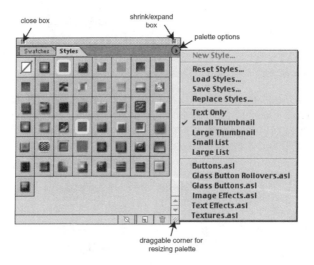

Menus

Photoshop's menu bar contains nine different menus: File, Edit, Image, Layer, Select, Filter, View, Window, and Help. We should already be familiar with the File and the Window menus. As you will have seen, different actions and commands are organized into different menus and submenus (to access a submenu follow the arrow that signifies its presence). If an option is grayed out, then this means that it is not available with the current selection or image.

The File menu is where files are opened, closed, saved, and printed. It is also where you exit Photoshop.

The Edit menu is where you can copy, cut, paste and transform images. It is also where the Preferences are accessed. The Transform submenu allows you to rotate, distort or change the scale of a selected area or image.

The Image menu allows mode changes, color adjustments, and size alterations to be made.

The Layer menu is where layers are managed. Layers can be added, deleted or filled. You will learn more about layers in Chapter 5.

The Select menu is where you manage your selections. More about selections in Chapter 3.

The Filter menu is where all the filters (special effects) are kept. You will learn more about the different filters in Chapter 9.

The View menu is where you can change the way your image is displayed. You will learn more about the View menu later in this chapter.

As you've already seen, the Window menu is where the different palettes are accessed.

The Help menu is where you go for help, and a variety of Internet links.

Navigating images

The View menu, the Navigation palette and the toolbox all offer us various ways to view our image. It is possible to see the whole image, part of the image close up, or the size of the image as it will appear once printed by going to Window > Print Size, or View > Print Size for Windows users. You can also see how it will look on the Web: Window > Actual Pixels, or View > Actual Pixels for Windows users.

This section should help you understand more clearly the issues of resolution and dpi. If you open shrine.psd and ask to see it at its print size it will probably fit on the screen. Ask to see it at its pixel size and it will become much larger. As explained earlier, monitors only display 72 pixels per inch but the resolution of shrine.psd is 200dpi. When you ask to see shrine.psd at its print size, it will not show all the information/pixels but when you ask to see the Actual Pixels, the pixels will be spread over the screen so the image appears much larger. When you are working on an image you will no doubt be zooming in and out.

> *It is good practice to keep viewing the image at* Print Size *if you are working on an image for print or at* Actual Pixels *if you are preparing an image for the Web*

This is `shrine.psd` viewed at Print Size:

Here it is viewed at Actual Pixels:

The View menu

The View menu contains commands that give different view of your image. The View > New View command opens a second window of your image. View > Proof Setup allows you to see the image in different color spaces, on different monitors and in different print modes, which again is useful for you to have a clear idea of how the final image will appear.

View > Gamut Warning allows you to check which colors won't print on a four-color press. It allows you to zoom in (CMD/CTRL+), zoom out (CMD/CTRL-), to make the image fit on the screen (CMD/CTRL 0), to see it at actual pixel size and at print size.

There are submenus in the View menu that display visual aids such as grids, guides and rulers. The View > Show submenu contains the commands for Selection Edges, Target Paths, Grids, Guides, Slices and Annotations. To change the units or colors that the grids and rulers are displayed at, go to Edit > Preferences > Grids & Guides / Units & Rulers.

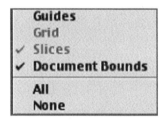

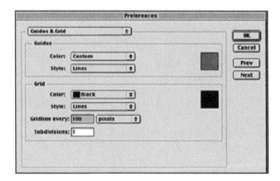

If you select the double arrows to the right of Guides & Grid, you will get a further drop-down menu, and be able to select Units & Rulers.

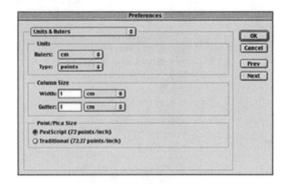

These displays are useful when making selections and there is the option to ask Photoshop to **snap** to a guide or grid (make the cursor/selection automatically cling to the grid or guide). This option is contained in the Snap To submenu.

Zoom and Hand tools

Near the bottom of the toolbox are two navigation tools: the **Zoom** tool, that looks like a magnifying glass and allows you to zoom in and out of the image, and the **Hand** tool, that allows you to move the image around in the window. As these tools are selected, the status bar changes and offers new view options.

Using the Zoom tool

1. Open `shrine.psd`

2. Select the Zoom tool by clicking on the icon in the toolbox (or press Z on your keyboard).

3. As you move the cursor over the image window it changes to a magnifying glass. On the tool options bar, make sure that Resize Windows to Fit is unchecked if you don't want the image window to resize as you zoom in and out. You can either check or uncheck Ignore Palettes, depending on whether you

want the image to fill the whole of the screen or not. Click to zoom in. As you zoom in, look at the title bar of the image window – the view percentage changes as you zoom.

4.   To zoom out again, press ALT or OPTION and you will see that a minus sign appears in the magnifying glass. This means that when you click it will zoom out.

5.   Zoom into a certain area by dragging a marquee with the zoom tool. The area you select will fill the image window.

> *If you want to quickly use the Zoom whilst another tool is selected, then hold* ALT/CTRL + SPACE *to temporarily switch. It will return to the tool you were using when you let go.*

Using the Hand tool

1.   Using either the Zoom tool or the shortcut command (CMD/CTRL+), zoom into the image, so that you only see part of it in the image window.

2.   Select the **Hand** tool by clicking the icon in the toolbox or by pressing H on your keyboard. The icon will change to a hand.

3.   Drag the hand across the image and you will see it move in the window. Alternatively use the scrollbars on the side of the image window.

4.   With the Hand tool still selected, press CMD (Mac) or CTRL (Windows) and you will see that the hand icon changes to the zoom in icon. Press OPTION (Mac) or ALT (Windows) and it will change to the zoom out icon.

5.   Double-click on the Hand tool icon in the toolbar to make the image fit back into the window.

> *If you want to quickly use the Hand tool whilst another tool is selected, then hold down the* SPACE *to temporarily switch.*

The Navigator palette

The Navigator palette gives other ways to zoom in/out, to move your image around and to see where you are in your image.

Using the Navigator palette

1. Make your image fit on the screen by pressing CMD+0 for a Mac, and CTRL+0 for Windows.

2. If it is not already visible, open the Navigator palette by going to Window > Show Navigator.

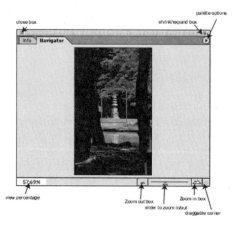

3. Drag the bottom right hand corner of the window until the window is at a size that you are happy working with. Notice that there is a view box around your image in the Navigator window (you can change the color of this box in the Palette Options, which you can find by clicking on the arrow on the top right hand corner of the Navigator palette).

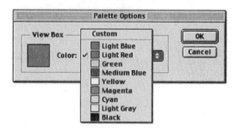

4. Use the Zoom slider or the Zoom in button to zoom into the image. Have a look in the image window and see how it is now magnified. In the Navigator window, the view box is smaller and in the center of the image.

5. Move your cursor over the box and the icon will change to a hand. Drag the box to another part of the image and your image will also move in the image window.

6. At the bottom left of the Navigator window you will see the zoom percentage. Highlight this and you can enter a new precise percentage.

View size shortcuts

Changing the view of the image you are working on will probably be the most common of your commands when you are using Photoshop. Learning the following shortcuts will therefore be very useful and save having to go through menus and change tools.

Command	MACINTOSH	WINDOWS
Zoom in (no window resize)	CMD +	Ctrl +
Zoom out (no window resize)	CMD -	Ctrl -
Zoom in (window resize)	CMD Option +	Ctrl Alt +
Zoom out (window resize)	CMD Option -	Ctrl Alt -
Actual Pixels	CMD Option 0	Ctrl Alt
Fit on screen	CMD 0	Ctrl 0

Screen display modes

When working in Photoshop, we are offered three different ways of viewing the screen. Some people find it distracting to have their desktop in the background or to see the edges of the window box. There are three different screen modes: **Standard**, **Full Screen with Menu Bar** and **Full Screen**. The buttons for the different screen modes are to the bottom of the tool bar.

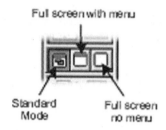

Full screen with menu

Standard Mode

Full screen no menu

Standard Mode displays the toolbox, menu bar, palettes and scroll bars on the image window.

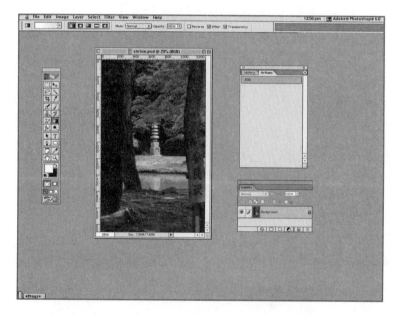

Full Screen with Menu Bars displays the image at full size (therefore no scrollbars) with gray around the image; you can change the background color by Shift-clicking on it with the Paint Bucket tool. This will then set this color as the new foreground color. This mode also displays the toolbox, menu bar and palettes.

Full Screen Mode displays the image at full size with black all around, toolbox and palettes (the menu bar is hidden).

The keyboard shortcut to use in order to toggle between the three screen options, is the F key.

If you want to hide the toolbox and palettes, press TAB. To hide just the palettes press SHIFT+TAB.

Saving files

Photoshop's many saving options are accessed through the File menu. They are Save, Save As, Save a copy and Save for Web. There are many formats which all have different characteristics – some are better for saving images for printing, some are better for saving images with layers, others work cross-platform (work on both Mac OS and Windows) and others are better for the Web. The different formats are explained in the Appendix at the back of the book. It is essential to be aware of the different formats and how you are saving your images, as important information can be lost if you save an image in the wrong way. If you were to save an image that contains layers as a TIFF for example, the layer information would be lost next time you opened the document. A native Photoshop document (.psd) holds onto layers, guides and grids, and color management profiles, as well as channels, saved selections, filter effects, styles and more.

Saving a new file

1. Go to File and then Save As. The Save As window will be launched:

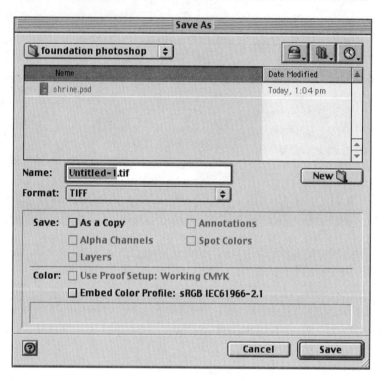

2. Enter a name into the Name box.

3. Navigate to where you want to save your image. It is good practice to be systematic about your saving and save all related work in folders.

4. Select a file format from Format (Mac OS)/Save As (Windows). The pop-up menu will only display the formats that the image can be saved in (this will depend on the image's color mode, and layers).

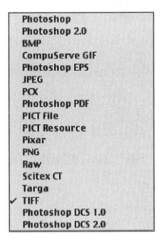

5. Check any of the other saving options you want such as Alpha Channels or Layers. If a format doesn't support an option then the box will be dimmed.

6. Press Save or ENTER/RETURN.

Saving an existing image

Go to File and Save (CMD/CTRL-S). This will automatically save over the last image.

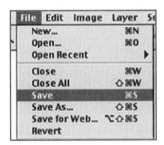

If the image has been changed since the last time it was saved, so that the image can no longer be saved in the same format, the Save As window will be launched. Our document, Tabula Rasa, should still be open on your desktop but it remains unsaved. Save it by activating it (click anywhere on the image window and press (CMD/CTRL-S).

If you want to save a version of your image at a certain state or in a different mode, use the Save As command.

To save a new version of an image

1.   Go to File and Save As (CTRL SHIFT S/ALT SHIFT S).

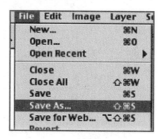

The Save As window will be launched.

2.   The name of the image will be highlighted. Type in a new name, unless you want to replace your original image. If you don't change the name it will save over the original image. Photoshop will confirm you want to do this by asking if you want to replace the image when you click Save. If you chose Cancel, then the Save As window will close, and you will need to navigate the menu again.

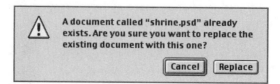

3. Navigate to where you want to save the new version of the image.

4. Choose a Format for the image and check any of the Save option boxes you want.

5. Click Save.

Notice that the name of the image has changed in the title bar. The original image has closed and will have returned to its last saved state.

Save As a Copy

Use Save As a Copy if want to carry on working on your image but also save a copy of it at its present state and/or in a different format.

1. Go to File and Save As.

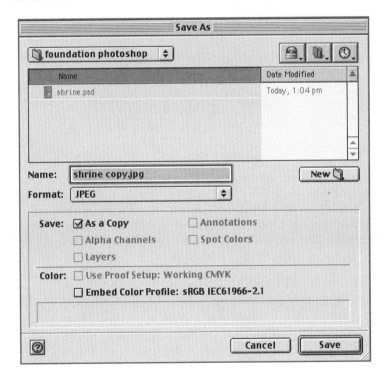

2. Check the As a Copy box. The word copy will appear after the name of your file.

3. Navigate to where you want to save the copy.

4. Select the format and any options you want for the copy.

5. Click Save and you can return to the original image and carry on working.

Revert

If you have been working on a piece, tinkering around with it, tweaking here and there, but have finally decided that you dislike all of your new changes, then this is a beneficial function.

Revert allows you to return to the last saved state of your image. To revert, go to File and Revert.

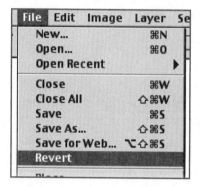

Summary

So, we have now covered the basics of Photoshop. We have looked at the basic interface, the menus, and palettes, and we have covered ways to manage the palette windows. We have also considered various ways in which to navigate our images, and how to use the Navigator palette. Finally we have discussed the various saving options in Photoshop. I'm sure that you are now keen to get started and, armed with a new-found understanding of where things are, you are now at the threshold of your Photoshop adventure, enjoy it!

2 Painting Tools

What we'll cover in this chapter:

- *Sampling Color using the info window, the Color Picker, and the Color and Swatch palettes*

- *Modifying, saving, and loading brushes*

- *Modifying brush opacity and pressure*

- *Fading strokes, wet edges, and auto-erase*

- *Painting tool blending modes*

- *The History palette*

Why paint in Photoshop?

Photoshop: its name firmly places it in the arena of all things photographic, and indeed its primary function is the manipulation of photographic images. However, it would be wrong to underestimate the versatility of the program, although never originally designed to produce natural media effects, it has developed into an excellent tool for producing hand drawn pieces, with authentic painting effects. In this chapter we will discuss how to use the painting tools effectively, focusing on dealing with color, brushes, strokes, blending options, and how to use the snapshot and history states effectively.

Many artists work with Photoshop to create pure, autographic illustrations, but many more use it as a means to combine photographic and autographic imagery. Stephen Walter's *New Parliament* is a good example of this. Stephen Walter makes work that comments on the urban landscape. In *New Parliament* he has added expressive, painterly marks to a scanned image of The Houses of Parliament in London using Photoshop's paint and color tools.

Photoshop has a number of different tools to simulate painting and drawing effects, all with many options that help create subtle and realistic painting effects. Some people find obtaining accuracy using paint tools difficult when using a regular mouse, but now, with the price of graphics tablets dropping, it is possible to make accurate marks and create sensitive drawings. These tablets give much more control to the artist as the stroke varies according to the pressure of the artist's pen. I personally have become addicted to my graphics tablet and now use it in all applications. If you plan to work a lot in Photoshop, I highly recommend the investment. There are many different kinds of drawing tablets available on the market. The most widely used and most reasonably priced tablet is made by Wacom (at the time of writing r.r.p. is $99.99). Not only is it USB, but it also comes in lots of lovely colors! To find out more about Wacom's tablets, visit their web site http://www.wacom.com

In this chapter we will work with `shrine.psd`. If you have not already downloaded this from the friends of ED web site then do so now, by going to http://www.friendsofed.com/code.html. We will also use a file created in the last chapter, `Tabula Rasa.psd` to explore the different tools and learn more about the use of color in Photoshop. Our Tabula Rasa, (or blank slate), will soon contain a masterpiece inspired by a Japanese shrine!

Sampling colors

There are many different ways to select and work with colors in Photoshop which we will learn about in this section. First, we will learn how to use the Eyedropper tool to sample and learn about the colors in shrine.psd.

Using the Eyedropper tool

1. Open shrine.psd

2. Select the Eyedropper tool from the toolbox or press I on your keyboard.

   The cursor will change to an eyedropper icon as you move it over the image.

3. Drag or click the cursor on different parts of the image. Notice how the foreground color in the toolbox changes.

4. In the *Eyedropper* options bar, located at the top of the interface, it is possible to change the area that the Eyedropper samples by changing the Sample Size. Point Sample selects the exact pixel that is clicked on, 3 by 3 Average makes an average of the colors in a 3 x 3 pixels square and 5 by 5 Average, an average of the colors in a 5 x 5 pixels square. These alternate options can be very useful when trying to pick the basic color of an area that is filled with noisy texture.

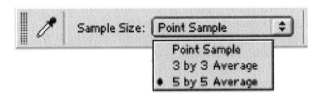

   You can use the colors that you have picked in the rest of your project, for instance to fill in gaps or to replace color.

Info palette

Open the Info palette (Window > Show Info). Move the palette so that the Image window, toolbox and Info palette can be seen at the same time.

As you move the cursor over the image, notice how the values in the Info palette change.

The Info palette tells us about the pixel currently under the cursor. It shows us the position of the pixel, and two sets of mode values, in this case, the RGB and CMYK values, but this is dependent on the color mode of the individual image.

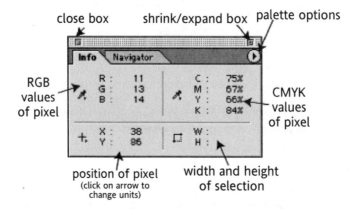

As we learnt in Chapter 1, RGB and CMYK are different color modes. **RGB** (red, green and blue) are additive colors (they combine to produce white) and are used to display color on monitors. **CMYK** (cyan, magenta, yellow and black) are subtractive colors used for four-color printing.

Not all the colors seen on a monitor can be printed, and not all the colors that can be printed can be seen on the monitor. Also, the colors of a **CMYK** image can only be simulated as all monitors work with **RGB** light. Not only do monitors not display true **CMYK** colors, but also, different monitors will display the same image differently due to monitor temperature, calibration and the surrounding light.

The Info palette, therefore, is very important if you want accurate color matching when printing an image. The Info palette tells us the precise RGB values and CMYK values of the color in an image and warns if there are colors in the image that won't print on a four-color press by putting an exclamation mark next to the CMYK values. Try moving the cursor over the trees in the top right hand corner of shrine.psd to see this warning. If you convert the image from RGB to CMYK then these exclamation marks will disappear.

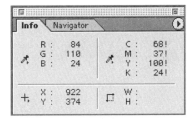

The size of a selection can also be seen in the Info palette, next to **W** (width) and **H** (height) in the bottom right of the palette. To change the units that the dimensions are displayed in go to the palette options. You can access the Info Options window by clicking on the arrow in the top right hand corner and going to Palette Options. This will allow you to select other Mode values such as Grayscale and Web Color. The Web Color option is useful as it shows you the hexadecimal code of a color. If, for example, our shrine image was to become an important part of a web site, we could pick color from it and use that color for other features in the site such as background color or text color.

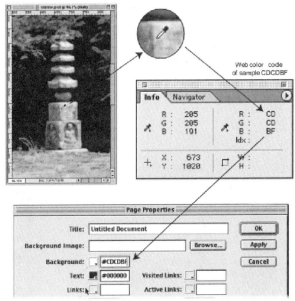

Page Property options from a Web design program with sampled values entered

Foreground and background colors

At the bottom of the toolbox are the Set foreground color, and Set background color boxes. The *foreground color* is the color that your paint tools paint in; the *background* style is the color that it erases to, when on the background layer. If you are using multiple layers, matters are slightly more complicated, but we'll cross that bridge when we come to it (in Chapter 5).

The ***background*** and ***foreground*** colors can be switched over by clicking the Switch Color icon in the top right hand corner above the boxes, or by using the shortcut key; x. To default back to white as the foreground color and black as the background color, click the Default Colors icon below the foreground and background color squares, or use the keyboard shortcut, D.

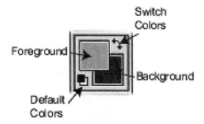

We have already seen that the Eyedropper tool can select foreground colors (for the Eyedropper to select background colors, press ALT/OPTION as you click). Other ways to select colors are using the Color Picker, the Color palette or the Swatches palette; we will discuss these three methods now.

Using the Color Picker

1. Open the Color Picker by clicking on either the Foreground or the Background squares.

2. The Color Picker window will be launched.

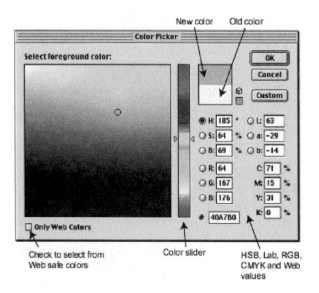

3. Pick a hue by moving the slider on the vertical color slider.

4. Pick an exact shade of the color from the box.

5. Notice how the box to the right of the color slider displays the old color and the new color that you have selected. If you were to click on the old color then it would restore the settings of the new color to those of the old.

6. If the color selected is one that won't print, then a gamut warning will appear in the form of a small box of color and a warning sign icon.

7. If you click on this, Photoshop will select the color closest to the one you have chosen that will print. Also, notice the mode value boxes, which show the exact values of your color.

8. Check the Only Web Colors box to see how the color box changes to display only web safe colors. If you don't have Only Web Colors selected than you can choose the nearest web safe color to the one that you have selected by clicking on the small box to the right hand side of the color box.

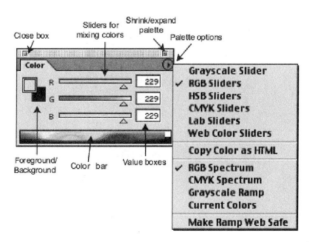

9. To the right of the window are different mode value boxes. Try keying in 255 into the each of the RGB to see how they add together to make white. Key 0 into the boxes, and they subtract to make black. You can also enter the exact values for a web color into the value boxes, including the hexadecimal one at the bottom. With the web safe color box checked, values entered will be rounded to the nearest web safe color.

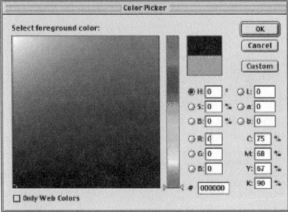

Once you have selected a color you want, click OK.

The custom color picker

The custom picker is used to select colors other than CMYK that are used by commercial printers. If, for example, you want to make an image that uses designated corporate colors, it is better to use the exact color ink rather than make the color by mixing CMYK inks. This depends on the final printing process used, which will be discussed later in the book. There are different ranges of ink that printers use, so if you do want to have something printed in this way, check with the printer as to which set of Photoshop custom colors to choose from. Also, as monitors cannot be relied on to display the color accurately, try to obtain a color swatch book, which will show you the colors as they will be printed. Custom colors are most commonly used for spot colors (these are explained in Chapter 6).

Using the custom color picker

1. Open the Color Picker by clicking on the Set foreground color, or Set background color box.

2. The Color Picker window will be launched. Click on the Custom button and it will change to the Custom Colors window.

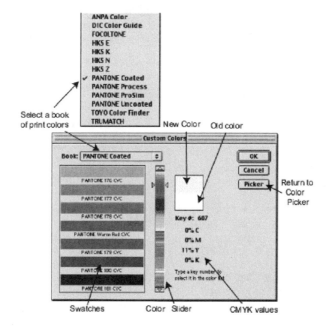

3. To select the book of colors you are going to print with, go to the pop-up menu at the top of the window.

4. Use the vertical slider to find the color range you want.

5. Select the exact swatch by clicking on it.

6. Click OK.

The Color palette

The Color palette offers another way to select colors. This method of selecting colors is more practical as it saves having to launch a window: it stays open on your desktop while you work so you can select new colors as you paint. It also allows you to mix a color yourself, which is a great opportunity to learn about the way colors work together.

Using the Color palette

1. Open the Color palette (Window > Show Color).

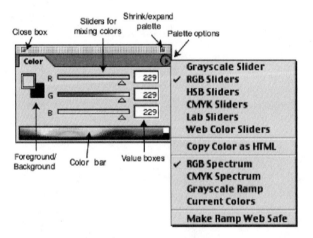

2. Click on the Set foreground color button in the Color palette to make it active.

Note: if you clicked on this button when it was already active, then you've probably opened the Color Picker *window, just close that window down, and go back to the Color palette.*

3. Click on the small arrow in the top right hand corner to access the Color palette options menu. In this menu you can choose a color model. As we are working with RGB images choose the RGB Sliders.

4. To select a color, use the sliders to mix the color that you want. Move each one up and down and see the color change in the Set foreground color box. Experiment with these sliders a little, and enjoy the unique feeling of being able to mix up a beautiful new color without getting paint on your hands.

5. Alternatively, click on the color bar or enter values into the boxes. To select black or white, there is a white area and a black area to the right of the *color* bar.

The Swatches palette

The Swatches palette differs from the Color palette, because it contains colors that have already been mixed. The palette holds a whole library of different swatches: swatches for custom colors (such as Pantone colors), swatches for Windows, swatches for Mac OS and swatches for the Web. Colors can be added and removed from the palette. It is also possible to create, and then save your own palette of swatches using the various color selection methods.

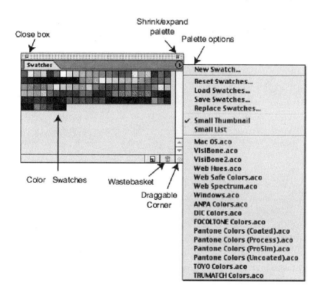

Working with the Swatches palette

1. Open the Swatches palette (Window > Show Swatches).

2. Select a color by clicking on a swatch. Notice how the Set foreground color square in the toolbox changes to the selected color. To easily select a new background color, hold down OPTION/ALT when clicking on the new color.

3. You can add new colors to your Swatch palette by using one of three methods. Either use the Eyedropper to sample a color from `shrine.psd`, mix a color using the color mixers in the Color palette or select a color using the Color Picker.

4. Once you have your new color, move your cursor over to the bottom, blank area of the Swatches palette. Your cursor will change to the Paint Bucket icon. Click once.

If you can't see the blank area, use the scroll bars on the side of the palette to find it. Also, you might not see any blank space if you are viewing the Swatches palette as a Small List, change this by going into the Swatches palette options via the small arrow in the top right hand corner, and check the Small Thumbnail option.

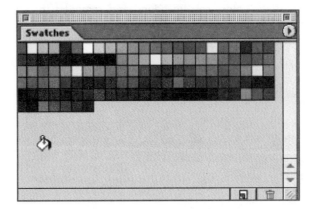

5. The Color Swatch Name window will be launched. Enter a name and click OK.

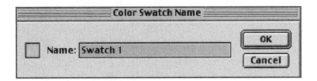

A new swatch of your chosen color will appear in the palette.

6. Select a new color.

7. Go to the Swatches palette and SHIFT CLICK on an existing swatch. It will change to the new color.

8. Delete a swatch from the palette by CMD/CTRL clicking on a swatch or by dragging it into the palette's trashcan.

9. Restore the palette by choosing **Reset Swatches** from the palette menu, and clicking OK or pressing ENTER/RETURN on your keyboard. This pop-up will also ask you if you wish to Append your amended swatch palette to the default colors, which can be quite handy if you wish to use both sets of swatches at the same time.

10. Using the Eyedropper tool, select a number of different colors from shrine.psd, adding them to the existing palette. Delete any colors that you don't like from the palette.

11. Save this palette by going to **Save Swatches** in the palette options.

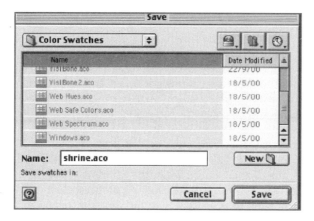

12. Save the swatches in the Color Swatches folder as shrine.aco. You will now be able to reload this palette of swatches into Photoshop at any time by going to **Load Swatches** in the palette options. You will also be able to load it into other programs such as Illustrator.

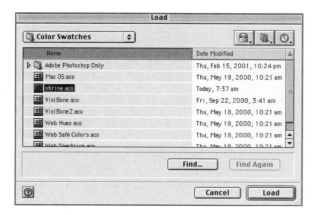

Painting Tools

Photoshop has a number of different painting and drawing tools, which can all be customized, giving the ability to create a great variety of marks. The ways that the Paintbrush, Pencil and Airbrush tools work and are modified are very similar. The difference is that the Paintbrush applies brush strokes, the Pencil draws lines and the Airbrush sprays paint. It can be difficult to tell which is which when they all have the same settings. Each of the tools' option bars offers a selection of different brush tips, various blending modes and Fade options. Options specific to the paintbrush are Opacity levels and the option of Wet Edges. Options specific to the pencil are Opacity and the option to Auto Erase. Options specific to the Airbrush concern Pressure.

Now, let's get to work on our Tabula Rasa using the colors we selected from the shrine.psd and Photoshop's Paintbrush, Pencil and Airbrush tools.

1. Open shrine.psd and Tabula Rasa.psd. If you do not have the Tabula Rasa file from the last chapter then shame on you for skipping chapters, but not to worry. Simply open a new document and call it Tabula Rasa.

2. Open the Swatches palette and load the swatches shrine.aco.

3. Select a swatch.

4. Select one of the painting tools: the Paintbrush, the Pencil or the Airbrush. The shortcut key for both the Pencil and Paintbrush tool is B, to toggle between the two, you need to press SHIFT + B, the shortcut for the Airbrush tool is J.

5. Drag the cursor across Tabula Rasa.psd. Hooray! You have now created your first mark in Photoshop!

6. Paint a straight line by clicking once where the stroke should begin, and then SHIFT-CLICK where it should end.

7. Go to the Options bar and click on the arrow next to brush. A menu of brushes will appear. Select a different brush and make a new mark on the screen. Continue selecting different brushes, and new colors, and applying strokes to Tabula Rasa.psd to see the different results. Anything that you don't like you can delete by going to Edit > Undo, although for the moment, we are just getting comfortable with tools so don't worry too much if it gets a little messy.

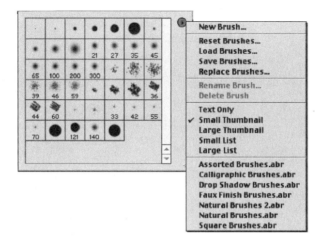

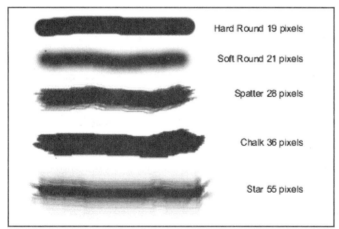

Hard Round 19 pixels

Soft Round 21 pixels

Spatter 28 pixels

Chalk 36 pixels

Star 55 pixels

Modifying brushes

1. Select a different swatch color.

2. On the Options bar, click on the Edit Brush button. This is the button that an image of the brush, with its diameter in pixels written on it.

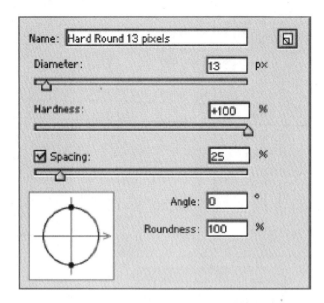

3. The New Brush window will appear. This allows you to modify the Diameter, Hardness, Spacing, Angle and Roundness of the brush:

● Diameter relates to the size of the stroke applied by the brush. To change the diameter of the brush, move the slider or enter a number between 1-999 pixels.

● Hardness is the percentage of the paint stroke's diameter that is opaque. To change the hardness, use the sliders or enter a percentage (1-100%).

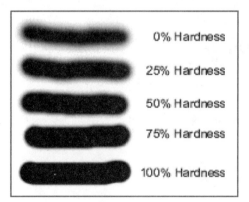

Spacing is how close or far apart the paint drops are. To change the spacing, use the sliders or enter a percentage. Alternatively, uncheck the spacing box so that the faster the mouse is dragged, the more paint drops will be missed.

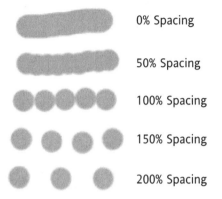

0% Spacing

50% Spacing

100% Spacing

150% Spacing

200% Spacing

■ Angle is the angle of the brush. To change the angle, enter a percentage or rotate the direction of the arrow in the brush preview box.

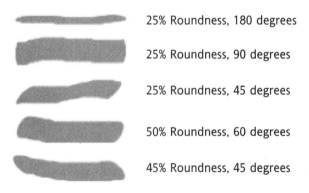

25% Roundness, 180 degrees

25% Roundness, 90 degrees

25% Roundness, 45 degrees

50% Roundness, 60 degrees

45% Roundness, 45 degrees

■ Roundness is how round the brush is. To change the roundness, enter a percentage or drag the dots in the brush preview box inwards/outwards. Experiment making different brush tips, testing their effects on Tabula Rasa.psd as you go.

Saving and loading brushes

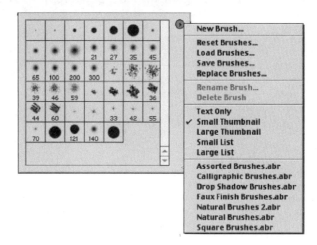

1. Create a new brush, either by modifying an existing brush and then clicking on the layer icon, or by going to the picker options and then New Brush.

    The brush will appear in the Brush picker.

2. Delete a brush that you don't like in the Brush picker by highlighting it and then going to Delete Brush in the picker options. You can also COMMAND-CLICK or ALT-CLICK on a brush that you wish to delete.

3. Save the set of brushes that you have created by going to **Save Brushes** in the picker options.

4. Call the brushes `shrine.brc` and click OK.

5. Open the picker options. To the bottom of the list are different sets of brushes that can be loaded into the brushes palette. Go through the different sets of brushes, testing them in `Tabula Rasa.psd`.

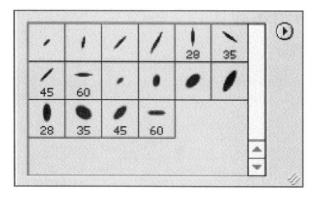

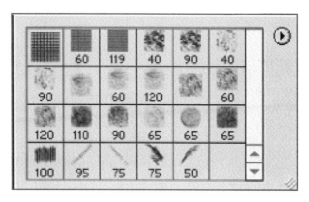

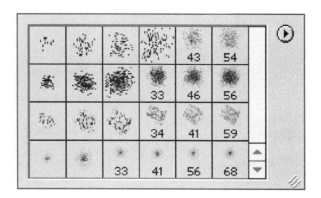

Further modification

Pressure and opacity

You can change the pressure of the Airbrush by entering a percentage in to the pressure box or by using the pop-up slider. Similarly you can alter the opacity of a brush stroke or a pencil line by entering a percentage in to the opacity box or by using the pop-up slider.

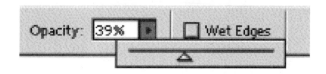

Fading strokes

To the right of the Paint tool Options bar, are the Brush Dynamics options. Here you can ask the stroke to fade in size, opacity or color as it ends. To make a brush fade at the end of a stroke, select Fade from the pop-up menus and enter a value (1-999 pixels). The higher the number the longer the stroke you can make before it fades completely.

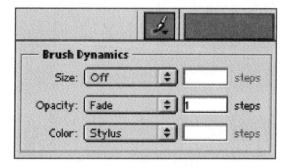

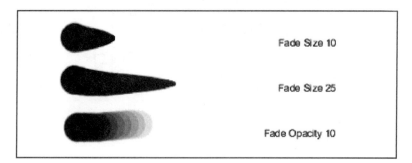

Wet Edges (paintbrush only)

To get paint strokes that have a higher concentration of color around the edges, similar to watercolor painting, check the Wet Edges box. When this box is checked the paint stroke is semi-transparent, to give a lovely fluid feeling to the brushstrokes.

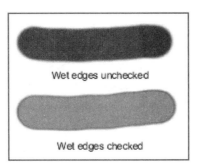

Auto Erase (pencil only)

Check the Auto Erase button to draw in the foreground color in the first stroke, and in the background color in the second stroke.

Painting tools blending modes

Finally let us learn about the Blending Modes that can be chosen for our paint tool. These modes are accessed via the small arrow to the right hand side of the Mode box, which will lead to a drop-down menu. The blending modes are the way the paint blends with canvas or existing image. The color that you are painting with is called the **blend color**, the color that you are painting onto (whether it be the blank canvas, or an existing image), is the **base color**. In the following examples, the horizontal strokes of paint are the blend colors, and shrine.psd is the base color.

Each of the modes affect the base color differently. As we go through each Mode option, test them out yourself so you can see the difference between each one, try using a range of dark and light blend colors, on the various elements of shrine.psd, and really familiarize yourself with these options.

Normal

This is the paintbrush's default setting. There is no blending with this option; the blend color replaces the base color.

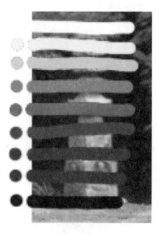

Dissolve

This creates a grainy, dry brush effect in paint that is being applied (the blend color). To increase the graininess of the paint, reduce the Opacity.

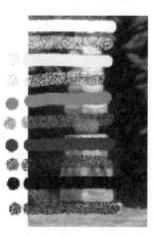

Multiply

This literally multiplies the blend color and base color. If you paint with a dark color, the base colors become darker, as the blend color removes any lighter parts of the base color. If you paint with a light blend color, it becomes very transparent and only slightly tints the base color. Multiply is like using felt tip pens.

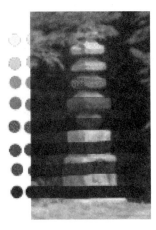

Screen

This lightens the base color; it lightens the dark areas and bleaches out the light areas. This mode works best with light blend colors.

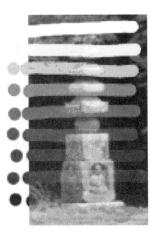

Overlay

Overlay is a combination of the Multiply mode and the Screen mode; it darkens the dark areas and lightens the light areas. This mode is very useful, as it doesn't affect black and white, so detail in an image is preserved. It tends to make base colors more dramatic.

Soft Light

Soft Light is similar to Overlay; it lightens a base color if the blend color is light and darkens them if the blend color is dark. When a light color is used it makes the base colors look flatter and more diffuse.

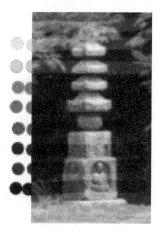

Hard Light

Hard Light works like Overlay but the blend color is much more opaque.

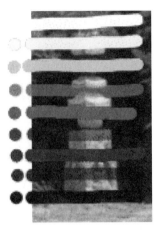

Color Dodge

Color Dodge brightens the base color if the blend color is light but has little effect when the blend color is dark. Midtone blend colors fill in the dark areas and tint the light areas of the base image.

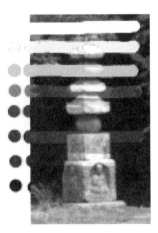

Color Burn

This is the opposite of Color Dodge; it darkens the base color if the blend color is dark, but has little effect if the blend color is light. Color Burn looks like ink spilled on to an image; dark inks obliterate the image, light inks stain.

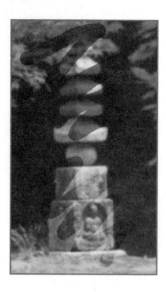

Darken

Darken looks at the blend color and base color and decides which is the darkest. The darkest color remains.

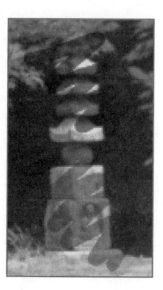

Lighten

This is the opposite of the Darken mode. If the blend color is lighter than the base color then it stays on the image; if it is darker then the base color remains.

Difference

Difference looks at the blend and base color, and subtracts the brighter color from the darker color. This results in the colors being inverted. The brighter the blend color, the more dramatic the negative effect in the base color.

Exclusion

This is very similar to Difference but there is less contrast in the areas of the color that are inverted.

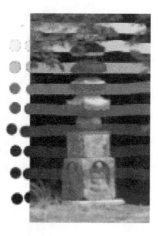

Hue

The blend color tints the base color. This is like applying watercolor wash. All colors work well in this mode.

Saturation

The saturation level of the blend color is applied to the base color. The brighter the blend color, the more saturated the base color becomes. The base color maintains its original brightness and color.

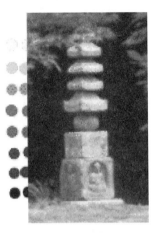

Color

The color and saturation of the blend color are applied to the base color. The contrast levels (amount of light and dark) in the base color don't change so detail is preserved. It applies a strong tint of the blend color to the base color.

Luminosity

Luminosity applies the grayscale value of the blend color to the base color (it ignores the blend color's hue and saturation). The saturation of the base color is unchanged.

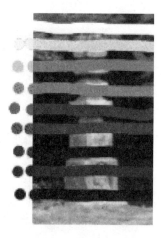

Using blending modes confidently takes a while, as their effects are often unpredictable. It is worth investing time in learning how they work, as they can be very useful and offer practical solutions to image retouching problems. To return to our shrine.psd image, we are going to transport the garden to fall-time, by painting the leaves with seasonal fall colors. By using the blending options we will be able to give our scene a real autumnal feel.

Using the blending mode

1. Open shrine.psd

2. Select a medium sized soft brush and change its Opacity to 30%.

> *It is a good idea to reduce the opacity when using blending modes as it gives more control and allows the effect to be built up slowly.*

3. First, make the leaves of the trees indicate the change of season by using the Color blending mode to tint them to an autumnal range of colors. Select Color from the Mode menu in the Option palette. Mix an orange as your foreground color. Paint this color onto parts of the leaves. Alternate through different shades of orange and yellow, slowing applying the paint to all of the leafy areas of the picture until you are satisfied that your tree looks as if it is in Fall.

4. To make the tree seem more three-dimensional, select the Darken mode from the options bar and a dark brown color as the blend color. Paint it onto the lower sides of the clusters of leaves (you may need to reduce the size of your brush for better accuracy).

5. Dull the light reflections on the water less by changing the mode to Luminosity and applying a mid tone blend color to the water.

6. Add more depth to the picture by using the Overlay mode and a dark brown/black blend color on the shrine and the grass around. Apply this to the water also, so that it reflects color of the Fall leaves. Make the foreground lighter by selecting the Soft light mode and painting a pale yellow/green around the roots of the trees.

7. You should now have a shrine in Fall. Save this as autumnshrine.psd and don't close it just yet.

Color mode
Orange, terracotta and yellow blend colours

Darken Mode
Dark brown blend colour

Overlay Mode
Dark brown blend colour

Luminosity Mode
Mid tone blend colour
Overlay Mode
Dark brown blend colour

Soft Light
Pale green blend color

The History palette

Before you close `autumnshrine.psd`, open the History palette (Window > Show History). Drag the corner of the box so that you can see all its contents. What you should see is a list of the last 99 states of `autumnshrine.psd` (although the number of past states listed depends on the Preferences settings in your individual copy of Photoshop). The History palette displays the oldest state at the top of the list, and the most recent at the bottom.

The History palette allows you to go back to any of these states by clicking on them. Try clicking on some of these states to see how the History palette returns to former states of your image in the image window. As you click back through the states notice that all the states after the one that you clicked on have dimmed. It is also possible to step back and forward through the states by going through the palette menu and selecting Step Forward or Step Back, or, by dragging the slider on the left side of the palette.

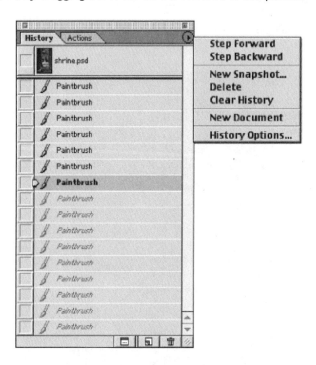

There are two different modes for the History palette: **Linear History** and **Non-linear History**. With linear history, if you click to an earlier state, and then start reworking the image, the dimmed states are deleted. With non-linear history, later states are neither dimmed, nor deleted. The new adjustments that you make to the image become the latest states in the palette. This gives the flexibility to try out a series of different effects and jump between them in the History palette.

To learn about the wonders of the History palette let's try again to make the leaves of the trees in shrine.psd autumnal. Using the History palette in non-linear mode will allow us to experiment with different colors and then compare the results quickly and easily before proceeding with the rest of the image.

1.   Open shrine.psd.

2.   Change the History palette to non-linear mode by going to the palette options and checking the box Allow Non-linear History. You will also notice the options to automatically create snapshots of your image. Snap shots will be explained later in this chapter. As you become more familiar with the History palette you may find it useful to check some of these options.

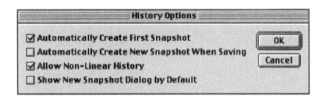

3.   Start applying an orange color as before to the leaves to make them autumnal. Notice that every time you use the brush, a new state is created. Once the leaves have turned orange, go back to the first state in the History palette. Notice that all the later states remain undimmed.

4.   Now, choose a yellow color and start working on the leaves again. In the History palette there is a black line where you stopped applying the orange color. The new states are being added to the History palette after this line.

5.   Once you have made the leaves yellow, return again to the first state and color the leaves with a red color. Again, a line will be created in the History palette and any new states are added after the line.

6.   The History palette should now contain a list of states divided by three bold lines. Click through the states above the lines to compare the effects of the different blend colors.

Now let's organize the History palette by duplicating states, creating snapshots and deleting unwanted states.

Duplicating a state

Duplicating a state will make it appear again at the bottom of the list, making it easier to jump back or forward to.

1. ALT-CLICK/OPTION-CLICK on each of the states above the black lines in the History palette that show the leaves in different colors.

2. The duplicated states will appear at the bottom of the list. It is now easier to step back and forward through our different colored leaves, as they are now together at the bottom of the list.

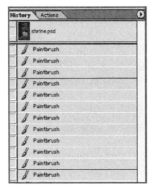

Creating a snapshot of a history

As the maximum amount of states stored in the History palette is 99, it is safer to create a snapshot of a state that we want to return to, as snapshots, unlike states, can't be pushed off the palette if the number of states exceeds 99.

1. Highlight the state in the History palette that shows the tree with yellow leaves.

2. Go to the palette menu and select New Snapshot. Alternatively ALT-CLICK/OPTION-CLICK the Create New Snapshot button at the bottom of the palette.

3. In the New Snapshot name box write Yellow Leaves.

    The snapshot, along with a picture icon, will now appear at the top of the History palette.

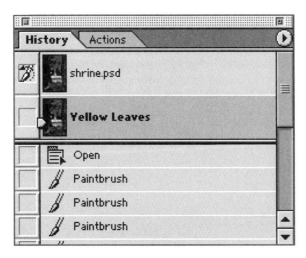

Deleting history states

The History palette now contains states and duplicate states that we no longer need. They can be deleted by highlighting the unwanted state, and then clicking the Trashcan icon at the bottom of the palette. Alternatively all the states, other than the snapshots, can be deleted by going to Clear History in the palette menu.

Creating a new document from a snapshot state

When an image is closed, snapshots and history states are deleted. It is possible, however, to make a new document of a snapshot or state.

1. Highlight the Yellow Leaves snapshot.

2. Click on the Create New Document button or RIGHT-CLICK/CONTROL CLICK.

3. A new window containing the state of the tree with yellow leaves will appear. The document will take the name of the snapshot.

4. Yellow Leaves can now be saved and returned to at a later time, even if shrine.psd is not open.

Summary

In this chapter we have learnt how to sample, pick, and mix colors. We have learnt to apply color using the different paint tools, learnt how to customize brushes and create a great variety of marks. Tabula Rasa.psd is now a documentation of your first journey through Photoshop's brush strokes, airbrush effects and pencil lines! Using the blending options we have created a shrine in Fall and you should feel confident enough to manipulate any image knowing that you can always use the History palette to return to any previous state and correct any mistakes.

If the idea of using these brushes to create your own artwork has caught your imagination, then you won't be surprised to learn that many designers use Photoshop to do just that. Links to some sites are included in the back of the book, but to be going on with, have a peek at www.tbns.net/rdgraffix/withoutacountry.html, a moody scene created using custom brushes by Rowan Dodds.

3 Selection

What we'll cover in this chapter:

- *An introduction to the concept of selections and why they are important to the Photoshop user.*

- *User-based, color-based, and contrast-based methods of selection, including the Marquee, Lasso, and Magic Wand tools, and we'll also take a look at the Color Range command.*

- *Methods of refining selections using the Quick Mask mode and the options available on the Select menu.*

- *An introduction to the concept of channels as a method of saving, retrieving, and editing selections.*

Right, you're nearly ready to start creating those wonderful masterpieces you've always dreamed of, but first you need to get your hands dirty with some real photo editing and composition. Before we can really let fly though, there's a little more we have to cover...

In this chapter, you'll be introduced to the concept of **selections** in Photoshop, and you'll soon realize that without selections, none of those ideas you have in your head could come to fruition. The fact of the matter is that, in contrast to the real world, objects do not exist in the basic Photoshop document. It's an optical illusion of sorts. Essentially, what we see on the screen is really a mass of tiny squares (more correctly referred to as **pixels**), all carefully colored and shaded by Photoshop to depict the image that we have imported.

 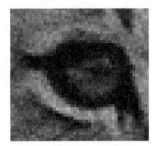

Look carefully at the images above. On the left, we see a photograph of a lion cub; but on the right, where we have zoomed in on one of the lion cub's eyes, what we see is what is actually there in the Photoshop representation; a collection of colored pixels that make up the image.

So why is this important, you ask? Well, the fact of the matter is that if we want to manipulate any particular part of an image, perhaps to apply a filter, or a color correction, or copy it for use in another image; we have to tell Photoshop that this is the collection of pixels to which we are referring (remember, there are no objects to select!), and the only way that you can do this is by making a **selection**. The selections we'll be talking about here refer to the piece of the image that we want to work on.

In Photoshop, we can create such selections by using one of a number of different selection tools, perhaps a combination of these tools, or even by using specific menu commands. As I said just a minute ago, the purpose of this chapter is to introduce you to and make you more familiar with these options, so that as your knowledge of Photoshop develops and you find yourself wanting to make more and more complex selections, you'll have the necessary skills with which to do so.

So, if you're sitting comfortably, we'll begin with...

The geometric selection tools

The most basic of the selection tools are those which enable us to create simple geometrically-shaped sections; and these are the Rectangular, Elliptical, Single Row, and Single Column Marquee tools.

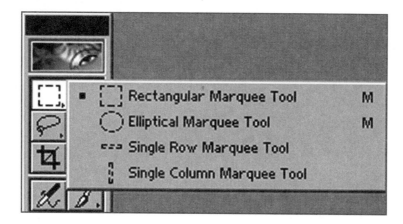

For example, to create a rectangular- or elliptical-shaped selection, we'd simply select the appropriate tool from the toolbox and click and drag on the desired part of the image. The selected area is marked by what looks like a moving black and white line, otherwise known as a **marquee**. On the other hand, if we decided that we could use either the Single Row or Single Column selection tools, we would click near the target area in the image, and then drag the marquee to the desired location. It's worth noting that unless we use special modifier keys (which we'll come to later), our selection will always start from the point at which we first clicked on the image. So, those are some of the tools available to us for making free-hand selections, but how can we use these tools if our selections need to be precisely symmetrical about some point?

Creating symmetrical selections

With a combination of the SHIFT and OPTION/ALT keys, we can control the shape of the selection. We can in fact also use keypresses (known as keyboard modifiers) to control how a selection that is being created interacts with any other existing selections, but this will be discussed later in the chapter. Let's just have a quick look at how we can create simple symmetrical shapes using the Marquee tools:

- To create a perfectly symmetrical rectangle (in other words, a square!) or ellipse (a circle), begin by selecting the appropriate Marquee tool. Next, we simply click and drag on the image to begin creating the selection, and then depress the SHIFT key, keeping it depressed until after we've released the mouse button.

■ To draw a rectangle or ellipse from the center, again, we begin by selecting the appropriate Marquee tool. We then click and drag on the image, and then depress the OPTION/ALT key, holding it down until after we've released the mouse button.

■ To create a perfectly symmetrical square or a circle starting from its center, once again we select the relevant Marquee tool, and then click and drag on the image to begin creating the selection. As we do this, we need to depress both the SHIFT key and OPTION/ALT keys, and hold them down until after we've released the mouse button.

Using the Tool Options bar

Whenever we change tools in Photoshop, the Tool Options bar, which by default is displayed across the top of our screen (below the Menu bar), updates to give us information on the tool that is currently selected. By choosing from the available options displayed on this bar before our selection is created, we are able to further clarify our selection – note that the options we choose will only apply to the next selection that we create. Here's how the Tool Options bar looks for the Elliptical Marquee tool:

With real estate on your screen at a premium, you may have chosen to close some of your palettes or even the Tool Options *bar. To restore the location of all palettes and this bar to their original position, choose* Reset Palette Locations *from the* Window *menu.*

Similarly, to reset all tools to their default settings, click and hold the mouse down on the selected tool icon on the extreme left of the Tool Options *bar. A drop-down menu will then appear, and from this you should choose the* Reset All Tools *option. It's often helpful to do this if tools do not seem to be behaving as you expected.*

You may notice, as you become more familiar with these selection tools, that Photoshop only allows one selection to exist at any one time. Now, there may be times when you wish to have more than one area of an image selected, or perhaps you may want to add to or subtract from a selection. To specify how new selections will interact with an existing selection in an image, Photoshop makes various options available to us. We can access these options by clicking on one of the following icons on the Tool Options bar, as illustrated by the following screenshot:

Creating smooth-edged selections

In addition to these options, this bar also offers a **feather** option, which enables us to create a selection that has a smooth transition between the selected pixels and the non-selected pixels. Entering a value here before we draw the marquee will cause our selection to have a blurry edge, dependent upon the value we input here and the resolution of our image. If our image is of a low resolution, entering a given value here will have a far greater visual impact on our image than if it is a high-resolution image. The following screenshots illustrate the difference between an elliptical marquee selection without feathering (on the left), and a similar selection utilizing feathering on the right:

The Elliptical Marquee tool also offers an option to turn **anti-aliasing** on or off. Essentially, this feature smoothes the selection by making the edge pixels of a selection semi-transparent. Have a look at the following images; the images show part of an elliptical marquee selection, without anti-aliasing (on the left), and with anti-aliasing (on the right) checked on the Tool Options bar:

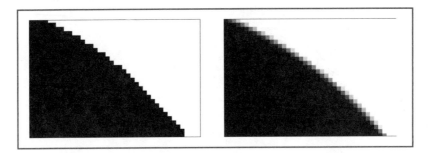

Using Styles in the Tool Options bar to draw selections

With the Rectangular and Elliptical Marquee tools, we can also choose different **styles** for our selections, and we can select different styles according to what effect we want to achieve.

- Use Normal to create a selection by dragging on the image.

- Use Constrained Aspect Ratio to create a marquee with a specific height-to-width ratio. With this style, click near the target area in the image, and then position the marquee by dragging it to the desired location.

- Use Fixed Size to stipulate absolute values for the marquee's height and width. As with the Constrained Aspect Ratio style, click near the target area in the image and then position the marquee by dragging it.

Transforming selections

Although the material mentioned here is relevant to all types of selections, I think it'll be useful to introduce **transformations** to you at this point. You see, once we have defined our selection border, we can still resize, rotate, and modify it by accessing the options on the Select menu.

For example, if we wished to resize or rotate our selection border dynamically, we would choose Transform Selection from the Select menu, and we would then see a series of cursors appear around our selection. These cursors act as handles, and we could then drag these handles on the bounding box to resize the selection border, or we could even drag the handle from a point outside the bounding box to rotate the selection border. To return to the normal selection border, we would then either double-click within the bounding-box, or hit RETURN/ENTER.

If we wanted to expand or contract our selection by an absolute value, we could select Modify from the Select menu and then choose either Expand or Contract. The amount that an image is affected is determined by the number of pixels that we specify at this stage, so we simply enter the desired number of pixels in the dialog box that appears, bearing in mind that the effect of a given value is dependent on the resolution of our image. For low-resolution images, the same number of pixels will represent a larger distance.

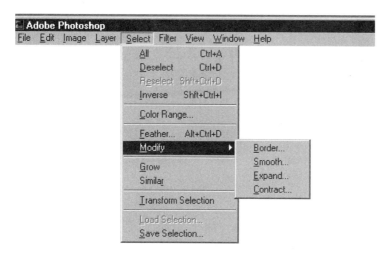

There are also a number of modifier keys, which enable us to manipulate these selection borders, and some of the more frequently used ones are as follows:

- To scale the selection border in proportion, select a corner handle and hold down the SHIFT key whilst dragging. Remember to release the mouse before releasing the SHIFT key.

- To scale a selection border from the center, select any handle and hold down the OPTION/ALT key whilst dragging. As with the previous modifier, keep the modifier key depressed until after you've released the mouse button.

- To scale a selection border, both in proportion and from the center, select a corner handle and hold down both the SHIFT and OPTION/ALT key as you drag. Once again, hold them down until after you have released the mouse button.

■ To rotate the border in 45° increments, move the cursor outside the bounding box until it changes into a double-headed curved arrow, and then hold down the SHIFT key as you rotate the bounding box.

Some selection tips and shortcuts...

■ To deselect a selection, click (but do not drag) anywhere else on the image with a selection tool active. If you are using either the Column or the Row selection tool, or any of the Styles other than Normal, this will not work. Alternatively, choose the Deselect option from the Select menu, or use the shortcut command: CMD/CTRL+D.

■ To reselect your last selection, choose the Reselect option on the Select menu, or use the shortcut command CMD/CTRL+SHIFT+D.

■ To reposition a rectangular or elliptical marquee selection border whilst drawing it, keep the mouse button depressed and hold down the SPACE bar. Drag to reposition, and release the SPACE bar only when the selection is in the desired position. Drag down with the mouse button to continue to create the selection marquee.

■ To reposition a selection marquee border after releasing the mouse button, ensure that you still have a selection tool active and either drag from inside the selection, or use the arrow keys to move the border in small increments. Holding down SHIFT in conjunction with the arrow keys will nudge the border in greater increments.

Creating basic geometric selections

With some of the skills for creating basic selections under your belt, it's time to put this knowledge to good use, as we have a little fun with filters and, at a later stage in the exercise, take advantage of an opportunity to fine-tune some of the painting skills that you've acquired in the previous chapters.

1. Open the file 3-1twirl.psd. You should see a swirl image, and whilst it may not look like much, it'll be just fine for our work here. By the end of this exercise, you will have transformed this lowly swirl image into something resembling an Escher-esque image of tropical birds. I remember when I started the exercise, I saw them as toucans, but then they became puffins, and finally there was no way to describe them other than as 'tropical birds', as they were quite unlike anything I've ever seen before! Oops, I'm diverging, back to the tutorial...

2. From the View menu, access the Show sub-menu and ensure that there is a tick next to Guides. Similarly, ensure that there is a tick next to Guides on the Snap To sub-menu. You should see that the image has been neatly divided into four equal quadrants.

3. Select the Rectangular Marquee tool and reset all the tools to their original settings by accessing the drop-down menu from the tool icon. Resize your view of the image on the screen so that you can see a gray expanse on all sides of the image.

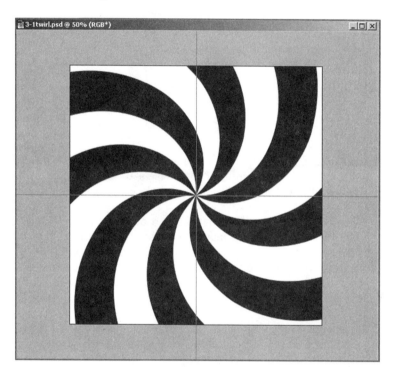

4. Click and drag with the Rectangular Marquee tool to create a marquee selection encompassing the upper-left quadrant of the image. The selection should snap to the guides on the image, but if your selection is not quite accurate enough, select Transform Selection from the Select menu and modify it until it's more or less spot-on.

5. Now, with this selection still active, select Filter > Distort > Twirl, enter a value of 419° for the angle and then click OK, as illustrated in the following screenshot:

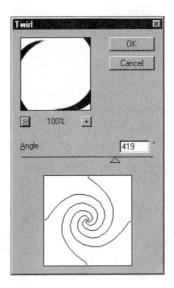

Look at the image, and with a little imagination you should be able to see a bird with its beak at the center of the image – or is it just that my imagination has spent a little too long roaming free in the creative world?

6. With the Rectangular Marquee tool still active, select the upper right-hand quadrant and move the cursor to the top right of the image. Hold down the mouse button and drag towards the center of the image. As you drag, depress the SHIFT button as well, and notice how the selection border is constrained to a square. You'll have to drag diagonally to get to the center of the image.

7. Apply the Twirl filter with the same values. Note that since this was the last filter we used, we can easily re-apply it by choosing Twirl from the top of the Filter menu, or by using the shortcut CMD/CTRL+F.

8. To apply the filter to the bottom left-hand quadrant, we're going to use one of the rectangular marquee styles we cordially introduced ourselves to at the beginning of the chapter. Choose Constrained Aspect Value from the Tool Options bar, and enter a value of 1 in both the Width and Height fields. Click and drag from the bottom left of the image towards the center. Notice how the border is being constrained to a ratio of 1:1 as you drag.

9. Re-apply the Twirl filter as explained above.

10. For the remaining quadrant, we'll specify an absolute value for the size of our marquee; choose the Fixed Size style from the Tools Option bar.

11. We need to set a value of 450 pixels (px) in both the Width and Height fields, so go ahead and do this. Now click on the image, and a selection border of that exact size will be created. Drag to position it accurately in the bottom right-hand quadrant, and once again re-apply the Twirl filter as explained in step 7.

12. Reset the tools by accessing the Reset All Tools from the tool icon on the Tool Options bar.

> *I would suggest that the above step is one you should quickly become accustomed to using when first familiarizing yourself with Photoshop. This will limit the number of occasions on which your tools seem to be behaving as if they have a mind of their own, on account of them having been set for an earlier task and still retaining the values they had been given.*

13. By now, your image should now look very (or at least fairly) similar to the screenshot shown below. Remember that you can hide the Guides by going to View > Show > Guides and removing the check next to the option, or by using the shortcut CMD/ CTRL +' (apostrophe).

14. To finish, save your file by choosing File > Save and then saving the file in a folder or directory of your choice. A piece of advice that you may have come across before, but that is always worth stressing, is that you should try to name your files concisely but sensibly. So for this particular image, a name like `swirl.psd` would suffice, unless the new image reminds you of anything else in particular!

Oh, and don't get too upset about leaving this aesthetically pleasing file behind – you'll be coming back to it soon enough to practice your increasing skills!

But, for now, let's move on to...

Creating user-defined shaped selections

After that thorough grounding in the basic machinery of the geometrically predefined shape selection tools, it's now time to introduce you to other ways in which we can define selections. The tools that will be discussed here are the Lasso and Polygon Lasso tools, which enable us to create basic freehand selections and freehand selections with straight edges. We'll then move on to look at the Magnetic Lasso, which functions according to the contrast within an image, basing selection on pixel color, as opposed to the methods used by the other free-form selections that we've seen so far.

Although you may find both the Lasso and Polygon Lasso tools useful in your initial exploratory stages in Photoshop, as you learn new and more powerful ways of making selections, you'll seldom use these tools except for making rough selections.

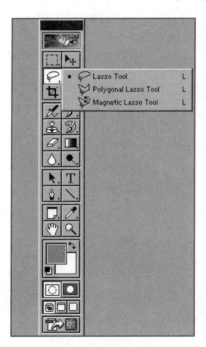

Creating simple shape selections with the Lasso and Polygonal Lasso tools

Choose either the regular or Polygonal Lasso tools from the toolbar, and as you do so, have a look at the options for both of these tools on the tool options bar. Notice how the bar changes as you select the tools, but that no new features are introduced. Also note how the options are more limited than those that were available when we were using the Rectangular and Elliptical Marquee tools.

To use the (regular) Lasso tool, select it and then click and drag on your image to create a selection of the desired shape. If the mouse button is released without returning to the original starting point, Photoshop will connect the end and start points with a straight line.

To use the Polygonal Lasso tool, select it and then click and release the mouse button at a point in the image. Continue clicking at certain desired intervals to extend the selection. To close the selection we can either return to our original starting point and click, CMD/CTRL+CLICK, or simply double-click at any point on the image, and then Photoshop will then close the selection by choosing the shortest route back to the starting point.

To temporarily switch from the regular to the Polygonal Lasso while drawing a selection, hold down the OPTION/ALT key and click. Keep the OPTION/ALT key down until you wish to return to the regular Lasso tool and continue clicking to create a straight-sided selection. To switch back to the regular Lasso tool, depress the mouse button, release the OPTION/ALT key, and continue to drag – this feature can be particularly useful when cutting out awkward shapes.

Creating contrast-based selections with the Magnetic Lasso tool

The role of the Magnetic Lasso tool is to make irregularly-shaped selections based on the contrast of color within an image. The theory is that we simply move this tool along the edge of the area in the image we wish to select, and the tool will snap against the edges of the desired area of color. However, before we discuss the merits of the Magnetic Lasso tool in any detail, let's first look at the options it offers us on the tool options bar.

Magnetic Lasso options

The Width parameter relates to the width of the area within which Photoshop will search for color changes in our image. In the past I've found it useful to switch to a **Precise Cursor** by depressing the Caps Lock key when using this tool, and then centering the hotspot (the little target in the middle of the cursor) over the edge of the area in which I want Photoshop to detect a color contrast, and this seems to work fairly well in most cases.

> *Remember: the degree of success that you have, and the size of your sensor area will always be dependent on the contrast factor in your image, and its resolution. In a 72 dpi image, a 10-pixel hotspot covers a far higher percentage of the image than it would on a high-resolution 300 dpi image.*

The next parameter is the Edge Contrast parameter, which describes the degree of sensitivity that we want Photoshop to detect in the change in colors as we move the Magnetic Lasso tool over an image. In a high-contrast image with strong, marked colors, this value can be increased, but if our image is full of subtle variations in tone, we'll have to bring the value down so that it notices the smaller changes in color within the image.

The Frequency parameter determines the rate at which the Magnetic Lasso will automatically attach fastening points to the edge of the contrasting area in the image. Once again, we may wish to increase the value if we require a detailed selection in a low contrast image.

To use the Magnetic Lasso, simply click in the image against the edge of the area you want to select and then move the mouse along the edge you wish to trace. It's not necessary to hold the mouse down, although if Photoshop does not seem to be placing sufficient anchor points for your liking, you can click to add your own. To close the selection accurately, return to the starting point (if you're in the **Precise Cursor** mode, the cursor will change back to the Magnetic Lasso icon), and click to end your trace.

Occasionally, this tool will seem to develop a mind of its own as it detects changes in color, and will tend to wander away from the edge you wish to trace, depositing anchor points as it goes. To delete these anchor points, and tidy up your selection, move the cursor back along the outline, hitting the Delete key to remove any errant anchor points as you pass over them.

Although the Magnetic Lasso can be useful in creating quick and easy selections in markedly contrasting files, I prefer to use the Magnetic Pen, which allows a far greater freedom for manipulation and accuracy once the initial outline has been created. This tool is discussed in more detail in the next chapter.

It's often the case that the Lasso tools are not particularly useful for creating an initial selection. Instead, they tend to come into their own when we use them to further refine a selection by adding to or removing areas.

Working with color-based selections

All of the selection tools discussed so far have all related to shapes, but in a real world of a myriad images, simple shape selections aren't going to get us that far, and so we need to add the **Magic Wand** tool and the **Color Range menu** command to our ever-expanding arsenal of selection options...

The Magic Wand tool

The **Magic Wand** tool is useful for selecting irregularly shaped objects in an image, especially if the object to be selected is of a similar color to its background, or if the image has subtle color variations throughout.

In practice, what this means is that if we click on a pixel in the image, the Magic Wand tool will look at the color of the selected pixel, and expand our selection to include any adjoining pixels that are colored such that they that fall within a range of colors, determined by the value set by us in the Tolerance field.

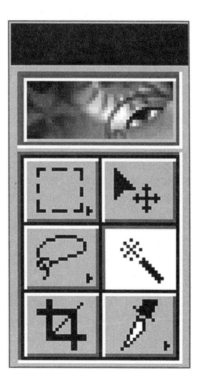

Sounds complicated? Honestly, it's not really – the only fiddly bit is deciding what value to specify in the Tolerance field (which be discussed in more detail in a second) and deciding where exactly to click in the image. As mentioned earlier, whenever we select a different tool, the Tool Options bar will change to reflect any options available for the active tool. As such, the bar for the Magic Wand will display three new features, which we can use to control how we make our selections. Click on the Magic Wand tool icon, and then take a look at the Tool Options bar.

Magic Wand options

I know, I know. You're disappointed that features such as *Produce White Rabbit from behind Handkerchief*, or perhaps *Transport Photoshop Genius Telepathically* didn't crop up when you opened this tool. So what have we got to work with?

Well, the first new field on the options bar is labeled Tolerance (this is the one we were talking about just a second ago), and the default value is 32. If your value is different, this is probably a good time to reset all of your tools to their default settings.

The term 'tolerance' refers to the range of color that will be included in our selection. The math behind the computation is a little involved, and knowledge of exactly how it works is not really necessary. You see, the bare bones of the matter is that if we click on a mid-green pixel with a Tolerance setting of 32, Photoshop will seek out all adjacent pixels which are approximately 32 shades lighter, and 32 shades darker. This is an over-simplification, because Photoshop actually looks at all the independent RGB or CMYK color values, but for our purposes the simpler definition will suffice.

So how do we decide when to change the Tolerance parameter? Well, that all depends on the particular image that we're working with. If we were working with a very low contrast image, with many areas of similar color, we would probably find that with a Tolerance setting of 32 we'd be selecting a greater area than we had wanted, and therefore would need to decrease the Tolerance value. On the other hand, if we were working with a high contrast image, with large blocks of strong color, a higher value would be fine.

I said earlier that the Magic Wand selects only continuous areas of similar color, but we are in fact able to adjust a value such that the tool will pick-up on areas of similar color anywhere in the image. With the Magic Wand at its default setting, there's a check next to Contiguous on the Tool Options bar, and it is this that limits the selection to adjacent, similarly colored pixels. If we deselect this, we'll select the same range of colors irrespective of where they are in the image.

The third option on the Tool Options bar gives us the opportunity to employ the Magic Wand in selecting similar colored pixels throughout all the layers in our active file, called, intuitively enough, Use All Layers. As we've not yet begun to work on multi-layered images, this feature may not make sense just yet – but don't worry, that'll all come with time. Essentially, checking this box allows the Magic Wand to ignore any question of layer and treat the entire image as if it were a flattened whole. Deselecting this option will ensure that the Magic Wand will operate exclusively on the active layer, encompassing even hidden areas of this layer.

Using the Magic Wand

"Enough of this theory..." I hear you say, "...let me at it, I want to practice!". This is just where I'm leading, as you can probably infer from the heading above. But let me warn you, however, that the image I've chosen as your introduction to the Magic Wand is not a 'walk in the park' example, with blanket areas of the same color. No! It's a challenging one! Maybe even a little mean at this early stage before you're fully equipped to tackle such an image, but there is method in my apparent madness, so please, stick with me!

Too often we rely on just one tool to make our selections, when a far better solution would be to use a combination of tools until we get the selection just right. So with that in mind, let's open the image and have a little dabble...

1. Open the file called `3-2elephant.psd`

We're looking at selections here, and what's the most obvious thing to select? The elephant, right? Well, at first glance, this selection looks easy enough. We want to select the elephant, and elephants are gray, so one click with the Magic Wand should suffice, right? Wrong! Nature, in all her wisdom, did not paint animals with blanket colors – their coloring is subtle and transient. OK, there may be some exceptions – but our friend here is not one of them, so no short cuts!

2. Armed with the Magic Wand, set with a default Tolerance value of 32, click somewhere in the region of the ear. While your exact selection may vary, it's likely that the top of the elephant's ear and head have been selected.

3. Now deselect by choosing Deselect from the Select menu, or by using the shortcut: CMD/CTRL+D. Change your Tolerance to 64, and click in roughly the same area. The result will be a larger selection, but possibly it has bled into the surrounding vegetation.

4. OK, that was just to demonstrate the effect of altering this value on a given image. Deselect again and return your Tolerance setting to 32. An easy way to access the Tolerance field is to hit RETURN/ENTER, and you'll notice that the numbers in the field have been highlighted so that you can type in the new value directly.

5. With your image Tolerance setting at 32 again, click in the same area again,and you should get a selection that is very similar to your previous one. We're going to add to this selection by using the Add to Selection option in the Magic Wand Tool Options bar, so go ahead and click this button.

6. Continue to click in additional places on the elephant to increase the area selected. If a selection bleeds into the vegetation at some point, undo that action by choosing Undo from the Edit menu (CMD/CTRL+Z), and feel free to change the values in the Tolerance field as you see fit.

You may notice that there are some pixels within your selected elephant that are not selected, and this is where using a combination of selection tools comes into its own. You may recall I said earlier that the Lasso tool is often useful for cleaning up selections. Well, we'll soon see if I need to be eating those words – it's time to put my theory into practice!

7. Select the regular Lasso tool (try using the keyboard shortcut: L).

As the book progresses you may notice more and more shortcuts being introduced. I assure you, they really do speed up your workflow, and I promise only to mention those that I have found to be very useful.

Notice on the Lasso Tool Options bar that the kind of selection to be made has reverted to the original New Selection icon.

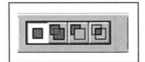

8. To save you time, do not choose the Add to Selection icon. Instead, simply depress the Shift key **before** clicking in the image. Notice that a little plus sign is appended to the cursor. This indicates that we are adding to our selection, so click and drag around those errant pixels to include them in the selection.

9. To remove pixels from the selection while the Lasso tool is still active, depress the Option/Alt key **before** you click and drag in the image.

Note that the shortcuts I've introduced can be used with any of the selection tools, and they are discussed in detail a little later in the chapter.

Often, when making selections with the Magic Wand, you may find that your incremental click goes too far and you need to revert to an earlier selection. The quickest way to do this is to undo your last action, either by choosing Undo from the Edit menu, or by pressing Cmd/Ctrl+Z. Remember that Photoshop has only one true undo action in its memory at any time, so it's imperative that you undo your command before you do anything else. The History palette, which will be covered in detail later will offer alternate ways for stepping back through your selections, but for the moment I want to keep you on your toes, so we won't discuss that just yet!

10. By now, it's likely that you've spent a fair amount of time refining this selection, and I dare say it still isn't perfect – but don't worry, we'll come back to it later. For the moment, save both the selection and the file. To save the selection so it can be used again at a later stage, choose Save Selection from the Select menu. The following dialog box should appear, and in the Name field enter: basic elephant, and then click OK.

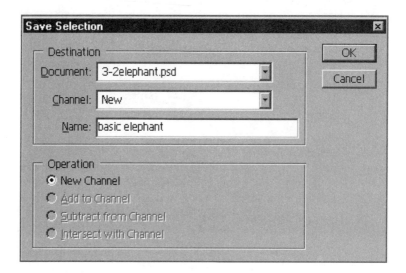

Even though we've saved the actual selection within the file, it's important that we also save the file at this point, because if we close the file without saving it, we'll lose the selection information and have to start all over again! With this in mind, select Save from the File menu, (CMD/CTRL+S) and save the file in a folder of your choice. That's it, we're done for now!

Using the keyboard to add to and subtract from selections

Earlier in this chapter, you were introduced to the icons on the Tools Options bar, which enable us to add, subtract, and intersect new selections with existing selections. There is however, a more efficient way of achieving the same end, and this involves using keyboard modifiers (or shortcuts).

Initially you may find using the shortcuts a little confusing, but my recommendation is that you persevere with them until you become familiar with them. The key to working well and rapidly in Photoshop is to take advantage of as many of the useful shortcuts as possible, to minimize the amount of time you spend selecting options from menus and tool bars.

Modifiers in practice

● To add to an existing selection, depress the SHIFT key before clicking in the image with the active selection tool. Keep an eye on the cursor when you depress the SHIFT key, you'll notice that there is a small plus sign, +, below the tool icon.

● To subtract from an existing selection, depress the OPTION/ALT key before clicking in the image with a selection tool. As with the preceding shortcut, the cursor icon will change to indicate that you are subtracting from the selection.

● To intersect the selection you are about to draw with an existing selection, depress both the SHIFT and the OPTION/ALT keys before you hold down the mouse button. You'll notice that the cursor now displays a small cross below the tool icon.

"Hold on", you may or may not be thinking, "I remember being introduced to very similar shortcuts a few pages back, which enabled me to draw circular and square selections, and to draw selections from the center..."

The difference in how these shortcuts behave lies in the exact moment at which you choose to hold down the modifier keys (SHIFT and/or OPTION/ALT). Essentially...

● If you want to add to a selection, depress SHIFT before you click in the image, and release it at anytime after you've begun the selection. Similarly, to subtract, simply depress OPTION/ALT before clicking in the image.

● To draw a symmetrical shape or draw from the center, click in the image with the selection tool first, and then depress the correct modifier key. Keep the key depressed until after you've released the mouse button.

Consequently, to add to a selection and draw a perfectly symmetrical shape, depress the SHIFT key, begin your selection; release the SHIFT key, then depress it again, keeping it down until after you have released the mouse button. A similar pattern is followed for the other options. This may sound confusing, but with practice it does become automatic, and it makes working in Photoshop so much more efficient.

Using the Color Range menu command

In addition to the Magic Wand, which creates selections dependent on the colors present in an image, there is also a menu command that provides us with very similar features and possibilities. To be honest, whichever of the two you choose to use is very much a matter of personal preference, but from my own experience I've found that while the Magic Wand can work perfectly well in cheap and cheerful situations, the Color Range menu command offers a far greater degree of control and accuracy when it comes to making difficult selections. Not only does the Color Range command enable us to select on color, but it also allows us to continually sub-select, until we get a selection that is very close to what we want, and as a result, very little tidying-up is needed.

Before we look at the options in any detail, it might be helpful for you to have an image open, as we'll need an image to work with a little later. The one I suggest you open is the `3-2elephant.psd` file, which is the one we worked with earlier on in the Magic Wand exercise. Once you've got it open, select Color Range from the Select menu, and a dialog box should appear on your screen:

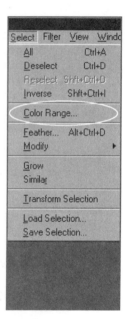

At the top of the dialog box you should see a drop-down menu containing the caption: Sampled Colors. Click on the down arrow to have a look at what options are available. What you should notice is that, in addition to sampling colors (which you can do by clicking on the image either in the preview box or on the image itself), you can also select specific colors or ranges of colors, for example: Highlights (light areas), Midtones, Shadows, and Out of Gamut (non-printable) colors.

If for example we wished to select all yellow tones in our highlights, we would open the dialog box once and select either Highlights or Yellows from the drop-down menu, and then click OK to close the dialog box. Without deselecting, we would then re-open the Color Range command, and this time choose Highlights if we chose Yellows previously, or vice-versa.

And there you have it – all yellow highlights would have been selected.

Moving on now, below the drop-down menu you'll see a slider, which claims to have something to do with Fuzziness. Well, if you can recall what you learned about the Tolerance value for the Magic Wand tool, this feature works in exactly the same way. You see, the way this works is that the higher the value, the wider the range of colors that will be included in the selection, and the lower the value, the narrower the range.

The benefit of this approach is that, unlike the Magic Wand, we can dynamically change the value if the selection is too small or large, without having to undo our selection. I've hardly begun to explain this feature, but I'm sure you're already seeing how much more powerful the Color Range command is than the Magic Wand.

Below the Fuzziness slider is a preview area, which we can use to display either our image, or our selection in black and white. Now, this is possibly your first introduction to the **Black and White** concept in Photoshop, but it's going to feature very prominently in the future as you delve deeper and deeper into the inner workings of the software.

With the plain eyedropper selected, and the preview image set to Selection, click in various places either on your image, or in the preview. Notice that the parts of the image that you select show up as white, those sections that are partially selected show up as gray, and what is not selected shows up as black.

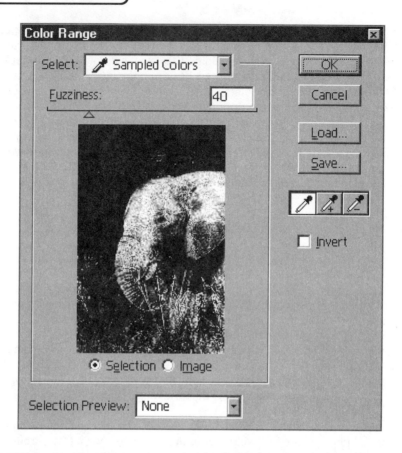

You can liken the white/gray/black scenario to white = light (so we can see), gray = lowlight (so we can only partially see), and black = night (and so we can't see a thing). Essentially, exactly the same logic follows for the Color Range command, alpha channels, and layer masks. Therefore, developing an understanding of what goes on in this preview box will give you an idea as to how the alpha channels in the Channels palette (still to come in this chapter) and layer masks work (we'll be looking at layer masks even later in the book).

Back to the dialog box, after that little aside...

On the right-hand side of the dialog box are three eyedroppers to be used for sampling colors:

The leftmost eyedropper is for creating a new selection, similar to the first click on an image with the Magic Wand. The eyedropper with a plus sign adds to the current selection shown in the preview window (if the Selection radio button below the image preview has been chosen), and the third eyedropper is for removing selected colors from the proposed selection. So, as you can see, unlike the Magic Wand, we don't have to deselect and try again if our selection goes too far!

However, like the Magic Wand and the other selection tools, there is no need to constantly switch between these three eyedroppers. Instead, we can remain with the regular eyedropper and then simply hold down the SHIFT key before clicking again to add to a selection, or depress OPTION/ALT before clicking to subtract from a selection.

The Invert option (note the check box below the eyedroppers) can come in handy for certain images. Take for example, an image of someone against a fairly uniformly colored background, and let's say that we wanted to make a copy of the person for another image. Trying to select the person with all the subtle variations in color would be difficult – far easier then to select the background and choose the Invert option.

Using the Color Range command

The only way to fully convince you of the power of this feature is to put it into practice so, without further ado, let's plunge in!

1. Ensure that you have `3-2elephant.psd` open, and that you have no active selections (CMD/CTRL+D).

2. Access the Color Range dialog box via the Select menu. Choose Sampled Colors as your color option at the top of the box, and leave the Fuzziness value at 40 for the time being.

3. Set the preview area to the Selection option, and what you should see is a predominantly black preview (remember the Black & White story?). Ensure that the Selection Preview option at the bottom of the dialog box is set to None.

4. With the regular eyedropper, click either in the preview area or on the image to get a basic selection of the elephant.

5. To add to your selection, either choose the eyedropper with the plus sign, or hold down the SHIFT key. Click, or click and drag, in either area until you have a reasonable selection of the elephant.

6. Drag the Fuzziness slider to the left to decrease the range of colors selected, or to the right to increase the range. Remember that whatever appears white is selected, and whatever is black is not.

7. Once you're fairly happy with the selection, click the OK button to return to the main window. You may recall that I said this was a fairly complex file to use, to introduce you to color-based selections, so don't be disappointed if it's not perfect! The foliage and background have colors in common with the elephant, and so you will not get a completely clean selection. This isn't too much of a problem though, as we'll use Quick Mask mode and also adjust the Alpha channels a little later on in the chapter to fine-tune our elephant.

8. Once you're back in the main Photoshop area, we'll use a handy trick to tidy up our selection a little more. Be careful with this one – too high a value will destroy the selection and you'll have to start again. Now, it's likely that in the bottom left of your image you have large areas partially selected which you don't really want selected at all. In Photoshop's mind, this is making your selection 'rough', because there are so many small areas that are selected. To get over this, choose Select > Modify > Smooth, and enter a value of 1 or 2 pixels for the Sample Radius parameter. In a high-resolution image, you could enter a slightly higher value. Let me guess – it's a little better, but it's not quite perfect?

9. If there are any large areas that you wish to deselect, you could use the OPTION/ALT key with either the Lasso tool or Rectangular Marquee tool to remove additional areas. Don't spend too much time trying to clean up the grass around the elephant's feet, as we have yet another weapon to help us there, and we'll get to that in just a minute.

10. For now, we can finish, so save your selection by accessing Save Selection from the Select menu. Ensure that you are creating a new channel, and call it Color Range Elephant, and then save the file to guarantee that the selection information is saved within the file.

And that's it – for now at least. You may be wondering where you've been saving these selections, and how you will access them again later. Don't worry – as soon as you hear the magic words 'Alpha channels', we're there!

Refining selections

At this stage, we've pretty much covered the most common ways of making geometric and color-based selections, so what remains for you to discover is how to refine and tidy up those selections. To do this we'll start by first introducing you to the Quick Mask feature, and then I'll give you a sneak peek at **Alpha channels**.

Using Quick Mask mode

The selection tools used so far have been fine for selecting geometric and freehand selections, or even making selections based on color, but remember how with our elephant image even these tools didn't quite make the grade. Neither approach has given us the means with which to tackle that pesky grass that surrounds the elephant's feet...

Enter Quick Mask mode! No, he's not a superhero able to change appearance instantaneously, in fact he doesn't even wear his underpants over his tights – but he is pretty handy when it comes to eliminating unwanted fine details from our selection.

So, with the elephant file open, have the elephant selection still active – if you've lost your elephant (a major achievement in any sphere, let's face it) don't worry. Choose Load Selection from the Select menu, and select the Color Range Elephant channel from the drop-down list.

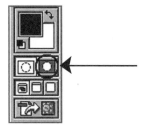

Click on the Quick Mask Mode button as indicated above, or better still, use the keyboard shortcut Q (I'm beginning to see a definite superhero connection here now – didn't James Bond rely on Q for help?). What you should see is that a large portion of the image is covered with a red, semi-opaque film. If this is not the case, double-click on the Quick Mask Mode button on the toolbox and set the parameters as per the following screenshot:

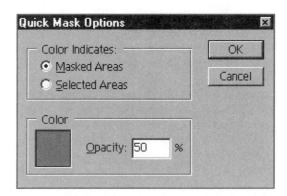

Unfortunately, you won't be seeing this screenshot in color, so you'll just have to trust me once again that the mask is indeed bright red. To set your color, click on the (you guessed it) Color box and select a particularly garish red to work with.

Now that we are all starting from the same point, have a look at your image on screen. The area covered with red is the area that is not selected, whilst the rest is the area that has been selected. Admittedly, in some cases it may be difficult to see what is and what is not selected, but resist the temptation to whack the color opacity up to 100%, it really doesn't help.

Should you wish to change the color of the mask, well that's up to you, who knows? It may even be desirable – for example, the bright red we have selected would not be suitable for working on an image of, say, a tomato!

Sometimes it's also useful to switch the color from indicating the masked areas to covering the selected areas, and it's often useful to switch between the two options to check a mask selection. Whenever making changes like these to the default settings, it's always good practice to return to the original values and colors indicated in the dialog box above on completion of the editing.

The joy of Quick Mask mode is that we can use almost any tool or menu option to further refine a selection, but for the purposes of this exercise we'll concentrate on using the Brush, Pencil and Eraser tools as these are tools with which you are probably more familiar.

You'll also find me pushing the shortcuts just a little more when we discuss the Quick Mask mode, as it's just so much quicker and easier to use these options, rather than constantly changing tools and options by selecting them from the menu and toolbars.

Whilst in Quick Mask mode, have a look at the foreground and background colors as indicated in the toolbox. You'll notice that according to this, the colors are black and white. Select the Paintbrush (B – another shortcut), and paint proudly across your image. Surprised? Black is the color with which you are painting, and yet the color added to your image is red. Choose Edit > Undo or CMD/CTRL+Z to undo that last action.

Switch the foreground color to white, and paint into the red area of your image. Once again, you may be surprised, because we have not in actual fact added any white to the image. Choose Edit > Undo or CMD/CTRL+Z to undo that last action.

Why? Well, it's all coming back to that 'Black and White' story again. If we paint with black, even though it shows up as red onscreen, we are removing areas from our selection (we don't see them, remember), and if we paint with white, we're adding to our selection (remember the analogy – when it's white, it's light, and we can see!). You can also use the Eraser to remove the red overlay from your image, but I'd suggest that you switch between painting with black and white to remove from or add to your selection. Not only does it keep the 'Black and White' analogy going, but also if I can convince you to use the keyboard shortcuts, you'll find this way of working a great deal quicker in the end.

Before we jump into another exercise, let's take a moment to see how we can use Quick Mask mode to clean up our selection:

- Use the Paintbrush or Pencil tool to paint onto the image in Quick Mask mode. Use the Paintbrush to paint a soft-edged area to a selection, or for sharp-edged, fine parts of the selection, use the Pencil tool. The shortcut to switch between the two tools once you have selected either one is SHIFT+B. Depending on the size of your hands, you may or may not consider this to be a shortcut. In my book, a shortcut is something that doesn't require that you remove your other hand from the mouse, so if you can't reach both keys with a single hand, you might be better off using the toolbox to switch tools.

- As you paint, you'll probably find that you need to adjust the size of your brush, and this is where keyboard shortcuts come to the rescue once again. You see, instead of using the dropdown list on the Paintbrush/Pencil Tool Options bar, the square brackets can be used to increase or reduce Paintbrush/Pencil size, [making the brush size smaller, while] does the opposite. Ensure that the cursor display is set to Brush Size (Edit > Preferences > Display and Cursors, and select Brush Size), so that you can more readily see what's going on with the size of your brush.

- To switch between painting with black (removing from the selection) and white (adding to the selection), either click the double-headed arrow above the foreground and background colors on the toolbox, or better still, press X to alternate between the two.

  To check on how your selection is developing, hit Q, or the Quick Mask Mode icon, to toggle between Normal mode and Quick Mask mode.

OK, ready to plough on? Then let's get into...

Using Quick Mask mode to refine selections

Back to the elephant image, and don't worry, it won't be long before I give you the choice between turning him into an pop-art type image, or manipulating the background so that we can fool viewers into believing that our sedate old elephant is actually a rampaging bull, and that we put our lives at risk taking the photograph.

1. OK, begin by ensuring that you have `3-2elephant.psd` open, and that you have your elephant selection active. If your elephant selection is no longer active, choose Load Selection from the Select menu, and select the Color Range Elephant channel from the drop-down list.

2. Switch to Quick Mask mode (if you're not already in it) by selecting the icon on the toolbar or pressing the Q key.

3. If you wish to change the color of the overlay, or to switch between having color show the Masked or Selected areas, double-click the Quick Mask mode icon on the toolbox.

4. Choose either the Paintbrush or Pencil tool (B), switch between painting with either black or white by pressing X, and change your brush size by using the [or] keys.

   Paint your image with black in areas where you want to remove elements from the selection (remember this will show up as a color on the screen), or with white to add an area to your selection and remove the colored overlay. Try switching between Normal mode and Quick Mask mode by switching between the two icons on the toolbox (or by pressing the Q key) to see how your selection is progressing. Keep going until you've cleaned up your entire selection, paying particular attention to that pesky, grassy problem area around the elephant's feet.

5. Save the selection as Quick Mask Elephant by choosing Save Selection from the Select menu, saving as a new channel and typing in the new name. Remember to also save the image file to ensure that the selection information is saved within it.

Feeling confident? You should be – we've covered quite a lot of ground already, so you may want to take this opportunity for a breather before we get started on a subject, the very mention of which brings a helpless gaze and a tear to the eye of many apparent Photoshop experts.

Have no fear – I'm not trying to increase the pace and accelerate away from you, this will be a steady and gentle...

Introduction to working with Alpha channels

"Why?" I hear you ask. Well, assuming that you are referring to our discussion of this topic, rather than expressing a deeper, philosophical query, I can tell you that introducing Alpha channels at this stage is meant for your overall Photoshopping benefit, not to punish you! Although there's many a seasoned Photoshop artist who has religiously avoided the subject, we are armed with the knowledge that what doesn't kill us will make us stronger.

I think at this stage I should point out to those of you now in the fetal position behind the couch that most of the complications of using Alpha channels are perceived, rather than real, and you'll soon find that all of their magic is available to you if you're prepared to tackle them head-on.

So, let's approach them cautiously at first, and take a look at what they *are* as well as what they *do* – it's a simple line of attack, and one that you should be used to by now. Let's strip off that cloak of mystery and air of superiority, and take the first step to putting Alpha channels at our creative mercy...

The brief

First off, the simple truth – Alpha channels are nothing more than a storage area for your saved selections.

Secondly, as with the Color Range command, the Quick Mask mode (both features with which you are familiar), and the Layer Mask mode (still to come), the bottom line is the Black and White story I mentioned earlier. In short, what is selected or visible is indicated by white, and what is not selected, or not visible, is indicated by black.

Gray areas are slightly more difficult to pin down (as they always are), but try to remember that the darker the gray in the Alpha channel, the lower the percentage of each individual pixel selected. Conversely, the lighter the gray implies a higher selected percentage.

Still with me? Just about? Good. Let's have a look at the Channels palette for our elephant file; so select Show Channels from the Window menu.

On this tab, you'll notice a number of color channels (RGB and so on), and these will be dealt with later in the book. Accompanying these, there are also 3 additional 8-bit (note the grayscale images, capable of displaying 256 levels of gray!) channels, and these are our selections, which have been saved at various stages throughout the chapter.

To view each channel in turn, click on the channel's name, and your screen will switch to display the channel, which in turn corresponds to the saved selection. Take a few moments, click through them a number of times, and remember that what is black is not selected, what is white is, and in the gray areas it depends on the density of the gray as to how much of that area is selected.

Three different beasts...

In the basic elephant channel, you've probably got a black and white image that is limited in detail and almost certainly contains no information pertaining to the grass around the elephant's feet.

In the Color Range Elephant channel, you should be able to make out a fair amount of detail in the grassy areas, with many of the pixels showing up as white, indicating that they are selected areas.

In the refined Quick Mask Elephant channel, you should see an image that is pretty much a combination of the two previous channels, and the detail in the channel depends very much on how much patience you had when you were painting in the individual grass strands. Do you notice any soft semi-gray areas in the channel? If you do, these indicate areas where you may have used the Paintbrush tool, while the hard-edged, fine areas indicate where you have used the Pencil tool to paint in details.

Viewing channels

To view an Alpha channel in conjunction with an image, ensure that the target channel is highlighted and visible (there should be an eye to the left of the channel name on the palette). Now click in the 'eye' area next to the composite RGB channel. Have a look at the following screenshot, here we can see that we have an Alpha channel both visible and active, and that we also have the composite RGB channel visible.

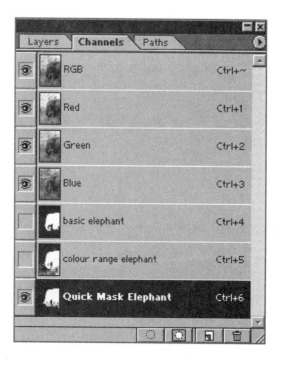

Does this look familiar? A little like Quick Mask mode? Well, it is, and the upshot of this is that if we wanted to skip the intermediate Quick Mask step, we could make a selection, save it as an Alpha channel, and then dive right in there and edit that – and we'll be doing some editing directly in Alpha channels a little later!

To return to Normal viewing mode, click on the RGB composite channel, there will be a highlight in the palette in the RGB, Red, Green, and Blue channels. Ensure that the eye next to the Alpha channel is no longer visible. This is achieved by clicking on the eye next to the channel you wish to hide.

If you wish to edit one of your channels, make sure that channel is both visible and selected (the channel name is highlighted), and edit with whichever tools suit your purpose. We'll use the Paintbrush and Pencil tools a little later, and paint in black and white (again).

All this discussion about channels has failed to answer what is probably one of your most pressing questions – "I can see the channel, but how do I load it as a selection?" Well, there are a number of ways in which this can be achieved. I'll show you three ways, but you can bet I'll be pushing the shortcut method! To load a channel as a selection:

1. Choose Load Selection from the Select menu and scroll until you see the name of the desired channel and then click OK.

2. In the Channels palette, make your target channel active and click on the icon as indicated in the following screenshot. Once you've done that, return to your composite image by clicking on the RGB channel and then ensuring that the eye next to the Alpha channel is switched off.

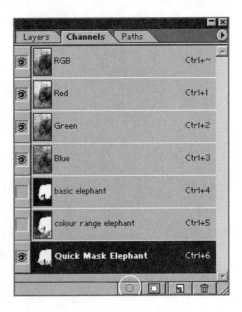

3. You just had to know there was a shortcut coming! So here it is. With the composite image visible, CMD/CTRL and click in the target Alpha channel on the Channels palette.

> *Another gentle nudge... I'd suggest that you learn how to load channels this way because this shortcut works not only for channels, but also for layers, layer masks, and paths as well – so it will come in handy even more as you become more proficient.*

Phew! All that information! I'm sure you're positively screaming for a chance to play, so let's kick off another exercise, and what better name for this than...

Working in Alpha channels to refine selections

1. Here we are, at the final stage in preparing our elephant image for the manipulation that is to follow. If you don't already have it open, start by opening `3-2elephant.psd`. Open the Channels palette and click on Quick Mask Elephant channel to make this channel both visible and active.

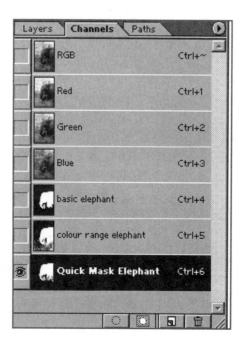

Look carefully at the black and white depiction – are there areas that are not as clean as they should be? White splotches in the black areas, or vice-versa?

2. OK, choose either the Paintbrush tool or the Pencil tool, and start to clean up any of these areas. Remember – painting with black subtracts from the selection, and painting with white adds to the selection. As you progress, you may find it useful to toggle the eye next to the composite RGB channel off and on to check your progress. When you're happy with your selection, save the file.

> *Because we're working directly in the channels, there's no need to follow the two-step procedure of saving the selection and then saving the file as we have done in the past.*

Once you're done, you should have a very clean channel that corresponds closely to your selected and non-selected areas, and we are in fact nearly finished...

3. However, we're not out of the woods yet. You see, we're going to need two variations on this theme, so we need to duplicate and then edit the individual Alpha channels. Now, to do this, we could follow the menu-driven option by accessing the contextual palette menu. We would do this by clicking on the arrow at the top right hand corner of the Channels palette, and then choosing Duplicate Channel from this menu, as illustrated here...

...or we could be brave and continue down the shortcut route by pressing OPTION/ALT and dragging the channel to be duplicated onto the New Channel icon which is located at the bottom of the palette (to the left of the Trash Can icon). Alternatively, we could CONTROL + CLICK (Mac) or right-click (PC) to access the context menu, which also offers an option to duplicate the channel. Whichever process you decide to follow, rename the channel Background Selection.

As it stands, the newly created Background Selection channel is not what we need, as it's the elephant that's white, and therefore selected, and we want the background to be selected instead. Let's set this straight.

4. With this channel selected on the Channels palette, choose Image > Adjust > Invert (CMD/CTRL + I) to switch the colors around. Now the background area should be white, and the elephant should be black, indicating that when we load the channel as a selection, it will be the background area and not the elephant that is selected.

5. The original Quick Mask Elephant selection may well include the tusks in the white (selected) area. If this is the case, use the Paintbrush and Pencil tools to remove them from the selection.

6. Save the file, and then make a duplicate of the file by selecting Image > Duplicate. Name this duplicate file popArt.

7. Now, with the original 3-2elephant.psd file active, it's time to load up the Background Selection channel, and manipulate that area of the image. You *could* load the selection by selecting Choose Load Selection from the Select menu, scrolling until you saw the name Background Selection, and then clicking OK. Like I say, yes, you could do it that way, but I'd sleep a lot more soundly in my bed tonight if you took the shortcut. Believe me, it's in your own interest. I know how hard it can be to let go of that mouse sometimes, but a simple CMD/CTRL+CLICK on the Background Selection channel on the Channels palette is not too much of a burden, I'm sure.

8. With the background foliage now active, go to the Filter > Blur > Motion Blur and input values similar to those shown in the dialog box below, and then click OK.

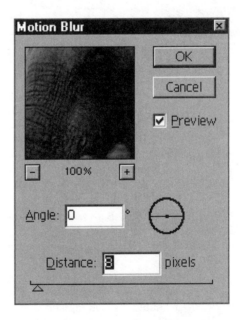

There you have it, one rampaging elephant! Save and close the file.

© 3-2elephant1.psd @ 100% (RGB)

9. Now switch to the pop art file that we created just a minute ago, and which should still be active on your desktop. Load the Quick Mask Elephant channel selection by selecting Choose Load Selection from the Select menu and choosing the correct target channel, or CMD/CTRL+CLICK on the Quick Mask Elephant channel on the Channels palette.

10. From the Swatches palette, select a color for the elephant, preferably something totally unrealistic (you've worked hard – you deserve a little fun!). To color the elephant, select Edit > Fill, and then set the parameters in the subsequent dialog that appears to be something similar to those shown on the next page:

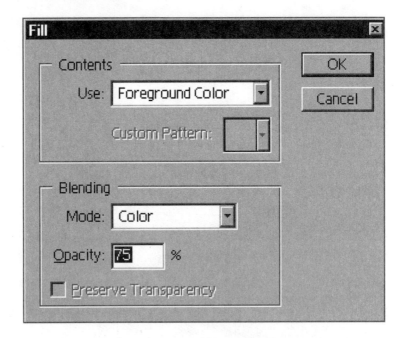

Note that in an attempt to retain some of the elephant's natural color, the Fill Mode has been set to Color, not Normal, and the opacity has been set to 75%.

11. Click OK, then save and close your pop-art style elephant.

Congratulations if you stuck with me through all that! As I warned you in the beginning, the image was not the easiest to make a clean selection from, but if you managed to create a fairly decent one and understood the process that was being followed, you're well on your way to mastering the skills you'll need to become a competent Photoshopper!

Using menu commands to refine selections

I can just see you sitting there, dusting your hands, mission accomplished, selections under your belt, smug smile on your face; and here I am saying there's still more to learn! Don't worry, we're just going to take a quick look at some of the Select menu commands, which can help you refine your selections, and then we'll relax and have some more creative fun.

Inverse

The first command to be tackled is the Inverse command. You may well be wondering why we would go to great lengths to accurately select an area of our image, just to ask Photoshop to select exactly the opposite. Well, as I mentioned earlier, when we were looking at the Color Range command, such functionality would be useful if we wanted to lift part of a multi-colored image from its background, if the background was of a fairly constant color it may well be easier to select that area, and then ask Photoshop to invert the selection so that we had the target area of the image selected.

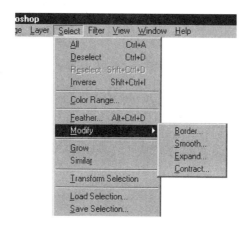

The Modify menu option

Looking at the Modify sub-menu, there are a few features that we've not yet discussed, which can be useful for manipulating selections. The Expand and Contract commands should be pretty self-explanatory, as they enable us to do exactly that to active selections. Bear in mind that all images in Photoshop are resolution-dependent, which means that the values we choose to insert in the dialog boxes will affect the file relative to its resolution. For example, 12 pixels in a 72 dpi image is a far larger area than 12 pixels in a 300 dpi image.

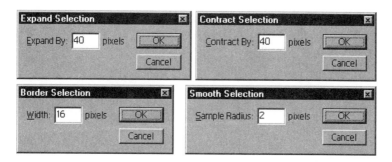

Earlier, I mentioned that the Smooth command can be useful for eliminating rogue pixels in a color-based selection. Remember back to when we started refining the elephant Color Range selection? Once again, the value we input is relative to the resolution of our image. Too high a value on a low-resolution image and your selection will lose all its detail.

The Border option should also be fairly self-explanatory. It replaces a solid selection with a bordered selection, thus removing the central part of the selection. If, using the value in the Border Selection dialog box (shown above), we chose to set a border width of 16 pixels, this would be centrally placed on the previous selection outline, with the border expanding in both directions by 8 pixels. Also, as for the above examples, these values are resolution-dependent, meaning that the actual physical size of the border is dependent on the resolution of the image. The lower the resolution, the greater the visual effect of the border.

Grow and Similar

Sounding a bit like a dodgy firm of lawyers, the Grow and Similar commands could be costly for you too, if you don't take the time to learn the difference between them. The easiest way to explain them is to liken them to the functionality of the Magic Wand tool and its options.

When using the Magic Wand command, remember how we had an option to increase the Tolerance value to select a wider range of colors in adjacent areas? Well, this is essentially what the Grow command achieves. For example, if you've made a selection, and then realize that you could have had a higher Tolerance value, using the Grow command will increase the selection area by increasing the range of colors selected. Be careful though, as you're not able to specify by how much you would like to increase the range of colors selected, and can often end up inadvertently ruining your selection.

The Similar feature behaves in a (dare I say it?) *similar* way to the Contiguous option on Tool Options bar of the Magic Wand tool. Once you've made a selection, you can use this feature to select pixels of similar color to those already selected throughout an image. But once again you have little control, and may find the option cumbersome in comparison to some of the features we've already discussed.

However, I'm not suggesting that you ignore either Grow or Similar – they can be very useful when you are making simple selections. All I'm saying is that you should not expect too much finesse and control from them.

Combining your new-found skills

Well, your Photoshop toolbox should have increased considerably in weight from the modified pencil case you keenly carried into the start of the chapter. Lest it get too heavy, let's lay this box down and arrange our tools neatly on the ground before us, ready to put them to use in the next exercise.

In the very first exercise in this chapter, we transformed a pretty regular black and white striped image into something that, with a fairly good stretch of the imagination, resembled four birds with their beaks touching. When we did this, I promised then that you would have a chance to come back to this image at some stage, and refine both your newly learned selection skills, and the painting skills acquired in earlier chapters. Well, here we are again. You've spent a long time straining your left brain with new concepts, it's time to switch to the right and give you a chance to enjoy and consolidate, before you move onto the case study, and then onto even more new skills. You may also notice an increased emphasis on keyboard shortcuts here. Don't doubt my persistence!

Putting it all together with the birds...

1. Open the file called `3-1twirl.psd`, which you saved earlier. It should look something like this:

2. From the View menu, access the Show sub-menu and ensure that there is a check next to Guides. Similarly, ensure that there is a check next to Guides on the Snap To sub-menu. Reset all the tools to their original settings by accessing the drop-down menu from the tool icon, and reset all palettes to their original screen locations by choosing this option from the bottom of the Window menu.

3. The first thing we'll do is save the entire black and white original as a channel to make some of your selections easier. Select the entire canvas by choosing Edit > Select All (CMD/CTRL+A), and then switch to the Channels palette.

4. Now access the drop-down context menu by clicking on the arrow in the top right-hand corner of the palette, and choose New Channel (or OPTION/ALT+CLICK on the New Channel icon at the bottom of the palette). Name the channel Total Image. The OPTION/ALT+CLICK shortcut enables us to create and name a channel without having to access the drop-down menu, or double-click on the channel in the palette at a later stage.

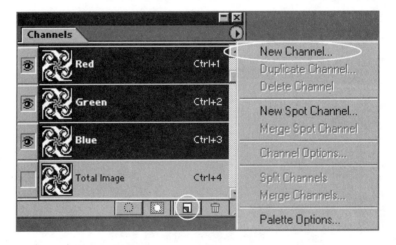

5. Return to the main image by clicking on the RGB composite channel at the top of the Channel palette. We'll create and save some other selections in channels for easy access to the original state as our image develops.

6. Now, select the Rectangular Marquee selection tool (M), and use it to draw a selection accurately around the top left-hand quadrant. We don't want to save the entire block as a selection, only the pristine white areas, so switch to the Magic Wand (W), hold down the OPTION/ALT key, and click in the black areas within the quadrant to remove them from the selection. Continue until only the white areas remain selected. Don't forget the little black areas against the edges of the quadrant.

> *To check that you have completed the selection, you may wish to switch momentarily to Quick Mask mode (Q). All the white areas should be clear of color, and the black covered with the red film. If all seems okay, switch back to Normal mode by pressing Q again.*

7. Save the selection as Top Left by accessing the Save Selection option on the Select menu. If you wish, have a look at the Channels palette to ensure that this has happened. Remember also to save the file.

8. Repeat this previous step another three times, saving the further selections as Top Right, Bottom Right, and Bottom Left (don't forget those little areas against the borders). When you're done save the file.

> *Alternatively, of course, we could have done a blanket white selection throughout the image, but we want to be able to color each bird independently, as well as practice our selection skills, so that's why I suggested we do it the other way.*

Creating the birds' eyes

So we've got our birds, and I figure it's about time we gave them some eyes, and guess what? You guessed it; we're going to use selections to make these too. We'll make and save the selections for use later in the exercise.

1. Select the Elliptical Marquee tool, and in the Tool Options bar, set a feather of 5 pixels. The feather value has been set because we wish to avoid having hard edges of color in our image. We're not going for realism here!

2. In the top left-hand quadrant, draw a selection with the Elliptical Marquee tool that corresponds roughly to what we would presume to be the eye area. Don't worry if it's not perfect, we'll use the Transform Selection command from the Select menu to help us with that.

3. Choose the Transform Selection command, and move the cursor outside the bounding box to rotate the ellipse as necessary. Drag on the handles to resize, and if you wish to reposition the selection, click and drag on the flashing boundary. Save this selection as TL eye.

4. To save unnecessary time and effort, switch back to one of the selection tools, position your cursor within the selection and drag it down to the bottom right quadrant. We've chosen to go here because the bird is at roughly the opposite angle, so we don't have to do any major transforming to the selection to get it to fit. Save this selection as BR eye.

5. Drag the selection to either of the remaining quadrants, transform as needed, and then save and repeat until all the eye areas are saved as selections, naming the remaining selections TR eye (for top right) and BL eye (for bottom left). Save your file.

6. Now have another look at the Channels palette. Click on one of the four quadrant selections, note the black and white areas, and remember that they correlate to what will be selected when the channel is loaded as a selection – white areas will be selected, black will not. Click on one of the eye channels and note that in addition to the solid black and white areas, there is also a transitional gray area. This is where the feathered selection goes from being totally selected (white) to not being selected (black).

Painting the birds

With those selections in place, we're ready to start painting. I'll give you suggestions for one of the birds, concentrating on varying the way in the selections are made and the manner in which the various painting tools are used. How many you wish to complete is entirely up to you, and the time you have at your disposal.

1. Load the TL eye selection by accessing the Load Selection command from the Select menu and choosing the correct channel. Select the Airbrush tool (J) and your choice of color for the eyes from the Swatches palette. With a fairly large brush and a low opacity, put a light coat of color in the area. Do not attempt to fill it with a solid color – you'll want some scope for manipulation as the image develops.

2. What else have birds got? Beaks, that's what, and we'll look at how to bring that into our project now, but we'll keep it simple. To create and fill the beak area, load the Top Left selection, and then with the OPTION/ALT key and the Magic Wand tool (M) click in the additional white areas, which effectively do not form part of the bird's body.

   In the next two steps of the exercise, we'll give the edges a soft appearance and try to keep some of the definition between the different regions.

3. With the area selected, click Select > Modify > Contract, and set the value to 2 pixels. Then set a Feather value of 4 pixels.

4. If you paint in this area now, you're likely to over-paint the eye area, but there's a very easy way to protect against this. I couldn't resist slipping in a variation on the Load Selection dialog box. So far, by default, we've always been loading New Selections, but here we want to *remove* the eye area from the active selection. With the bird's body still selected, go to the Load Selection dialog box, choose TL eye as the channel, and instead of leaving New Selection as the active operation, choose Subtract from Selection, and click OK.

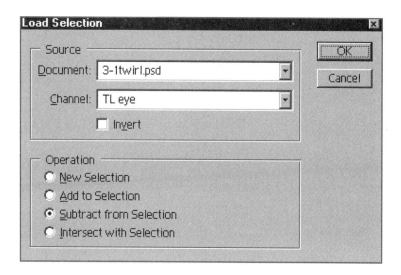

This should have effectively removed the eye area from the active selection. It may be that you're beginning to see now, why we followed that long process of saving the selections as channels earlier. To try and select the areas once we've colored them would be far more difficult.

Continue to paint the area, switching colors and tool opacity at will. Once again, don't cover the area entirely with color, and don't worry if it still looks a little blotchy. We'll use a cheap and cheerful trick to smooth that out.

With the area still selected, choose Filter > Blur > Gaussian Blur.

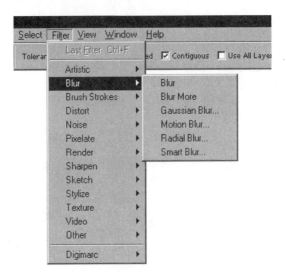

5. In the dialog box that follows, change the radius setting until you've gently blurred your painted areas. This filter can be memory-intensive, so you must give the computer time to catch up as you change the filter values. To view a specific area of the image in the preview window, click in the image with your cursor.

6. To select the black area of the bird's body in the upper left quadrant, ready for painting, simply click on one of the black areas with the Magic Wand tool, and then SHIFT+CLICK to add the other black area to your selection. Once again we'll maintain those soft, defined edges by contracting the selection by 2 pixels, and then feathering by 4 pixels. You should be familiar with the location of these options on the Select menu by now, but if are unsure, you may wish to refer to the earlier instructions.

7. Paint this area as before, and run a Gaussian Blur filter to soften any rough areas in your painting. When you are happy with it, save your file.

Feel free to go ahead and have a play with your image – you'd be surprised at some of the effects that can be generated using the tools we've familiarized ourselves with.

Case Study

In the case study, which runs from the end of chapter three to eleven, we are going to build a postcard and companion web page for a fictitious company called Exotic Imports. We are going to take some of the new skills you just learned out "for a spin" in the real world. This will have a twofold reward:

- It will reinforce what you just learned

- It will provide a vehicle for you to begin to think of ways to apply your new skills

You don't have to create exactly what you see in the case study, I encourage you to use your own images and create something unique. Apply the principles and techniques and create something 100% yours! The photos used are from the Corel "Exotic Cars" royalty-free CD and if you want to stick with the exotic car theme, but don't want to buy the CD, similar images can be found at www.hemerastudio.com. (There is no breach of copyright if you download these images for personal use only, but you are not allowed to distribute them.)

For this project assume we have a job order. The client is launching a new branch at Irvine California, they need a postcard to mail out, which introduces their line of fine imported automobiles, and they would also like a simple companion web site.

In this first part of the case study we are going to prepare two images for use on the project:

- For one image we will create a vignette effect for the picture. This means the edges will be soft and blend into white for a nice clean look. We are going to use this image for our postcard AND our web page. This is a very nice effect that you will use often in your career and you will soon discover that it is an easy effect to create.

- For the second we are going to remove an object from its background using the Extract tool. We are going to use this image later in a collage, so it will be sharing a background with another picture on the home page.

We are going to use two different methods for removing pictures from their backgrounds in the course of this case study. In this section you will learn how to use the Extract tool (introduced in Photoshop 5.5). The Extract tool is really good for removing a complex shape or a shape with irregular soft edges from a multi-colored background (I would choose the Magic Wand or the Color Sampler tool for an image with a solid background color). In the next part we will look at using the Pen tool. This is the slowest way, but the Pen produces the sharpest edges, I usually use the Pen tool for high resolution printing, because the details are very noticeable in print work, as compared to web work, which is a lot more forgiving.

Softening the border

1. We will begin by preparing the background image for our postcard. We would like to have soft edges, fading into white. I used an image of the back-end of a Porsche for this. (Open image `29071.jpg` – from Corel "Exotic Cars" CD)

2. With the Rectangular Marquee tool, draw a large border around the photo. We are marking the edges of the new border.

3. Now we want to soften the selection, so that we don't get a hard edge: Select > Feather, add use a radius of 10 pixels.

4. Now if we deleted the selection, we would lose our main picture and just keep our border. The solution is to inverse the selection, so that just the outside area is selected. Select > Inverse (SHIFT+CTRL/CMD+I)

5. Press the D key to reset the Foreground/Background colors (or the black on white icon in the tool bar). Now, to fill the border with white, open the Fill dialog box: Either Edit > Fill or SHIFT+BACKSPACE. Select Background Color and press OK.

Press CTRL/CMD+D *or* Select > Deselect to turn off the selection. We now have the image we will use for our background.

6. Now that we have created the effect on the edges of our picture, we will save it for use later. Save it as exotic imports.tif. The reason we are saving as a TIFF is that this format is lossless which means that the original photo quality is maintained.

For this project I suggest you create a directory called FP Case study with three more subdirectories under the case study directory, called Working, Website and Final.

A note about workflow and housekeeping: It is very important to organize your files. Usually when I am working on a project I create the initial directory (or folder) for a client, then I create separate subdirectories for each part of the project. Within those subdirectories I create 3 more subdirectories, called: Working, Final and Output.

- Working is where I keep my files that are under construction and not yet finished, sometimes I call this "junkyard" because it can get filled up with all kinds of junk pretty quickly.

- Final is where I keep all the finished PSD files.

- Output is where I put the files in the final output formats; TIFF, EPS, PDF etc. When I am designing for the Web I will call this web and put my HTML files and images there. (Note I will create another subdirectory called images to keep all the pictures in when I create a web page normally.)

Once I've finished a project, I usually dump my junkyard/working folder (all the final PSDs should be saved under the final folder). And save the final and output folders to a CD for archiving. I remember a long time ago when I didn't do this, I had a hard drive failure and lost months of work! Just about every professional designer has horror stories, but I also have a positive one! About a year ago I got a nasty virus that wiped out all my JPEGs. This could have caused me to go into major stress, but because of my habit of archiving everything to a CD, it didn't affect me beyond a few hours cleaning off the virus and restoring my system.

A very good thing to remember is to save, save and save again. Whenever I finish a major transformation to my image I save it because of the "unlikely" (ha ha) event that my computer will crash or lock up.

You should also get into the habit of naming your layers. I am bad at this one, but when working on a document with a lot of layers I generally name the folders (layer set) and put whatever layers are relevant to the folder there.

Removing the car from the background

1. I decided to use the image of an Aluma Coupe for the collage on my homepage (open `29024.jpg`). We are going to remove it from its background using the Extract tool.

2. Bring up the window for the Extract tool (Image > Extract... or ALT+CTRL/CMD+X). Since this image consists of hard edges I used a (fairly small) 19-pixel brush, which will limit the transition size.

The trick to using this tool is to use a large brush size for soft edges like hair and fur, and a small brush for hard edges. I usually keep all the other settings as default because I don't want to waste too much time in the Extract box; it's often quicker to clean up the images later on. You can use the [ ] keys to enlarge and shrink the brush while you draw. Draw around the entire object. I've found, for a cleaner extract, it's best to try to keep one third of the brush inside the object and two-thirds on the outside. This area is the transition area, where Photoshop makes the decisions about what to keep and what to throw away.

3. Now select the Fill Bucket (top left) and fill the areas that we want to protect. Make sure you don't forget the front wheel.

Click OK and you will have a loose cutout image. We will need to clean it up a bit now. Notice that there are bits missing from the object.

4. We can paint them back in using the History brush. Open the History palette, select the History Brush and click to the left of the Open state. A History Brush icon appears, telling us this is the state that will be painted (the original image when we first opened the file).

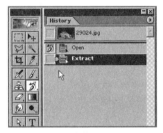

Begin to paint back the areas that were accidentally erased. Use a hard-edged brush so that you will get a sharp clean edge. For larger areas, use a larger brush (30+ pixels) and for fine details use a smaller brush (5 or 10 pixels). Zoom in closer if you need to see more detail.

There will also be some areas that have been left over, that should have been erased. Clean these up with the Eraser tool. If you erase too much, you can switch back to the History brush to replace it. Vary your brush size depending on the detail you are working on and you may need to go over some parts of the outline, like the roof, which may be partially transparent.

Take your time with this step, it's important to get the image as clean as possible. You can usually tell an experienced designer from a less experienced one by the quality of their extractions. When you are done, you should have something that resembles this.

5.   Save the file in your working folder as `yellow car.psd`, we'll be using it later in our web page. It's important to save as a PSD because this is the standard Photoshop format and it maintains all the layers, channels, paths and layer styles.

Summary

Hopefully, this chapter has consolidated your initiation to the secret skills possessed by every successful Photoshopper – in particular, the ability to make accurate and neat selections within an image. It doesn't matter how creative your imagination is, or how complete your knowledge of other features in Photoshop, if you can't make a good selection, you're stuck at the starting line.

So, just to review, in this chapter we've looked at:

- The major selection tools – their characteristics, strengths, and weaknesses

- How to use these tools to create aesthetically pleasing effects

- How to combine different selection features to maximize their potential

- The Channels palette – the hidden storage area of saved selections

- The concept of Black (deselected) and White (selected) in Photoshop selections

- The 'gray area', and how this relates to how much of a section is selected

In the next chapter we'll be looking at another way of creating selections by introducing the concept of vector graphics and paths.

4 Paths

What we'll cover in this chapter:

- *An introduction to vector graphics*

- *The nature of paths*

- *Introducing the Pen tool*

- *Using the Paths palette to organise your paths*

- *Using the magnetic Pen tool to make selections*

- *Manipulating paths*

- *Loading paths as selections*

- *Creating clipping paths*

- *Copying paths from one file to another*

- *Drawing Bezier curves*

- *Transforming paths*

- *Creating clipping paths to export 'transparent' images for print*

An introduction to the concept of vector graphics

Welcome to the wonderful world of vector graphics, in this chapter you will be introduced to the various pen tools as a means of not only making more accurate freeform selections in your images, but also as a way of drawing vector shapes in your Photoshop images.

There are some experienced Photoshop users who have shied away from learning about paths and the Pen tool, but with the latest innovations in Photoshop 6, including support for vectors, this attitude is an outdated one. The Pen tool and the Paths palette are powerful tools for creating and manipulating freeform shapes, once mastered they allow us an enhanced level of creative freedom to create images that are a wonderful mix of both raster images and vector shapes.

You may already have some questions forming, for instance:

- What is a vector shape?

- Why am I learning to draw in a photo-editing application?

- Isn't learning about paths before I learn about layers and shape layers, putting the cart before the horse?

This chapter will answer these questions. We will learn all about Bezier curves, paths, anchor points and more. But first, a little bit of background...

Vector graphics in Photoshop

Earlier versions of Adobe Photoshop established the product as the de facto application for photo editing, but probably the most innovative feature added to the latest release was the addition of the shape tools and the shape layers with extensive support for the creation and manipulation of vector shapes.

Prior to this release, if we wanted to create an illustration, that is, a mix of sharp-edged vector graphics and continuous tone (photographic) images, our workflow was a little convoluted. The scenario would be to open a vector-based illustration application such as Adobe Illustrator or Macromedia Freehand, create all our shapes, export the file in a format compatible in Adobe Photoshop, open it in Photoshop and continue. Then we'd realize that we wanted to make a ground-level change to the illustration, so we'd open up our drawing application again, make the changes, export again...and so the cycle repeats itself.

With support for scalable vector shapes, life is just so much simpler. Create the illustration from the ground up in Adobe Photoshop using vector shapes and shape layers. Scale, transform, and manipulate these shapes without worrying about degrading our image, and the whole process is relatively stress-free.

Pixels versus Vectors

In the previous chapter you were introduced to the concept of pixels, and that in order to manipulate any part of the image you had to make a selection. This was a slight over-simplification of the matter because with the introduction of support for vectors in Adobe Photoshop 6, the situation has changed. Let's clarify the situation now.

Photoshop 6 supports two very distinct types of graphics: **Pixel images** (also referred to as **raster**, **bitmap** or **continuous tone images**), and **Vector graphics**.

- **Pixel images:** You have been introduced to these already. These images are composed of tiny squares, more correctly referred to as pixels. The pixels are colored and shaded by Photoshop to represent the image you have imported. These images are **resolution-dependent**, which simply means that they are composed of a fixed number of these pesky pixels, and if you scale the image or even part of the image, what happens is that your little squares become bigger squares, and the resulting image will look jagged when printed.

- **Vector graphics:** These images are the complete opposite. They are composed of lines and curves defined by mathematical formulae. This means that we can scale and transform these graphics at will without any loss of resolution or detail. Unlike bitmap images, they will not become jaggy when scaled, they will retain their clean lines irrespective of how much we scale them, or at what resolution they are printed; and as such, they are called **resolution-independent** graphics.

When do we use paths?

Probably the oldest and most traditional reason for creating a path was to enable you to demarcate areas that should be invisible when an image is exported and placed in a page-layout application such as Adobe InDesign or Quark XPress. An image in Photoshop is always rectangular in shape, and no area is transparent when it is exported in a format suitable for placement in these applications. To eliminate the unwanted background, we could draw an outline around the portions of the image we wanted to display, and save this as a **clipping path**, a process that you will learn later in this chapter.

Alternatively we may want to draw and paint in Photoshop rather than manipulate a photographic image, and to control our shapes more accurately, we would create paths and then fill them or stroke (outline) them. Or we could draw a path round part of our image, and load that shape up as a selection to be saved in our Channels palette for further manipulation. Finally, we might just want to use the new features in Photoshop 6 to create scalable, resolution-independent graphic shapes.

The nature of paths

A few points about paths before we begin:

- Rather than creating selections with the tools you used in the previous chapter, the Pen tool creates path segments that are anchored in position by aptly named **anchor points**.

- As you draw a path with any Pen tool, a **work path** is created.

- Paths can be manipulated by moving the individual anchor points, anchor point handles or the path segments with the Direct Selection tool. More about this later.

- Like selections, these working paths can be saved with a file. But unlike selections, they are not saved in the Channels palette, but in the Paths palette, as illustrated below:

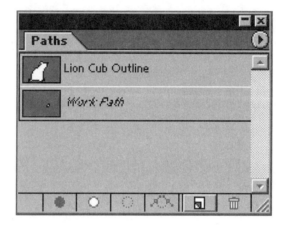

Introducing the Pen tool

As mentioned earlier, there's many an experienced Photoshop user who has never quite got to grips with drawing Bezier curves with the Pen tool, and to be honest, when you first start using it, you may find it clunky and quirky. My advice to you is to not give up, but to persevere with the tool, and soon you'll come to appreciate how useful and accurate it is in drawing shapes and paths in your image.

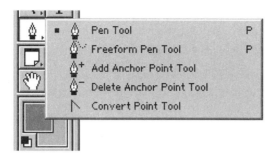

The Pen tool is actually a number of different tools: the Pen, the Freeform Pen, and the Magnetic Pen are all useful drawing tools. The Convert Point tool is ideal for editing paths that we have already created, and as you will see later, the Pen tool comes in very handy when editing paths too. In order to give you a full introduction to the concept of paths we will first of all concentrate on drawing the paths, then we will consider using the Magnetic Pen tool to make selections, and finally we will consider how to use the various Pen tools to edit and manipulate paths.

Using the Freeform Pen tool

To launch you into working with the Pen tool, we'll start using the Freeform Pen, which bears a certain similarity to drawing with a real world pencil. You draw the line, and Photoshop will automatically deposit anchor points along the path for you. It's a friendly introduction to the concept, but the disadvantage of the Freeform tool is that you seldom manage to draw a path that perfectly suits your needs, also this tool tends to put down far more anchor points on the path than are necessary.

Let's begin by looking at the Options bar for this tool. The first two icons which toggle at the extreme left of the bar determine whether you are going to draw a new shape layer or a path to be saved into the Paths palette. We will discuss shape layers a little later, so for the moment, ensure that the Create new work path icon is depressed.

If you cannot see the Create new work path button, but instead can see four buttons on the left hand side of the Options bar, then this could be because you have already made a mark in the document. If you want to start from scratch then press the Dismiss target path icon (it looks like a check mark) on the right hand side of the toolbar, and you will return to having a blank screen and just two buttons on the left hand side of the toolbar.

The Curve Fit option determines how closely the final path imitates the path you draw with your mouse. You can enter a value between 0.5 and 10 pixels, with the lower value creating a path which more closely follows your mouse, but that is more complex and has more anchor points.

By checking Auto Add/Delete, you do not have to switch to the Add Anchor Point tool or the Delete Anchor Point tool (more of which later) to add or delete anchor points from the active path. This means that once you have drawn the path, and it is still active, you will be able to edit it without changing tools.

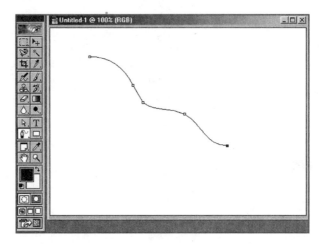

Once you have created a path, the Options bar display will change, showing four new icons on the left hand side.

These four icons determine how any new sub-paths that you draw will interact with existing active paths, from left to right. They are:

- Add to shape area: Any areas encompassed by a new path will be included with areas in existing sub-paths. The keyboard shortcut for this function is +

- Subtract from shape area: As you draw with the Pen tool, if you overlap onto areas that were previously surrounded by a sub-path, those areas will be subtracted. The shortcut for this is -

- Intersect shape areas: Only the areas common to the preceding sub-path, and the one you are drawing, will remain.

- Exclude overlapping shape areas: Areas common to the existing path and the newly created path will be excluded.

As you draw on the image, what is happening with the various options might not be clear, and I suggest you keep an eye on the Paths palette to help you visually. The areas depicted by white in the palette are those areas that form the areas encompassed by the path.

The Dismiss target path icon (the check mark) at the extreme right of the Options bar dismisses the target path. This means that the path is no longer active. You would click this if you were unhappy with your path, and wished to start again, or just wanted to de-activate the work path. Remember that if you choose this option to deactivate the work but wished to keep the path, you must go to the Paths palette and save it. If you can't see the Dismiss target path icon at the extreme right, maximise Photoshop so that it is covering your entire screen, and then it should appear.

The Magnetic Freeform Pen tool

The Magnetic Freeform Pen tool is a variation of the Freeform Pen. It is an extremely effective means of selecting an area of an image, rather like the Magnetic Lasso, which we looked at in the last chapter. To select the tool you need to first choose the Freeform Pen tool from the Toolbox, and then check the Magnetic box.

Setting the Magnetic Freeform Pen tool options

The Magnetic options for this tool offer a similar functionality to those offered by the Magnetic Lasso, with the only real difference being the limit on the rate for frequency, the Magnetic Pen tool is pegged at a ceiling value of 40 pixels. To set these options click on the Magnetic Pen options button on the Options bar.

- Width: as with the Magnetic lasso, this refers to the size of the area that will be searched below the mouse for color contrast as you move your cursor over the image.

- Contrast: this value is the percentage by which pixels need to vary in color for Photoshop to determine whether to put down an anchor point.

- Frequency: this relates to how often Photoshop will automatically add an anchor point along a path as you draw. The higher the value, the more accurate, but the more complex the path will be.

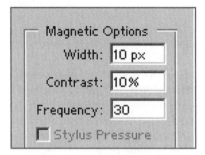

Comparing the Magnetic Pen tool and the Magnetic Lasso

i) Making selections

Enough of theory, let's put it to the test. In the chapter on selections, you were introduced to the Magnetic Lasso tool as an option for creating freeform contrast-based selections around objects. You may remember that, as a conclusion to the discussion of that tool, I suggested that you may find the Magnetic Pen tool a better option, because it offers a far greater freedom for manipulation and accuracy, once the initial outline has been created. We're here to prove that point now.

In this exercise we will use both the Magnetic Lasso tool and the Magnetic Freeform Pen tool to create a selection in an image. After you have completed the exercise, you will be well aware of the similarities and differences between the two tools, and in a position to make an educated decision on which tool will better suit your needs in a particular situation.

1. Open the file called `lioncub.psd`, which you can find on the friends of ED web site: www.friendsofed.com/code.html

2. Immediately after you have opened the file, duplicate the image (Image > Duplicate) so that you can compare your final results. Name this duplicate file `Lioncub Pen`.

3. In the original file, `lioncub.psd`, select the Magnetic Lasso; we will compare it with the Magnetic Pen. In the Options bar set the Feather to 0; check the Anti-aliased box; set the Width to 10, the Edge Contrast to 10%, and the Frequency should be set to 57. Switch CAPS LOCK on to get a precise cursor.

4. We're going to draw a selection around the lion cub in the center of the image. Use the Zoom tool to zoom right in on the lion cub, to give you greater precision when tracing around it. Click in the image against the edge of the cub's outline and move the mouse along its edge. Remember, it is not necessary to hold the mouse down, although if Photoshop does not seem to be placing sufficient anchor points for your liking, you can click to add your own. The best advice for doing this kind of outline is just to take it really slowly, but don't worry too much if it looks a little messy; we're going to be tidying the images up later on.

5. To close the selection, return to the starting point and click to end your trace. If the cursor wanders off away from the edge you wish to trace, depositing errant anchor points as it goes, move your cursor back along the outline, hitting the DELETE key to remove any unwanted anchor points as you pass over them.

6. Save your selection by choosing Select > Save Selection and name the selection LioncubOutline. Remember that selections are saved in the Channels palette, and you might wish to have a look just to reacquaint yourself with the palette. Save the file as Lioncub Lasso.psd, but don't close it, as we'll return to it later.

    Now, we'll create a similar outline in the Lioncub Pen file, using the Magnetic Pen tool.

1. Select the Freeform Pen tool from the toolbox, and set your options as specified below.

2. Click on the Magnetic Pen options icon on the tool bar to display the specific options for this tool, set them as indicated in the screenshot, and switch CAPS LOCK on to get a precise cursor.

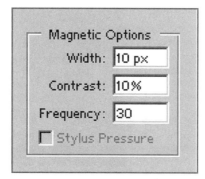

3. Click in the image against the edge of the cub's outline and move the mouse along its edge, as you did in the previous exercises. At this stage the Magnetic Pen tool functions almost identically to the Magnetic Lasso tool, so follow the same procedure for drawing the outline, adding and deleting points. Close the outline by returning to your starting point, and click to end your outline.

4. Locate the Paths palette, and note that a Work Path has been automatically created in the palette, but it has not yet been saved. As with selections, a Work Path is a temporary creation, unless you choose specifically to save that path. Do so now, by choosing Save Path from the drop-down menu on the Paths palette. Remember that to access this menu, you click on the arrow located at the top right-hand corner of the palette.

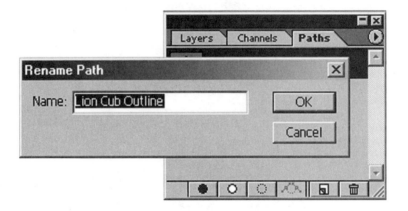

Save the Path as Lion Cub Outline, and save your file as `Lioncub Pen.psd`, but don't close it yet, because we'll be returning to it later.

Manipulating a path

Unlike an active selection, which can be modified only in a limited number of ways, individual components of the path can be modified and reshaped. When you create paths in Photoshop with either the Freeform or the Magnetic Pen tool, Photoshop automatically creates the anchor points for you, whereas if you create a path using the Pen tool, you can create the points manually.

More on this later, but suffice to say at this stage that, with a path created, we can modify the outline so that it suits our purpose more closely before we turn it into a selection. To accomplish this, we need to introduce another tool – the Direct Selection tool.

The Direct Selection tool

You use the Direct Selection tool to modify the shape of specific segments of a path after you have created it with one of the Pen tools. With this tool, you can select individual anchor points, direction handles or path segments, and manipulate them at will until your path is the exact shape you want.

The Path Component Selection tool

The Path Component Selection tool, however, does not see individual points, but rather paths and sub-paths as a complete object. If you are familiar with Adobe Illustrator, the comparative tool is the Selection tool. This tool can be used either for selecting the contents of an entire path, by either SHIFT-CLICKING on individual path outlines, or by marquee dragging with the tool over the path.

The Pen tool

Although we use the regular Pen tool and Freeform Pen tool primarily for drawing paths, we can also use them to edit paths by checking Auto Add/Delete, in the Pen tool Options bar. This means that you do not have to switch to the Add Anchor Point tool or the Delete Anchor Point tool to add or delete anchor points from the active path.

The Convert Point tool

The Convert Point tool allows you to convert an anchor point from a corner point to a smooth point, or vice versa. To convert an anchor point from one option to another, there are four main methods:

- To convert from a corner point to a smooth curve point, click and drag on the anchor point with the Convert Point tool. Be careful not to twist the handles. If you find this happening, do not release the mouse, but drag in the opposite direction to which you started.

- To convert from a smooth curve anchor to a corner, click and release the mouse on an anchor with the Convert Point tool.

- To convert from a smooth curve to a corner with handles that are able to move independently of each other, click and drag on a handle with the Convert Point tool.

> *Before you begin to manipulate a path, first select the Direct Selection tool, and then the Pen tool. Photoshop will remember that the last selection tool you used was the Direct Selection tool. To toggle between the Pen and the Selection tool, simply hold down the CTRL/CMD key. This saves you having to constantly switch between tools as you edit. To access the Convert Point Tool while the Pen tool is active, hold down the ALT/OPTION key; and then release it when you wish to return to the standard Pen tool.*

Anatomy of a path

Controlling the path and handles can be a little tricky the first time you attempt it, so before we start, we'll just take a moment to dissect a typical path and its components.

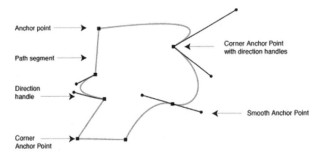

- **Anchor points:** These are the points created either manually by the user or automatically by Photoshop when you create a path

- **Path segment:** This is the part of a path which falls between two anchor points

- **Corner Anchor Point:** Anchor points connecting either straight path segments, or sharply curved path segments

- **Smooth Anchor Points:** Smooth anchor points connecting smoothly curved path segments. Their direction handles tend to work like propellers. If you change the angle by dragging a smooth direction handle, its counterpart on the other side of the anchor point will also move

- **Direction Handles:** They control both the length and direction of a curve

ii) Manipulating paths

Now we'll have a look at the selections previously created in your lion cub files. Ensure that both Lioncub Lasso and Lioncub Pen files are open.

1. In the Lioncub Lasso file, load the selection called Lion Cub Outline using the Load Selection command from the Select menu.

2. Zoom in closely on the edge of the selection Note that, depending on where you look, this selection may not accurate, and may need extensive manipulation either in Quick Mask mode, or by painting directly in the channel. Remember that if you load a selection from a channel, and then edit it in Quick Mask, you must resave the selection.

3. Keep the selection active. Duplicate the file, and call it Lioncub Lasso 2. Inverse your selection by choosing Select > Inverse (COMMAND/CTRL+SHIFT+I). You may need to re-load your selection in the duplicate file.

4. Everything except the lion cub is now selected; hit the DELETE key to remove the existing background. Notice the harsh lines around the edge of the lion cub, and possibly even areas where you have lost part of the cub. Save the file as Lioncub Lasso 2.psd. Remember that if you load a selection from a channel and then edit it in Quick Mask, you must resave the selection.

5. Return to your original Lioncub Lasso file. Ensure that the selection is still loaded. This time we'll expand the selection and feather it before we delete the background.

6. Expand your selection by 6 pixels (Select > Modify > Expand); and then feather this selection by 12 pixels (Select > Feather). The shortcut keys for this are CONTROL+ALT+DorCOMMAND+OPTION+D

7. Invert your selection by choosing Select > Inverse (COMMAND/CTRL+SHIFT+I) and delete the existing background. Because we chose to expand and feather the selection, thus softening it, the fact that it may not have been accurate does not present us with a problem. Save the file as Lioncub Lasso.psd.

A quick mention here about layers, if your image were on the background layer then the feathering would not take place. In our example, we are not on the background layer, but bear this point in mind if you have had difficulty in feathering an alternate image. More on layers in the next chapter!

Returning to your Lioncub Pen.psd file, you'll now spend a fair amount of time fine-tuning your path outline. Not only by manipulating the shape of curves via changing the position of path segments and anchor points, or by moving and changing direction handles, but also by adding and removing anchor points where necessary.

> *A word of advice here – it's better practice to have as few anchor points as possible, and use their positioning and the length and direction of handles to manipulate the path, than to just add numerous anchor points to the path. Adding unnecessary points to your path often makes your path less smooth, and can create a larger and more complicated clipping path for use in other applications.*

1. In the Lioncub Pen file, locate the Paths palette and activate the path called LioncubOutline by clicking on its name. To indicate that the path is active, the path should be highlighted in the palette, and if you look at the image onscreen, you should see a thin line surrounding the cub. This is the path you drew earlier with the Magnetic Pen tool.

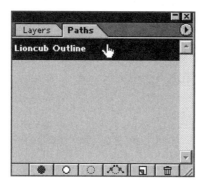

2. Switch to the Direct Selection tool and click on the path outline to make the anchor points on the path visible. Note that the anchor points are displayed as hollow squares; this indicates that they are not selected. If by chance you happened to click on an anchor point when you selected the path with the Direct Selection tool, that particular anchor point is displayed as a solid square. If no anchor point is active, click on one now.

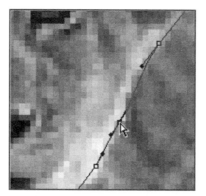

3. Zoom in closely on the edge of the outline and you may notice that this path is very similar to your initial lasso selection. But it is here that you can make changes. Instead of saving the selection and modifying it either in Quick Mask mode or in a channel, creating a path allows you to edit it before you convert it to a selection. If you wish, have a little play with the anchor points to try and refine your path.

4. Click and drag on an anchor point to reposition it slightly to improve the outline.

5. Pull gently on a path segment between two anchor points and watch how it behaves. It will depend on what type of anchor point is at each end of the segment, but if there are handles, notice how they move as you gently pull and push on the segment. Do not attempt major changes with this method; it is too crude because it reacts too quickly.

6. Be brave. Select a direction handle, drag it along its existing angle and notice how the curve responds. Keep the direction handle the same length, move it to change its angle in relation to the anchor point, and again, watch how the curve responds.

7. To add or remove points along the outline, switch to the Pen tool or the specific Add Anchor or Delete Anchor Point tools. Position your cursor carefully over the path. Notice that the cursor will change and display either an addition or minus sign at the bottom right below the pen cursor to indicate that you are over the path. Click to add a point.

8. If you notice kinks in the path where you would like to have smooth curves, click and drag on the anchor with the Convert Anchor tool. Remember you can toggle this tool by holding down the Option/Alt key while the Pen tool is active.

9. If there are smooth curves where you want sharp corners, click on the anchor point with the Convert Point tool

10. And if you have smooth curves, and want to keep the handles but need to have a sharp kink in the outline use the Convert Anchor tool to click and drag on a direction handle.

11. When you are satisfied with your outline, save the file.

Hang in there. We're nearly ready to complete the lion cub exercise so that you can compare the results. At this stage you may be thinking that the whole process of creating and manipulating a path, and then converting it into a selection is such a long-winded approach, but bear two things in mind:

■   This is a new skill for you, so you will be slower initially. As you practice more and more, not only will you find this a preferable route to take, but you will also become more proficient at it.

■   As your images become more complex, using the Lasso tool to create a cut-out just won't do. You won't get the result you want, and will spend as much time if not more in Quick Mask mode or editing in channels to refine your selection, often with inferior results.

Loading a path as a selection

To load a path as a selection, you must have the Paths palette visible, with the targeted path active.

Once you have the path active, there are a number of methods by which you can load the selection, and your final choice is up to you, although I do have my own particular preference, as you'll notice as we investigate the options:

Firstly, access the context menu from the Paths palette and choose Make Selection. You'll notice that the path outline is now overlaid with a selection. Click in the empty gray area of the palette below the active path to de-activate the path.

Alternatively, with the path still active, click on the Load Selection icon at the bottom of the Path palette as indicated in the screenshot below. To de-activate the path, click in the empty gray area of the palette below the active path.

Finally, my favorite method is CTRL/CMD+CLICK on the target path, in the Path palette. This is an efficient way of loading a path as a selection for a number of reasons:

- The target path does not have to be made active before it is loaded as a selection, as in the preceding two options.

- This shortcut for loading works not only for the Paths palette, but also for the Channels palette; and, still to come, the Layers palette.

- If you adopt either of the first two approaches, the path is still active. This can cause confusion if you decide to copy your selection contents, because with the path active, it will be the path, and not the contents that are copied.

- If you begin to draw another path with one still active, a new distinct path is not created on the Paths palette. Rather, the new path is added as a subpath to the active path.

- There is no need to click in the empty gray area of the palette below the active path to de-activate the path, as it was not made active.

Specifying settings for a loaded selection

The procedures followed above work perfectly well in most situations. There may however be times when you want to control how the loaded selection interacts with selections that are already active in the image, and also take the opportunity to set feather settings at the same time if they are desired.

In order to do this, the target path must be active (highlighted in the palette and on the screen). Then you'd need to ALT/OPTION+CLICK on the Load Selection icon at the bottom of the palette.

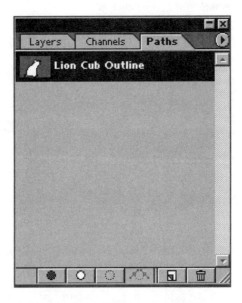

This action displays the Make Selection dialog box that allows you to choose options for how the path will be loaded.

You can set Feather Radius options for the selection to be loaded, and also determine whether or not to anti-alias the selection. Remember that doing so helps to eliminate jagged edges around the selection.

The four options in the lower part of the dialog box allow you to specify how your selection will interact with any existing active selections. There are no options for modifying your selection by expanding or contracting it, thus this approach will only be suitable if your path to be loaded as a selection is the exact required size.

- **New Selection:** This loads your path as an entirely new selection, and deselects any existing selection

- **Add to Selection:** Any areas encompassed by a new path will be converted to a selection and added to any existing selection

- **Subtract from Selection:** Areas included in the path to be loaded as a selection will be subtracted from an active selection

- **Intersect with Selection:** Only the areas common to the existing active selection and the area which will be loaded as a selection will remain

Loading paths as selections

Let's now apply what you have learned about loading a path as a selection to your previously created Lioncub Pen.psd file.

1. If the Lioncub Pen.psd file is not open, open it now.

2. Ensure that the Paths palette is visible, and load the path as a selection. Remember that if you opt to use either of the first two approaches explained in the preceding section, it is good practice to de-activate the path by clicking in the empty gray area of the palette below the active path.

3. Keep the selection active. Duplicate the file, and call it Lioncub Pen 2. Inverse your selection by choosing Select > Inverse (CTRL/COMMAND+SHIFT+I).

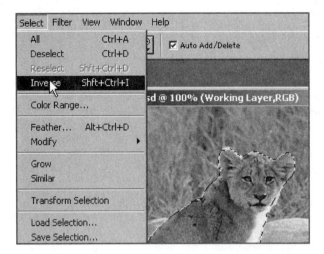

4. As before in the Lioncub Lasso files, only the background is selected. Depress the DELETE key to remove the existing background. Notice the harsh lines around the edge of the lion cub. Depending on how accurate the path you drew and manipulated was, this should be a far more accurate outline of the cub than that created with the Magnetic Lasso tool. You might wish to open the Lioncub Lasso 2 file and compare your results.

5. Save the file as `Lioncub Pen 2.psd`.

6. Return to your original `Lioncub Pen` file. Ensure that the selection is still loaded. This time we'll expand the selection and feather it before we delete the background.

7. Expand your selection by 6 pixels (Select > Modify > Expand); and then feather this selection by 12 pixels (Select > Feather).

8. Inverse your selection by choosing Select > Inverse (CTRL/COMMAND+SHIFT+I) and delete the existing background. As with the Lioncub Lasso file because we chose to expand and feather the selection, thus softening it, the accuracy of the original path is not that critical. Save the file as `Lioncub Pen.psd`.

Creating clipping paths

You may recall in the beginning of the chapter we mentioned that one of the purposes for creating paths in Photoshop was to enable you to export the path as a **clipping path**. You would want to use a clipping path if you wanted to export your lion cub image to a page-layout application, and only wanted the areas which you previously defined using the path to display and print.

To export an image with a clipping path, you must first create a named path. In the screenshot below, you will notice that there are two paths, one named Path 1, and one called Work Path. You would be able to create a clipping path from Path 1, but not from Work Path, because it is not a named path.

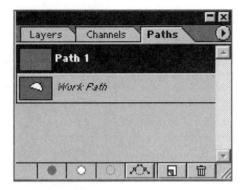

There are three alternative ways to create a named path suitable for use as a clipping path:

- Create a work path by drawing on the image with the Pen tool. Once the path is completed, either choose Save Path from the palette's context menu or double-click on the words Work Path in the Paths palette and name the path.

- Click on the New Path icon on the bottom of the Paths palette before you begin to draw with the Pen tool on the image. A new path automatically named Path 1 will be added to the Paths palette. If you wish to rename the path, double-click on the path's name in the palette and enter the new name in the dialog box that appears.

- ALT/OPTION+CLICK on the New Path icon on the bottom of the Paths palette before you begin to draw with the Pen tool on the image. Enter the new name in the dialog box that appears. A new path with the specified name will be added to the Paths palette.

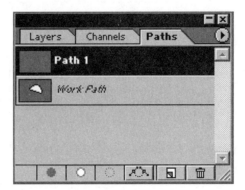

Converting selections into clipping paths

Previously you were shown how to load a path as a selection, but you can also do the exact opposite, and save an active selection as a path. This can be useful if you want to create a geometric shaped clipping path, but I would not suggest this procedure for an intricate path unless you are prepared to do intensive manipulation on the path before you use it as the basis for a clipping path.

With an active selection, click on the Make work path from selection icon at the bottom of the Paths palette. Once you have created a work path, remember you will need to convert it to a named path before it can be used as a clipping path.

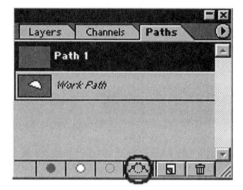

Once you have created a named path, the procedure for converting it into a clipping path is relatively simple. On the Paths palette menu, select Clipping Path. In the dialog box which appears, choose the required clipping path from the drop-down list, which will display all named paths in the palette.

The Flatness value dictates how **PostScript** will create the curved line segments in your path by creating a series of connected straight lines. For most images, there is no need to input a value here; this will print the image using the printer's default value. It is only when you experience printing problems with complex clipping paths that you may need to input a value. By the way, PostScript is a page description printing language, you will learn more about it in Chapter 6.

To indicate which path has been converted to a clipping path, the name will appear slightly emboldened (or in outline on a Mac) on the Paths palette. Note you can only have one clipping path in a file.

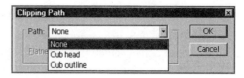

Once you have created a clipping path that needs to be interpreted by a page-layout application, save your file either as an **EPS** (Encapsulated Postscript), **DCS** (Desktop Color Separation) or **PDF** (Portable Document Format) and import into the desired application. Again, don't worry if you don't understand these terms right now, you will encounter them in more detail in Chapter 6.

Creating a clipping path

Back to our lion cubs for the last time! As you recall, I mentioned earlier in the chapter that there were times when the Magnetic Pen tool was far superior to the Magnetic Lasso tool; and creating accurate clipping paths is just such an instance.

1. Open both the `Lioncub Pen 2.psd`, and the `Lioncub Lasso 2.psd` files. These were the files where no feathering was introduced to the selection, and you consequently have hard edges defining your selection.

2. Look closely at the outlines of each file, and determine for yourself which one has the better edges for use in a brochure or other such printed material. I'm betting it's the Lioncub Pen 2 file, but this depends on how much time you spent manipulating the path before you converted it to a selection.

3. With the `Lioncub Pen 2.psd` file active, access the Paths palette, select the LioncubOutline path and convert it to a clipping path by choosing Clipping Path from the drop-down menu on the Paths palette.

4. Save the file, and then save a copy of the file (File > Save As) in the Adobe Acrobat (PDF) format. Name it `Penclip.pdf` and accept the default settings in the PDF dialog box.

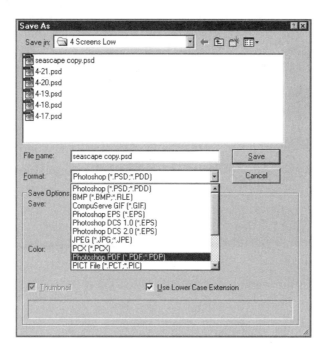

5. With the `Lioncub Lasso 2.psd` file active, load the LioncubOutline from the Select menu. Convert the selection to a path by choosing the Makes work path from selection at the bottom of the Paths palette.

6. Once the path becomes a named path, convert it to a clipping path. Save the file, and then save a copy of the file as Lassoclip in an Adobe Acrobat (PDF) format.

7. Launch Adobe Acrobat Reader or Adobe Acrobat, and open both the `Lassoclip.pdf` and `Penclip.pdf` files. Have a look at the edges defined by the clipping paths you created. Do not zoom in too closely and be too critical, you have been working with low-resolution files, and if you zoom too much, the edges will be exaggerated.

8. Close Adobe Acrobat and return to Photoshop. Close your lioncub files.

Copying paths from one file to another

In order to copy a path from one file to another, both the source file and the target file must be open, and visible on the stage. In the target file, ensure that no path is active, as dragging a path into this file when a path is active would add the new path to your existing active path. In the Paths palette of the source file, select the path you wish to copy, and drag it into the destination file. Simple as that. You'll know that you have copied the path correctly, because the Paths palette will change to reflect the path contents of the target file.

Drawing a seascape: the ocean

Now let's learn something about the tools by trying them out for ourselves.

1. Download and open the file seascape.psd from the friends of Ed web site.

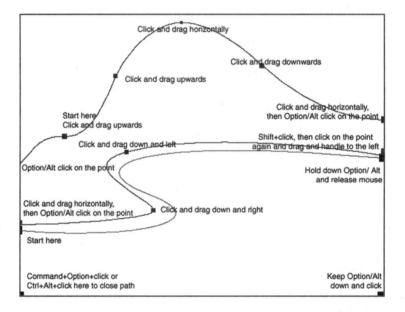

2. Ensure that you can see the Paths palette, as you will need it often to save and manage your paths. In this first session you will draw the ocean at the base of the image and the landscape. The guide for the ocean has been drawn in red, and there are some instructions to help you.

3. With the Freeform Pen tool, set the Curve Fit to 2px and ensure that Auto Add/Delete is checked.

4. Click on the far left of the red line (marked Start Here) and, keeping the mouse button depressed, follow the red line to the right hand edge of the screen.

5. At the edge, hold down the ALT/OPTION key and release the mouse button. You can now click on the bottom right hand corner, and Photoshop will draw a straight line between the two points.

6. Still holding the ALT/OPTION key, hold the CTRL/COMMAND key as well, before clicking in the bottom left hand corner. This will close the path by drawing a line back to the start point.

7. Switch to the Direct Selection tool to select anchor points, handles, or path segments in order to edit them. Have a little play with the anchor points to try and refine your path, if you're not happy with it.

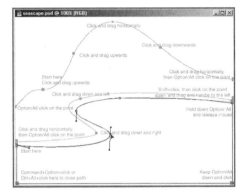

8. Once you are happy with the shape double-click on Work Path in the Paths palette and name the path Ocean. You have effectively saved the path, and will be able to re-use it later.

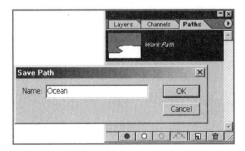

9. Save the file.

Drawing Bezier curves

The most accurate method of creating paths in Photoshop is to use the regular Pen tool, which allows you to place anchor points wherever you wish upon a path, and to control how they create the path. If you are familiar with the Pen tools from another illustration package such as Adobe Illustrator or Macromedia Freehand, you should find that there are a great many similarities, and you'll be able to create precise paths after little practice. If you are new to the concept of Bezier curves, don't worry, it's just going to take you a little longer.

Let's first look at the Pen tool Options Bar:

As with the Freeform Pen tool, you have the option of creating either a Shape Layer or a Work Path. Ensure that the second icon, Create new work path, is depressed; and that Auto Add/Delete is checked.

The only additional option here is the Rubber Band. Whilst many people familiar with the Pen tool find working with the Rubber Band option a little disconcerting, I would strongly recommend it for the person new to Bezier curves. Essentially when you draw a curve, Photoshop does not display that path segment until you have clicked to create an anchor point after it. With the Rubber Band option checked, Photoshop will display the segment so that you have an idea of the direction your path is developing before you commit to adding that anchor point.

How to use the Pen tool

To create a straight line with the Pen tool, click and release the mouse button, move the mouse to the point in the image where you wish to complete the first path segment, and click and release again. Continue in this manner until you have completed the path.

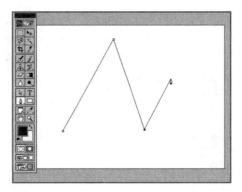

To constrain a straight line to 45° increments, hold down the SHIFT key when you click with the mouse button.

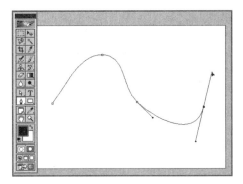

To draw a curve, click and drag with the mouse button in the direction in which you would like the curve to go, release the mouse when the angle and strength of the curve is to your liking. To continue the curve, click and drag elsewhere in the image. Photoshop will play join-the-dots for you.

- To split a pair of Bezier handles 'on the fly' – i.e. as you are drawing the path – click and drag to create your curve, and then without letting go of the mouse button, hold down the ALT/OPTION key and drag the direction handle to a new position.

- To pull a handle out of a square corner point 'on the fly' – place the point simply by clicking and then ALT/OPTION+CLICK directly on the anchor point and drag a direction handle out.

- To force Photoshop to retract the second direction handle in a curve point whilst you are drawing the path – ALT/OPTION+CLICK on the curve anchor point immediately after placing it on the page.

Tips for drawing curves

Keep the following guidelines in mind to help you draw any kind of curve quickly and easily:

- Always drag the first direction point in the direction of the bump of the curve, and drag the second direction point in the opposite direction to create a single curve. Dragging both direction points in the same direction creates an "S" curve.

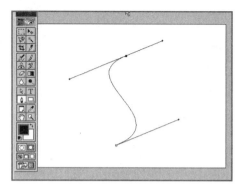

■ When drawing a series of continuous curves, draw one curve at a time, placing anchor points at the beginning and end of each curve, not at the tip of the curve. Use as few anchor points as possible, placing them as far apart as possible.

Too often novices with the Pen tool make nearly every anchor point into a corner with handles because they find it easier to control individual handles. The end result is a path with many unnecessary hard kinks in it. Persevere with the smooth propeller type anchor points and their handles. Your paths will be so much better for it. ALT/OPTION key; and then release it when you wish to return to the standard Pen tool.

Drawing a seascape: using the Pen tool to draw the hills

Now a chance to practice drawing those Bezier curves. I mentioned earlier that you may find the Bezier tool non-intuitive, clunky and quirky, but I also encouraged you to persevere with it. You'll complete this section of the exercise with a few directions as to how to place and drag the anchor points, and then later on, you practice by tracing over images.

1. Open the file seascape.psd if it is not already open. The guide for the landscape has been drawn in blue, and there are some instructions to help you.

2. Display the Paths palette, as you will need it often, to save and manage your paths.

3. With the Pen tool, check the Rubber Band and Auto Add/Delete options.

4. On the Paths palette, ALT/OPTION+CLICK on the New Path icon, and name the path Landmass.

5. Attempt to follow the outline as closely as possibly. But this is your first attempt, and you can manipulate the anchor points after you have created the path. As with the ocean path, your path should reach to the outer extremities of the image area, if only to avoid gaps at the edges of the image. Don't worry if this happens, you can always move the anchor points later.

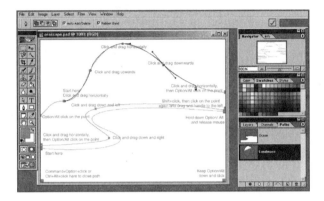

6. Remove or add anchor points to refine your path as necessary, but remember it is good practice to have as few points as possible.

7. Switch to the Direct Selection tool to select anchor points, handles or path segments in order to edit them.

8. Save the file.

9. There are an additional two files called boat.psd and tree.psd available for download on the friends of ED site for you to practice your skills. Remember to save the paths in each file. If you do not have time to do so at the moment, you may wish to try them another time. We will be using those files next, but I have created paths for you to use if you do not get a chance to do them yourself.

Drawing a seascape: importing the palm and the yacht

To further develop your seascape, you are going to bring the paths from both the boat.psd and the tree.psd files into the seascape file.

1. Open the seascape.psd, boat.psd and tree.psd files

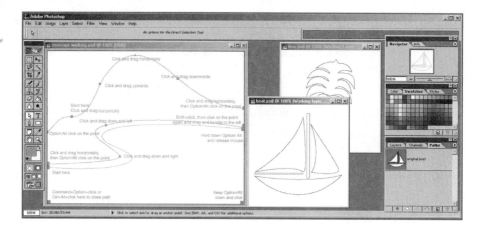

2. Arrange the files on the page so that at least some of each file is visible.

3. Ensure that no path is active in the seascape file by clicking on the gray area below the paths in the palette.

4. In the boat.psd file, select the boat path, either the original boat path that was created for you, or the one you created yourself (if you've been a bit more adventurous), or if you wish you can bring both paths in.

5. Drag the boat path from the Paths palette onto the image area of the seascape file. Once you're sure it's there, close boat.psd. After each 'dragged' path procedure, you must remember to deactivate the path. You'll note that it doesn't appear in an especially artistic position on our seascape, but don't worry, we'll sort that out soon.

6. Repeat the procedure for the tree.psd, and bring the path(s) into the seascape file. Close tree.psd.

7. Save your seascape file.

Duplicating paths

Often, as with our seascape image, you will wish to use a number of different variations of the same path as you develop your image. There is no need to redraw the path, or to copy and paste one path's contents into a new path.

With the Paths palette visible, either choose Duplicate Path from the palette's context menu, or drag the targeted path onto the New Path icon at the bottom of the Paths palette. Double-click on the new path in the Paths palette to access the dialog box that will allow you to rename the path.

Alternatively, you could CTRL+CLICK (Mac) or RIGHT-CLICK (Windows) on the active path in the palette to access a context menu with a Duplicate Path command, or hold down ALT/OPTION, as you drag the targeted path onto the New Path icon, and enter the new path's name directly at this stage.

Transforming paths

As paths are defined vectors and thus resolution-independent, you can scale them at will without any loss of detail or clarity, unlike if you scale your 'image' portions of your Photoshop file.

To transform a path, it must be activated by clicking on the path in the palette, then go to Edit >Transform Path. If these commands are grayed out, it is because you have forgotten to activate the path first.

You may still find that some of the options are grayed out; this could happen if the file you were working on had only one layer.

Once you have your path activated, you have a wide variety of transformations that you can apply to it far more than you found with the Transform Selection command in the preceding chapter.

Most of the options as illustrated in the menu should be self-explanatory, except perhaps for Skew, and the Rotate 90°CW and Rotate 90°CCW options. When you Skew a path, you distort it by slanting it, and CW means clockwise, and CCW means counter-clockwise, now I'll bet they make sense.

Once you have selected an option to transform, two changes will occur on the screen. Firstly, the Tool Options bar will have changed to reflect the fact that you have chosen a Transform option, and you may note that irrespective of whether you chose to scale, rotate, skew, distort or apply a perspective to the path, the same options appear on the Tool Options bar; and secondly, your path is encompassed by a bounding box.

Working from left to right, the initial icon allows you to set the Reference Point location. What this means is that the point from which the transformation will be affected. The default setting is that transformations will happen from the center, but by clicking on any of the remaining eight points, you could set a different reference point.

For example, if you wish to scale an object but keep the top left hand corner of the path pegged to its original position, you would click on the top left hand corner of the icon to highlight it. Effectively, this would translate to a real world analogy of sticking a pin in at this particular point and thus fixing it, with all transformations happening relative to it.

The X and Y options on the bar indicate the position of the reference point relative to its place on the X and Y axis of the image area, with 0:0 being at the top left hand corner of the image area. By clicking the triangular shape between the two values, you will be using the position of the reference point as a zero position instead of its position within the image.

The width and height values (W and H) are shown in relative percentage values, allowing you to transform the object numerically, as opposed to dynamically by clicking and dragging on one of the handles on the bounding box. The link chain icon between the width and height values constrains the transformation proportionally if it is depressed.

The rotation icon allows an exact numerical value to be input, as opposed to transforming the rotation value dynamically by dragging the bounding box if the Rotation Transform option had been selected.

Similarly, the horizontal and vertical skew angles can be entered as absolute values.

Finally, the check mark or cross icons at the right of the bar would be clicked if you wished to accept or reject the transformations that were performed either by entering values in the options bar or dynamically transforming the path. To reject the transformation using the keyboard, hit the ESCAPE key; to accept it, you can either hit RETURN/ENTER, or double-click within the bounding box.

Once you select a Transform option such as Scale, Rotate, Skew, Distort or Perspective, your path appears surrounded by a bounding box with handles and a target point in the center of the active path representation, as indicated in the screenshot below.

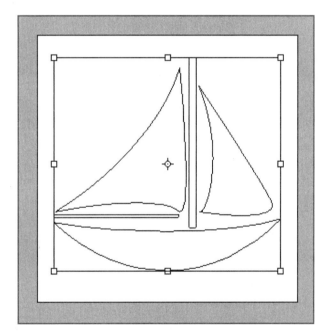

To dynamically apply the transformation command selected, you would click and drag on the bounding box handles as shown above. To reset the reference point location to a point other than the eight accessible through the Tool Options bar, click and drag on the target in the center of the bounding box to reposition it. Note that the target for the reference point location can be dragged outside of the area encompassed by the bounding box.

Using the Free Transform command

In many instances, when you feel the need to transform a path, you may not be certain whether Scale or another Transform option would better suit your purpose. For this reason, I really recommend that you become familiar with the Free Transform command and the associated keyboard shortcuts. Furthermore, if you're an Adobe Illustrator user, you'll find that the shortcuts are exactly the same in both applications.

After you have chosen the Free Transform (Edit > Free Transform Path) command (CTRL/CMD+T), use the following keyboard and mouse combinations to transform your path.

- To rotate the path, move the cursor just outside the bounding box. You'll notice that it turns into a double-headed arrow. Click and drag to rotate your path, holding down the SHIFT key to constrain the rotation to increments of 45° if so desired.

- To scale the object disproportionately, click and drag on any of the bounding box handles. If you wish to constrain the transformation proportionately, drag on a corner handle while holding down the SHIFT key.

- To scale the object from the center, hold down ALT/OPTION+ click and drag on any of the bounding box handles.

- To scale an object proportionately from the center, hold both the SHIFT and the ALT/OPTION key down as you drag a corner handle. As with all these transformations, remember to release the mouse button before you release any of the keyboard modifiers.

- To skew an object dynamically, select any of the four side handles on the bounding box and begin to drag. Without releasing the mouse button, hold down the CTRL/CMD key and continue to drag. Your path should now begin to skew. To keep the skew to the same parallel as the original, add the SHIFT key to the CTRL/CMD key.

- If you wish to freely distort the path, click and drag on a corner handle. Once again, without releasing the mouse button, hold down the CTRL/CMD key and continue to drag.

- Finally, if you wish to apply a perspective transformation to your path, put down anything you may have in your other hands because this is an 'all hands on deck' keyboard action. Click on a corner handle and began to drag, depress the CTRL/CMD key, and the ALT/OPTION key and the SHIFT key. You don't need to depress all the keyboard modifiers simultaneously. Just remember to drag before you start to depress the keys, and to hold them down until after you have released the mouse button.

If all of that seemed a little complex, and you're wondering how on earth you're ever going to remember it all, and get your fingers to obey you, don't worry. Think back to when you first started driving a car, and wondered how you would ever remember all the things you were supposed to do, and now it's just automatic. With practice, the same will happen here; and we'll give you that first practice session next.

Drawing a seascape: transforming the paths

1. Ensure that the `seascape.psd` file is open, and the Paths palette is visible.

2. Select the Original Boat path in the Paths palette and choose Edit > Transform Path > Scale.

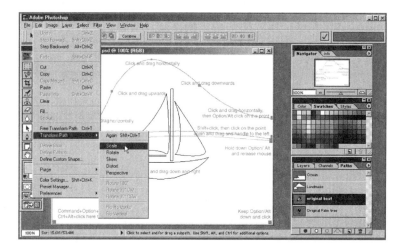

3. You'll notice that the boat is now surrounded by a bounding box with handles in the corners, and along the sides. Click one of the corner handles, and reduce drag it to reduce the boat to a more artistically appropriate size. If you hold down the SHIFT key, the proportions will be constrained and the boat won't end up looking squashed. Remember to release the mouse button before you let go of the SHIFT key.

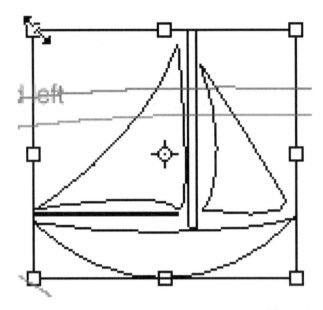

4. If you move the pointer over the shrunken boat you'll notice that it goes black. Click and drag from inside the box to re-position the boat, perhaps somewhere near the foreground and off to the right.

5. Click on the check mark icon on the tool options bar, or double-click inside the bounding box, or press RETURN/ENTER to accept the changes you have made. Click on the cross icon on the tool options bar, or hit the ESCAPE key to reject your changes.

6. Now activate the Original Palm Tree layer. This time, select Edit > Scale and instead of altering the size by dragging, use the tool bar to specify the percentages. By clicking on the chain button in the center either before you enter any values, or after you enter the first value, you can constrain the dimensions.

7. Possibly you think a palm tree should look as if it is blowing in the breeze. You could accomplish this by activating one of the palm paths, and then selecting Edit > Transform Path > Skew. Remember you must tell Photoshop whether you wish to accept or reject the transformation as explained in step 5 above.

8. Some of your boats could be traveling from a different direction. To achieve this, select a boat path boat.psd, and use the Flip Horizontal command on the Edit > Transform menu, to introduce a little more variety.

9. Continue in this fashion building up your seascape. If you wish, feel free to create more duplicate boat and palm paths. Practice using the Scale, Rotate, Skew, Distort and Perspective commands, flip a few more boats and Palms to change their direction.

10. Now for the brave bit, try selecting a few different paths and using the Edit > Free Transform Path command with some of those shortcuts mentioned above. Remember, that if you don't like the transformation you can always reject it by hitting the ESCAPE key, or clicking on the cross on the tool options bar.

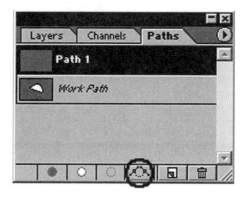

11. When you are happy with your seascape, save the file, and we'll move on.

Filling and stroking paths

You've spent a fair while learning how to create, manipulate, transform and duplicate paths; but surely they must have some greater use within your Photoshop image other than creating clipping paths? Of course they have. Like selections, paths can be loaded and then filled or stroked as desired to create your image.

It is important at this stage that you realize that the paths loaded from the Paths palette act very much like stencils when you activate and then fill or outline them. If you decide to make a change to the original path after you have filled or stroked the active one in the image, any future changes to the path will not affect the previously filled area, it will only affect the path the next time you activate it. The stencil analogy could be continued here; if you create a stencil and spray through it onto your wall, and then decide to make modifications to the stencil, the original artwork on the wall will not be affected by this change, only consequent uses of the stencil would show the new image.

Furthermore, once you either fill or stroke a path, the resultant colored area in your image is no longer vector-based, and is therefore resolution-dependent. So it's a good idea to apply transformations to the path before you fill or stroke it.

If you wish to fill a path, ensure that the path or sub-path is selected before you attempt to do anything else. Once the target path is active, you have one of three options:

- You can access the Fill Path or Fill Sub-path option on the context menu, and interact with the resulting dialog box.

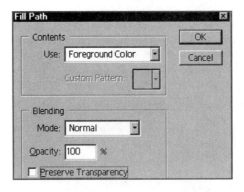

- You can also click on the Fill Path icon at the bottom of the Paths palette or drag the path onto the icon but beware, this approach does not give you the option of changing the way your object will be filled. The values used will be those used the last time you filled a path or selection.

- Finally, in a combination of the above approaches, ALT/OPTION+CLICK on the New Path icon. This will bring up the Fill options dialog box for you to set options.

  Stroking (or outlining) a path follows exactly the same process as the one detailed above for filling paths. Menu options will look slightly different:

- You can access the Stroke Path or Stroke Sub-path option on the drop-down context menu on the Paths palette, and select your preferred tool. Note however, that the weight of the stroke applied to your path is dependent on the options last set for the tool you use to stroke your path. In other words, if you select the Pencil tool; and the last brush used was a 36 point one, that will be the size of your stroke.

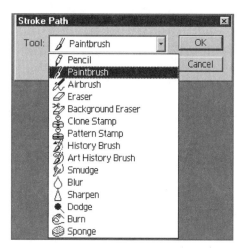

- You can also click on the Stroke Path icon at the bottom of the Paths palette, or drag the path onto the icon; but this approach gives you no opportunity to choose either the tool or the stroke weight. The tool used to stroke your path will be the last one used from amongst those in the drop-down list, and with the options set for that tool previously.

- Finally, in a combination of the above approaches, you can ALT/OPTION+CLICK on the New Path icon. This will bring up the Fill options dialog box for you to set options. Once again the weight or pressure of the stroke will be the value set for that particular tool when it was last used.

Drawing a seascape: duplicating paths

In building up your seascape, it's pretty obvious that having just one yacht and one palm tree in your vista doesn't make for a very exciting picture. So, in this exercise, we'll concentrate on populating the landscape and sea with a number of boats and trees. This will also give you an opportunity to practice your transforming skills which were introduced earlier.

1. Ensure that the seascape.psd file is open, and the Paths palette is visible.

2. Activate the Original Boat path in the Paths palette, and duplicate it by accessing the context menu on the Paths palette, and choosing the Duplicate Path command as illustrated in the screenshot below. Call the path boat 2. If your duplicate paths are all on top of the original, don't worry, this is natural. What you are doing is building up a number of paths, which you can then transform and move.

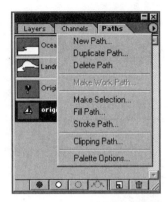

3. Create another duplicate boat path by dragging either of the boat paths onto the New Path icon at the bottom of the palette. Double-click on the new path in the Paths palette, and rename it boat 3.

4. Create a duplicate of the original Palm tree path by CTRL+CLICK (Mac) or RIGHT-CLICKING (PC) to display the Duplicate Path command, and name this path, palm 2.

5. Finally, duplicate another Palm path by dragging either of the existing Palm paths onto the New Path icon at the bottom of the palette. Hold down ALT/OPTION as you do this, and name the path as palm 3.

6. Save the file

Creating shape layers

Since you started reading this book, all the exercises have taken place on single-layered files, but the time has come to make that move to multi-layered compositions; and what better way to introduce you to the concept than by leading on from paths to the new approach of creating **Shape Layers**. However, this will only be a cursory glance at layers, and details such as Layer Blending Modes and Layer Styles will be covered in detail later in the book.

The ultimate difference between the approach of creating and filling paths and creating shape layers is the whole issue of scalability. We have said that paths are vector-based, and therefore scalable without any loss of detail; but what happens if you decide you wish to transform an area which has been filled via use of a path? The 'sprayed' area is now a bitmap area and therefore any scaling could result in a loss of clarity and detail in the image.

This is where Shape Layers enter the picture. They keep the scalability of these vector areas even after they have been filled, filling happens pretty much automatically as you create the path on the Shape layer. The entire layer is filled with the selected foreground color, but this color is only visible in areas that have been marked on the Shape Layer using the Pen tool.

To create a Shape layer, select your desired foreground color before you begin to draw on the image area, then with either the Pen or the Freeform Pen tool, click and drag to draw your path on the screen. You may notice in the Paths palette, that a temporary clipping path is displayed while you draw your path. This allows you to see through to the layer beneath, so, although it looks like the shape is filled with color, in fact it is not. The path is creating a window through to the layer below. Therefore if you scale the clipping path, it is the vector shape that you are scaling, and I think you're beginning to become familiar with this idea of vector paths being completely scalable without loss of quality.

Drawing a seascape: creating a Shape Layer

For the last time, we're going to be working with the seascape file; just to add a few finishing details to the sky area, a seagull or two could fill a few empty spaces!

1. Open the `seascape.psd` file if it is not already open.

2. Select a foreground color from the color picker or from the swatches for your birds.

3. Select either the Freeform Pen tool or the Pen tool to draw your birds, and ensure that the Make Shape Layer icon is selected on the Tool Options bar.

4. Click and drag with the pen tool to create shapes suitable to represent your birds. Remember to switch to the Direct Selection tool if you need to select and manipulate individual points, or segments, or handles. Note that in order for your birds to have some color, they cannot be those single lined shapes we drew as children!

5. Continue creating as many birds as you wish.

6. Finally, save and close the seascape file.

Case Study

In the last part of the case study we removed an image from its background using the Extract tool, now let's look at another way of extracting an image. This is the most accurate way to do it. The Pen tool gives us the cleanest edges and allows for more options, but it is also more time-consuming and requires more practice. I would recommend practicing using the Pen tool, as this is one of the most indispensable skills you can have in Photoshop. Over time you will improve and become faster and more accurate using this tool. Your skills with these Bezier tools will also carry over into many other graphics applications, like Illustrator, InDesign, QuarkXpress, Corel Draw etc...

I am planning to use this image in a page layout program and put it against a solid white background, so the edges must be very sharp. It will also ultimately be for the web page we are constructing.

Making a selection with the Pen tool

1. I chose a picture of a Lamborghini Diablo for this part of our project (open 29058.jpg).

2. Select the Pen tool in the toolbox.

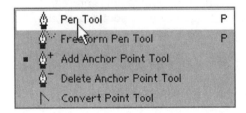

Make a rough selection around our object. Click at the beginning and end of each major curve, just like joining the dots when you were a kid, except you are making the dots.

3. Now that we have made a rough selection, it's time for us to go in for a closer look and get really accurate. Use the Zoom tool and the Navigator palette to move in close-up and move around the image.

The red box indicates the viewing area of your image. You can just drag the box around to view different areas of your image. This is a great tool for moving around your image when you are doing very detailed work. (You can also hold down the spacebar to pan around your image.)

4. Switch to the Add Anchor Point tool, found *under* the Pen tool.

Here is the way I use the tool - it works very well for me!

To move an anchor point, just click and drag it. To add a curve, click in the middle of the line that you want to curve around an object, then release the mouse button.

Now click again in exactly the same spot and drag out the curve.

Another way of fixing the curves is to grab one of the handles and drag that.

Finally after a bit of trial and error and perhaps a bit of frustration, you will have your object with a nice tight path. Don't worry, as I said before; you will get better at this with practice and you can actually get pretty fast at it.

5. OK, now let's save the path. This is the path that we are going to use that will tell us where the edges of the image are. In the Paths palette, click on the little arrow in the top right and select Save Path.

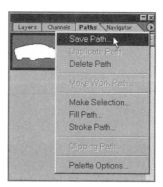

Keep the name path1, it will work fine in this case, click OK. Generally you will want to give each path a meaningful name so you will be able to tell the different paths apart. But in this case we only have one path, so this is not so important.

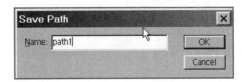

6. Finally save the picture as `black car.psd`. Save this to the working folder too. This will be used later on in our project.

Congratulations, you have now successfully practiced drawing a path and defined it in Photoshop. You have just practiced a very important Photoshop skill. I would advise you to keep practicing this technique, don't be discouraged if it takes you a while to get comfortable with the Pen tool, it does require a lot of practice.

Summary

And there you have it, an introduction to the concepts of the Pen tools and paths in Photoshop; and even a little peek at layers. Add the skills you have been introduced to your knowledge on painting, and creating, and saving selections, and you are well on your way to becoming proficient in the application.

If you found working with Bezier curves a little foreign, I do urge that you continue practicing as much as possible, it does become much more intuitive in time. A good way of practicing is to scan in simple images from children's coloring books and to trace them. Even better still, flip the images vertically and/or horizontally before you start to trace, so that you can concentrate on the shape of the lines as opposed to the entire object.

5 Basic Layers

What we'll cover in this chapter:

- Working with layers and the Layers palette

- Linking and merging layers

- Applying and editing layer styles

- Creating layer sets

- Working with type layers

Understanding layers

Way back in 1994, the release of Photoshop 3.0 prompted a great deal of excitement over a brand new feature called **layers**. In fact, it wasn't long before layers completely revolutionized the way that users approached Photoshop. Before the introduction of layers, all Photoshop images would consist of a simple grid of pixels – a so-called **flat image**. Whenever you modified an area within the image, you were directly changing the color of the pixels that made up that part of the image, and overwriting whatever was there before, almost as if you were painting onto a piece of canvas. Unfortunately, this meant that any alterations you made would effectively destroy a part of the original image.

So, if you wanted to change anything later (perhaps you noticed a typo in the text you'd placed) you would either have to be very good with the rubber stamp tool, or start all over. In those days, some of the most horrifying words I'd hear from a client were "could you just move that over to the right and down a bit?" Well, yes I could; the only problem was that it would leave a gaping hole in my image – I might as well have used a Stanley knife on a photograph!

As you can well imagine, my tiny little hard drive would quickly get filled up with files containing the various different elements making up an image, not to mention all the different versions of the composite image in varying degrees of completeness. What I really needed (along with many other graphic designers in the same position) was some way to bundle all the picture elements together, so that they could be viewed (and saved) together, but manipulated separately. Ideally, we'd have them all stacked on top of one another, so that we could touch them up and move them around as much as we wanted, without sacrificing all the precious information in other elements within the image. Fortunately for us, this is precisely what Photoshop layers let us do.

The figures below illustrate how our image might look if we could view it in three dimensions: the first is a flat image; the second, the same image constructed from three separate layers, each containing a complete element.

One good way to visualize layers is to think of painting onto sheets of acetate (clear plastic). We could paint separate elements onto each sheet, and then move individual sheets around, restack them, even remove and replace them, without having to worry about any of the other elements in the image.

Of course, this is a real technique that's been in use for decades to create animated cartoons. By separating static backgrounds from moving characters, animators save themselves from having to recreate the background for every single frame.

Say we want to create a nice pastoral landscape, containing the following elements:

- Sky
- Clouds
- Mountains
- Forest
- Field
- Tree
- Cow

We'd probably start off by painting a blue background. We could then paint some clouds onto a sheet of acetate and lay it on top of the background. On a new sheet of acetate, we'd add the mountains, and then paint a forest, a field, a tree, and a cow, each on their own sheet of acetate. Finally we'd stack these layers on top of each other to produce the finished image.

There are a few things to note here:

- Each layer (apart from the background) will contain transparent areas, through which we can see other layers.

- The topmost layers (the cow and the tree) will hide certain parts of the background. However, the background is very much there, so we can safely reposition them without having to cover up any unsightly holes.

- The topmost layers feature elements that are nearest to the viewer's position within the scene, while lower layers show elements that are further away, and therefore obstructed.

In order to depict a similar scene, in which the cow stands just behind the tree, we simply exchange the topmost two layers. Now the tree will be on top, and parts of the cow will be hidden behind it.

Even on its own, the ability to work on each element separately gives us a formidable amount of control over our images. Not only does it make our lives a lot easier, it helps us get our work done a great deal quicker! All the same, this is just the tip of the iceberg with Photoshop layers – as we're going to see, there's a whole lot more we can do than shuffle stacks of pictures.

Let's not worry about all these other features for now though – we will get to them soon enough. First, let's build up a good practical understanding of how layers work before we delve into all the exciting nooks and crannies in the Layers palette.

Working with layers

In my opinion, layers are undoubtedly the most interesting, exciting, and darned useful feature in the whole Photoshop package. It's therefore important that you get a good grasp of how they work. If you're still confused by the time you reach the end of this section, I advise you to read it again, and keep playing with Photoshop until you're really comfortable (and happy) using layers.

Introducing the Layers palette

Before we launch into our first worked example, let's take a quick look at the Layers palette, which you may have already noticed lurking at the bottom-right corner of the main Photoshop window (by default, that is – if you can't see it, you can select Window > Show Layers to call it up). In this palette, you'll see a list of all the layers that make up the currently selected image.

Of course, there won't be anything to see here until we have an image open, so we'll create one now. Let's make it 300 pixels by 300 pixels, and since it's only for use on screen (and not for printing) we can give it a resolution of 72 pixels/inch.

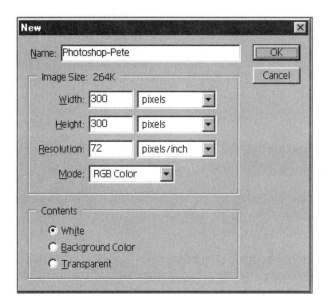

As we know, the Contents buttons let us pick a color for the new image: in this case, let's choose White. Then press OK and save the file as Photoshop Pete.psd.

The PSD format is perfect for this project, as it stores complete information on all the layers we're going to be creating. Saving to almost any other file format will automatically flatten the image, and all layer information will be lost.

You should now see a single list entry in the Layers palette, called Background. You'll see that it also sports a plain white square (a **thumbnail**) illustrating the contents of our background layer, an 'eye' icon (indicating that it's visible), a 'paintbrush' icon (indicating that it's currently selected – okay, the fact that the whole entry is highlighted is also just a bit of a giveaway), and a 'padlock' icon (indicating that this layer is locked and cannot be moved or edited).

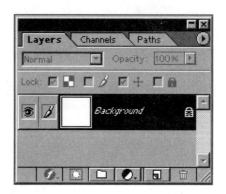

Creating Layers

We're now ready to create a new layer – as usual, Photoshop gives us a number of different ways to do this:

- via the Menu bar – Layer > New > Layer
- via the keyboard shortcut CTRL/CMD+SHIFT+N
- via the Layers palette – click on the little arrow at the top right of the palette window; when a fly-out menu appears, click on New Layer

A dialog box should now appear, allowing you to name your layer (let's call it face) and specify a number of other properties, which we'll gloss over for now, but return to in this and later chapters. For now, let's accept the default values as shown on the next page.

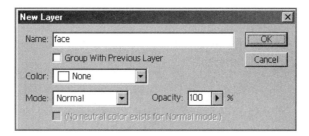

There's actually another way to create a new layer, which bypasses this dialog completely, and uses default settings (including a name Layer 1, Layer 2, Layer 3, etc.):

- via the Layers palette – click on the new layer icon at the bottom of the palette window (second from the right).

If you use this method, you may well want to change the layer's name once it's in place. This is very simple, as you can access the layer's name and color settings from the Layer Properties entry in the palette's fly-out menu.

Of course, it's largely a matter of personal preference as to which one you use (I personally prefer the last method), but it's worth familiarizing yourself with all of the options, so that you can pick the one that's best suited to your own working habits.

Take another look at the Layers palette, and you should now see your new face layer:

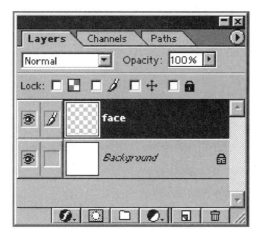

Congratulations! You've just created your first layered image. Note that the paintbrush icon (which indicates the active layer – that is, the one that's currently being edited) has moved up to the new layer, and that the thumbnail image shows a check pattern, which indicates an area of transparency (as requested). That's why we haven't seen any change to the image itself.

Before we do anything else, let's make the palette thumbnails a little larger, so we can see more clearly what we're doing. Once more, click the little arrow at the top of the Layers palette, and our new friend the fly-out menu will fly out for us again. This time round, click Palette Options, and the dialog shown below should appear:

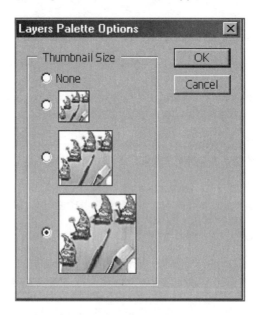

From here, you can select one of four different thumbnail display options – small, medium, or large size thumbnails, or none at all. As I'm using quite a high-resolution desktop (1152x864), everything on my screen looks rather small. By picking the largest thumbnail size, I should be able to identify each of the layers on the list without straining my eyes too much. On the other hand, if I find that they take up too much space on my screen (or I want to see many layers listed on my screen at the same time), I can always pick the smallest size.

Well, right now, our new layer is still blank, and there's not really much to demonstrate while that's the case! So, without further ado, let's start adding some content.

Adding objects to layers

Throughout the rest of the chapter, we're going using a variety of techniques to construct a picture of our eponymous hero: Photoshop Pete. Along the way, we're going to see a whole stack of Photoshop's most useful layer techniques in action.

1. Let's start by creating a rough head shape. Select the Elliptical Marquee tool by clicking on the Marquee tool icon holding for a moment, and then selecting the

appropriate entry from the fly-out menu that appears. Make an oval selection on the face layer (like the one shown below) and fill it with a fairly light color – I used a light purple, with RGB values (230, 115, 235).

2. Remove the selection (Select > Deselect) and take another look at the Layers palette. You will see that our oval is now showing in the thumbnail for the face layer. Look carefully, and you'll also notice that the check pattern remains in place all around the oval. In fact, it's easy to view this at full scale – just click on the Background layer's eye icon to make the white background invisible. Click on it again, and the white background reappears. Simple!

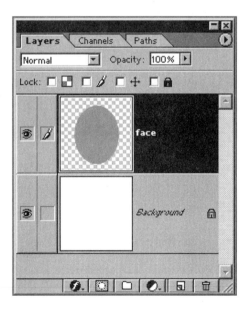

3. Let's create another new layer, using the new layer icon at the bottom of the Layers palette. A new layer called Layer 1 will appear above the face layer.

4. Note that you were not prompted for a name – if you're in a hurry and don't need terribly descriptive names, this method is undoubtedly the fastest. All the same, we can (and ideally should) give this layer a proper name, and we've already seen how to do this via the Layer Properties dialog. A quick way to call this up is to hold down ALT/OPTION and double-click on the name of the layer.

5. When the dialog pops up, rename this layer as eyes.

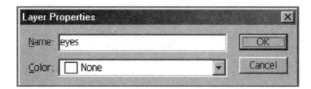

A glance at the Layers palette will reveal that we now have three layers, with the eyes at the top.

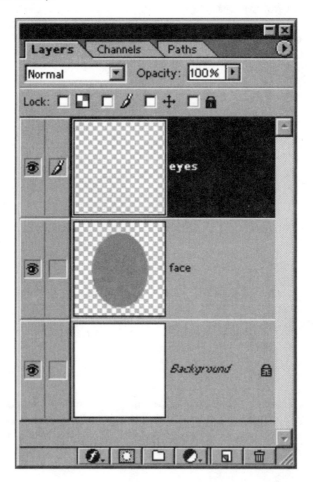

Now would be a good time to save your file again – frequent saving is a very useful habit to get into. You can save yourself a great deal of frustration and wasted time by keeping an up-to-date copy of your work safe on disk. Especially where I work in Southern California, rolling blackouts can take out a computer at a moment's notice!

Duplicating objects in layers

1. Now that we have a layer for them, let's draw some simple eyes. Using the Elliptical Marquee tool again, make a small oval (as below) and fill it with white. Don't hit Deselect just yet.

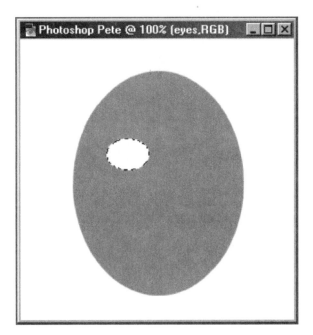

Now, check out this cool trick for duplicating an object on the same layer:

2. Select the Move tool, hold down the ALT/OPTION key and click on our new eye (the white oval). You'll notice that the mouse cursor changes to a double arrow – this indicates that we are about to duplicate an object.

3. Hold down the mouse button and drag to the right; you'll now see two white ovals.

4. While you're doing this, hold down the SHIFT key (yes, of course you still have a free finger!) so as to help you keep the copy vertically aligned with the original. You wouldn't want Pete's eyes to end up on different levels, would you?

5. Once the second eye is in position on the right-hand side of the face, you can deselect.

   You should now have a face that looks something like this:

6. Now create a new layer called pupils.

7. Make sure the new layer is selected, and use the Elliptical Marquee tool (while holding down the SHIFT key) to make a small circle. Fill the circle with black.

8. Duplicate the pupil (just like we did with the eyes), and place the copy over the right eye.

Your picture and Layers palette should now look like this:

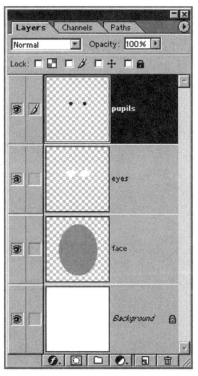

So far, so good – but Pete's lack of a mouth is sort of conspicuous. Let's make one.

9. Create a new layer and call it mouth. Draw an oval on it, and fill this selection with white.

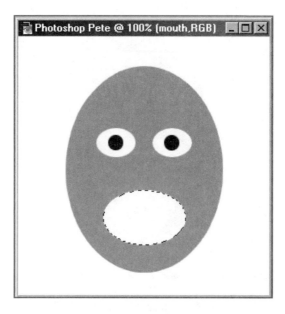

10. Switch from the Elliptical Marquee tool to the Rectangular one, and draw a new selection across the top half of the circle.

11. Press the DELETE key, and you'll find that you've deleted the top half of the white circle, making it look more like a simple mouth.

This is one of those handy things that we can only do because we're using layers. Since we're only working on the contents of the mouth layer, a DELETE (which would normally obliterate everything within the current selection) only takes out parts of the mouth that are within the selection. Despite the fact that it's apparently selected, the purple oval of the face stays completely unaffected!

12. Finally, Deselect (CTRL/CMD+D), and you'll find yourself looking at the happy fella below:

Duplicating layers

So, we now have a little experience of duplicating objects on a single layer. What about duplicating an entire layer then? Well, as usual, Photoshop gives us a stack of different ways to do it – easiest by far, though, is to drag and drop your existing layer onto the new layer icon.

We want to add a little detail to Pete's eyes – in particular, we want to give him some nice colorful irises. The easiest way to do this is to modify a copy of the pupils layer that we just created.

1. Select the pupils layer from the Layers palette, then click on it again and drag it over to the new layer icon. Release the mouse, and you'll see a new layer added to the list: pupils copy.

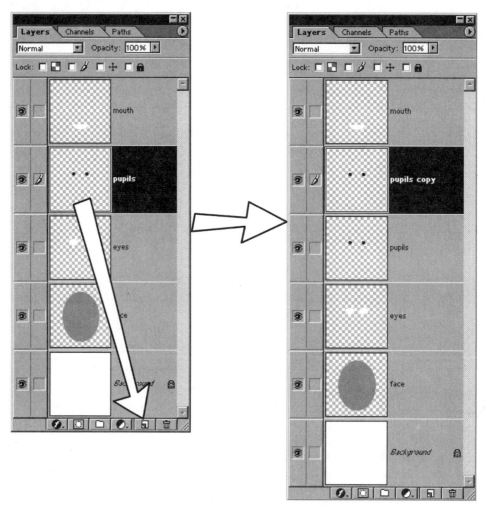

2. Before we do anything with it, let's rename this new layer as irises.

Now we want to make the irises slightly larger than the pupils, give them some color, and place them *behind* the pupils.

Free Transforming a layer

Well, first things first – to make all the contents larger on the whole layer, we can use Photoshop's Free Transform method. There's quite a lot we can do with this technique, and our irises layer is a little restricted as far as demonstrations go (for a start, it's rather on the small side!) So let's take a quick detour first, and try transforming a nice illustrative image; in this case, we're going to use a block of text, which we'll create using the Type tool.

1. Create a new image at 500 pixels by 200 pixels, with a resolution of 72 pixels/inch and a white background.

2. Select the Type tool so that we can insert some text, and click inside the document. You will see the toolbar at the top has changed to show you various Type options.

Don't worry about creating a new layer, as the type tool creates a special **type layer** for itself.

3. Select a font and type size (I've used Arial Black, 48pt) and make sure that the color is set to black.

4. Now type "Photoshop Pete", and you should see the words appear in the image area.

5. Hit the check button at the top right of the toolbar to confirm the text you've entered; alternatively, you can press the cross to cancel the effect.

You'll see that a new layer called Photoshop Pete has been added to your image, with a small 'T' icon in place of the usual thumbnail – this denotes a type layer, which is reserved exclusively for typography. Type layers contain vector objects, so they can be scaled up and down without loss of quality. What's more, you can edit the text at any time, as well as applying most of the usual layer tweaks. However, there are also limitations – principally, that you can't use filter effects and many of the distortions it's possible to apply to a normal layer. Fortunately for us though, the Free Transform feature is one that's still available to us.

6. To start our transformations demo off, go to Edit > Free Transform or hit CTRL/CMD+T. You should now see a bounding box around the two pupils, with 8 squares (called **handles** or **nodes**) around the edge: one halfway along each side, and one on each corner.

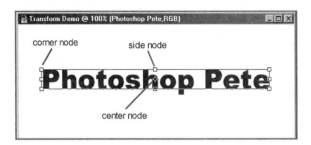

Simple transforms

1. When you move your cursor over any of these nodes, you will see it change to a double-ended arrow, or by dragging them around, you can resize the box, and your image will automatically stretch to fill it. A node on the side of the box lets you adjust the position of that particular side (along an axis set at 90 degrees to it), affecting either height or width.

2. Meanwhile, a corner node (fairly predictably) lets you move the relevant corner, adjusting the height and width of the box at the same time. If you want to maintain the proportions of the box, just hold down the SHIFT key.

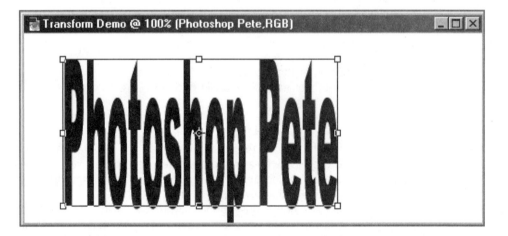

3. You'll also see a node at the center of the box. This is used as a point around which you can rotate the box. If you move your cursor around outside the box, you'll see it change to a rotate cursor. Click and drag when you see this cursor, and you'll find the whole box spins about the center point.

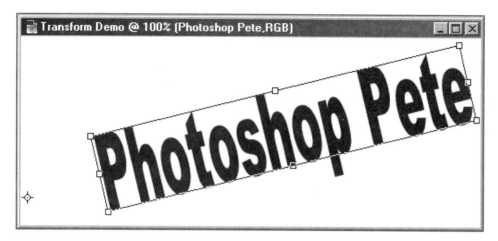

4. The center point has one more use: if you hold down Alt/Option while you're resizing the box, you can force it to resize about the center point. If this is positioned at the exact center of the box, you can resize the text symmetrically

> *Note that while you're transforming, you can't access any other functionality, but you can hit ESCAPE to cancel any changes you've made.*

5. Various other options can be accessed via the context menu, which you can call up by right-clicking (Windows) or CTRL-clicking (Mac). We've already looked at the first two options (scale and rotate), so we'll skip past them to Skew, which applies a horizontal or vertical skew to the bounding box (along with whatever's inside it). The horizontal skew I've applied in the image below (by dragging the bottom side node to the left) has the effect of making the text lean over to the right:

6. Although the nodes still appear as they were before, you can now only drag them *along* the axis of the line they're sitting on, rather than perpendicularly (as we could before).

7. The fixed Rotate options are fairly self-explanatory, giving you precise rotations of 90 or 180 degrees either clockwise or counter-clockwise. Meanwhile, Flip horizontal and vertical allow you to produce a mirroring effect.

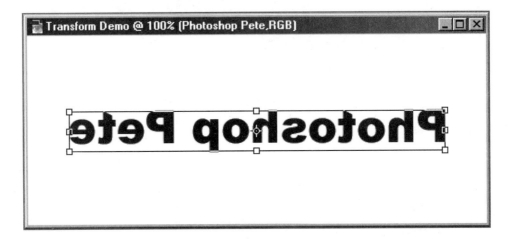

Advanced transforms

1. You'll find that the Distort and Perspective options are initially both greyed out because they are not available for type layers. We must therefore convert our text to a raster-based image before applying them. Hit Escape to duck out of Free Transform mode, select the Type Tool and right-click (or Ctrl-click) to call up its context menu.

2. The entry Rasterize Type will convert the type to purely pixel-based information, which means we can now apply more complex distortions to it, using Distort and Perspective transforms:

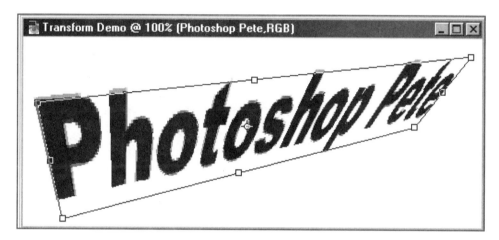

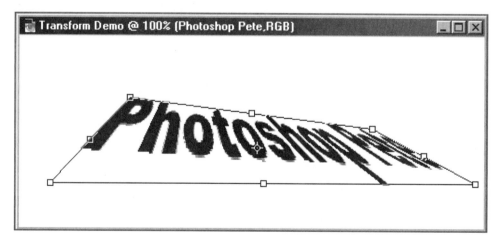

Note however, that this rasterized text doesn't scale nearly as cleanly as it did before. We'll take more of a look at the Distort and Perspective transform options in the next chapter.

Transforming Pete's eyes

Before we get too carried away with all these possibilities, let's get back to our ongoing project. To recap, we wanted to adjust Photoshop Pete's irises so that they would be visible behind his pupils.

1. Select the irises layer and hit CTRL/CMD+T to switch into Free Transform mode.

2. Hold down Shift (to constrain proportions) and Alt/Option (to resize symmetrically about the center) and drag one of the corner nodes out just a little, so that the irises are about 50% larger than the pupils.

3. Finally, press ENTER to apply the transformation.

Layer transparency

1. Well, Pete certainly looks more bug-eyed than he did before – I'd say it's time to fill his irises with a different color. There's another cool trick we can use here, that'll help make this a cinch:

2. Use the Color Picker to select a nice light-blue color (I've used R=0, G=180, B=180):

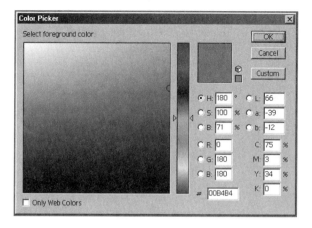

3. Make sure that the irises layer is selected, and press ALT/OPTION+SHIFT+BACKSPACE

As you may recall, ALT/OPTION+BACKSPACE fills an area with the current foreground color. By pressing the SHIFT key at the same time, we add transparency protection. So, we can fill all areas of our selected layer that contain pixel information, while automatically preserving transparent areas – the simple upshot of which is that Pete's irises turn blue, just as we wanted. Remember though, that this trick *only works on layers*.

Another way you can do this is to **lock** the layer's transparency and perform a normal flood fill on each of the irises. Simply select the appropriate layer and put a check against the transparency lock at the top of the Layers palette.

While we're on the subject, let's take a quick look at each of these layer locks, and what it means if they're checked:

- **Lock Transparent Pixels** – you can't change pixel transparency in the layer

- **Lock Image Pixels** – you can't change pixel colors in the layer

- **Lock Position** – you can't move the layer around

- **Lock all** – this prevents any editing, as if all of the other boxes were checked

All of these options are new to Photoshop version 6.0.

4. Okay, let's get back to our face image again. We still have a small problem with Pete's eyes. The pupils layer (on which we based the irises) should be right at the front – right now they're being obstructed. It's nothing major though; we can very easily change the stacking order by dragging the irises layer down the layers palette list, so that it's just underneath the pupils layer.

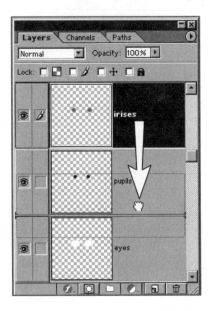

5. As you can see, the black circles are now in front of the blue circles, looking more like the pupils and irises they're supposed to depict.

6. Let's add a nose now. Create a layer called nose, make sure that it's the topmost layer, and draw another oval in the center of the face – I've used a dark blue color (R=0, G=0, B=180).

7. We should also add some ears, so create another new layer called ears, and add an oval to the side of Pete's head. You might want to use the Eyedropper tool to pick the same color as we used for the head, so that it joins on seamlessly.

8. Now use the Move tool and ALT/OPTION+SHIFT+drag to duplicate the selection and position the left ear. Finally, deselect, and you should end up with a two-eared chap looking rather like this:

Unless you've been saving your work every ten minutes as a matter of course (a fine example to all Photoshop users!) this is probably another good point for us to commit `Photoshop Pete.psd` to disk, as we've just about finished the groundwork for our picture of Pete, and we're about to launch into some of the truly exciting things you can do with layers. It'd be a shame if a sudden power cut sent you back to the top of the chapter after all that hard work!

Working with more than one layer

Since we started playing around with layers, you've probably been thinking, "it's all well and good breaking images up into separate elements, but what if I want to work on more than one at a time?"

Say, for example, we decide to tweak our picture of Photoshop Pete so that he seems to be looking upwards. Ideally, we'd like to drag the pupils and irises upwards as a single element – it would look rather odd if the former moved and the latter didn't!

Linking layers

In this case, the best solution is to **link** the two layers. Take a look at the Layers palette, and you'll see a small box just to the left of the thumbnail for each layer. This is where you'll sometimes see a paintbrush icon displayed, indicating the current active layer. Try clicking this box for an inactive layer, and you'll see a little chain icon appear in it:

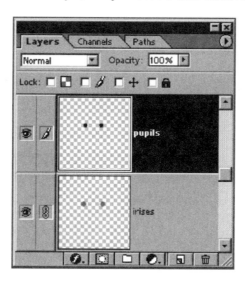

This indicates that it is linked to the active layer, telling Photoshop that you want to manipulate these layers together. For example, if you resize the active layer, any linked layers will also be resized. Likewise, if you change its position, all linked layers will move along with it. You might like to try linking the pupils and irises, and moving them around together.

Merging layers

Although linking lets us work with multiple layers at once, it's important to remember that you're still working with separate layers – try painting on the layers you just linked, and you'll see that it's still just the active layer that gets affected. If we want a more comprehensive connection between the contents of two layers, we can always **merge** the layers.

9. For example, it would be useful to join Pete's ears to his face; as we're unlikely to need to work on them separately. Essentially, we can take several layers (in this case, just two) and merge them together as a single layer. The first step is to link them, as we did before. So, with the face layer selected, click on the link box for the ears layer – you should see the chain icon appear.

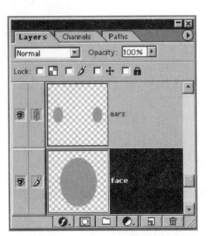

10. Note that I've pulled the ears layer down the list so that it's immediately above the face layer. This is simply in order to keep the above figure nice and compact – otherwise you'd be looking at a very tall, thin image, showing lots of miniscule (and illegible) layer entries. This change in ordering won't have any effect on the process so it's not a problem if you choose not to bother with it.

11. Now that we've established a link between the layers, we're ready to perform a Merge Linked operation – either select Layer > Merge Linked from the menu bar (or from the Layers palette fly-out menu) or simply press Ctrl/Cmd+E. This takes all our linked layers and throws them together in a single layer, which adopts the name (and layer position) of the previously active layer – in this case face. Now is probably a good time to rename this layer as head.

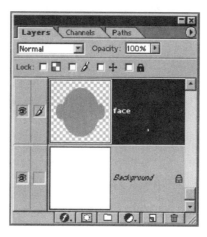

Great! Now that we have a largely feature-complete head, let's look at sprucing it up a little.

Selecting layers

1. We're going to start by adding a few highlights to Pete's face, so as to give it a little depth. Before we do that though, let's darken our background layer a little, in order to help the highlights stand out a little when we apply them. We simply need to select the Background layer (be sure to deselect any outstanding selections) and flood-fill it with a medium gray (R=128, G=128, B=128).

2. Now create a new layer called highlights and place it just above the head layer in the Layers palette. With the highlights layer active, hold down the CTRL/CMD key and click on the thumbnail for the head layer. You'll now see the familiar line of "marching ants" that Photoshop uses to mark the currently selected area – they should be marching round the edge of the purple shape that we're using

for Pete's head. (Okay, we couldn't actually get them to move in the screenshot below; guess you'll just have to take my word for it...)

3. Select the highlights layer (thus making it the active layer) and check the lock transparency box at the top of the Layers palette – this will help us to get a really smooth edge.

4. Now we're ready to paint around the edges with a large black airbrush. I'd suggest you use a brush size of 100-200 pixels, with a pressure of 35%. Okay, at first glance, this probably seems *way* too large; after all, the image itself is only 300 pixels across! However, there is a little method in this madness: if you use the brush from well outside the image area, and spray *around* the image, only the soft edges of the brush will actually apply any paint. This method helps us create a very smooth airbrushed effect.

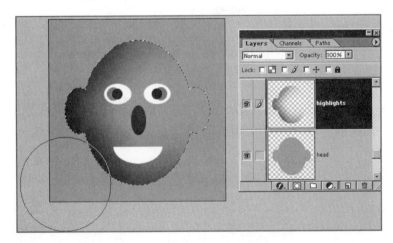

5. When you've finished brushing in the shadows, switch to a smaller brush (around 50 pixels), and add in a few white highlights. This starts to add a bit of depth to the image, without affecting the face itself in any way – all the highlights are limited to the highlights layer.

The screenshots below show you my efforts with this technique – the first is the original image; the last, the finished product; in between, the highlights layer on its own.

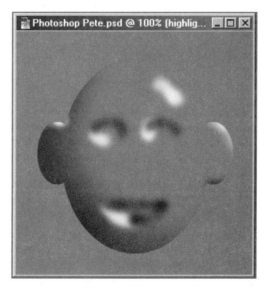

Don't worry if your first few attempts don't look too great; there's a lot of trial and error involved in getting this technique to bear fruit, and no single 'right way to do it'. If you have the time and patience, I'd encourage you to play about with different highlights and shadows, just to get comfortable with the tools and methods. If not, don't panic, because there's another way to give the image depth, and once you get the hang of it, it only takes a moment...

Layer styles

In this section, we're going to start looking at a very powerful feature that Photoshop 6.0 provides for use with layered images. As we just saw, there are times when the application of a few effects to a simple layer can make a tremendous difference to the overall impact of the image as a whole. Just how useful would it be if we had a whole bank of effects ready on tap? Well read on, and you tell me – because that's precisely what we have got, in the form of **layer styles**.

1. Before we apply any Layer Styles to Photoshop Pete, let's tuck away the highlights we created in the last section. The easiest way to do this is by simply hiding the highlights layer by clicking on its eye icon in the Layers palette. Another option (if you're in a particularly destructive mood) is to delete the layer completely – just select Delete Layer from one of the usual collection of menus. Alternatively, you can drag the layer over the trashcan icon in the bottom right corner of the Layers palette.

The Layer Style dialog

Right now, down to business. Let's start out by making the head layer active, and double-clicking on its Layers palette thumbnail. You'll hardly fail to notice the appearance of a huge dialog box called Layer Style – no doubt you've already launched it once or twice by accident!

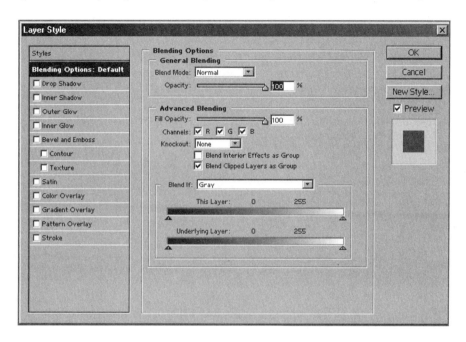

The first thing to note here is the menu on the left – let's run quickly down the options here:

- The first entry is called Styles, and shows us a list of the preset styles available for us to apply to the current layer. If you click on it now, you'll probably see some twenty styles (most of them not particularly exciting) that are bundled along with Photoshop 6.0 in a file called `ImageEffects.asl`.

- Next, we have the Blending Options entry, which is either Default (if you leave it be) or Custom (if you change any of the settings shown to the right). These settings determine how the currently selected layer effects are blended together with the underlying layer. Most of the control we're likely to need at this stage is available elsewhere, so we won't look too closely at this dialog – feel free to play around with it though.

- The rest of the list shows all the layer effects available to us. To apply one, simply check the box next to its entry in the list, and there's no limit to the number you can apply at the same time. I'd suggest just playing around for a while with all these effects, to get a feel for what they can do for you.

On the right hand side you can see a preview window, which (if the Preview box is checked) will show the overall effect of the style you're creating, as applied to a gray square. Note that you may have to move the Styles box over to the side so you can see what's going on. We refer to this overall combination of layer effects as a **layer style**. Later on, we'll see how to load and save these styles – for now, we'll concentrate on creating and editing them.

We're going to start off our exploration of layer styles by applying a simple bevel effect to the head layer; the plan is (once again) to add a little depth to Pete's face. This effect will simulate a beveled edge all around the face, with highlights and shadows cast roughly as they would be in reality.

2. Check the box by Bevel and Emboss and you will see the image change as the default bevel is applied to it:

3. Okay, we have a bit of a bevel – but it's still sort of flat, making the face look like a gingerbread man. We really want more of a rounded look. No problem, we just need to adjust the effect to suit our requirements. In the Layer Styles dialog, click on the words Bevel and Emboss to highlight the effect and bring up the relevant editing controls:

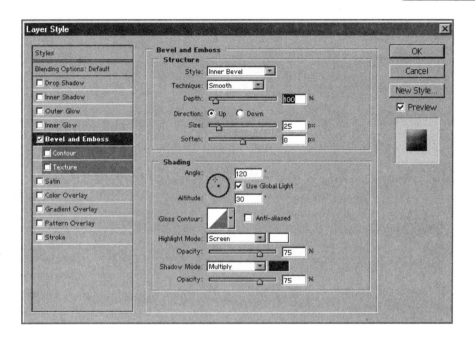

As you can see, there are an awful lot of different options here for tweaking the bevels. Once again, it's well worth playing about with them, just to see what sort of effects you can produce. For now though, we're only interested in three of them:

- **Depth**: the relative depth of the beveled edge, and the resulting strength of shading

- **Size**: the width of the beveled edge

- **Soften**: the smoothness of the bevel

4. For the next image, I cranked up the size to 25px. While this gives a far larger bevel, it was a little too harsh for my liking, so I also increased the Softness to 8px – you can see what a difference it makes! Of course, you might like to alter it if you prefer a slightly different look – once you're satisfied, just press OK to apply the effect.

You may have noticed a couple of new features appear on the Layers palette when we started applying layer styles. The head layer now has a pair of icons alongside its name and thumbnail, as well as a mini-entry immediately below, listing the names of the effects we just applied to it (in this case, just the one):

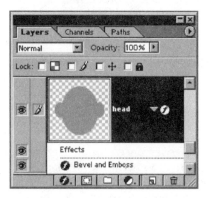

As you can see, there is a little icon and an arrow pointing down to the layer styles information, which you can collapse or expand by clicking on the arrow. Any time you want to change the style, simply double-click and make your adjustments. You can turn off a layer effect in the same way as you would a layer: click on the eye to the left of the effect name.

5. Now back to Photoshop Pete – I think we should cut the mouth out of the face so that it doesn't look quite so flat. In doing so, we can demonstrate a useful

technique, namely making a selection based on one layer, and using it to manipulate another layer.

6. We already know how to create a selection based on the contents of a layer. With the head layer still selected, CTRL/CMD-click on the mouth thumbnail to load the selection. You should see the marching ants around the mouth.

7. Turn off the visibility of the mouth layer so we can see what is happening (by clicking on the appropriate eye icon). You should now see the face minus a mouth, with an army of ants marching round the place it used to be.

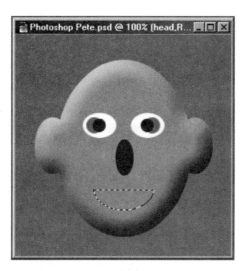

8. Ensure that the head layer is still active, and press the Delete key to remove this selection from the face.

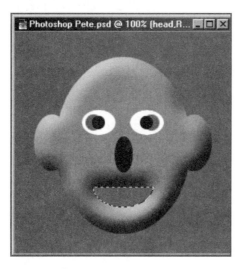

Notice how the layer style is automatically applied to the new area? That's one of the most useful aspects of the layer styles: they are what are called 'live' effects, changing as the image changes and updating themselves automatically. This not only saves us an enormous amount of time when making alterations, but makes it very quick and simple to experiment to your heart's content!

Let's apply this technique once again, this time to Pete's eyes:

9. Keep the head layer active, and Ctrl/Cmd-click the eyes thumbnail to select them.

10. Press the DELETE key to cut the eyes out of the face. As the bevel will be applied to all the edges of that layer, you will now see some beveling around the eyes.

11. Finally, remember to deselect!

Reusing effects

Well, we're certainly adding depth to the face with this bevel effect, but don't you think the nose is still looking a bit flat by comparison? Let's add a bevel to that as well. Since we want the nose to look as if it's standing proud of the face, we need a different approach from the one that we used for the eyes and mouth. In fact, we need to apply a brand new bevel effect to the nose layer.

But why recreate a bevel effect when we have a perfectly good one in place? Can't we just copy the layer style across from the face to the nose? Yes we can, and once again our good friend "drag and drop" comes to the rescue.

1. Click on the word Effects on the head layer and drag it up to the nose layer. When you see a line appear between the nose layer and the layer immediately beneath it, you can release the mouse button to deposit the effect there.

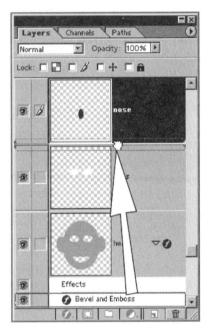

Alright! You've just duplicated a layer style – really not that hard at all. But what if we need to copy a layer style to several layers at once; do we have to drag and drop it onto every one of the new layers? Fortunately, we don't. This is another situation where layer linking comes in handy:

- Make the source of your layer style the active layer

- Link all layers to which you want to copy this layer style

- Select Layer > Layer Style > Paste Layer Style to Linked

You'll find that this is a great time saver, especially if you need to apply uniform effects across many layers. You can also use this technique if you decide to modify one of the parameters of a layer style that's been duplicated – changes can be applied quickly to all the duplicates without any trouble. This is a really important technique that sees a lot of use in the real world, as it saves a lot of time, and is very straightforward to use once you know what you're doing.

Color overlay

Assuming you're still working in color, you can't have failed to notice that Pete's nose is a different color to his face. What can we do about this then? Well, it just so happens that we have a layer style called Color Overlay, which allows us to change the color of all the contents in the layer.

1. Select the nose layer and open up the styles dialog (by double-clicking on the thumbnail or layer name).

2. Now click on the word Color Overlay in the style dialog. The effect will automatically be applied, and options for the color overlay will be activated.

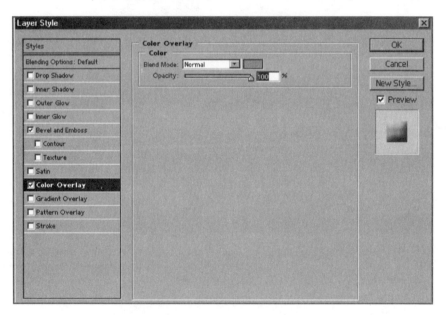

Although the default color is red (which is why 'Pete' currently looks more like 'Rudolf'), we can change it to anything we want. As it happens, we want to match the nose color to that of the face:

3. Double-click on the red box at the top of the dialog (right next to where it says Blend Mode: Normal). This will open a color picker dialog.

4. We could now select a color directly from this window; however, we want to match the color of the face. If you move the cursor outside the picker window, you will see that it changes to an Eyedropper tool. Click on an evenly colored part of the face, and the Eyedropper will pick up the color and apply it. Click OK in the Color Picker and once again in the Layer Style dialog.

The colors should now match perfectly. You can also see that a new Color Overlay effect has been added below the nose layer.

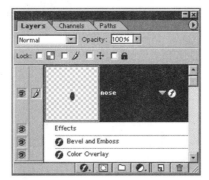

Modifying a layer style

Well, that's looking a bit better. As we've already observed, one of the really nice things about layer styles is that if you don't think they look quite right, it's very easy to go back and change them. Let's say we want to change the direction of the lighting on our beveled layers; nothing could be simpler!

1. Open the Layer Style dialog for the head layer (by double-clicking on the thumbnail).

2. Double-click the Bevel and Emboss entry, to call up the relevant editing controls.

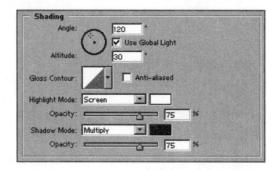

You'll find the control we're after in the lower half of the dialog, as shown here. Shading Angle controls the orientation of the virtual light source that Photoshop uses to simulate shadows and highlights. The main control takes the form of a crosshair inside a circle, which can be dragged around to control the point at which light hits the object.

The circle represents a hemisphere of points on which you can place the light source, so when the crosshair is centered, light will appear to come from directly above. On the other hand, if it's on the circle's circumference, the light will appear to be coming from the side of the image.

You can also control the orientation of the light source using the two text boxes to the right of the circle control. These give you a much greater degree of fine control than the crosshairs do, letting you specify precise angles for the horizontal angle and altitude. The images below should give you a good idea of how different values correspond to crosshair positions and the final appearance of the layer:

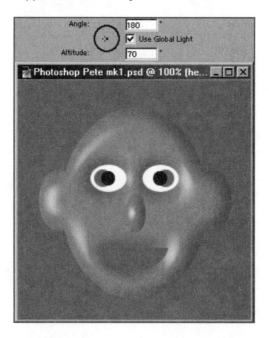

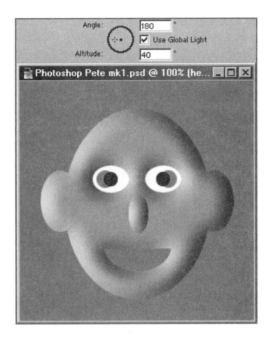

You may have noticed something rather curious going on here – although we're editing styles for the head layer, the bevel lighting on the nose layer is changing as well. It's just as well it is actually, or it might look rather odd! Between the two textboxes, you'll see a checkbox marked Use Global Light. The purpose of this is fairly self-explanatory: when it's checked (as it is, by default), you're using the **global light**, whose settings are independent of the layer you're working on, and even independent of the particular layer you're working with. Any layer styles that use the global light will get automatically updated when you change its settings.

Of course, there's nothing to stop you from turning it off – we might well want to use a different light source on one of the elements in our image. In this case however, that's possibly not such a good idea, unless we especially want to give Pete a receding nose...

By lighting the nose layer from the left, I've actually made it look more like a hollow cavity being lit from the right (like the rest of the face). No, this isn't really what we want; I'd suggest putting it back to using the global light source before we move on and look at some other layer effects and styles.

Inner shadow

1. I now want to introduce you to another layer effect, along with a new way to apply it. Let's add some depth to the eyes by applying an inner shadow effect – this places shadows *inside* an object, so that it appears to have been cut out of the page. With the eyes layer active, click on the icon at the bottom of the Layers palette; up pops a menu, listing all the same effects as the layer styles dialog box. Select Inner Shadow....

I'm personally rather fond of this effect, particularly when used with type, giving the appearance of text cut out of a page.

I guess you've been thinking for a while, "what's with those goofy eyes?" Although the irises are in roughly the right place, they're still a little out of kilter with the pupils they're meant to match. Let's see if we can do anything about this.

2. First we want to make them bigger and place them centrally under the pupils. Select the irises layer and open up the Free Transform menu again (remember the shortcut? It's CTRL/CMD+T or Edit > Free Transform). Hold down SHIFT (to constrain proportions) and ALT/OPTION (to transform symmetrically about the center node) and drag out one of the corner nodes until the irises enlarge to almost enough to fill the eye sockets.

3. Drag the bounding box over to the right, so that the left eyeball is centered under the left pupil. Remember that you can hold down the SHIFT key while you do this, to help keep the original alignment.

4. Finally, apply the transformation.

We now have a new problem: if I try to line up the right iris, the left one will move out of position, since they are joined together! If only there was a way to separate the two for just a minute... Of course, there is. If we ignore for a moment the fact that we're using layers, the solution is perfectly obvious: create a selection around the right hand iris, and drag *that* into the correct position.

5. Use the Rectangular Marquee tool to draw a square around the right iris.

6. Now use the Move tool to drag it into position. As you begin to move the iris, you'll see the selection contract around our circle of non-transparent pixels – there's no point in moving a transparent area because there's effectively nothing there.

7. Finally, deselect the right hand iris.

Here's how the fruit of our labors looks now – much neater, I'm sure you'll agree:

Preset styles

Now I'd like to demonstrate another way to apply special effects to a layer with layer styles. Select Window > Show Styles, and you will see a new palette appear with lots of little colored squares on it. These are all the preset layer styles that you can apply to your layers with a single click.

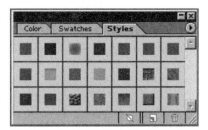

In fact, I have rather a lot more styles in my own palette than are shown here. That's because I've loaded many additional styles, and created quite a few of my own. A number of these extras are shipped with Photoshop 6.0 as standard, and if you click on the top right arrow in the Styles palette, you'll see a fly-out menu featuring a list of .asl files; each of these contains definitions for several different styles. You also have options to load styles from an external source (many are available via the Internet, and Appendix A lists some of the sites on which you can find them) and to save modified styles. For now, let's just make use of the Large List option, which puts the layer styles in a vertical list, alongside their names.

Using a preset style

We're now going to apply one of these preset styles to Pete's irises, so as to give them a little more texture.

1. Make sure that the irises layer is active, and begin clicking on some of the styles. You will see all kinds of effects instantly applied to the blue circles. Choose one that you like; I decided to opt for a subtle but effective one called Snow.

    When you apply the style, you'll see that all the effect information appears in the Layers palette, just as it did before.

    Note that some styles (including the one I picked) will only use one effect – in this case, a Pattern Overlay effect – whereas others will use several at once. We'll see plenty of examples of these as we progress through the book.

2. There's nothing to stop us from adding our own styles to this list of presets – since we've used the purple bevel style to such great effect here, we might want to keep it safe for future use. That's not a problem: just select the nose layer (which is where we defined the style we're after), call up the fly-out menu from the Styles palette, and select New Style.

3. In the dialog that now appears, enter a suitable name for the style and deselect the lower of the two checkboxes. We haven't modified the default Layer Blending Options, so there's not much point in saving them as part of the style. Hit OK and you should see a brand new addition to the palette's list of preset styles, which we can now use just like the others.

Organizing layers

1. Since we've been adding layers and styles to our project like crazy, the Layers palette is really starting to get rather crowded – it's time we did a bit of tidying up, so let's make the thumbnails small again. Just hit the top right arrow in the Layers palette, and select Palette options.... Pick one of the smaller images, and hit OK.

    That's one way to make things a little clearer for us; but bear in mind that we're still only looking at a relatively small number of layers – what about when we're working on projects with literally hundreds? Imagine an image depicting a crowd of faces, all based loosely on Photoshop Pete. Surely a recipe for confusion!

2. Well, there's one rather handy way to make things a little clearer: we can color code each of our layers using (you guessed it) layer colors. You've already seen the Color setting in the Layer properties dialog (hold down Alt/Option and double-click on the layer whose properties you want to check out).

    As soon as you change the Color setting, you'll see the first couple of columns in that layer's entry in the Layers palette change color to match. If you want to make particular layers clearly identifiable then this might be just what you need. Likewise, if you're dealing with a lot of layers that can be easily sorted into eight or fewer categories, it might also be helpful.

However, there's another factor to consider when we start thinking about projects with very large numbers of layers: we don't actually need to see every layer in the project listed in the palette; all the same, we want to be able to access them all should the need arise. Surely there's some way for us to bundle layers together, so that we can treat Photoshop Pete as a self-contained entity (and hide the gory details of his constituent elements when we need to), distinct from his friends Photoshop Bob and Photoshop Mel. Of course, there is.

Creating Layer sets

Photoshop 6.0 has introduced a new feature called **Layer Sets**, and believe me, it's long overdue! I have worked on images with more than 100 layers, and I'm sure it comes as no surprise, but things do start to get just a little bit confusing after a while, trying to remember which one fits in where, how it relates to other layers, what it contributes to the overall project. Layer sets let us arrange our layers into folders, and even assign a different color to each set.

We can do this two ways:

1. Click on the file folder at the bottom of the Layers palette (third from the left). This will create an empty folder as a new entry in the list. You can then drag and drop any of your layers into this folder (apart from the background, which is immovable).

2. Link all layers except for the background. Select New Set From Linked... from the Layers palette's fly-out menu. A dialog box pops up asking for a name, so call it Pete and press ENTER. A new folder will appear in the Layers palette; but where have all our layers gone?

3. Press the arrow on the layer set Pete, and the folder will open up to display all the missing layers. There's no limit to the number of layer sets you can have in one document, and you can even copy a layer set from one document to another by dragging and dropping between the two documents.

   Another thing to note is that layer sets also support a colors property, so we can color-code them in just the same way as we did our individual layer earlier on.

Drop Shadow

1. Let's finish off the face with my all-time favorite effect: the good old Drop Shadow. There is nothing quite like a nice soft shadow to add depth and realism. Let's check out all the editing options first – select the head layer, open up the Layer Style dialog, and select Drop Shadow.

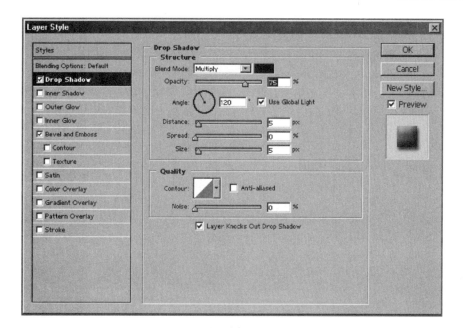

The main settings to take note of (and, of course, play about with) are:

- **Opacity:** The opposite of transparency (that is, how opaque the effect will be); the lower the opacity, the more transparent the image will become. I usually drop this to between 30% and 50%.

- **Distance:** This is how far the drop shadow will be from the image – the distance by which the shadow is offset. The further away it is from the image, the further the object seems to be away from the background.

- **Size:** The distance over which the shadow is blurred. As well as affecting the size of the shadow, this also controls its softness. I usually end up increasing this a little from its default setting.

2. In this case, I left everything at the default setting except for the Size, which I increased to 9px. Let's apply a drop shadow to the nose as well – either use the default settings, or copy the effect directly from the head layer. Here's the result on the next page:

I know it's not quite the Mona Lisa, but it's helped to illustrate some important techniques, and you should have learned a lot about layers in the course of creating it. You should be pretty comfortable working with layers by now; if not, it's probably worth going back and walking through this example again. We will cover some of the more advanced layer techniques in a later chapter.

Type layers

We haven't quite finished with layers yet. Although we touched on the Type tool earlier on in the chapter, we didn't really do much with it. So, just for fun, let's add some text underneath our picture of Photoshop Pete. The first thing we need to do is to make a bit more room for the text. The simplest way to do this is to shrink the head and move it up a little.

1. Select the layer set Pete and link one of the layers – you'll find that all the others are automatically linked.

2. Use the Free Transform tool to scale the head (holding the SHIFT key down to keep the proportions intact). Now shift it up to the top of the canvas.

   Since all the layers are linked, they all transform and move as a unit. Pretty cool, huh?

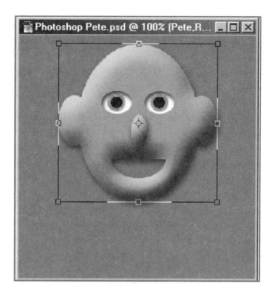

Now let's put in a caption for the picture — we may as well use the fella's name.

3. Press the "T" symbol in the toolbox to access the Type tool.

4. Select Arial, 30 pt; for the color choose black and type "Photoshop Pete". You may find that it helps to turn off the gray background layer, as the cursors used by this tool are also gray, and therefore don't show up very well at all.

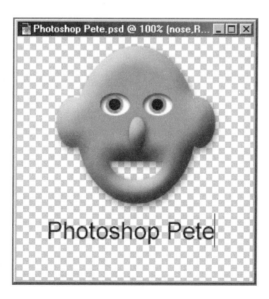

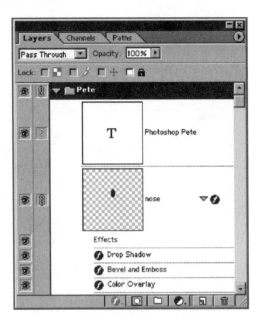

5.   Finally, hit the check button on the type tool options bar.

As we'd expect, the text appears in the image area, and a new layer called Photoshop Pete appears in the Layers palette. Remember, the "T" icon indicates a vector-based type layer, which can be scaled and edited (in terms of the text, style, etc.) without fuss or loss of quality, and to which we can apply a rather neat warping effect.

Editing text

One of most useful features of type layers is that they let you edit your text in situ, even after you've applied all sorts of fancy effects to it. Whether it comes down to fixing a typo, or producing umpteen different variations of a single design, with different text in each one, this is without doubt a fantastic time saver. Now we're going to see how to do it.

1.   Make sure you have the Text tool selected, and that the appropriate text layer is active.

2.   Click at the beginning of the text and drag the mouse across until you have all the words highlighted. Alternatively, you can double-click on the text to select a word, or triple-click to select the full text. Now that it's selected, we're ready to edit.

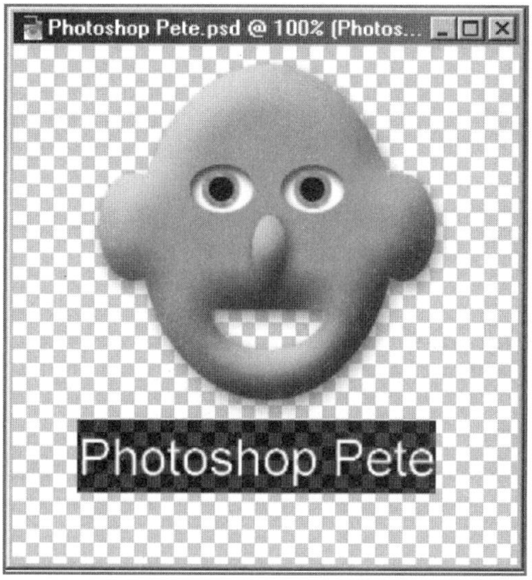

3. If the Character palette isn't visible, click on the button in the tool options bar.

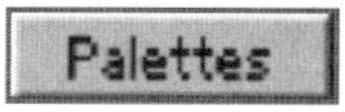

4. Use the Character palette to change the font to something a little thicker. Here's a very handy tip for when you're picking fonts – if you select the drop-down menu of font names, you can cycle through the entries using UP and DOWN cursor keys. The selected text in the image will automatically switch to the current font, so you can very quickly look at how a lot of different fonts will look in context. You can either select the size from the drop down menu, or type it manually into the box – I ended up using Impact, 33pt.

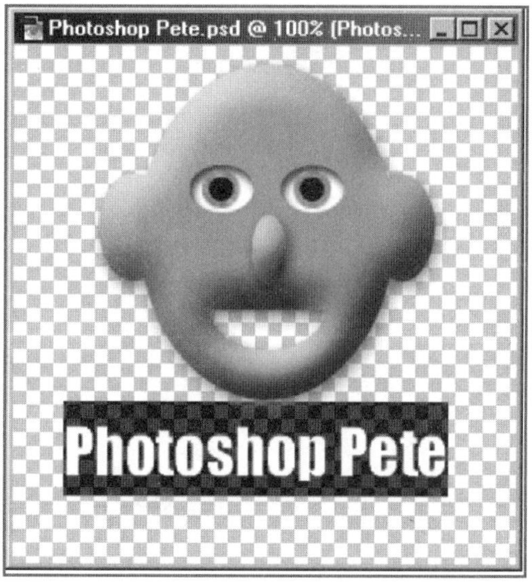

5. If your text isn't properly centered, you can use the Move tool to drag it into position.

   Now that we're happy with the font and type size, let's have some fun with our text:

6. Select the text, and click the icon on the Text tool options bar – this launches the Text Warp dialog.

   This is a fun little tool that's been introduced in Photoshop 6.0, that lets us warp text in a variety of different ways. It's probably more instructive to *show* you what it does rather than to try to explain it!

7. Select Arc from the Style drop-down – this will warp our text around a circular arc. By default, this will be arcing downwards (Bend: 50%). To arc it upwards, change the bend setting to –50%. Note that you can drag your text around the window while this tool is active, which helps you to position your text while warping it.

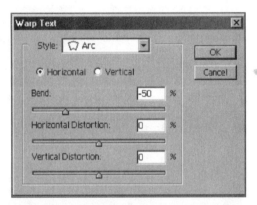

8. Press OK to apply the effect.

Finally, let's apply some effects to our text.

9. Double-click on the Layers palette entry for the Photoshop Pete layer (noting that the icon being used in place of a thumbnail has changed to reflect the fact that this layer now contains warped type) to call up the Layer Style dialog.

10. Apply Outer Glow and Drop Shadow effects.

As you can see, we can apply styles and effects to your type, and even change the font. As long as the text is defined in a type layer, it is fully editable. However, we also know that this has a few drawbacks (we can't use filters and certain distortions on a type layer), so it's sometimes necessary to convert a type layer to a regular layer. We'll come back to these issues in Chapter 10, where we'll discuss more advanced layers techniques.

Case Study

All right, now that you are starting to get the hang of layers, we can start to do some really cool stuff. Let's start off by creating a logo for our company. We are going to add a color gradient and depth to our logo by using layer styles. This is going to be the logo that we will use on all the pages of our fictitious company. We will save this logo on a transparent background so it can be easily copied onto our images.

For the last part of the case study we will add our newly created logo to the image of the Porsche and resize it. We will use this logo many times through the course of the case study.

Creating our logo

1. Open `logo elements.psd` (available for download from the friends of ED web site) or create your own with the Type tool on a new file with a transparent background. If you create your own you'll need to rasterize it before we can apply all our effects and transformations. To do this, simply right-click on the name of the layer and select Rasterize Layer. The font I used was "Gunship", which can be found at 1001freefonts.com, I like this font because it is very modern and industrial looking; perfect for automobiles. The "X" was skewed a little bit for effect: Edit > Transform > Skew and drag the side handle up a bit.

2. Let's put the words "Exotic Imports" on a separate layer so that we can edit them separately from the "X". Of course, if you created your own type they will already be on a separate layer. Make a selection around the words with the Rectangular Marquee tool.

3. Press SHIFT+CTRL/CMD+ J (Layer > New > Layer via Cut) to move the selection to a new layer. This is a very useful shortcut, that you'll find yourself using time and again, so best to learn it now! Let's give the layers more appropriate names; name the new layer Exotic Imports and change the old layer to X.

First we will work on the X layer. With the layer active, hold down the CTRL/CMD key and click on the layer thumbnail to load the selection for "X".

4. We want to cut a groove around the "X" and make it look like metal. Choose Select > Modify > Contract and enter 15 pixels in the dialog box.

Now choose Select > Modify > Border and enter a setting of 5 pixels.

Press the DELETE key and the "X" should look like the image below. Deselect.

5. Load the new selection for the "X" by Ctrl/Cmd clicking on the X layer thumbnail. Select the Gradient tool, Foreground to Background, and fill the "X" with a linear gradient from the bottom to the top.

6. Now open the Layer Style box (click on 'f' icon at the bottom of the Layers palette) and apply the settings shown below. The Drop Shadow is just the default setting, but I changed the Bevel and Emboss settings; I have turned off the Global Light box so that I can change the altitude without affecting the angle. Increase the Depth, change the Angle and the Altitude, and select Ring-Double for the Gloss Contour. You can play around here, to find settings that suit your taste.

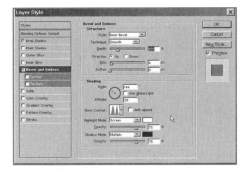

There, the "X" is looking much better, let's work on the "Exotic Imports" now.

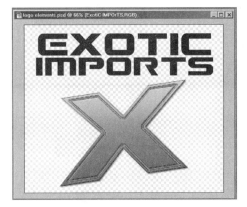

7. Select the Exotic Imports layer and set the foreground color to a dark blue by clicking on the black square in the toolbox. I used the settings below: R=45, G= 0, B=175.

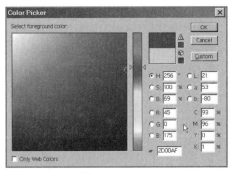

Load the selection by CTRL/CMD clicking on the layer thumbnail and fill with a white to blue gradient.

8. To complete the effect, drag the layer style we created for the "X" to the Exotic imports layer. To do this, simply drag and drop the word Effects from just below the X layer and drop it right at the bottom of the words Exotic imports. The effect is now duplicated.

9. Deselect and move the words down so they are placed on top of the "X" using the Move tool.

Great, we have a nice 'car badge' feel. We need something that represents the world to complete our logo. What better than a circle?

10. Create a new layer and draw a large circle with the Elliptical Marquee tool, hold down Shift to constrain it to a circle.

Let's just fill the outline; we don't want to compete with our "X".

11. Edit > Stroke..., choose a setting of 8 pixels and use the Color Picker to select an orange/red color, now press OK.

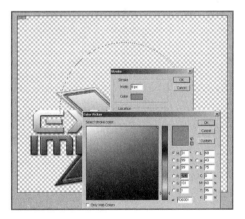

Deselect and the result...

12. To complete the effect, I decided to mutate the circle, press Ctrl+T (or Edit > Free Transform). Scale, rotate and position the ring as shown.

13. Save the logo as `logo.psd`.

Adding the logo to our exotic imports document

1. We are going to add our logo to the main image now. Link all the layers together, so that they will stay together. Open the document `Exotic imports.tif` that you saved earlier.

2. Drag and drop the logo into the exotic imports document.

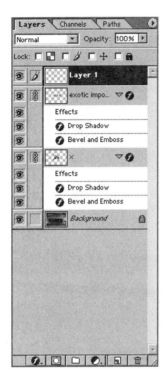
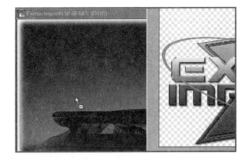

Notice that it has copied over with all the layers and styles intact, assuming both documents are using the same color space. Save and close the logo document.

3. Using the Free Transform tool again, scale and position the logo onto our image.

4. Select the Type tool and, using the settings shown, (or something of your own), create a caption for our postcard with a light gray colored font.

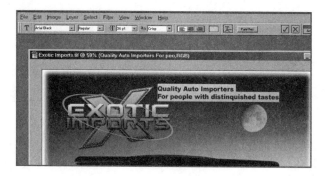

To finish off, add the address, phone number and web site address on the bottom (I used Arial Narrow).

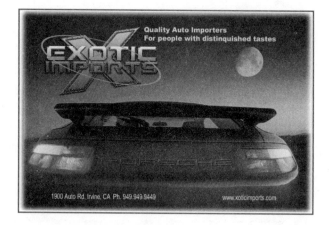

You have done well! Your postcard is almost done. Don't worry, the next part of the Case Study will be shorter. Be sure to save your file; you don't want to lose all your hard work! Save it as exotic imports.psd.

Summary

This chapter introduced us to the notion of layers, an integral feature of Photoshop 6.0 that enables us to create separate image elements as independent images, and arrange them dynamically within Photoshop. We learned that layers were stacked in a specific order, with elements at the top of the stack concealing those further down. By varying the transparency of layers, we can combine their contents in a variety of useful ways.

We started out by familiarizing ourselves with basic techniques for manipulating layers: creation, ordering, locking, duplication, and modifying visibility. Aided by the trusty character of Photoshop Pete, we looked at a variety of other techniques that can be used to manipulate elements contained within layers: free transforms, and a number of useful selection techniques.

We then looked at working with multiple layers, linking and merging layers, and applying various layer styles. Finally, we considered layer sets (and some of the organizational issues that they solve for us) and rounded things off with a satisfyingly fancy (but useful nonetheless) demonstration of text warping.

We've covered a lot of ground in this chapter, and you should now be fairly confident at finding your way comfortably around an image based on multiple layers. Make sure you remember what you've learned here, because we'll be making plenty of use of layers throughout the rest of the book. In particular, you will need a solid foundation for the advanced layers chapter, in which we're really going to make Photoshop fly!

6 Color and Printing

What we'll cover in this chapter:

- *Capturing images*

- *Optimizing the Preferences for higher performance*

- *Color theory – how the human eye sees color*

- *The difference between additive and subtractive color*

- *RGB Channels*

- *CMYK Channels*

- *Grayscale*

- *Pantone color matching system*

- *Spot colors and how to prepare them for printing*

- *Duotones, tritones and quadtones*

- *Hue/Saturation*

- *Cropping and creative cropping*

- *Image resolution*

- *Print file formats*

Capturing images

Scanning

Apart from a CD, the most common way to get an image into Photoshop is through a scanner. There are many different types that range from cheap $50 flatbed scanners through to drum scanners that can cost well in excess of $100,000. The most common type is now the flatbed scanner. These can produce remarkably good quality scans and are available for very reasonable prices.

They work like this: you put a picture face down on the glass plate (bed). A diode passes over the image and digitally samples it as it goes. The older types were called triple pass scanners and they would scan the page 3 times, once for red, once for green and again for blue colors. The majority of the flatbeds on the market today are single pass, meaning that the diode only has to pass once to capture all the color and image information. This saves a lot of time.

To scan into Photoshop, first set up your scanning software, then click on File > Import. You will see a list of devices that you can import from. Your scanner should be on the list once you have set up your software - you might have to check the documentation that came with your scanner if it's not showing up in Photoshop. Mine is a Microtek scan wizard for USB.

When you click on that option, your scanning software will launch in Photoshop. Every manufacturer has different software for scanning, so explaining my scanning software will not help much. However there are a few options common to all scanning.

Colors

```
2 bit = 4 colors
3 bit = 8
4 bit = 16
5 bit = 32
7 bit = 64
8 bit = 256 colors
16 bit = 65,000 colors
32 bit = 16,000,000
36 bit = 68.7 billion colors
```

Choose at least 32 bit color for all color scanning to get the best results. If your scanner doesn't support 32 bit, then choose the highest available. 16 bit is sometimes referred to as having 32,000 (+) colors. This is because older computers did not have the full range of 65,536 available in the color palette. Choose 8 bit (256 shades of gray) grayscale for grayscale images (no color!).

Resolution

There are 3 common resolutions to be aware of:

- For Web and multimedia use 72dpi

- For output to an inkjet printer use 150dpi. Any lower and your image would look pixelized. Any higher and the ink saturation would be too high, producing a muddy image

- For output on a commercial printing press, select 300dpi

There is really no advantage in going any larger unless you plan on enlarging the image (as you increase resolution, you are increasing file size). If you do plan on enlarging it, increase the dpi resolution accordingly. For example if you want to double your image size and commercially print your work, then scan at 600dpi instead of 300dpi. If the scanner has a scaling option, then use that and leave the resolution at the optimum for your media output.

Digital cameras

When shooting pictures, people think that the larger the file, the better the picture. The largest would be an uncompressed TIFF (UT) or RAW image (which requires the manufacturer's software to process). Most cameras come with a 16MB card. With a 3.1megapixel camera, you would normally only fit one UT image (depending on the image size), but from a 5.1mp camera, you can't even fit one UT on a 16MB card!

The UTs are also very slow, taking about 25 - 45 seconds to download from camera to card and the same amount of time to the computer.

It's much better to use the JPEG option. Choose the highest quality. This will allow approximately 7 images on a 16MB card, of course the amount will change if you are using a CD or disk. Once in Photoshop, you would be hard pressed to see the difference between a high quality JPEG and the TIFF image. The next level down is **Normal**. Normal mode now gives 14 images to 16MB card and the quality is almost as good as Fine or UT. For print output it's not advisable to go any lower. However, for web you can usually get away with a fairly small file size.

When uploading the pictures into your computer you can use the USB cable or purchase a card reader. These are better for convenience and speed.

For image management, I recommend Extensis Portfolio to look after photos, but the low-cost Cameraid ($15 shareware) is what I turn to first.

Open a JPEG image in Photoshop and you will find it is very large. It should be resized before it can be used. Use Image > Image Size to turn off Resample Image for print, and change the resolution to 300dpi. For online use, you could turn on resampling and just make the dimensions smaller since you don't need the image to be more than 72 dpi. Save the file as a TIFF so as to keep the quality. I don't recommend changing to a JPEG again until we Save for Web…. We will look more at image resampling at the end of this chapter.

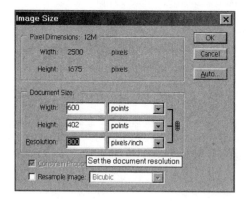

Optimizing your preferences

Click on Edit > Preferences > General and the dialog box below will come up. These are the Photoshop preferences. Clicking on the Next button will enable you to cycle through the different screens. Most of them will be fine at the default settings but there are a few that you should be aware of and may need to change.

General

If you have very little free hard drive space and are low on RAM, reduce the History States, otherwise I would leave it alone. Uncheck Export Clipboard, or it will slow down your exit time from Photoshop and fill your clipboard. The general preferences are also the place where you reset your tools.

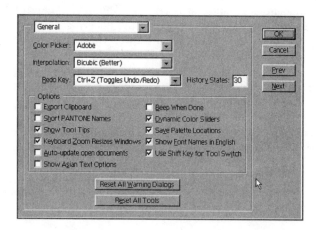

Saving files

Image Previews are nice. They are the little thumbnails of the image that display in your file explorer or finder. Maximize backwards compatibility in Photoshop format should be turned off, unless you plan on opening your image with Photoshop 2.5 or below. All that does is save a composite image with the file so that it can be displayed on a version of Photoshop that doesn't support layers. It just bloats your files otherwise.

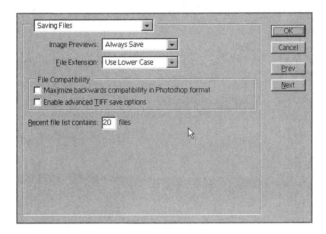

Displays & Cursors

I like to choose Brush Size for the painting tools; it lets me see exactly where I will be painting and shows the width of the brush. I choose Standard for the other tools so I have a visual on what tool is in use. I like this option best, and if I ever need the precise tools they are only a keystroke away: press the CAPS LOCK to toggle between the Precise cursor (which is a tiny crosshair) and back again.

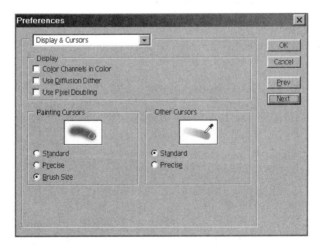

Plug-Ins & Scratch Disks

Generally speaking, you would put all your Plug-ins in your, er, plug-ins directory. If for some reason you have another directory for plug-ins then you can also specify that path.

The Scratch Disks warrant attention. When Photoshop runs out of RAM for a specific task it uses hard disk space as temporary RAM. Photoshop uses approximately 10 times the size of the image you are working on in RAM and scratch disk, as a rough rule of thumb. Always set your fastest hard drive as the first scratch disk. If you have multiple drives, set them all into the Scratch disk so that Photoshop can use them. A lot of users have a hard drive installed to use as a dedicated scratch disk. This can boost performance and save a lot of "scratch disk full" errors. However, with today's increasing drive sizes it is becoming less of a problem.

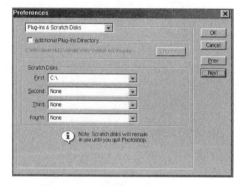

Memory & Image Cache

Physical Memory Usage assigns how much of your RAM is available for Photoshop to use. If you experience out of memory errors, I suggest changing the settings here. If you run other programs like I do at the same time, you probably don't want to go much above 80%. If you are just using Photoshop then you could crank it up a bit higher. This would also depend on how much RAM you have. I wouldn't use Photoshop with any less than 128 MB, 256 will improve performance a huge amount – the more the better. The old saying, 'you can never have too much RAM' stands true.

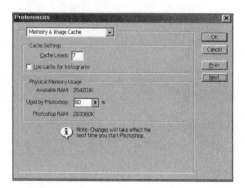

Color settings

There is also another set of preferences for you to be aware of. This is where you set your color profiles under Edit > Color Settings….

You will see a drop-down menu when you select Settings. Choose the best option for the work you will be doing. Web Graphics Default will be a good starting place if you are doing multimedia and web-related work. If you are doing print work, choose the appropriate Prepress option for your region. Or if you don't care, or find it annoying, select Color Management Off.

In the other options, the only real change I make is to choose Adobe RGB (under Working Spaces) instead of the ancient RGB default. You will notice your images become much richer-looking. I also turn off the Profile Mismatches (they ask to convert the images to the chosen color profile) to avoid converting every image I open in Photoshop, and the dialog boxes get annoying after a while. If you are doing print work, it is advisable to keep them on so you get consistency between your images. The good thing is you can turn them on or off whenever you want. It only takes a few seconds and unlike the main preferences box, you don't have to restart Photoshop for the color changes to take place.

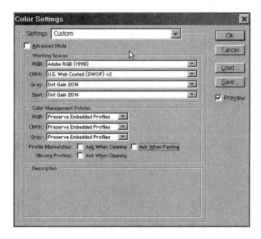

Color theory

OK, you'd better fasten your seatbelts because we are going to take a crash course through color theory at warp speed. Understanding color is a vital piece of knowledge for your graphic design career. The color section of your Adobe manual has some really good information on this, so if you are one of the tiny percentage of people who actually read their manuals, you'll have a jump on most Photoshop users. This book is not designed to replace the manual, rather to give you a real world approach with things that you can really use. Because of that, there are some technical details that are not covered and should not be covered here.

Having said that, let's look at color. I will divide it into 2 parts; displayed images such as those on your monitor, and color used in print.

There are 2 types of color, one called **additive** and one **subtractive**. With additive color all the colors added together make white. As the sunlight reflects off objects they absorb different colors. What is left over is the color that our eyes perceive. This type of color is what occurs in the real world. For example (in terms of primary colors: Red, Yellow, Blue) when sunlight hits an orange, the orange absorbs the color blue. As a result, yellow and red are left over and, combined, make up an orange color visible to the eye. In other words, take white and remove blue and you have orange.

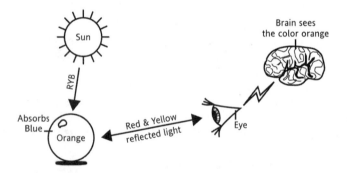

Of course, in the real world we are dealing with more colors than just the three primary colors. Take a rainbow and you will see all the colors in the spectrum. A prism is another example; shine a pure white light at just the right angle and you will see the color split into red, orange, yellow, green, blue, indigo and violet. The same process occurs, using raindrops as prisms, when a rainbow appears.

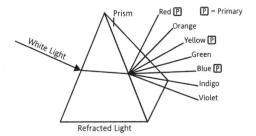

Another example is the ocean. Have you ever wondered why everything deep in the ocean appears to be blue? That is because the colors red, orange, yellow and green are less dense than blue and are filtered out by the time they reach a certain depth. That is why underwater photographers carry a large flashlight, to restore the colors in the depths of the ocean.

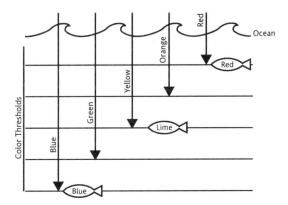

A good way to demonstrate this would be to take a round piece of cardboard and paint red, yellow and blue on it and spin it really fast, you would notice that as it spins, the colors mixed together become white.

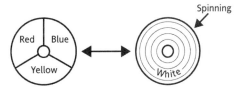

A monitor works a little differently, in that the primary colors used are Red, Green and Blue. That is where the name RGB comes from. These colors are called RGB primaries. There are three guns inside the monitor shining these three colors onto the screen that we see. These three colors mixed together form the various colors possible on a color monitor. A monitor is an example of **additive color**.

The old masters used RYB color, but this does not produce all colors (seems like the art teacher was wrong!) – for example, they had problems creating a genuine black. Isaac Newton first described the full spectrum, and as color theory developed, it was found that RGB could produce a greater variety of colors than the old RYB primary color system.

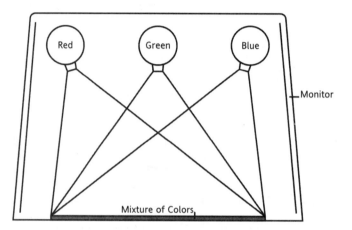

The second type is called the **subtractive color**, where we subtract color to make up white. We are most familiar with this color model when we mix paints etc. This is also how a printer works.

However, a commercial printing press works a little differently. It uses a CMY color space. This means that the primary colors used are Cyan (bright blue), Magenta (purple-red), and Yellow. Because these three colors mixed together make up a weak black, the color black is also added. That is where we get the name CMYK, blacK is represented as K so we don't get it mixed up with blue. This is the information we need to know when we are designing for a commercial print job.

When we print on a four color commercial printing press, it's actually called four-color process printing. We will go into this in more detail in Chapter 13. In a nutshell, the four colors are arranged into different dots at varying sizes and angles to fool the eyes into seeing the different colors. If you look at a printed piece with a magnifying glass you will notice that the image is made up of tiny dots.

Each color mode is called a color space. The range of possible colors with each color space is called a **color gamut**. Gamuts are there because a human eye is capable of seeing more colors than are presently reproducible on a monitor or print. The gamuts are the colors that are reproducible. A CMYK color space is smaller than that of an RGB, meaning that there are fewer colors available. The reason that the CMYK gamut is smaller than that of the RGB is because you cannot reproduce with ink all the colors you can produce on a monitor. You will notice that you will lose some brightness and vibrancy when converting to CMYK. The image below shows the available colors in each color space. This should be overlaid on a color wheel.

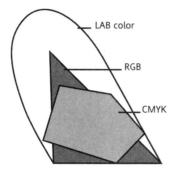

In the Color Picker you will notice an out of gamut warning: a little triangle. More about CMYK printing in chapter 13.

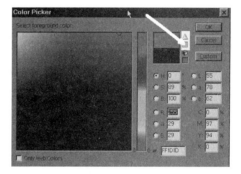

RGB channels

Imagine three sheets of clear plastic on top of each other and a piece of white paper on the bottom. We now take small pieces of tinted plastic, one is red (R), another in green (G) and yet another in blue (B), and we paste a piece of colored plastic onto each clear sheet in the shape of an object.

We paste the red in areas we want to appear red in our red channel. Do this on the green and blue channels also. We now have three sheets of plastic, with areas covered respectively in colored plastic.

Now take a flashlight and shine a light through from the top. The composite layer is just a white sheet of paper. What you will see on the white sheet of paper is the result of the colors blended together as a color image, kind of like a slide, except there are 3 slides, one for each primary color. This is over-simplistic, but I hope you understand the concept.

Channels (RGB) Additive 16.7 million colors

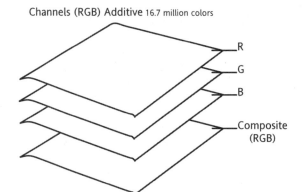

R
G
B
Composite
(RGB)

Open the Channels palette and see how Photoshop displays color channels. Each channel would be like the separate sheets of plastic in the above illustration. The channels are where Photoshop stores the color information for each primary color.

Each channel has 256 levels of gray. Solid white would represent full intensity of the color that is represented by the channel. Solid black would mean that none of that color would be displayed at all.

Starting with an RGB image, I have made a color bar of pure red, green and blue so you can see how each color channel affects each color.

This first image is the composite image. You can download the PSD (channels rgb.psd) in color from the friends of ED web site.

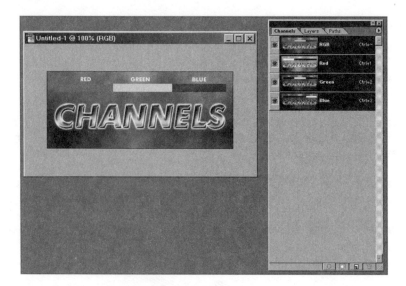

First of all look at the Red channel. You can display just a single channel by clicking on it in the Channels palette. If you do not see RGB channels, select it from the main menu Image > Mode > RGB Color.

You can also display more than one channel at a time by clicking on the little eye to the left of each channel thumbnail. Try some combinations to start to get a feel for how they interact with one another.

Notice the color bar in each of the channels: where it is red, the Red channel displays pure white. This means that there is a solid red color displayed.

Here is the Green channel, notice the green on the color strip.

And the Blue channel.

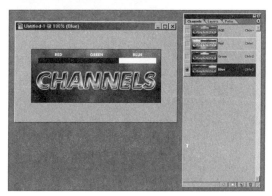

I hope you are starting to get a grasp on how Photoshop handles color and how RGB additive colors work. To summarize, RGB has three channels consisting of 256 levels of red, 256 levels of green and 256 levels of blue. Combined these colors give a possible combination of 16.7 million colors. That's 256 x 256 x 256.

CMYK color channels

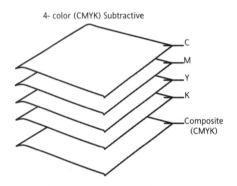

4- color (CMYK) Subtractive

With CMYK, there are four plates that make up the color.

Here is our image again. This time I have replaced the color bar with cyan, magenta, yellow and black (`channels cmyk.psd`). To change to CMYK mode in Photoshop, click on Image > Mode > CMYK Color.

The thing to notice with CMYK is because it is subtractive color, the color channels will be displayed in the opposite way to RGB. Each channel still has 256 levels of gray, but now black indicates color and white an absence of color. Just notice how the color bar interacts with each of the different channels here:

Here is the Cyan channel:

The Magenta channel:

The Yellow channel:

And finally the Black channel:

Grayscale

Another option you will see on the Image > Mode menu is Grayscale. This is a mode that has only one channel. There are no colors displayed, only 256 levels of gray. Not surprisingly this channel is called gray.

Pantone

Pantone is a color-matching technology that enables us to take a color swatch and match it exactly to an ink color. This is important for getting precise color. You can use the Pantone system for printing one-color jobs. Produce a Grayscale image and specify a **PMS** (Pantone Matching System) **color** for the printer, for example, PMS 72 is reflex blue, a very common call.

You can also use the PMS colors to give you accurate colors in your CMYK images. You can load the Pantone colors into your color swatch by clicking on the little arrow in the top right of the Swatches palette and loading Pantone colors. Make sure you load the Process Pantone, for four-color process printing. Coated and Uncoated refers to the paper. If it is coated, it is referring to a treatment to the paper that prevents the ink soaking into the paper too much. This is typically a glossy paper, whereas an example of uncoated paper would be newsprint.

1. You can switch to Small List view to see the names of the colors displayed.

If the Pantone options are not available, load them by clicking on the Load Swatches option in the same fly-out menu.

You should be taken right to your Photoshop directory. If not, navigate to your Photoshop installation directory, find Presets > Color Swatches > Adobe Photoshop Only and double-click on Pantone Colors (Coated).aco to load it.

2. If you use Pantone colors, you should have a printed swatch. Look down it and locate a suitable color.

3. Now find the corresponding color in your Swatches palette in Photoshop. Don't worry if the colors don't look exactly the same on screen, the color on the printed swatch is what will, all things being equal, print on the press (though not all Pantone colors are reproduced perfectly by CMYK printing).

4. To load the color into your document, click on the color in the Swatches palette and it will appear as the new foreground color. Notice the Color palette will also display your color with its CMYK values broken down.

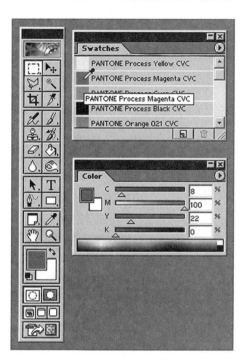

5. Be sure your document is now in CMYK mode and then select an area and fill with the foreground color. You can be pretty sure that the color will print very close to the swatch color if not exactly right (depending on how good the pressman is).

Spot color

If you really want accurate color, for example you are doing a job for Coca-Cola and there is no room for "close enough" in the red for their logo, you would use a **spot color**. With spot colors you are able to specify a certain color ink to be printed in specific places. When you specify a spot color on a CMYK document it will be run on a 5-color press or higher, depending on the number of spot colors specified. You can use metallic inks and varnish for spot colors too. These are typically used on very high-end print jobs because they are very expensive to print. Of course, you could specify a spot color to a grayscale image too, and do a cheaper two or three-color job.

To add a spot color

1. First make a selection around the area you want to apply the spot color.

2. From the Channels palette options, select New Spot Channel.

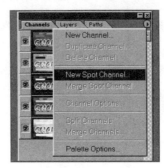

3. Immediately you will see a dialog box asking you to specify a color to be used as the new spot color.

4. Load the Pantone palette by clicking in the Color box and selecting Custom from the Color Picker. Select the color you want to use and click on OK.

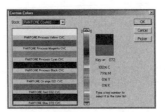

5. You will now see a new channel displayed. The name of the channel will be the same as the Pantone color used. The Pantone color will be applied to the area you selected.

6. Looking at your image window, you will see your color, but it will be mixed with the other channels if there is already color applied to that portion of the image. The problem you have here is that your color is **overprinting** the other colors. In some cases this may be the effect you are after. In most cases though, you would rather have your color **knockout** the other colors. Knockout means that you remove all the other colors from that region.

7. The way to do that is to CTRL-CLICK on your spot channel to load the selection.

8. Then go to the Layers palette and delete all the other color information in that region.

9. You will be able to see the layers that overprint the area. Just click on those layers and press DELETE with the region still selected. You will now have a clean spot color.

> When the job is being printed, sometimes the paper will shift on the printer leaving gaps around the color, this is called **misregistration**. You can compensate for this by a technique called **trapping**. Trapping is when you intentionally go over the lines slightly to allow for the slipping on the press. Good page layout software automatically adds trapping, but Photoshop doesn't have that ability yet. You can use this method to get around it fairly easy. When you select your channel go Select > Modify > Contract and input 1 pixel. When you delete the overprinting colors, you will now have a small margin for error.

10. When you save the document, be careful to have Spot Colors checked in the Save Options section. Make sure you communicate with your printer that you want to use a spot color and specify the PMS color in your spec. sheet.

Duotones

As we have just learned, a grayscale image has only 256 shades available. So how do they get those rich black and white images like you see in photography books, you may ask? Imagine Ansel Adams (www.adamsgallery.com) in 256 shades of gray! That would be an insult to his genius. Duotones are a way to increase the tone depth of an image. By combining more than one channel we can increase the richness of the image. We can assign a PMS color to the added channel if we wish. Duotones also enable us to do some interesting color effects. We can adjust the tone curve of the image too. This allows us to apply certain colors to certain tones. Duotones are really good for the aged look or the trendy retro feel.

Converting an image to duotone

1. We start with a grayscale image. If we wanted, we could start with a color image and convert it to grayscale. I've used `EiffelTower.tif` from the Photoshop Samples folder.

2. To convert to duotone mode, go to Image > Mode > Duotone.

3. In the Type box it will say Monotone. Change it to Duotone. Click on the color thumbnail of Ink 2 to open the Color Picker. Click the Custom button and find a suitable Pantone color. I chose 122, which is a yellow color. Click OK to apply it.

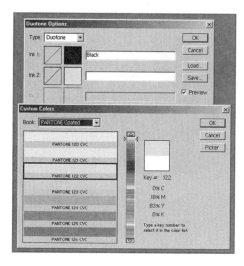

4. Now let's modify the curve. To do so, click on the diagonal line (representing the curve) for the tone you want to modify. This works in exactly the same way as the main curve box in the adjustments. Experiment until you get the desired result. Then press OK to apply the color and enrich our grayscale image.

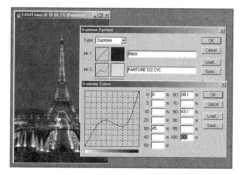

5. We can go beyond a duotone and produce a tritone or a quadtone. They are exactly as they sound. Tritone is three channels while quadtone is four. Here I added another channel to produce a tritone. You can really see the difference this made to our humble grayscale image. (The source file is EiffelTower tritone.psd).

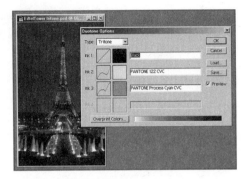

6. You would then save this image as an EPS for printing purposes.

Hue/Saturation

We just discovered that we are not forever stuck with black and white images. There is another way to colorize images apart from duotone. This is the powerful filter called Hue/Saturation. This filter gets right into the nitty-gritty of the color of the image. It has 3 main controls:

- **Hue**: Changes the actual color. The slider will take you through the entire color spectrum.

- **Saturation**: This controls the amount of color applied to the image. At -100 your image is grayscale, and as you slide it up there is more color applied. Generally speaking, zero is about normal saturation, though don't be afraid to push it up well past there. This is also a great way to remove color from an image. This is called **desaturation**. You can completely desaturate an image by pressing CRTL/CMD+SHIFT+U.

- **Lightness**: This controls the overall brightness of the image. I generally only use this when colorizing pure black and white. When it comes to adjusting the brightness of an image, I prefer the levels control. The difference is like having a tone control on your radio compared to a 3-band. In other words, the levels give a higher degree of control over brightness.

There are two more controls I would like to mention.

- Colorize box. When this is checked, the image will be converted to a monotone image. Monotone is the same as Grayscale except that instead of black being the base color, we can adjust it with the hue and saturation controls.

■ On the fill controls, you can apply the effect to the entire image or just a particular channel or color range.

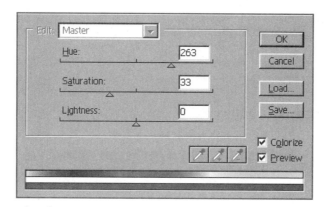

Using Hue/Saturation to color a grayscale image

1. Open a grayscale image. Once again, I have used the picture of the huge oil rig in Paris. The first thing we need to do is change the mode from grayscale to RGB (Image > Mode > RGB Color). Sorry, this doesn't magically make all the colors appear. What this does is provide the two extra channels needed for a color image.

2. Open the Hue/Saturation controls using Image > Adjust > Hue/Saturation or CTRL-U. Check the Colorize box and see how our image takes on a color tint. Slide the Hue slider and watch the color change. Increase the Saturation and notice how the color gets stronger.

3. I finally settled on this setting, which produced a nice purple color.

4.   Press OK to apply the color correction.

Alternatively, you might want to save the settings for later, or perhaps you have a series of pictures you would like to apply the same colors to. Maybe you are working on a low-resolution 'comp' image and you want to supply the settings to an outside source who will be scanning with a drum scanner. A comp or composition is a final design, with low-resolution images placed in the layout, sometimes these images are marked FPO (For Position Only) and the printer is expected to substitute the high-resolution images at a later time. It's very simple, just click on save, then navigate to a place you would like to save your settings to on your hard drive. Give it a name (I called it tower), and press OK to save the settings.

To load the settings is a very similar procedure: Open your image. Open the Hue/Saturation box and click on Load. Now navigate to the place you saved the settings, or to a floppy disk if you have received it from someone else. You will find your settings with an .ahu file extension. Select it and click Load. The settings will be automatically applied to your image. This powerful save and load feature is available in many of Photoshop's dialog boxes.

Hue/Saturation also works on full color images. You can use it to change the entire image's color or just select a particular color and shift that only. I will keep saying it, experiment!

Cropping

The Crop tool has grown up in Photoshop 6. We will look at some of the new functions in this section, as well as basic cropping. You will see the crop tool third down on the left of the toolbox.

First of all, I will show you its most basic use.

1.   Open an image that you want to crop.

2. Draw the same way you would with the Rectangular Marquee tool. If you click on the Shield cropped area in the tool bar, you will notice that the area outside the cropping zone is grayed out. You can adjust the size of the box just like with the scale command by dragging on any of the eight 'handles'. On the tool options bar you will notice there is an option to delete or hide the cropped area. If you click on Hide, instead of deleting the cropped area, a layer mask will be applied. More on layer masks in Chapter 10. This option is only available on a layer.

3. When you are satisfied with your crop shape and size, press either the check mark icon on the top right of the tool options bar, double-click inside the crop or just press ENTER on the keyboard. If you want to cancel the crop, press either the cross on the tool options bar or the Esc key.

Now the rest of the image is deleted outside the crop area. This is cropping in its simplest form. Let's look at a couple of creative uses of the Crop tool now.

Crop-rotate

1. Notice that this Eiffel tower is looking a bit more like its rival landmark in Italy, the Leaning Tower of Pisa. This can be easily fixed with the Crop tool.

2. Make a selection around the image with the Crop tool. Don't crop right up to the edges, rather leave some space around the image.

3. By clicking and dragging on the canvas outside the crop area, we can rotate the cropping area. Remember that the image will be cropped to the rectangle, so line it up carefully with the image's true horizontal plane.

4. Press OK and you now have a nice level image. You can do all kinds of things with this option, from fixing images to applying wide angled crops.

Perspective

I took this photo in Germany, while taking a European vacation. The problem with this huge building is that the perspective came out over-exaggerated. Notice how everything leans in towards the top. This is a very common condition but, yes, Photoshop allows us to fix this too! You can download the image `germany2.jpg` from the friends of ED website.

Correcting an image's perspective

1. Make a selection around our building with the Crop tool. In the tool options bar you will see an option called Perspective. Check the box and now you will notice that when you drag in a corner node, that corner will move independently to the others. Drag the 2 top ones in until they are parallel with the walls in the image.

2. Press ENTER and you now have a much more realistic looking image. A tip here: I never totally remove the perspective, or the image would look too unnatural. Just reduce it to an acceptable level.

Image resolution

Imagine 300 people all jammed inside one VW Beetle! Arms and feet dangling out everywhere, people yelling and screaming... I think you got the picture! I know it's impossible, but you won't forget this illustration. Now imagine the same 300 people in Madison Square Garden. They take up a lot more space now, but they are still the same 300 people right? Sure they are. The crowd size is still the same but the area is now larger.

It's exactly the same with resolution. Now instead of people, let's take pixels, or we will call them dots for the sake of clarity. At 300dpi (dots per inch) the 300 dots would occupy a space of one inch (the VW). At 72dpi, the same 300 dots are now spread out at a comfortable 4.167 inches (Madison Square Garden). The amount of dots is still the same (300) but the area is now larger (4.167 inches)

Take this image for instance, it is 600 pixels across:

It is being displayed at 100%, 600 X 450 pixels at 72 dots per inch. Its print size is 81/4 inches at 72dpi.

The print size of the image is only two inches wide at 300dpi. There is still the same number of pixels in the image but they are denser so the image takes up less area. The file size of the two images is identical: 707K

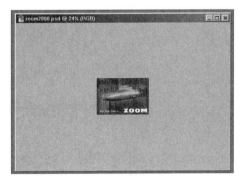

Now, to make the **area** of the image the same as the first at 300dpi would require 2,500 pixels across and a whopping 12 MB file size, (the equivalent of filling Madison Square Garden with people at the same density as they were in the VW).

So as you can see the actual screen size of an image (at 100% zoom) depends on two things:

- Number of pixels in an image

- Resolution (dpi)

Basically there are three resolutions that you should be aware of at this point:

- 72 dpi for online work, web and multimedia

- 150dpi for printing to an inkjet printer

- 300dpi for printing to a commercial printing press

> *dpi is the term used for ink and printing. With scanning, digital cameras and on screen there are no real dots, they are called pixels, so the correct term is ppi (Pixels Per Inch). We are calling them dpi here just to avoid confusion. 300 dpi and 300 ppi are implying the same thing.*

Image resampling

Resampling really means changing the amount of pixels in an image. **Resizing** is when we change the density but keep the same amount of pixels. In the previous three illustrations, the first image was the original, the second was resized and the third was resampled.

As a rule, you should never resample up like we did, adding pixels to an image. You should only resample down, reducing the pixels. Otherwise there is not enough image information to build the larger picture and pixelization occurs, otherwise known as 'the jaggies' i.e. the image looks like Lego.

To resize an image in PhotoShop go to Image > Image Size. Enter the resolution you desire and make sure the Resample Image option is unchecked and Constrain Proportions is checked.

To resample an image, do the same, but also enter your desired final size (use either pixels or inches), check the Resample Image box and the actual pixels will be changed, either some added or some subtracted.

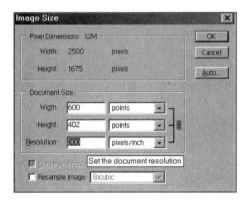

File formats

Now that we have all our images scanned and resized/resampled, we are ready to save them to our hard drive. The question now pops up, what file format do I use?
There are really 2 options for print use, EPS and TIFF.

Print

- EPS (Encapsulated Post Script). Postscript is a printing language invented by Adobe to bring compatibility to printing. I'm sure you are aware of the fonts and printers that use Postscript. This is definitely the option to use for any vectorized images, particularly Adobe Illustrator files. BMP formats do not store color information like an EPS can. I would use an EPS for some Photoshop files. EPS is the only format that supports clipping paths (a complete walkthrough of clipping paths is included in Chapter 13). It can do this because an EPS has the ability to store a channel mask (more about them also in Chapter 13).

- TIFF (Tagged Image File Format). This is the format I use to save the majority of my files. A TIFF is a 'lossless' format, meaning that you don't lose any image quality when you save and resave the file multiple times, unlike JPEG. TIFFs also have the ability to embed a color profile into them. This stores the color setting information to bring uniform color across different devices. A new feature with Photoshop 6 now allows us to attach our layers to a TIFF file. Photoshop also gives you the ability to save alpha channels in a TIFF.

We will be looking at web output formats in the next chapter.

Case Study

Phew, after all that theory is your head spinning? Have a nice hot cuppa if you need to! I promise this bit won't be so tech heavy. Just think about all the things you know now. You really are shedding the status of newbie very quickly!

It's time to prepare our postcard for printing. We are going to take our Exotic Imports picture and create a document that will be ready for print as a high-resolution full color project.

Preparing for print

1. Open our project file: exotic imports.psd. The first thing we need to do is size it correctly. We will be printing onto a 6 by 4 inch postcard on a 4-color process printing press (Standard commercial full color press).

2. Image > Image size (shortcut is ALT+I+I). Keep the Constrain Proportions and Resample Image boxes checked. Change the Resolution to 300 and enter 6 inches into the Width. Notice that the height changed to 4 inches automatically. That is what Constrain Proportions does, it makes sure that everything doesn't get stretched and weird.

The ALT+ *keyboard option only works on the PC, and can be used to get to ALL menu items. When you hold down the* ALT *key you will find a letter underlined for each of the main menus and for each of the options within that menu. Try it! You might find some useful shortcuts...*

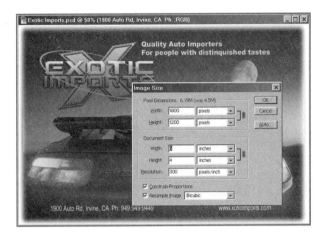

Yikes! The layer effects changed their appearance. How did that happen? Simple, the image is a different size, but the effects we set earlier are for the larger image. I actually like the "X" better now, but the words need some work. If you wanted to avoid this, you could flatten the image before resizing it, but then you wouldn't be able to alter the effects on each layer.

3. "They thought of everything", there is a simple solution (and a handy toy)! On the Text layer, right click on the words, Effects and you will see an option, Scale Effects.

I like the results at 31%.

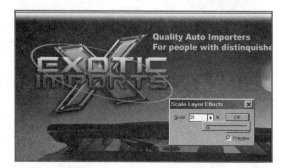

4. We have to have a flattened image for printing to a commercial printing press, so let's lock everything in by flattening the image. But first, save your PSD, so that you can return to it later. Then go to Layer > Flatten Image, or you can use the drop-down menu in the Layers palette.

Save it under a new name: Exotic Imports rgb.tif. The reason I am doing this is so that I have a backup copy of the RGB file for use on the Web. Once we convert to CMYK, some colors will be lost.

5. Now let's convert it to CMYK: Image > Mode > CMYK Color. This prepares the file for print it as a 4-color process print job.

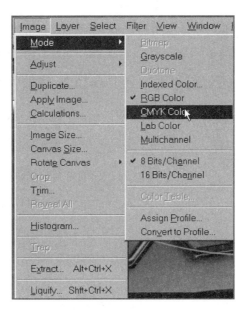

6. Now save the CMYK file as Exotic Imports.tif. You could either place this file into a page layout program or just give it to a printer for your postcards to be produced. It's ready and it will print on a 4-color press.

Congratulations, you have completed your first commercial color print job! If you sent this file to a printer they would be able to produce beautiful full color postcards right from this file.

Summary

In this chapter, we have learned how to capture images for Photoshop using a scanner or digital camera. We've learned how to optimize your Photoshop preferences, then we got down to the nitty-gritty of color theory. We wrapped things up with a look at some creative cropping, image resolution and printing file formats. In the next chapter we'll be looking at output for the Web.

7 Graphic Elements for the Web

What we'll cover in this chapter:

- *What makes a great web site?*

- *Image file types:*
  - *JPEG*
  - *GIF*
  - *PNG*

- *Saving for the Web*
  - *Previewing in a browser*
  - *Preview menu*
  - *Working with transparencies*

- *Overview of vector graphics*
  - *Importing vector files from illustration software*
  - *Shapes tool*
  - *Shapes in design*

- *Working with color*
  - *Web-safe color*
  - *Creating a swatch*
  - *Working with the swatches palette*

- *Simple web logos*
  - *Placing a logo in the background*
  - *Placing a logo in the title bar*

▶

Incredible as it now seems, the Web actually started out as a purely text-based medium, little more than a collection of network-accessible text documents that could cross-reference one another using the simple but powerful mechanism of hyperlinks: addresses hidden in the body of a page. Of course, while it is still quite possible to view web-based content in this way (text-only browsers such as Lynx are still relatively popular in certain circles), most contemporary users now experience the Web almost exclusively via richly graphics-enabled interfaces such as Netscape Navigator and Internet Explorer.

This has given designers a totally new, rich, and constantly evolving medium in which to work, and there are various issues we need to consider when preparing images for a web site. In this chapter will we explore these issues.

Although it may be tempting to think otherwise, it's not enough to judge a web site's visual design solely in terms of aesthetics. First and foremost it has to work – not just when seen in full 32 bit glory on a 1600x1200 desktop via a 21-inch flat screen monitor, but in whatever circumstances a visitor will actually see it. Depending on the target audience, and the purpose of the site, these circumstances will include a number of different factors, including connection speed, screen size, color depth, plug-in availability, browser type, and the patience of the user.

For now, we're going to concentrate on issues that affect the individual visual elements that we might contribute to a typical web page. Later on in the book (in Chapter 11) we'll start bolting these elements together, and consider how we can ensure that they work together effectively. We'll also look at how Photoshop 6 can help us build complete web pages.

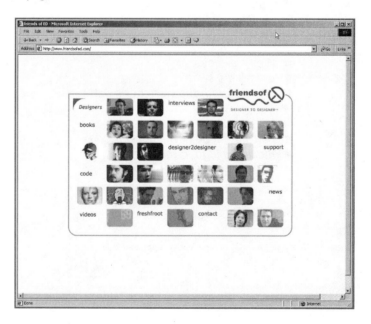

What makes a great web site?

When you're cruising the Web, why does one site get added to your Favorites list almost instantly, while another barely registers on your mental radar? The most obvious answer is that a good site gives you what you're looking for, whereas a bad one doesn't. It's as simple as that.

1. **Content** and **Functionality**. The most important ingredients of any web site. Content may be in the form of text, images, links to other sites or file downloads, audio, video, or any number of other variations and combinations of the above. Functionality can also come in many shapes and sizes – in fact, there's not a lot you can't do on a web page (assuming you've a fast enough connection or the patience of a saint!)

   While it may seem that neither of these really have much to do with the design of a site, they actually have *everything* to do with it. They're the primary reason for the site's existence, and everything else that goes into the site should be designed to make them as accessible and user-friendly as possible.

   What's more, if the content of the site includes images, it's important to ensure that these are suitably prepped for display on the Web. As we're going to see, an image that looks great on your desktop can easily suffer in the clutches of a web browser, and quickly jam up a network connection if it's been saved inappropriately.

2. **Fast download**. It doesn't matter how good a site is if you hit Stop before it's even loaded up. Even if the front page loads okay, you won't hang around long if you're left waiting while incredibly cool but bandwidth-guzzling images get loaded into the browser with each new page. Think about how long it would take your site to load on a 56K connection.

3. **Information.** You want information about the site and what it has to offer, so that you can quickly decide whether or not it's worth sticking around.

4. **Easy navigation.** Is it clear how you're supposed to navigate your way around the site? Are the links designed to look like links? Is it obvious what's at the other end, should you choose to click on them?

5. **Aesthetics**. What's the overall visual impression of my site? Does the color scheme work – is text legible, and does it reflect the intended tone of the site? Are the images pixellated and grainy, or are they smooth and seamlessly joined together in both color and design? Does the color scheme of bright pink and cyan inflict a nasty migraine on the visitor?

6. **The 'Wow!' factor**. What is it about the design of some web sites that simply blows you away? While there are plenty of folks out there who are doing a perfectly good job of designing sites that are based on tried and tested patterns, there's nothing quite so satisfying as discovering a new way to approach something that you'd never thought of before. How on earth did they do it? Could I make that work on my site?

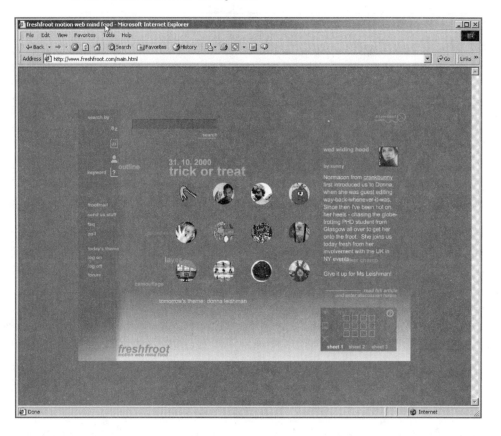

So, how can we use Photoshop to feed into this vision of a pleasing, effective, and memorable web site? Well, a quick glance at points one and two directs us towards one very straightforward answer: we can manipulate each of the site's graphic elements so that the resulting files are as small as possible, while at the same time, they retain all the clarity and range of color required.

Let's consider some of the properties we might want to tweak:

- Resolution
- Color depth
- File format and compression settings

So, if I'm looking for fast download speeds, I need to avoid using high-color images and keep detail to a minimum, right? Well, not necessarily. In fact, the most important player in the 'keep your file sizes down' game is the last one on the list – what *type* of file we choose to save the image as – and for that reason, we'll discuss it first.

Image file types for the Internet

Whenever you work with an image in Photoshop, a tremendous amount of data gets shuffled around inside your computer's memory in order to present a useful (and current) representation of that image on the screen. Besides everything else that Photoshop needs in order to work its various shades of magic, every single pixel in every single layer has a number attached to it, describing properties such as color and opacity with extraordinary accuracy.

Thankfully, we don't need to concern ourselves with how it does all that, and just get on with the job at hand. However, when you stop and think about the sheer quantity of information that goes into describing even the simplest of images, it can make you stop and catch your breath! How the heck does the Web cope with all those numbers?

There's a very simple answer: it doesn't have to. When we save our images to disk, a vast proportion of this information can be thrown away (unless we want to carry on editing at a later date, in which case we can save it as memory-guzzling PSD Photoshop document). Photoshop gives us a wide range of file formats to choose from, each with their own characteristics, each suited to particular applications. When it comes to saving images for the Web, there are really only three contenders: JPEG, GIF, and PNG.

JPEG

This format, named after its originators – the **Joint Photographic Experts Group** – was devised to compress tone-sensitive images (such as photographs) enough to be practical for use on the Web, while minimizing the perceivable loss in picture quality. It manages to do this by exploiting certain limitations of human vision: in particular, the fact that our eyes don't register small variations in color to the same extent as they register similar variations in brightness.

The elements of image data are sorted according to how much each one contributes to our overall impression of the picture. We can then choose how much of that information we want to throw away, without having to compromise color depth (fixed at 16 million colors = 24 bit) or image size. However, because of the photographic slant, sharp edges are amongst the first features to get thrown out, so line drawings and lettering suffer quite noticeably.

Since JPEG compression involves discarding information (albeit selectively) from an image, we refer to it as a **lossy** form of compression. Once discarded, it's impossible to retrieve this information, so JPEG files are ideally used for final output only.

A rule of thumb here would be not to save as a JPEG unless you intend to save the image as a smaller file than the original: once the pixel data is gone, it can't be recovered. Keep the original just in case!

While Photoshop saves JPEG files with the extension `.jpg`, most web browsers will recognize the alternative extensions `.jpe` and `.jpeg`.

CompuServe GIF

GIF (**Graphics Interchange Format**) is a **lossless** format designed by CompuServe, which supports up to 256 colors, making it ideal for simple, low-color images such as cartoons and labels. All the pixel information you put in the image is exactly what you'll get out. The name is a reference to its original application as a hardware-independent format for the online transmission and interchange of raster images.

The color of every pixel in a GIF must be taken from a palette of 256 colors. However, since the palette is redefined for each file, and its colors can be chosen from a 24 bit range (each palette entry can be any one of 16 million different colors) this isn't nearly as much of a limitation as it may initially seem.

The original GIF87a standard was updated as GIF89a, which allows you to specify one of the 256 colors in the palette as being transparent, and also supports the creation of animated GIFs. It's therefore very easy to use GIFs to display irregularly shaped elements, and even simple moving pictures.

GIF uses a lossless form of compression called LZW, which identifies continuous sequences of pixels that use the same palette entry, and describes them collectively (rather than duplicating information for each one). For images containing large blocks of one color, this sort of compression is particularly effective.

PNG

The **Portable Network Graphics** format was developed as a patent-free alternative to the GIF. As with GIF, PNG offers lossless compression and transparency.

Although PNG currently has only limited support from mainstream browsers, it is rapidly gaining in popularity with web designers, as it can support high-color images and lossless compression (and still without turning in impractically large files).

PNG files also come in two varieties:

- **PNG-8** uses 8 bit color, compressing solid areas of color and maintaining sharpness along the edges. This format is ideal for illustrations and line art. File sizes in PNG 8 can be smaller than GIF images, with no loss of resolution due to the lossless (and open) compression utilized by this format. The only real drawback is the lack of browser support.

- **PNG-24** supports 24 bit color, and is therefore useful for images that feature subtle tonal variations, such as photographs. However, since the compression is lossless, this will produce file sizes that are significantly larger than the equivalent JPEG compression.

  This format also supports transparencies, but unlike GIF and PNG-8, it can preserve up to 256 levels of transparency. It therefore allows you to create much smoother edges to your irregular images.

Bear in mind that although PNG is a very useful rich format, not all browsers support multi-level transparencies; indeed, some have yet to incorporate PNG viewing into their software at all.

So which file type is best for my needs?

The format you should use depends on the content you're saving. Here's a quick summary:

- JPEG and PNG-24 are best for photos due to the wide range of color variations they support. JPEG loses information from the original; PNG-24 maintains information but is not supported by all browsers. JPEG does not support transparencies; PNG 24 supports 256 levels of transparencies.

- GIF and PNG-8 are best for images with solid swatches of color or less color variations. Both formats support transparencies. PNG-8 produces images with higher quality than GIF, often at smaller file sizes, but not all browsers support PNG 8.

It is up to the designer to weigh up which file type would best suit a particular image, and a firm knowledge of Photoshop's Save For Web command is vital.

> *PNG is not supported by all browsers, and has not been yet been globally accepted. If you have many visitors from overseas or using earlier browser versions, they may not be able to view the PNG format and, as a result, surf to a different site. Until acceptance of PNG gets a bit closer to universal, GIF and JPEG are your best bets.*

Saving for the Web

Now that we've an idea of the main image file types we have at our disposal for use on the Web, our next step is to learn how we can optimize those images. Remember, we're aiming to get the best possible image quality in the smallest file size; this is where Photoshop's Save For Web feature proves very useful.

We're going to have a look at a simple image in the Save For Web dialog. You can download this file from the friends of ED web site.

1. Open the Save for Web dialog by going File > Save For Web, or use the keyboard shortcut ALT/OPTION+SHIFT+COMMAND/CTRL+S.

2. Notice the four tabs at the top:

Original will display our un-optimized image in the viewer. Optimized displays the optimized image, and we can look at multiple optimized examples in varying formats by selecting either the 2-Up or 4-Up selection tabs. By changing the settings in the control area to the right for each frame, we can instantly view both quality and file size for each selected format, comparing them to the original.

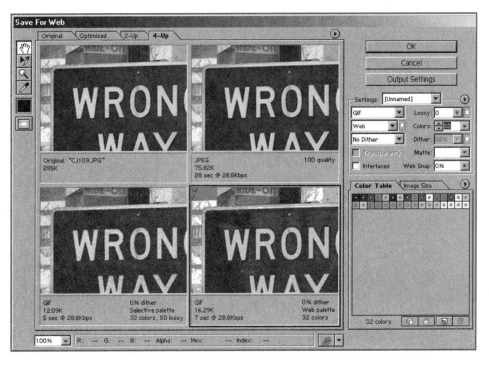

3. In the bottom left hand corner of the dialog window we find the image size value. Keep an eye on this portion as we continue, as we want that number to be as low as possible and still maintain a quality image in the viewer.

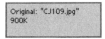

4. Select the Optimized tab. The optimized image will now appear in the window. Note how the image size value will change.

5. Open the Settings drop-down menu. Select the different file types one at a time, viewing both the image quality and file size.

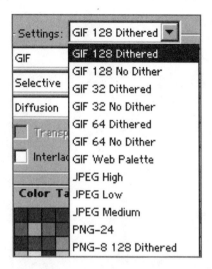

6. Choose GIF 32 Dithered to see how this affects your image.

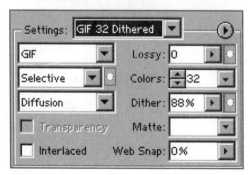

The examples on the previous page represent the image and settings when using GIF 32 Dithered. The resulting file size is 27.29. Not great, not too bad, but the image has become very grainy. Don't worry too much about the term, Dithered, we will learn about this later.

7. Now let's take a look at a JPEG example, choose JPEG Medium, in the Settings menu.

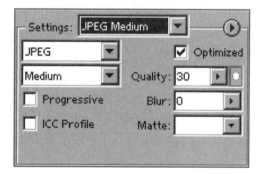

When switching to JPEG Medium, the quality and clarity of the image is much higher than the GIF setting, and even produces a smaller file size (10.31K) with increased quality. JPEG quality ranges from 1 at the lowest level, to 100 at maximum quality. When trying to find the optimum level for saving for the Web, you should experiment a little; reduce the quality to the lowest point with the image still looking good. This will ensure the lowest possible file size.

Previewing in a browser

Another cool feature you can find in this palette is the Preview in Browser command. This icon is located along the bottom of the dialog box, and allows you to instantly check the image quality in a browser. By default, only Internet Explorer will appear as an available browser, however you can add other browsers by clicking on Other. When designing web sites, previewing in alternate browsers is an important part of the process.

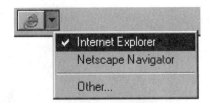

```
Format: JPEG
Dimensions: 360w x 270h
Size: 7.532K
Settings: Quality is 7, Non-Progressive, Optimized on


<HTML>
<HEAD>
<TITLE>CJ109</TITLE>
<META HTTP-EQUIV="Content-Type" CONTENT="text/html; charset=iso-8859-1">
</HEAD>
<BODY BGCOLOR=#FFFFFF>
<!-- ImageReady Slices (CJ109.JPG) -->
<IMG SRC="TargetPreview.jpg" WIDTH=360 HEIGHT=270>
<!-- End ImageReady Slices -->
</BODY>
</HTML>
```

All the pertinent file information for the selected preview is displayed, along with some basic HTML pertaining to the image. It is **always** good policy to check the image in a browser prior to posting, because as I'm sure you know by now, there can be a lot of discrepancy between the way an image appears on your screen, and the way it will appear in a browser. This feature makes such checks intuitive.

Preview menu

OK so you can see how the image will appear, but what about the amount of time it will take to download? If you want to know how a browser will react to an optimized image, the Preview menu gives you many options to test it out. Click the small arrow to the upper right of the viewer window. Out pops a menu that allows you to apply Browser Dither, Color Profile and connection speed to the image or selected example when in the 2-Up/4-Up modes.

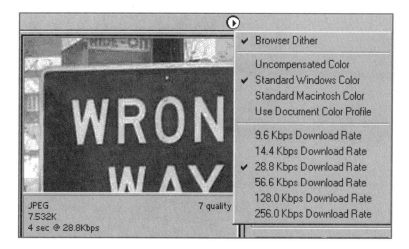

Below the image example the download speed will adjust accordingly, and the example itself will change to reflect the settings. No guess work here: Photoshop shows you what your visitors will see, and gives a reasonable estimate on the time it will take for your image to load.

Working with transparencies

You are most likely familiar with transparencies, but let's go over them a bit anyway. Transparencies let us see the background of a web page around the central image object. The image itself is still rectangular; there is no way around that as of yet. But certain pixels of that rectangular image are rendered invisible.

For creating transparencies, we turn to GIF, PNG 8, or PNG 24. GIF and PNG-8 support only one level of transparency: that means the pixels are either fully transparent or fully visible. PNG-24 supports 256 levels of transparency: this multilevel system allows you to vary the amount of transparency, similar to the opacity levels of a layer.

How to preserve background opacity in GIF and PNG-8

1. Create an image that has a transparency, we have used moneyTransparent.gif, which is available for download at the friends of ED web site.

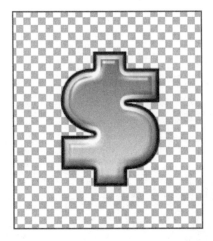

2. Open the Save for Web dialog. Select the Optimize tab, in the control panel on the right hand side, choose GIF or PNG-8 as your file format.

3. Check Transparency.

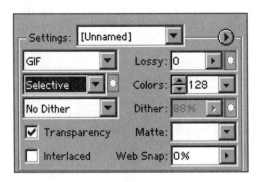

4.   Zoom right into the image and you should be able to see that some of the pixels are partially transparent, this won't translate well when you put the image onto our web site as you could end up with a halo effect around the image.

5.   You now need to decide what to do with these pixels. If the background to your web site is a solid block of color then you can blend the partially transparent pixels into this color, using the Matte feature, this will give your image a smooth edge. However, if your background is patterned you cannot do this, but you can convert the semi-transparent pixels into solid blocks of color.

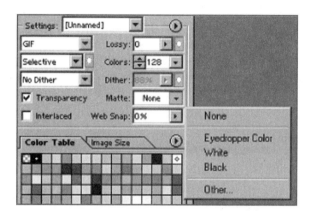

Image characteristics and development

Photoshop 6 and ImageReady 3 allow us to work with two image formats. These formats are **raster** (or bitmap) images and **vector**-based images. Photoshop 6 offers us a great deal more support and versatility for importing, creating and working with vector-based images than any of its predecessors. Why is this important to designing for the Web? Let's take a look at the difference between vector-based images and raster images and see if we can find an answer.

Raster images (Bitmap) are based on discrete pixels; tiny squares of varying colors that, when arranged a certain way, determine not only the image they represent but also the quality of that image when viewed. We call this **resolution**. The quality of the resolution is based on pixels per inch calculations, lower resolution images have more jagged edges, whereas high-resolution images have smoother edges and color blends.

Vector based images are not composed of pixels, but rather are mathematically shaped by paths and curves, or series of points to generate a shape. These mathematical points are known as vectors, hence the name. The shape is then filled with color. Due to the math involved, the shape may be re-colored, resized or repositioned and not lose any resolution.

The advantage of using vector images is that we can take a shape created in Photoshop or imported from an illustration program such as Adobe Illustrator or Macromedia Freehand (see 'Importing Vector Images' in Chapter 13) and, with a little careful manipulation have a GIF or PNG image ready for viewing on the Web. As vector images do not deal with large color variations, GIF or PNG formats suit them just fine.

Vector Shape options: Photoshop versus ImageReady

ImageReady is a very useful partner to Photoshop, and is ideal for creating rollovers, and animations. However when we consider drawing or shapes as a part of our web design process, we should remember that Photoshop has many advantages over ImageReady:

- Photoshop allows us to create Work Paths

- Photoshop allows us to use the pen, polygon and custom shape tools

- Photoshop allows us to draw multiple shapes in a layer

- Photoshop allows us to select how the shapes on a layer will interact with one another

- Photoshop allows us to edit shapes after they are drawn or placed in a layer, whereas Image Ready only allows for repositioning and transforming the shapes.

So when we decide to add shapes to the mix, clearly Photoshop gives us much more control and should be the primary tool for the job

Shape tool

The Shape tool allows us to create vector shapes in a manner similar to other illustration software. It also allows us to create perfect selections of abstract items, such as polygons or rectangles with rounded corners. This expands the range of drawing tools immensely; no longer are we restricted to ovals, circles and rectangles.

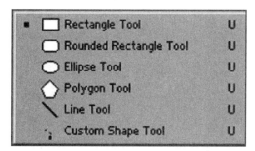

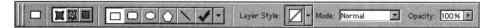

Photoshop 5 allowed us to work with Shapes, but Photoshop 6 gives us the additional Custom Shape tool. With it we can define virtually any selection as a shape to be incorporated into an image or saved and used later.

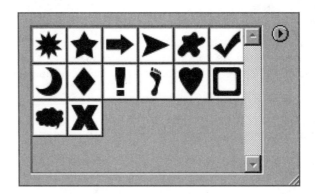

Shapes in design

We've measured some differences between Photoshop and ImageReady, and even taken a brief look at a few tools at our disposal. The meat, however, lies in demonstrating how shapes, and therefore vector images, might be incorporated into the design of web graphics.

Designing a button using the Shape tool

1. Open a new file, and make it large enough to place a few buttons on, say 300 x 500 pixels.

2. Create a new layer (SHIFT+ CTRL/CMD+N).

3. Select the Shape tool in the toolbox, and select the Rounded Rectangle tool from either the toolbox or the Shape tool options bar.

4. Use the rulers to help you size the shapes, by going to View > Show Rulers (COMMAND/CONTROL +R). When laying out buttons, it is often a good idea to work with guides in order to keep everything in line.

5. Set your corner radius for the shape in the tool options bar. The greater the value, the rounder the corner. Generally, for a nice pill button shape a radius of 5px works, but it will of course depend on the size of your button.

6. Set the Shape tool to Create a new work path. Draw your buttons by clicking and dragging the mouse in the new layer. Do a few of them for a practice run, until you have a path that you are happy with. Delete the shapes that you don't like using the Path Component tool.

7. Copy and paste your chosen button shape. In order to line the buttons up in a neat row, you can click and drag out the horizontal and vertical rulers to act as your guide when placing your buttons.

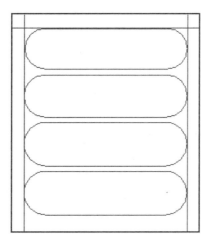

8. Go to your Paths palette and select the path you just created. Now click the Loads path as a selection icon, which is third from the left at the bottom of the palette:

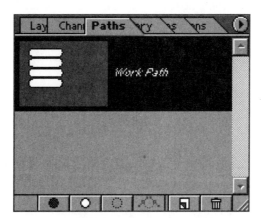

9. Click on the Fills path with foreground color icon, which is the button 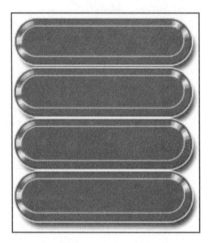 on the far left at the bottom of the Paths palette.

10. Apply a Layer Style of your choice to the buttons, by going to the Styles palette. Try experimenting with the Button Styles that shipped with Photoshop 6: you can find them in the Photoshop 6 > Presets > Styles folder.

11. Get rid of the guides, by going to View > Clear Guides.

Now you only need apply text for some quick buttons! See Chapter 11 for more on buttons and creating rollover images.

I did that first example the long way for a reason; so you would get used to working with selections. You need not convert the shape to a selection, however. Instead, you could choose the Create Filled Region icon from the tool options bar prior to drawing the shapes, and then merely apply the style to the shapes layer. This is similar to applying a style to a type layer rather than a type selection.

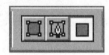

Shapes with no Style

Same Shapes, Style Applied

Custom shapes

Custom shapes can be created from imported vector images, clipart or Photoshop generated images. Say you have a logo you want to display in various areas of your web page. When you define the logo as a custom shape you can actually draw with the logo!

Creating a custom shape

1. Draw or import your logo. The image below (logo.psd) is available for download at the friends of ED web site.

2. Select the dark area with the Magic Wand.

3. Open the Paths palette. Open the Path menu and click on Make Work Path; set your tolerance to 0.5 pixels.

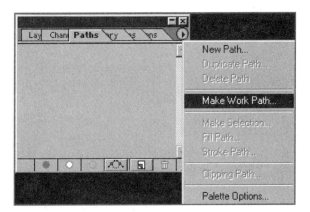

4. Go to Edit > Define Custom Shape. When you do this a dialog will pop up, allowing you to name your shape.

5. Now if you select the Custom Shape tool, and then click on the Custom Shape drop-down menu, in the tool options bar, you will find your shape sitting there.

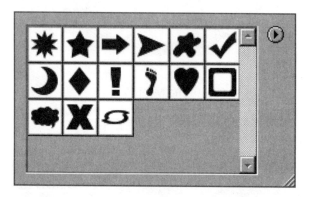

You can now insert paths in the form of your logo directly into your web images. Better still, you can size them accordingly just by dragging with the mouse.

Working with color

When designing for the Web, sometimes less is more, particularly when it comes to color schemes. By avoiding wide variations in color, you can decrease file size, save space on the server, and maintain an overall professional appearance.

We can help the process by learning a bit about the color table, and manipulating it to suit the job before us. The color table has a maximum of 256 colors. More may be added to the palette, or you may delete colors, lock colors into the palette to prevent deletion or convert a set of colors to **Web-safe colors**.

Web-safe colors

The concept behind web-safe color is to ensure that your web site will display the same colors no matter what kind of computer monitor or browser is viewing it. The cross platform (Windows and Mac OS) web-safe palette contains 216 colors that will display non-dithered, and consistent, when viewed in 8 bit color.

> **Dithering** *is a process that arranges pixels in such a way as to give the illusion of another color, or one not in the color palette. By canceling dithering, people with low-res monitor settings will not see grainy, pixilated images caused by color variations their monitor can't recognize, but will have smooth, solid colors instead. Though originated by Netscape, Microsoft now recognizes the web-safe palette, and Adobe has adapted it into their color schemes too.*

When selecting color in Photoshop we can specify the web-safe palette, choosing the Make Ramp Web Safe option from the Color palette menu. We can also check the Only Web Colors box in the Color Picker.

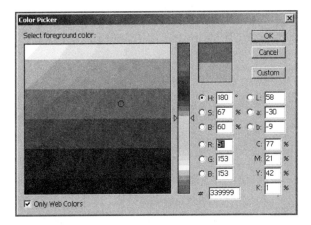

We can also return to the Save For Web feature, which will give us a color table generated by the colors found in the image. This is found in the lower right hand corner of the dialog box.

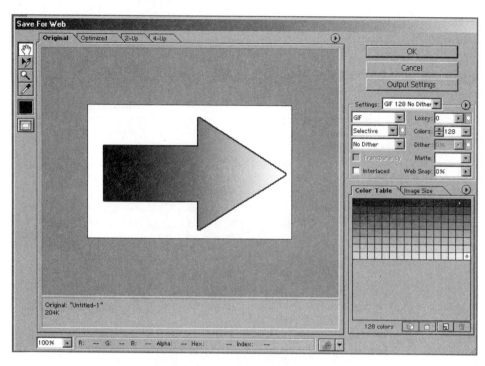

In this image we have an arrow filled with a gradient.

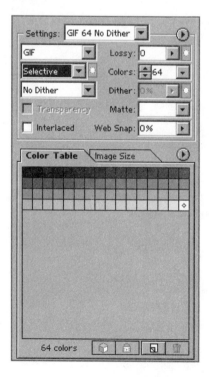

The settings in the Color Table display the relatively smooth image of a gradient arrow seen above. Were I to change the number of colors to 256 or so, the gradient would be even smoother and truer to the original image, but the file size more than doubles. In this example each color is arranged in the palette in order of luminance; that is, from darkest to lightest in color values, but we could change this by going to the Color Table menu.

Wait a minute. We are using a selective palette of 64 colors for this example, but our goal is to display this on the Web. Are any of these colors considered web-safe? Can we find out?

Sure we can. By opening the Color Table menu, we can highlight all web-safe colors in the palette.

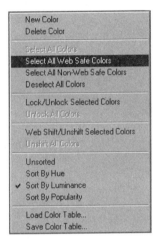

Now let's take a look at the Color Table:

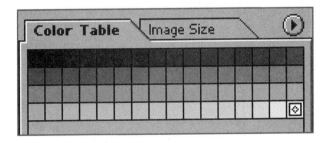

None of the hues in the Color Table are highlighted, so none must be considered web-safe. We change this by going up to where it says Selective in the settings area, opening the menu and choosing Web.

Now our palette is filled with web-safe colors, not all of which are used by the image. We can find out the primary colors in the image by again going into the Color Table menu and sorting the colors by popularity.

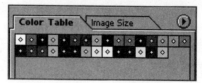

You will see a few extra colors, but the first few will be the most prevalent. Now we have web-safe colors in our image, so we must be ready to save, right? Wrong. Take a look at the viewer:

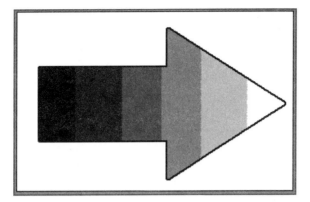

When we reduced the image color palette by choosing web-safe colors only, we were reduced to the six web-safe colors available from black to white. We've managed to reduce our original image from 204K down to 2K, but sacrificed the smooth transition of the gradient.

I walked through that, as I mentioned before, to prove a point. When working with gradients in grayscale, *never* use web-safe colors! Selective colors work much better. As there is a much wider variation in color gradients and the web-safe color palette, you may be able to find a happy medium. But for grayscale gradients, web-safe is not your friend. Your color palette is severely restricted, creating nasty looking gradients like those in the example. Web-safe only displays those colors that it recognizes, so if you have a gradient with 100 colors, perhaps six might be displayed. The other colors are replaced by something the palette will recognize.

Working with web-safe with our arrow as a solid gray reduced the file size from 204K to 1.76k in PNG 8. Photoshop chose the closest web-safe gray to fill the arrow, but overall it achieved the desired result; solid, un-dithered colors that will work online in a wide range of browser resolutions and reduce my file size.

Color coding

For a long time, some may say way too long, web pages consisted of a hodge-podge of garish color contrasts. Hey, we all had to learn web design somewhere!

One way to clean up those messy, over-indulgent designs is to limit yourself to work with a restrictive color swatch. A good portion of Photoshop users rarely delve into swatches, but a well laid out color plan can be extremely helpful in web site development.

So how do we create a color swatch? Or more specifically, how do we create a 'restrictive' color swatch to aid us in our web page design?

Creating a swatch

1. Open the Swatches palette.

2. Go to the Swatches menu, Replace Swatches. **Load the swatch named** Web Safe Colors.aco.

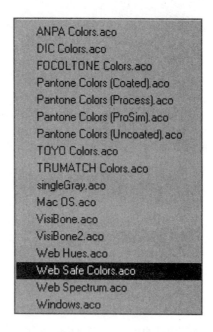

3. Do you already have a color scheme in mind? Perhaps dark brown to light tan? Delete every swatch that doesn't meet your color scheme. Try to keep it to as few colors as possible.

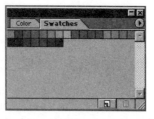

4. If you would like more colors added to your swatch, change the foreground color. Move the cursor over the Swatches palette. When your icon changes to the Paint Bucket, click the mouse, name your swatch, and the new color will appear in the Swatches palette.

5. Save your swatches.

Now when you restrict yourself to these colors, you will notice that your design will appear crisper and, dare I say it, more professional. If you think the site looks slick, chances are most of your visitors will as well.

Simple web logos

Remember that logo we turned into a Custom Shape a few pages ago? Let's revisit that guy and see if we can't dress him up a bit for our web site. There are a number of ways we can use it, and most marketing gurus will tell you that the more a customer sees your logo the more likely they will be to make a purchase. If you sell quality goods, the logo will come to stand for quality in the customer's eye.

Placing a logo in the background

1. Open a new image. We want something that will tile well and allow us to display a faint copy of the logo, so let's use 256x256 pixels, 72 dpi.

2. Fill the image with your background color.

3. Create a new layer, (SHIFT + CTRL/CMD + N).

4. Open your logo image. Put the logo on its own layer and resize it to fit within the background image, leaving some space along the sides. Edit > Transform > Scale should work nicely for this exercise.

5. Copy the small logo and paste into the background image. Center the logo.

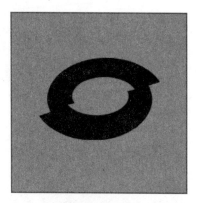

6. In the Layers palette, set the Logo layer's Opacity to 5%.

7. If you would like a bit more contrast, let's add a Pillow Emboss. Do this by going to Layer > Layer Styles > Bevel and Emboss, and then select Pillow Emboss in the drop-down Styles menu.

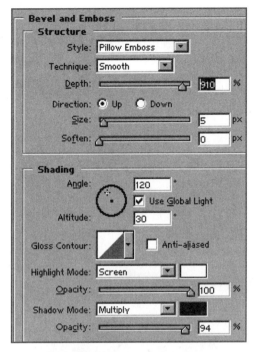

Sweet, subtle, and you should be able to read text right over the top of that logo!

Placing a logo in the title bar

Some web pages develop elaborate title bars for their pages, but here's a quick example of using a dressed up logo for a header or even navigation.

1. Open a new image. Make sure it is of sufficient size to create your header in, 560 x 200 pixels should be good.

2. Using the Paint Bucket tool, fill with your background color.

3. Repeat the process of copying the logo from the previous tutorial. Paste the logo into the header image.

4. Again, go to Layer > Layer Style > Bevel and Emboss, this time choose Inner Bevel to add to the logo.

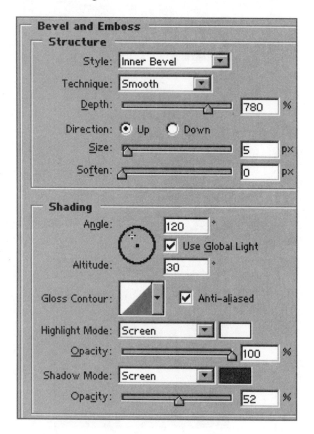

For my finished example I've also added a drop shadow and a radial gradient overlay, both using the Layer Styles palette. I then dressed up the header using the Shape tool techniques we learned earlier, a pattern overlay, layer mask and several fainter copies of the logo. For all of this, wherever a color was required, I used the colors generated for the restrictive swatch palette.

I'm not going to take you through all these steps, I think you should let your own imagination loose, and create your own knock 'em dead header.

We can also follow a similar process to create logo buttons for the page, though you may decide too many logos are overkill. At the end of the day, it's your call, but with Photoshop on board you'll be well equipped to achieve the desired result.

Case Study

Let's create a simple splash page for our web site. This is the page that people will see first; it is designed to tease the people into visiting the site. A lot of designers have stopped using splash pages to cut down on loading time, but they are still commonly used on the Web and you never know when a client is going to request one. The fun thing about splash pages is that they are a great way for you to express your artistic skills because they are purely for show (except when they are used as preloading pages, like in a Flash site), so the better looking the better.

We will be using the same image that we used for the postcard. You will practice resizing the image and then creating links and slices in Photoshop. We will then output the image as a functional web page using the save for web feature. In a later chapter we will be doing a similar task in ImageReady.

Preparing for the Web

1. Open the Exotic Imports rgb.tif that we saved earlier.

2. We now have to change the size and lower the resolution for use on the Internet. Go to Image > Image size. Check the Resample Image box and type 72 for the Resolution. Check Constrain Proportions and select 800 pixels for the Width. Press OK.

3. Save it as `index.jpg` under the `FP Case study > working folder` we created at the beginning of the case study. For Quality select Maximum because we don't want to lose any quality at this stage.

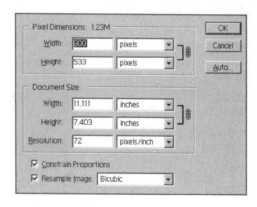

Great! The image is now the correct resolution for the Web. You may have to zoom in on the image a bit, as it will now appear smaller on the screen.

We are going to attach a slice here, so that we can make a link to the image. When you click on the picture on the web site, it will lead us to the home page. I am not going to get into the Slice tool much or explain it here, as it will be covered in detail in Chapter 11.

4.   Select the Slice tool.

Right-click (Mac CTRL+click) on the image and a window will pop up, choose Edit Slice Options.

The Slice Options box will open. All we want to do is put a URL (web address or link) to the image. This will make a link when the user clicks on it. For the URL enter `home.html` and for the Alt Tag type splash.

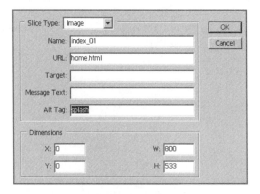

Press OK and you will now see a blue box in the top left corner with the number 01. This is telling you that there is a slice on the image.

5. Go to File > Save for Web…. Looking at the 4-Up display, we get to choose a good compromise between quality and file size. I chose the 38 for the quality of the JPEG.

> *You can alter these settings as you wish; what you are looking for is the smallest possible file size (so that it downloads quickly) with acceptable picture quality. The size that your image will appear on screen is also important – if it were only going to be small, then you could lower the image quality.*

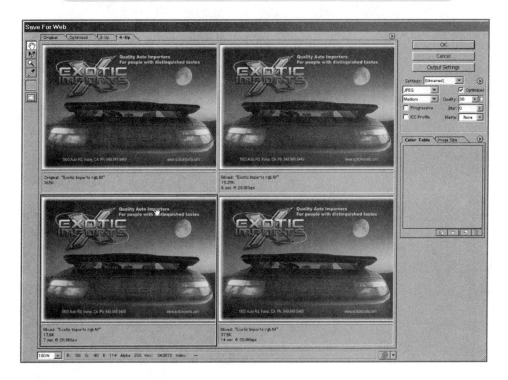

6. Let's save the file and create the web page. Click OK and the Save Optimized As box will come up. Save to the FP Case study > Website. This will keep the pictures and HTML documents together. Change the Save as type to HTML and Images. Name the file `index.html` and press Save.

We chose index as the name because this is the default name that a web browser looks for at a URL. For example, say our file was http://www.xoticimports.com/index.html the visitor would only have to type http://www.xoticimports.com and the index.html is found automatically. Index is the standard name used for the main page on most web sites today.

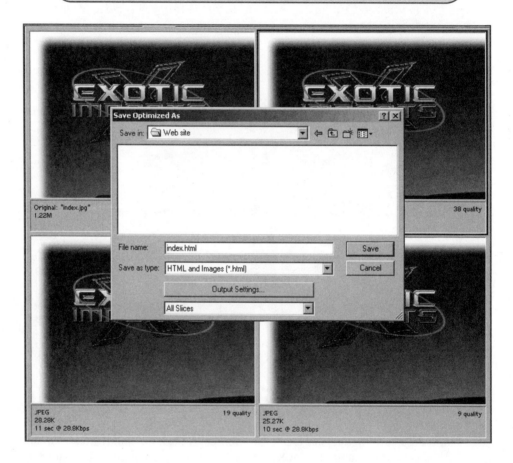

You now have a fully functional splash page. When you open it in the web browser you will see the image and when you click on it, it will take you to home.html – don't worry, we will build the home page soon.

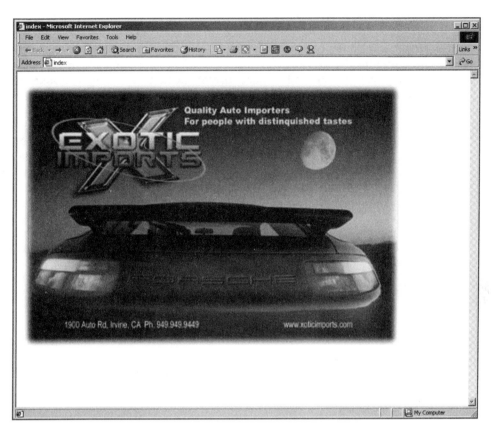

Congratulations, you have now created a basic splash page for the Web in Photoshop.

Summary

So there you have it, in this chapter we have looked at some of the fundamentals of using graphic elements effectively for the Web. Our emphasis has been on the web site's content and functionality. With this in mind we have covered the best ways to prepare your images for the Web, and have considered the three main image file types to be used for the Web: JPEGs, GIFs, and PNG.

You should now be familiar with using the Save For the Web feature, and the benefits of previewing in a browser. We have also looked at the Shape tool, and seen how this can help us to design nifty buttons for our site. We have also considered aesthetic appeal, and the important role of color on the Web. You should now be aware of the web-safe color palette, as well as understanding the importance of limiting our color range in order to create a stylish site.

When you develop an overall plan to your design and stick with it, the chances of the site attracting attention increase considerably. Word of mouth is a powerful force, in both business and on the Web. Chapter 11 continues in this vein, going into more depth on topics such as slicing, creating rollovers, animations, and applying HTML to your designs. With a good grasp of Photoshop, your site will be one of those with a definite "Wow!" factor.

Color Section

This section comprises of a selection of images from the book

Color mode
Orange, terracotta and yellow blend colours

Darken Mode
Dark brown blend colour

Overlay Mode
Dark brown blend colour

Luminosity Mode
Mid tone blend colour

Overlay Mode
Dark brown blend colour

Soft Light
Pale green blend colour

Page 67

Page 57 Auto Erase example

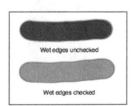

Wet edges unchecked

Wet edges checked

Page 57

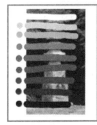

Painting tools blending modes

Page 58 Normal

Page 58 Dissolve

Page 59 Multiply

Page 59 Screen

Foundation Photoshop 6

Page 60 Overlay

Page 60 Soft Light

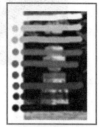

Page 61 Hard Light

Page 61 Color Dodge

Page 62 Color Burn

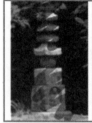

Page 62 Darken

Page 63 Lighten

Page 63 Difference

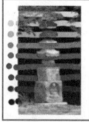

Page 64 Exclusion

Page 64 Hue

Page 65 Saturation

Page 65 Color

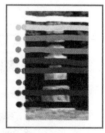

Page 66 Luminosity

Page 91

Page 123

Page 142

Page 147

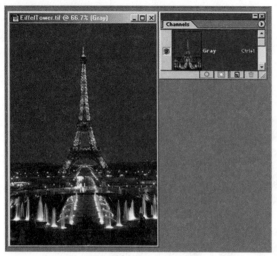

Page 274 Grayscale Image

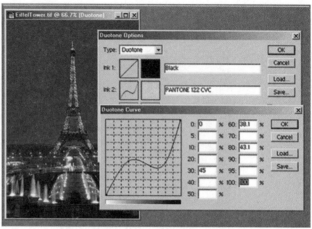

Page 275 Duotone Image

Page 276 Tritone Image

Page 277

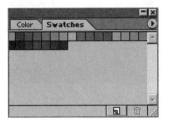

Page 318 Restrictive color swatch

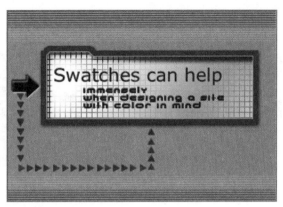

Page 319

Page 323

Page 346 Original Image

Page 346 After Auto Levels

Page 347 After Selective Color

Page 351

Page 352

Page 352

Page 354

Page 355

Page 355

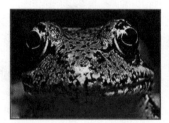

Page 357

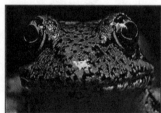

Page 357

Page 358

Page 361

Page 362

Page 362

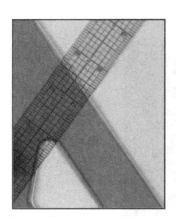

Page 364

Page 367

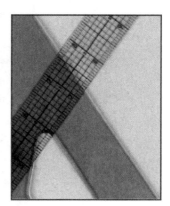

Page 365

Page 420 Original Image with Scan Lines

Page 421 After De-Interlace Even Fields

Page 421 After De-Interlace Odds Fields

Page 467 Difference Layer Blending Mode

Case Study

8 Image Correction

What we'll cover in this chapter:

- Setting up for image correction

- Color editing tools

- Color correction tools

- Correcting specific colors

- The Image > Adjust menu

- Editing specific color regions

- Editing pixels

Image correction

Photoshop gets its name from its ability to apply traditional photographic techniques digitally. This was a godsend to graphic design; in the old days photographs were altered via a messy process that invariably involved lots of chemicals and a darkroom. Needless to say, this process was both time consuming, and prone to variations in the final effect. Photoshop allows digital processing of the same image, and this leads to a much finer level of control and massive increases in production speed. Because we are working in the virtual digital world of the computer, not only can we easily apply photographic image correction effects, we can also add effects that are not possible with traditional methods.

I'll bet if you sit down and consider for a moment, you could pick two primary categories to divide **Image Correction** into: **Color** and **Contrast**. When we tweak images in Photoshop using commands primarily residing in the Image > Adjust menu, we are either trying to control the definition, or clarity, of an image (affecting edges and contrast) or manipulate the color mix in the image to create something closer to what we see in the real world. Granted, these same commands can and are used for special effects, but for the purpose of correcting images we want clarity and realism. Photoshop goes further than that though; as well as correcting for bad exposure or questionable colors in our photo (or any other bitmap), we can also change the content or purpose of our graphics;

- Just like Trotsky disappeared from Soviet historical photographs via the magic of the politically controlled airbrush, we can remove parts of our images; a Vogue cover girl can have even the merest hint of wrinkles electronically removed, and the telegraph poles that accidentally appeared in the background of our fashion shoot can also be made to go.

- We can add things to the image that were never there in the original. As well as correcting imperfections in the image, we can also make it look *better* than real life. For example, we could remove a gray sky and replace it with a clear blue one.

- We can take our image into totally different directions. Photoshop allows us to bring our images closer to reality, but why stick with boring old reality? The creative use of image correction frees us to make drastic changes that are not concerned with realism, but with *creativity*.

- We can make corrections to our images that allow us to *re-purpose* our work. For example, we may want our image to be converted to an animation in Macromedia Flash. Flash thinks in terms of simple vectors, and successfully changing a photograph to a low bandwidth vector requires a major change in its appearance. Photoshop is versatile enough to help us do this. In many ways, Photoshop has diversified from simple photographic correction towards a general graphic tool that allows us to rework images for *any* application.

Setting up for image correction

Before we can get into image correction, we need to look at how we actually get the image into Photoshop, and once it's on our monitor, we need to be sure that the image we are looking at is identical to the one we will see when we print the final work.

Input devices

To make full use of Photoshop and its color correction facilities, you first need to capture your images in a digital form. There are a number of choices:

- **Digital cameras:** A digital camera allows you to output directly to digital files. Although digital cameras are fast, they are still expensive, particularly if you need to produce print quality images (300dpi or better), and most don't support the input format that Photoshop expects (which is TWAIN). Most digital cameras are aimed for home use (family snapshots) and are only good for 100-200dpi, unless you are happy to look at postage stamp sized pictures! Additionally, many digital cameras save each shot in a lossy compressed format (such as JPEG) rather than a print quality format (such as the lossless TIFF format) to conserve camera memory. The JPEG format is not much use for professional print jobs, so it is advisable not to use a digital camera in such applications.

- **Flatbed scanner:** A flatbed scanner works rather like a color photocopier except that the copy is saved as a digital file. There are several advantages of using a scanner. For a start they have a wide price variation, starting from 'cheap and cheerful' (less than $100 dollars) up to print quality and beyond. As well as taking scans of photos, you can scan anything else on paper; personal sketches, textures (cloth, stone, etc) for use in your compositions.

- **Pro level scanners:** Professional scanners come in all sorts of shapes and sizes, and although you will probably never buy one, you might find them if you ever use Photoshop in a commercial environment. You may come across drum-based versions (which can cost upwards of $10,000), as well as specialized scanners that scan photographic slides or negatives.

For those of you wanting to get into image correction, a quick trip to the local computer or electronics store and purchasing a cheap flatbed scanner is strongly recommended.

Memory

A second consideration is memory. Scanned images can start to get very big, and Photoshop will quickly eat up further chunks of memory via undo features, setting up layers, and so on. Systems with less memory will very quickly start using virtual memory, which involves reading and writing from the hard-drive, and this will slow Photoshop considerably. 64Mb is perhaps the bare minimum. Memory is currently very cheap, so get it while it's hot!

Color bit depth

The number of distinct colors that your monitor can display is dependent on the **bit depth** of your screen. Each color is represented by a number of bits, and the more you assign to the color of each pixel, the more different colors you can describe per pixel. The maximum number of bits you can define depends on the amount of screen memory your graphic card contains. It can also depend on the screen resolution you select; the lower the screen resolution, the more colors your graphic card may be able to display.

To select a bit depth in Windows, right click on any empty area of the desktop and select Properties > Display Properties, and then the Settings tab to bring up the graphic card settings; if you are a Mac user, you need to go to the Apple Menu > Control Panel > Monitors.

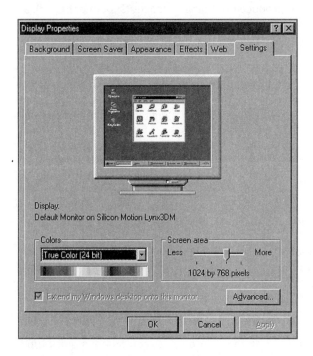

The Colors slider allows you to select the number of colors.

In general, you should select 24 bit (PC) or millions of colors (Mac) because this is close to the maximum number of colors that the human eye can perceive (which is why 24 bit color is sometimes referred to as 'true color'). Many modern graphic cards now also allow 32 bit color at no loss in speed.

Please see the Monitor Calibration Appendix to find out about calibrating your monitor to prepare for image correction. To find out more about color theory turn to Chapter 6.

Color editing tools

There are a large number of color correction tools available in Photoshop, and almost all of them are available in the Image > Adjust menu. The typical workflow in color correction is as follows;

- Capture the image

- Correct the image for errors introduced in the capture process

- Correct or enhance the image towards the finished final effect

Image capture

Buying a scanner

The device most usually associated with Photoshop is the scanner, and you cannot really use the full capabilities of Photoshop without one. This comes in many shapes and sizes, but as a beginner, you should start with a cheap flatbed scanner. Your scanner should meet the following minimum spec;

- An *optical* resolution of at least 300dpi. The optical resolution usually appears in the small print; the resolution in big letters is the *interpolated* resolution, and is not related to the underlying accuracy of the scanner. If you cannot find the optical resolution, divide the interpolated resolution by 4. 300dpi is the usual resolution used in print, and you need to be able to input content at this resolution to be able to output to print at the same quality and size.

- A TWAIN compatible driver. Photoshop (and most other professional editing software) cannot receive data directly from the scanner unless it has a TWAIN driver. Some other image grabbing devices (video recorders, etc) also allow output via TWAIN, and the setup is the same.

- 24 bit color accuracy. This means that the scanner is at least as sensitive to color as the human eye itself.

At the time of writing, you should be able to pick up such a device, complete with cables for around $100 - $200.

Scanning an image in Photoshop

To scan an image into Photoshop, assuming your scanner is all plugged in and ready to scan, the procedure is as follows:

1. Place the image to be scanned on the scanner bed. Scanners use a very bright light, and this may actually capture the *reverse* side of the page as well as the image on the front (especially with thin paper such as newspaper or magazines). To combat this, you can place a piece of black card on top of the image to be scanned. Close the scanner lid.

2. Select File > Import > and select the TWAIN source, choose your scanner from the list. You scanner may actually appear more than once (you might see stuff like myScanner_twain16, myScanner_twain24, myScanner_twain32) because it may be set up as a number of different TWAIN devices; one per output bit-depth. If this is the case, you should consult your scanner manual and select the output device that gives the best reproduction.

3. You are now ready to scan. Select File > Import > TWAIN... You will get a pop-up that varies with the type and make of scanner (it actually depends on the exact form of the drivers that come with your scanner), but you should see a button marked **Start Scan**, some means to select the scan resolution (in dpi) and some means to select the scan type (grayscale, color, scan reflective, scan transparency, etc). Once you have selected the scan resolution (anything from 72 to 300 will do, depending on the job) and the other settings, hit the start button and your scan will start.

You may sometimes get an annoying pattern over your scan called *Moire*. This is caused by interference between the scan rate for the scanner (in dpi) and the original dpi of the image. There are two ways to lose this effect:

- Scan at a higher resolution than you need and scale it down after scanning with the Image > Image Size option.

- Rotate the page on the scanner by about 5 - 10 degrees. This sometimes breaks the interference, and you can rotate the scanned image back in PhotoShop with interactive transform (select the whole image and then using Select > Transform Selection rotate the image back).

Once completed, you should see a window with your scanned image. Before you move on, it's best to save your file so far with File > Save As. Select a lossless file format such as TIFF. Lossy formats (such as JPEG) should be avoided because they will add fringes of incorrect colors at color borders (which is the sort of thing you are trying to remove!).

Correcting for capture color imperfections

Your scanner may have added a color cast or changed the brightness/contrast during the capture process. It may also capture textures from the page itself that you don't want. Let's see how to correct these imperfections before we move on;

Removing color imperfections.

You can remove any color imperfections that the scanner may have created because you have the original for comparison. To compare the scanned image with the original, you need to have a properly calibrated monitor, see the Appendix about this.

We can produce a ballpark correction by using the Variations window (Image > Adjust > Variations...). The window allows you to quickly remove noticeable color casts and changes to brightness:

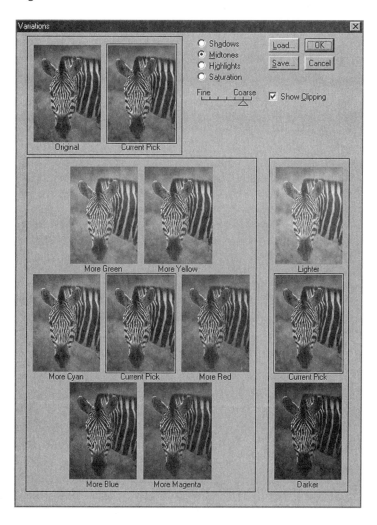

To bring the color of the scanned image closer to the original is simply a case of clicking on the image that looks closest to the original, until the Current Pick is as close to the original as possible.

> *At this stage you are not trying to make the scanned image better than the original. You want to make your scan as close to the original, warts and all. This will give you a good starting point for later corrective actions; you know that the initial scan is close to the original.*

The controls (top right) allow the following features;

- The Shadows, Midtones, Highlights and Saturation radio buttons allow you to apply variations to particular tonal groups of the image plus saturation. Most scanners are not linear in their color distortion, so you should look at each aspect of the picture separately.

- The Fine/Coarse scale allows you to control the level of variation. A fine variation level will produce a more subtle variations matrix, and you should usually select a mid to fine variation level, and set it more fine as you get closer to your target.

- The Load/Save buttons allow you to load or save a variation, as an `.ava` file. You can create a Scanner Calibration of sorts by scanning in an image of something with a large range of colors in it. I use an artists color wheel, which has the full range of printable colors on it and is produced to very accurate print standards. Once you are happy with the changes, you can save the Variations change as `Scanner Correction.ava` and apply it to all subsequent scans (or load it as the starting point).

- The Show Clipping checkbox will show pixels that are at the end of the color scale in a contrasting color. If you see this, don't click on the variation that includes it; doing so will mean that you will start to lose color information from your image.

The Variations window is very useful, as it allows you to make quick corrections to color and brightness. You can make more accurate and specific changes using some of the other tools though, and most of the time you would use the Variations window for broad brush changes only.

Cleaning up noise

You may also have to clean up the image if you have scanned in things you would rather not see, such as:

- The texture of the paper that the image is printed on.

- The ink dots that make up the image.

You can correct these via the filters found under Filter > Noise, but before you do so, it's always advisable to try rescanning a few times first. It is easy to assume that the higher the scan resolution you take, the better the final scanned image will be, but remember that most images are actually printed at a fairly low dpi (usually around 300 but less for newspapers and some magazines). Scanning at too high a resolution means that you will actually pick up all the imperfections in the original, plus any minor creases and dints in the page itself. Sometimes less is more!

The noise filter effects should be used with caution and you should not use high settings or repeated use of the same filter. They all work by averaging pixels and this may turn previously solid colors into *color gradients,* which may:

- Make it much harder to select colors or make selections based on color later on.

- Noticeably blur your image, which will result in a loss of information if used excessively.

- Inadvertently lose pixels forever if there are a lot of dark or white areas in the composition, which will become merged together to form a solid color.

The image below shows the effects of a recent scan I took of one of my oil paintings (circa the student years), which I wanted to resize and color correct. The larger image is the scanned image. The scanner picked up the canvas surface textures, which I didn't want (and would have also made Magic Wand selections very difficult). The right side of the zoomed area shows the texture in detail. Use of the Filter > Noise > Median... filter removed the texture to acceptable levels; you can see this on the left side of the zoomed area.

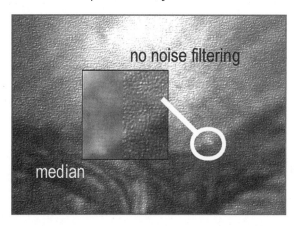
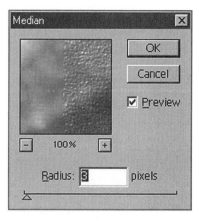

You are now ready to start correcting your image. Photoshop has a number of different color correction tools, and we will take a quick tour through them.

Color correction tools

Correcting levels using the Image > Adjust menu

There are a number of ways to alter the brightness and contrast of your image. The 'auto' filters make a 'best guess' as to what the picture should look like, and require no manual intervention. We will also look at how to use a manual method of achieving the same end result, but which gives you the final say.

Auto levels

(Image > Adjust > Auto Levels)

When applied to an image, this effect takes the darkest and lightest levels in the image and remaps them to black and white. It then spreads all the colors in between along the new range. It effectively normalizes the colors in the image, and may get rid of extreme contrast and/or color casts. It is useful sometimes to use this instead of Variations immediately after scanning an image. It doesn't always work however, and may actually make the image worse (but this is very rare). The image below left is the 'before' image, and the image to the right is the after. It perhaps still needs a little work, but is looking much better already.

*I am scanning currency because they are actually some of the most complex images; they are specifically designed to **prevent reproduction**, making them a good test for your scanner and software, and contain subtle colors and many faint areas with complex patterns... but remember that trying to spend one of your scans is a major felony!*

Auto Contrast

(Image > Adjust > Auto Contrast)
This is the same as Auto levels, but it works with contrast. Left image is the 'before'.

The two auto correction effects are quick and easy to use and go a long way to correcting bad midtones caused by bad photography or poor lighting, but Photoshop will make a mess of it if all the colors (including the brightest and darkest, which the auto corrections base their effects) are wrong. In these cases, we need to sit down and look at the distribution of color levels ourselves. To do this we need to go to the Levels window.

Levels

(Image > Adjust > Levels;
Levels allow you to control the brightness and contrast in an image by manipulating three components: shadow (black), midtones/gamma (gray), and highlights (white).

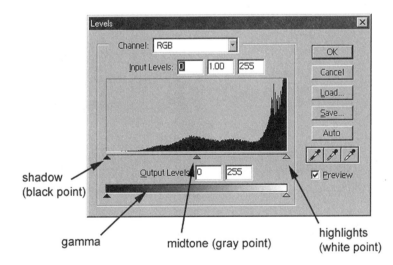

The middle area of the Levels dialog box is a histogram showing the distribution of each brightness level from black (extreme left) to white (extreme right). You can also select individual channels of the RGB model with the Channel drop-down menu, but this is not recommended until you have had some practice, because it tends to create color casts if you are not careful. Moving the shadow (black point) and highlight (white point) Output

Levels sliders toward the center of the histogram has the effect of increasing contrast in the image (darkening some pixels, lightening others). What you are doing here is similar to the auto levels effect; except that this time you're manually specifying the new darkest/lightest shades. Moving the pointers on the gamma slider will either lighten or darken the entire image.

The histogram is basically a breakdown of where various tones of image pixels lie. For the image this histogram represents, the overall tone is concentrated in the highlight areas, with little or no shadow or midtones.

The image below has a black point that is not representative of the actual levels in the histogram.

 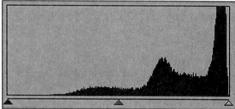

By moving it to a more representative position we get the image shown below. The darkest point of our image (the text) is now a true black.

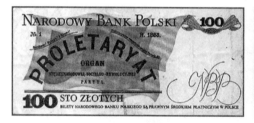 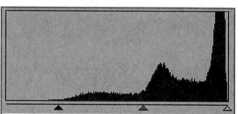

If (like me), you prefer not to bother with looking at the graphs but would rather use a more direct method, clicking on the three Eyedroppers to the right of the Levels window allows you to select the black point, the gray (mid tone) point and the white point directly.

> *If your image has no gray in it, don't select the midpoint using the Eyedroppers, but instead use the sliders.*

white point

black point

gray point

The concept behind Levels adjustment is fairly basic: The image carries with it information in the form of pixels, with each pixel carrying a color value. Levels help to redistribute that tonal information within the image to bring out sharper contrasts between the three areas. Though not a stand-alone miracle cure, much can be accomplished by simply working with the sliders/eyedroppers in the Levels dialog box.

> *The* Auto *button is another way to apply the auto levels effect. By doing this as soon as you open the* Levels *dialog, you can use Photoshop's 'best guess' as your starting point, and then manually tweak as necessary.*

The effects so far allow us to make global changes to the relative light levels of our image. What if we want to isolate and change particular colors rather than the whole image?

Correcting specific colors

The Variations window is cool, but when you use it, it affects *all* color. For example, if you wanted to make blues more prominent, the variation would also change the greens and reds. How can we be more specific and target individual colors in isolation? Well, there are several ways of doing this, and we will look at one of the easiest:

Okay. Here's an image just crying out for color correction (next page). It's not a scanned image this time, but a *rendered image* of a dolphin. I actually created it in a 3D program with virtual lighting. The trouble with the virtual world is that you can create extremes that do not exist in the real world, and I've gone overboard with the red sky here! Something a little more 'real-world' is called for.

The first thing I need to do is go to Auto Levels (Image > Adjust > Auto Levels). Compare the two pictures to see the effect. This gets rid of the green cast on the image (Auto Levels is very good at getting rid of casts, but occasionally, it seems just as good at creating them so a little manual judgment is always necessary to offset the 'auto' part, as defined by an unthinking machine).

see color signature   *see color signature*

I want to tone down that red sky, whilst keeping everything else the same. I could do this via a grayscale quick mask, but that would take ages to set up correctly. And anyway, there is something better I can use; *Selective color* (Image > Adjust > Selective Color). The drop-down menu allows me to target all primary and secondary colors, plus levels (blacks, grays, whites).

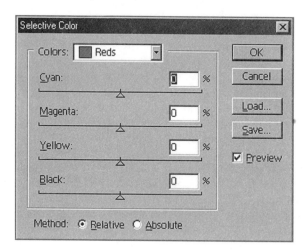 

Because I am targeting red only, I can go to town in eradicating it. Taking out all magenta and yellow, and ramping up the cyan will probably turn the red into a more realistic blue. I will probably have to do something to black as well to get the right shade to make my blue blend into the cyan at the horizon. After moving the sliders about to achieve this, I end up with a much more subtle effect.

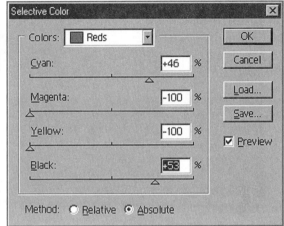

see color signature

Much better! Notice how the sea and horizon has remained the same color and shade; we have changed the sky only. If you try the same change using the Variations window, you will soon see how special selective color is and how much time it saves – most other methods require quick masks with gradients, or some very precise color picking and all sorts of other scary stuff.

Sometimes you don't want to replace color, but selectively get rid of it all together (to create a grayscale). To do this, you would use Image > Adjust > Hue/Saturation, which works in a similar way.

Most Photoshop images are built up via layers. We can be even more selective than this by targeting specific layers as well as targeting specific colors within each layer. To do this we need to set up an **adjustment layer**. To show you an example, we will first set up a few layers of color.

Create a new image (File > New) 500 by 500 pixels in size (RGB, with a white background). Create three new layers and call them red, green, and blue. Using an Airbrush, create a splodge of color with the same color as the layer name per layer, and make them overlap each other.

Suppose we wanted to make the red splodge brighter. At the bottom of the Layers palette, right click on the fourth icon from the left to bring up a menu of effects, and select Brightness/Contrast.

You will now see a new layer. This is an adjustment layer, and only those layers below it will be affected by the effect. In the Brightness/Contrast window, set brightness to +70 and hit OK. You will see the red blob become brighter.

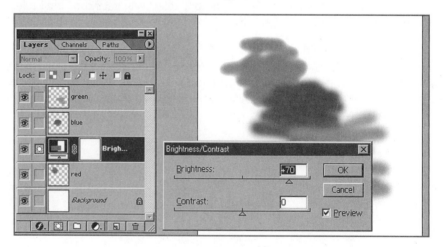

Because our effect is tied to a layer, its brightness effect can be switched off by clicking its eye icon. If you move the layer up in the layer order, the brightness will affect more layers, and the final image will change. Adjustment layers are great, because you can make almost every color correction on an adjustment layer; this allows you to temporarily undo the effect, or change its scope of effect. Even better, the adjustment layer acts just like any other layer with the opacity, blend and layer groupings all working as with normal layers containing type or pixels. Cool!

Curves

(Image > Adjust > Curves)

You've seen how effective using Levels can be for bringing your photos to life, with Levels we were only affecting three areas of the image: Shadows, Midtones, and Highlights. Curves, on the other hand give us much finer control in image correction, as we can change any point along a 0 – 100% scale, without affecting up to 15 other values. Even a slight change in the Curves dialog box gives noticeable results, so this is a tool that deserves more than a little respect and temperance in use.

Curves are great for adding contrast to an image, but they are also useful for tweaking neutral color values in an image, adjusting color casts and other operations that require a 'gentle' touch. Of course, if you don't want a naturalistic effect, you can intentionally over-adjust the Curves, to achieve a really psychedelic look.

There is one downside to working with Curves. We are not provided with a histogram as with levels to see where the balance of color lay. What we are given instead is a tonal line graph where points can be manipulated, raised and lowered, and more points added as needed.

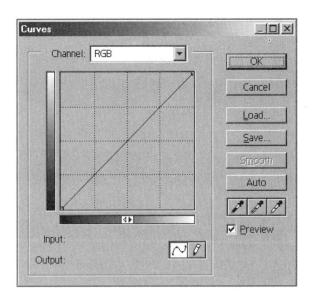

When we look at the tonal graph in the Curves window, we are actually seeing the image plotted in two ways. The horizontal axis represents the image information prior to alteration; the vertical plots the image information after adjustment. In other words, a straight line from lower left to upper right indicates the image has not been altered from its original state. When points are moved and added to the line, the image has undergone correction. The new position of a point on the graph indicates the new value for the portion of the image that point represents.

By moving the left point up the scale, we affect the lightness of the overall image. In turn, the rightmost point, when moved down the scale, affects the overall darkness of the image.

You can adjust all the channels simultaneously (RGB). You may, however, make adjustments to the separate color channels by clicking on the drop-down menu at the top of the Curves dialog box and choosing either the Red, Green or Blue channel when in RGB. The same goes for CMYK, etc. By adjusting the curves we are in fact editing the grayscale value of that channel.

The graph, by default, is represented as a 4 by 4 grid. With this representation we can determine where to insert points that will change the color value of shadows (extreme left), and highlights (extreme right) and all the tonal values inbetween. You may change this grid to 10 by 10 by going OPTION/ALT+CLICK on the graph.

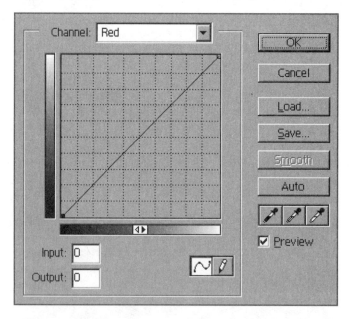

Below the grid we see what appears to be a gradient. This represents every possible tone, black to white. Clicking the small arrows icon switches between reading brightness values (RGB) to halftones (primarily for print). Photoshop defaults are set to read brightness.

- Input/Output: These two fields indicate the point's settings before and after moving them on the grid.

- Point Tool/Pencil Tool: The point tool allows you to select points and drag them on the grid. The pencil tool allows you to 'draw' the curve. The point tool is by far the easier to manipulate.

- Eyedroppers: Similar to the Eyedroppers found in Levels, these allow you to set endpoints as well as midtone values.

- Smooth: This is for 'smoothing out' a manually drawn curve, applying points to the curve line. Continuing to click Smooth will flatten the line in increments.

- Auto: Applies Auto-Levels

Let's have a look at this little turtle. Can Curves help us straighten the poor guy out? He looks a little pale as he sits. No problem amigo, we'll fix you right up!

By adjusting the output of our quartertone and three-quarter tone, we can clean up the photo by getting rid of some of the white fuzz and increasing the contrast overall.

see color signature

Adding more points to the curve and making minor adjustments, including increasing the halftone values, can bring our buddy into even clearer contrast.

see color signature

Using Curves can also help clean up scans and digital images that have picked up strange tones, or color casts, during the conversion from one media to the computer.

Color Balance

(Image > Adjust > Color Balance)

This is one tool at your disposal that does exactly what the name implies. By adjusting the sliders in the Color Balance dialog box, you can add and subtract hues from the various elements of an image.

Though not very powerful, this is a good tool for quick adjustments, and working with it is fairly intuitive. Say I want to add Blue to the image, I can either move the third slider toward the word Blue, or I can subtract both Red and Green to increase the overall blue in the image.

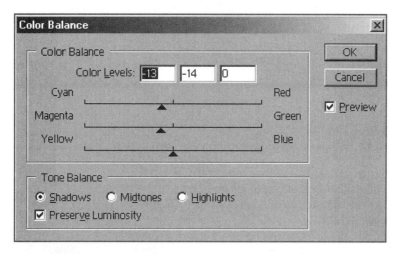

We can adjust Shadows (above 75%), Midtones (25-75%) and Highlights (below 25%), though not with the same amount of control as we had with the Curves.

Preserve Luminosity: This preserves the original lightness value. With this unchecked we affect both color content and tonal balance.

Brightness/Contrast

(Image > Adjust > Brightness/Contrast)

This is what I'd call a 'beginner's' editing tool. Moving the sliders on this tool affects the tonal balance of the entire image. There is no way to separately control the Reds, the Greens or the Blues, nor the shadows, midtones and highlights. Everything changes value at the same time with this tool, so it should be used sparingly if at all.

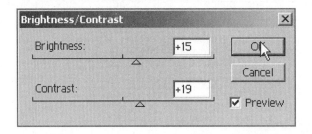

Hue/Saturation

(Image > Adjust > Hue/Saturation)

This command is unique from the others we've looked as it uses the **HSB** color model (**Hue/Saturation/Brightness**). We might also call these 3 areas color, intensity and tone, as that is what they represent.

I love this tool. With it we can alter the color, depth and brightness of specific areas of the image without changing other colors, depths, or highlights a bit. Or we can choose to alter the entire image, or master.

see color signature

If we make an adjustment to the Master, or entire spectrum of this image's HSB, the entire image is changed accordingly.

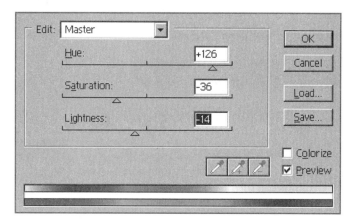

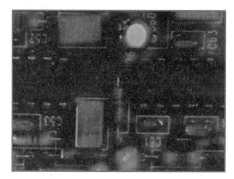

see color signature

All tonal values were altered based on the amount of change from their original values. If we select Colorize, when altering the Master, all original color values are replaced with a single hue set to varying saturation levels.

see color signature

When we decide to edit specific color regions, our control over the editing process becomes much more precise.

To demonstrate, I'll work on this image and provide a walkthrough for you to try on a photo of your own; choose something with a variety of color at different saturation levels.

Editing specific color regions

1. Open your image. Bring up the Hue/Saturation dialog box.

2. In the drop-down menu, choose the Reds channel. Select the Eyedropper tool and click it in an area best representing a red hue. This sets the center point of a color range representing red or hues of red, indicated in the gradient bar below the sliders.

see color signature

3. Now any hue falling into the range seen on the slider is defined by that point of color, and can be adjusted accordingly by changing position of the sliders.

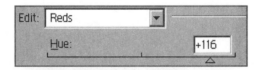

see color signature

4. We can also tweak the image by moving the slider bar on the gradient.

5. Try setting points for other areas of color, such as blue, magenta, and green. Move the sliders around and watch the changes made to the image.

Quick sepia tones

Here's a simple way to apply a sepia-style tone to your image:

1. With the image open, open the Hue/Saturation dialog box.

see color signature

2. Check Colorize.

3. Move the Hue slider until you get a nice, overall 'tan' cast to the image.

see color signature

4. Adjust the saturation and lightness levels to taste.

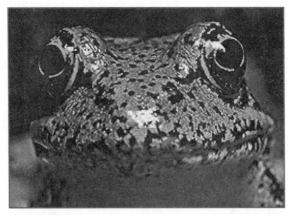

see color signature

There is one powerful feature in the Hue/Saturation dialog box that has been long overlooked. Though the drop-down allows you to pick and affect several colors, you need not be constrained merely to these ranges. You may, via the slider bar between the 2 gradient bars, increase the color range affected when manipulating one of the other colors in the drop-down menu. Similarly, by decreasing the distance between the range guides, we can narrow the color range affected by the sliders.

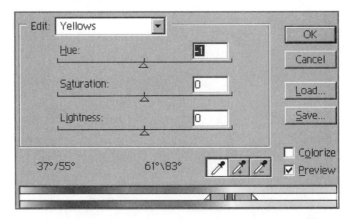

For this example I've narrowed the range of colors affected in the yellow range. Now a much narrower range of color values will be changed when I move the hue slider.

see color signature

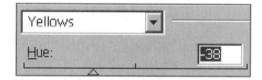

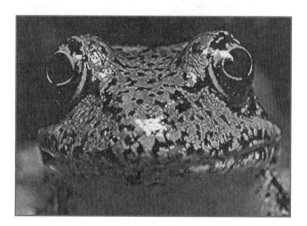

So what happens when we widen the range? That's right... we affect a wider gamut of color when the sliders are moved.

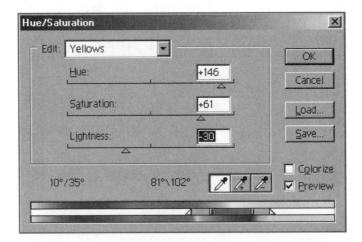

see color signature

Note the background color is still unchanged, as it did not fall within the range of color we set in the guides.

Desaturate

(Image > Adjust > Desaturate)

This command removes all color information from an image, converting it to shades of gray. All colors are reduced to a saturation of 0. This effect may also be applied by going to Hue/Saturation dialog box and moving the saturation slider to the far left, or you could use the Channel Mixer control.

Replace Color

(Image > Adjust > Replace Color...)

The Replace Color command allows you to select a color range and change it using the Hue, Saturation, and Lightness sliders.

With this tool you select the color range you want to affect by choosing a color range with the Eyedropper tools. You expand or contract that range with the Fuzziness slider located at the top of the Replace Color dialog box.

When using the Eyedropper to select a color range, you don't have to guess what color you are choosing by clicking in the black/white viewer window, but you may actually choose your color range by clicking within the image itself. Also, as with the selection tools, you can SHIFT+CLICK with the Eyedropper to add to your selection.

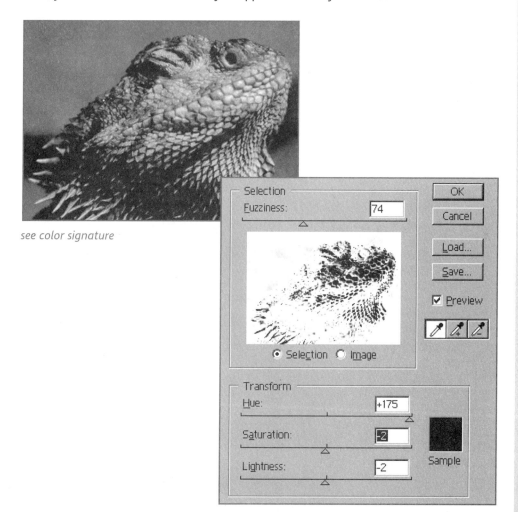

see color signature

see color signature

Selective Color

(Image > Adjust > Selective Color...)

This command allows you to change the CMYK values of regions of color. Though it functions in the realm of CMYK (where it is most effective), you may also use this function to correct RGB images. Selective Color correction is primarily used by separation programs and high-end scanners to adjust the amount of primary color in an image.

Selective Color is similar to Color Balance, but instead of targeting percentages you are targeting areas of color (Red, Blues, etc.).

Here's a quick demonstration of how this works.

OK, admittedly I've altered the lizard a bit, but this will help me demonstrate the process. The background appears to have a reddish purple tint to it, but I'm not entirely sure I want that much magenta in the mix. Bringing up the Selective Color dialog box, I'll choose Reds from the drop-down menu and reduce the magenta by adjusting the slider that corresponds to the color. I can also add and subtract color with the other sliders until I feel I have a good mix visually.

see color signature

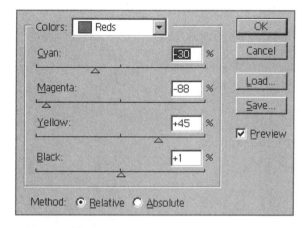

see color signature

The main problem with Selective Color is it leaves the user to guess when the mix is correct. Instead of having the capability of measuring the color levels and balances, the success of this process rests on the users ability to 'eyeball' the color changes.

Channel Mixer

(Image > Adjust > Channel Mixer...)

This function allows you to combine values from channels and use those values to replace the value of a single channel. In this manner you may totally replace the values of the green channel (move the green slider to 0) with the values of the red (increasing the red slider value to above 0).

For example, the image on the right has a fairly generous mix of red.

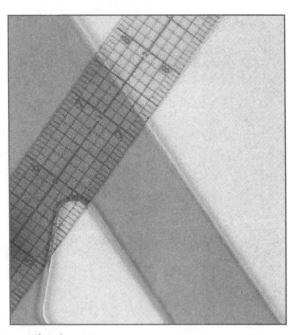

see color signature

When we bring up the Channel Mixer dialog box for the Red channel, the slider position will indicate 100% for Red, and 0% for Green and Blue.

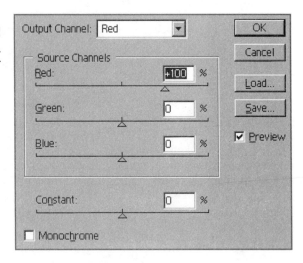

By moving the Red slider to 0 and increasing the Green value to 100%, the red channel adopts the information from the green channel setting.

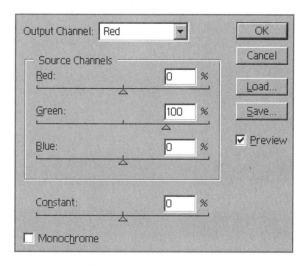

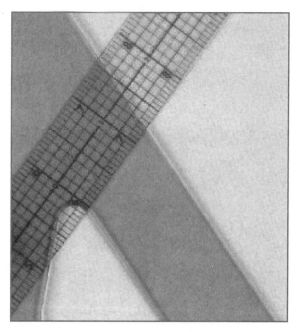

The Channel Mixer is an excellent tool for creating realism in black and white photos that far exceeds the effect given by merely converting an image to grayscale. To do this, check the Monochrome box to adjust the image.

This image was converted from RGB to Grayscale:

In this version, the RGB image was adjusted with the Channel Mixer:

About Channel Mixer

We should take a look at a few items concerning this tool. First and foremost, the Composite Channel, for example RGB, must be selected in the Channels palette in order for this to be available. Selecting a single channel will cause this selection to be whited out in the menu.

Another point is that only color channels may be adjusted. You cannot select an alpha channel, quick mask or layer mask.

As with most other commands in the Adjust menu, the settings for Channel Mixer may be saved for use on other images, or even distributed to other users. The saved file uses a .cha file extension.

Gradient Map

This tool actually desaturates an image and then re-maps the color values of an image or selection, replacing them with the color values of a selected gradient. The tonal values in the image are swapped with those of a gradient, which may be edited real-time.

This is another very cool function, especially for generating not-so-lifelike effects. Here is the original image:

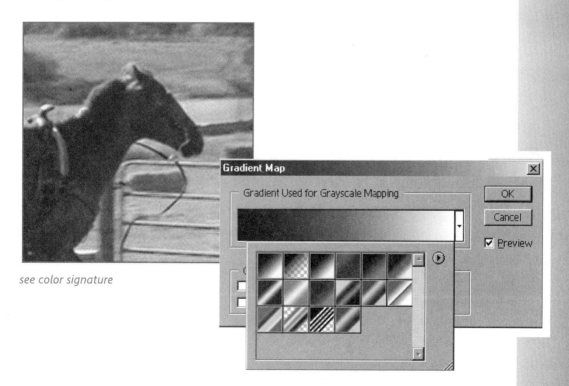

see color signature

Here's the same image after applying Copper with Reverse checked:

see color signature

Editing pixels

So far we have looked at image correction purely in terms of color, however, the final set of correction features don't involve color, but changing pixels themselves. You would use the following techniques to:

- Restore old or damaged photos

- Remove objects that spoil the image

Both tasks involve using the Clone Stamp tool; a tool that is often underestimated, but we are now going to learn all about its power.

Using the Clone Stamp tool

1. Open a new image 500 pixels by 500 pixels. Select the Airbrush (50% opacity) and airbrush three blobs of color (red, green and blue) using one of the patterned brushes to create some texture within the blob.

2. Now select the Clone Stamp tool.

3. The Clone Stamp tool allows you to sample pixels from one part of the image and place them somewhere else on the same (or even another) image. To select the area to sample (clone), ALT-CLICK or OPTION-CLICK in the center of one of the color blobs. Now, you can CLICK-HOLD in a blank area of the canvas and start painting.

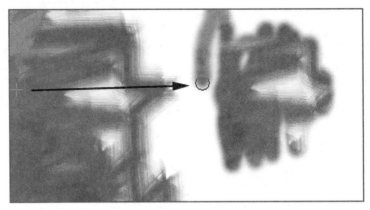

see color signature

The Clone tool copies pixels from the area you ALT-clicked on (signified by the crosshair), and copies it to the current cursor position. The Clone tool also allows you to copy with opacity and select any of the Airbrush tools.

4. Set the opacity to about 20% and use a shaped brush to mix the blue areas into the red. Unlike the airbrush, the Clone tool paints with existing pixels, and any textures in the original pixels are carried across to the new pixels.

see color signature

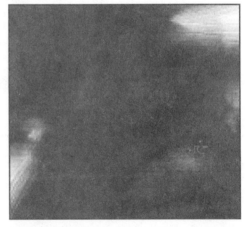

see color signature

5. Keep changing the clone position (ALT-CLICK). This will keep using new areas of the original, thus ensuring that the new pixels never look like the existing pixels they were sampled from. The overall effect starts to look almost painterly because we are carrying across the original pixels, complete with textures.

OK, so you might be thinking 'nice trick, but a bit limited'. Well yes, but imagine if the sampled pixels were from a real painterly image; such as a work by Rembrandt. You would be painting new colors, but based on brush strokes by the Old Masters! Try it sometime by drawing a pencil sketch, scanning it in, and then coloring it in with pixels cloned from color areas from original paintings. You can make the clone area from another image simply by ALT CLICKING on a second scanned image of, say a Da Vinci.

But that isn't the real power of the Clone Stamp tool, because the last exercise was just a taster to get you into understanding how the tool works. The real power is that you can hide areas of an image that contain 'bad' pixels by overlaying them with 'good' pixels sampled from elsewhere.

Restoring images

1. Take a photo or picture in a magazine and tear it in half. I've used a photo of a Christmas tree from last year. Make the tear obvious. That's the easy part.

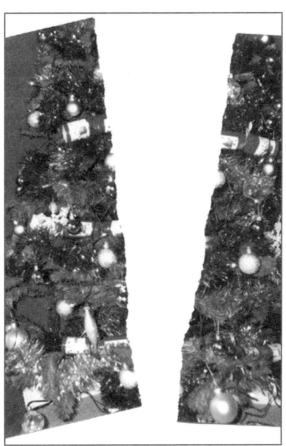

2. Next we will put it back together. Scan the two halves of the tree. Place them next to each other, or you might try to scan each separately and composite them together (which will allow you to put them closer together.)

3. I have left the two halves a fair distance apart to demonstrate what we are doing, but in real life you would try to nudge the two halves closer together. We will use the Clone Stamp tool's ability to sample pixels from one part of an image to another to fill in the tear. You would do the same sort of thing as in the next few steps to restore old photos via removal of tears, filling in holes or areas where the picture got scraped away, etc. This seems like a tall order for our image; there are baubles that are split in half across the tear, and a cracker that is in two halves. It's a hard job but someone's going to have to do it.

The cracker

4. The cracker is actually an easy one to fix. Simply ALT -CLICK in the red areas close to the crack and paint them into the tear. Use an opacity of about 80 to 90% with a feathered brush (a feathered brush should always be used unless you get to a border, such as the cracker edge, where you should now use a non-feathered and smaller round brush) and make small horizontal left to right strokes across the tear. Select a new clone area every two or three strokes, and make the brush size smaller as you reach the edges of the cracker and its label. The secret is to zoom in quite close and clone small areas at a time.

The bauble.

The bauble is a harder beast, and probably one of the more difficult mishapes to correct; a steady hand is required!

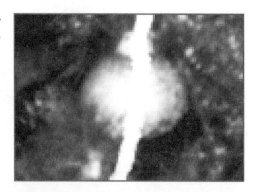

1. First, you need to copy pixels across from the left hand side of the bauble to the center tear. Don't worry about keeping it round at this stage.

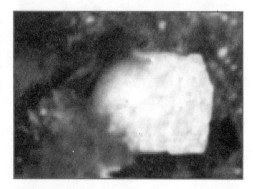

2. Next comes the clever bit; to give us our round bauble again, you need to start cloning pixels from the tree areas to the right of the bauble to 'carve out' our round edge... To get the smooth gradient (caused by the curvature of the bauble) select a very low opacity (around 10-20%) and clone dark areas of the tree along the bauble edge.

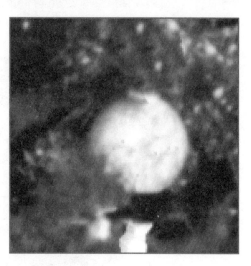

3. You would never know it was ever broken!

An alternative way to do this would be to copy the right hand of the bauble (using the Magic Wand or a Quick Mask selection), and then paste and nudge it back towards the left half. You would use the Clone Stamp tool to fill in any blemish at the join, and finally, correct the background around the bauble. I have used the Clone Stamp tool in isolation because it is the tool we are looking at. With practice, you will be able to string together different techniques to find quicker routes. Photoshop is very open ended in this way, and there are many options. As you will realize when deadlines loom, the 'best' method is usually the quickest!

4. All that remains now is to clone the greenery of the tree into the rest of the tear. Use an 80-90% opacity, and change the clone region (the ALT-CLICK position) often; this is the key to successful seamless cloning.

The picture below shows the cracker and bauble plus surrounding area finished. The tear has gone. The only clue that we have stitched it all together is that the cracker is perhaps too long, but this is just a consequence of placing the torn sides much farther apart than normal to show off the technique.

We now need to check how well we have done, and this is where a good knowledge of color systems comes in. Depending on whether the image is destined for print, check each color in turn to ensure that the tear is well hidden for each color channel. You need to do this because the dominant colors (in this case greens and yellows) may be hiding errors in the other channels (such as blue).

5. Using the Channels palette, look at each color in turn and look for any blemishes in the corrections. If you do find any, fix them in the same view mode as the one you found them in. I am using RGB, but you could just as well use CMYK if you were working towards print.

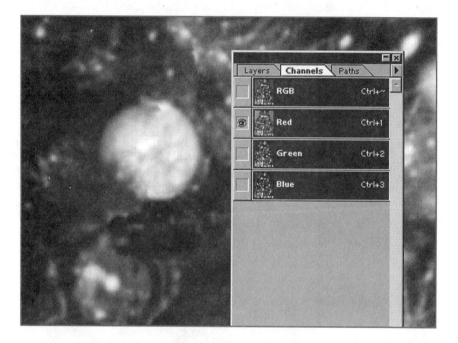

6. We now have to look at the lightness channel, and to do this; we have to convert to Lab mode. Do this via Image > Mode > Lab Color. Using the Channels palette again, show the Lightness channel only. Search for anything that sticks out as odd.

Aha! There are some dark areas that look as if they have been introduced by our tear fixing, and I have pointed them out with the arrows on the next page; there are areas of dark tones that still follow the tears outline, and some dark areas that look out of place.

Although looking at the color image only is what the average beginner would think to do, you must always look at the effects of pixel based color corrections in each color channel in isolation, plus the Lab Lightness channel to check brightness levels are okay. Your image will be used in many different applications, and may be later messed about with by other Photoshop operators, and some of them may apply effects that show up the shortcomings.

Additionally, the image may be reproduced in print using many different ink systems, and some of them may tend to show up blemishes that are hidden on your monitor.

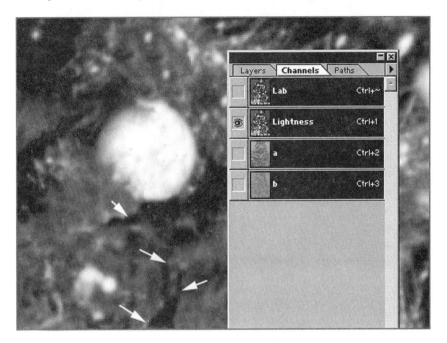

7. To clear up the dark areas, select a feathered brush at a low opacity (10-15%) and smooth out the dark edges by cloning lighter areas over them. By then superimposing lighter foliage textures over the offending areas, we create a much better seam.

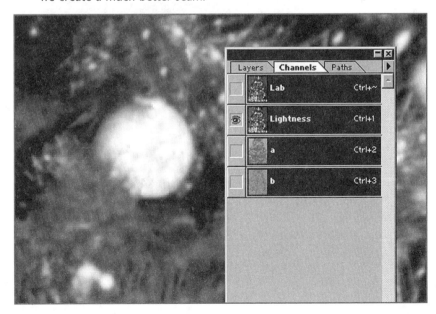

8. Okay, finished. Time for a before and after:

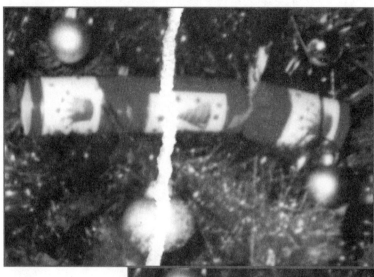

Who ever said the Clone Stamp tool was useless!

Airbrushing out objects

How many times have you taken the perfect picture, only to later realize that you missed the fact that there are telegraph poles spoiling the image, or a tree that is behind your subject, but in the picture seems to be sprouting out of their head? Hmmm. Obviously your photography skills are as good as mine then. It's a good job we have Photoshop to hide a multitude of sins.

The image below is spoiled by the idiot jumping up and down in the foreground. High time he was removed.

1.   By using the Clone Stamp tool, we can start deleting his legs. It's the same technique as before; 80-90% opacity, feathered brush, and don't forget to change the clone source area often.

2.   We hit a problem as we approach his upper leg; there are tracks in the sand that need to continue behind him after we have got shot of him. The paths of the tracks in question are shown below.

3. Of course, this isn't really a problem at all; simply select 100% for your opacity, and copy the tracks as shown below, using brush strokes that follow the path of the track. Once you have got the track, go down to 10-20% opacity to blend in the new track. Easy!

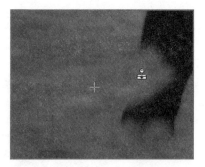

4. He doesn't stand a chance! Five minutes later, and his leg has all but disappeared, with the track now magically appearing behind him

5. You then need to follow the checking procedure using Lab Color once you have finished airbrushing our hapless web/graphic designer out of the picture. Another easy bit of Photoshop magic.

Case Study

Now it's time to practice your new skills on our case study. Let's do some preparation of our images for use on our project.

We are going to work on three of the images. The first two we are just going to do some simple adjustments to the contrast and color balance. On the third image we are going to remove the color and prepare the base image for our home page.

Altering the Contrast and Mid Tones

1. Open up the image we saved earlier as black car.psd. Looking at our picture of the Lamborghini, we need to add some stronger shadows and more contrast.

2. We are going to alter the image using levels: Image > Adjust > Levels or CTRL/CMD+L. You should now see the histogram of the image. Slide the left triangle in to the right a little bit and the right triangle into the left slightly. This will give brighter whites and darker blacks. Be careful not to overdo this step or you will blow out the image detail (try it and you'll see what I mean!).

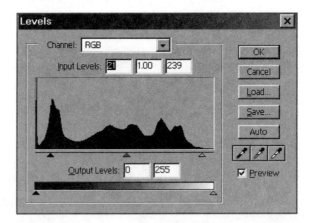

3. Save and close the image (choose the highest available Quality).

4. Open image 29052.jpg (or another picture with similar lighting problems). The contrast is good on this image but the mid tones need to be lightened a little bit. Open the Levels box again and slide the middle slider to the left a little bit.

5. Save this image as info.jpg (highest available Quality again). This is going to become the information page for our web site.

This time let's have a little fun with the next image.

Desaturating and adding a tab

1. Open up image 29087.jpg. If you are following the case study, but with a different theme, choose an image that strongly represents your product.

We will use this image as the background for the home page of our web site. We are going to prepare it for use as a base image. In a later section we are going to add our navigational elements to this page. The first thing we need to do is to crop the borders down because this image has a black border running around it. This is undesirable for our project, as it makes the picture look too raw and unprepared. Save it as home.jpg.

29087.jpg @ 50% (RGB)

2. This step is optional and is totally up to your personal preference. Let's remove the color from this image just for creative effect. It is sometimes a good idea to remove color from a picture used in a collage because the image can become very busy with shape and form. Being busy with color too can make a composition look a bit overdone. By removing the color (or converting to monotone) it can make the additional images blend better with the overall composition and avoid the main image from becoming too dominating. Image > Adjust > Desaturate (SHIFT+CTRL/CMD+U).

3. Now we want to draw a selection around part of the image. This is going to be for a purely aesthetic reason. At some point, you must have seen the tab type design that is really popular right now. Let's add a touch of that to our image. Select the Polygonal Lasso tool. (Normally you would create this on a new layer, but as I am sure it is going to be part of the background of the image, I decided to keep it on the background layer.)

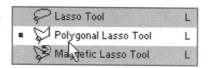

This tool is another join-the-dots type of effect. When you click inside the image, an anchor point is left, when you click again a straight line is drawn between the dots. You keep clicking until you go back to the beginning point, after that your selection becomes a closed polygon shape. Holding down the SHIFT key as we go constrains the angles to 45 degrees. This is really the key to creating these types of effects.

Draw the shape as shown here.

4.   Invert the part of the image that we have selected. Press CTRL+I (Image > Adjust > Invert).

5. Deselect and save the image again.

You just had a little practice in image correction. We also have our base image prepared for our home page. All our pieces are coming together, but we still have a few more touches to add to the images for our case study. In Chapter 9 we will add some filter effects to our info page. In Chapter 10 we are going to complete our home page and then wrap it up in Chapter 11, when we publish it as a web page.

Summary

As you may by now have gathered, the camera should never be trusted, at least not with Photoshop around. You can correct most things with the large number of tools available, and this is a major set of abilities to have when working with Photoshop.

Moving on

The best way to detect a photographic fake is to look at the lighting and contrast; shadows and changes of tone usually show an image to be a clever cut-and-paste job, so you really have to make full use of Lab color to sort out the lighting, and this lets you add shadows without changing the color.

Additionally, use of masking with the correction tools really adds a greater flexibility into the mix, so it's something to start looking at.

And just a final thought; If you look at the works of top Photoshop designers, for example, in the friends of ED book, New Masters of Photoshop, one thing that sticks out is that they tend to leave all the cuts, scratches and blemishes in, or make more of them. This is to break the coldness of a digital image by adding some random textures into the mix; the perfect blemish-free photo is not always the artistic goal.

9

Real World Filters

What we'll cover in this chapter:

- Photoshop Filters menu

- Artistic Filters

- Using the Blur tools

- Sharpening your images

- Filters for texture

- Stylizing

- Custom filter creation

- Embedding watermarks

- Correcting video images

- 3rd party filters

Photoshop attempts to be exactly what the name implies: a digital photo-processing workshop. When I think of the title the image of a darkroom dances through my head, complete with chemical trays, acidic smells burning the nostrils and damp photo paper hanging about. A strikingly powerful image, considering I've been in an actual darkroom perhaps twice in my life.

Of course there are no chemicals involved with Photoshop. Nor are there perspective-altering lenses that need be fumbled with. Photoshop has a full range of professional filters (some useful, some not as much) that we can apply digitally to any image opened with the software.

In this chapter, we will take a look at some of the more useful filters at our disposal, as well as some handy ways to apply them.

The Filter menu: first glance

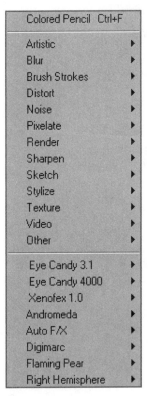

The Filter menu is divided into 3 groups (from top to bottom):

- **Last filter used**
- **Production/creative filters**
- **Third Party Filters**

You must have an open RGB image in Photoshop in order to have access to all of the filters.

Last filter, as the name indicates, re-applies the last filter used to an image or active layer. Clicking this will use the last settings for that filter, without giving you the option of changing those settings. To access the filter's dialog box in order to change these settings, hold down the Option (Mac) or Alt (PC) key when choosing Last Filter from the menu.

Artistic filters

This section contains 15 filters. The principle for this grouping is to duplicate (or at least attempt to recreate) artistic techniques found in real world art forms. Whether or not these succeed I'll leave you to decide. Though they may not render a true effect in every case, these tools can be incredibly effective with a little imagination and Photoshop finesse.

Colored Pencil...
Cutout...
Dry Brush...
Film Grain...
Fresco...
Neon Glow...
Paint Daubs...
Palette Knife...
Plastic Wrap...
Poster Edges...
Rough Pastels...
Smudge Stick...
Sponge...
Underpainting...
Watercolor...

The Artistic filters are alike in operation in that they grab similar colors from an image or selection and group them into a single, solid color. Depending on the filter this could have the effect of color blobs (Sponge) or stark edges (Cutout) with the overall result causing the image to appear painted or drawn.

Using Artistic filters

When used alone the Artistic filters give a reasonable semblance to their namesake. For instance, if you apply the Cutout filter set to 5 levels, the end result will be an image that appears to have 5 layers of stacked color roughly resembling the original image.

The same can be said for the Brush Strokes and Sketch filter groups. Though not exact, they certainly come close to the intended artistic style.

Later in this chapter we will use a few artistic filters in conjunction with other Photoshop functions.

Blur filters

This set of filters is incredibly useful and has a wide range of uses. Let's run through some definitions, and then venture into a few practical applications of the Blur group.

```
Blur
Blur More
Gaussian Blur...
Motion Blur...
Radial Blur...
Smart Blur...
```

Blur: Averages the pixels between stark contrasts in color.

Blur More: Same effect as Blur, though the effect is 3 to 4 times stronger.

Gaussian Blur: Averages the colors within a specified radius, giving the specific area a blurred effect. The effect is a hazy appearance to the selected area.

Motion Blur: Blurs pixels in a set direction.

Radial Blur: This filter takes the image and blurs the image outward, from the center, creating either a zoom or spin effect, depending on the options chosen

For example, if we have a photo and we want to draw attention to a certain area of the image, we would open the photo and duplicate the image in a new layer. Then we would Select All and go to Layer > New > Layer Via Copy, or simply drag the background layer to the new layer icon at the bottom of the Layers palette. Next we'd create a selection around the area you want people to focus on. You may use any selection tool you want.

Finally we'd inverse the selection (Select > Inverse) and apply the Radial Blur filter.

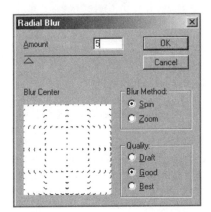

You can further the effect by adjusting the **brightness/contrast** to the background (by Image > Adjust > Brightness/Contrast). Darkening the blurred area will help bring out the subject of your photo, as on the following page:

Smart Blur: Have an image with a bit too much grain for your liking? This is the filter for you. Smart blur preserves the sharp edges within an image while averaging areas of more gradual color.

Photo before Smart Blur:

After applying Smart Blur:

Other Applications:

As mentioned before, there are many useful ways to utilize the Blur filters. They may be utilized to adjust the focus of selections and photos as shown above, give the illusion of movement or add realistic texture to type and interfaces.

Simulating movement

For this example we will use an image that implies movement, in this case a bull and rider shortly after the ride has begun.

1. Open your image (you can download the one from the friends of ED web site if you like).

2. Duplicate the background layer. Select All and go to Layer > New > Layer Via Copy, or simply drag the background layer to the new layer icon at the bottom of the layers palette. It seems this point is reiterated a lot, but I rarely, if ever, alter an original. This is because you could easily change around an original image and not have another saved version to revert back to.

3. Make a selection around the central character(s) using the Polygonal Lasso tool, with feather set to 2-4 pixels (Select > Feather). In this case, the background will be the moving object, giving the illusion of the bull and rider being in motion.

4. Now inverse the selection (Select > Inverse) and apply the Motion Blur filter, with Angle set to 0, with a Distance of 10 pixels:

Time in motion

Motion Blur can also be used to dress up your studio images for print and ad designs. Let's take a look at a 'Time in Motion' effect. This image is called 'time.psd'.

From this point on, I'm assuming that your image is open and you are working on a duplicate of the original image.

Here we are going to apply a motion blur to give the illusion that the watch is moving. This will be done by airbrushing away a normal layer to reveal a blurred layer.

1. Copy your image layer.

2. Apply a Motion Blur to the duplicate layer: Angle 0, Distance 40.

3. Go to Layer > Add Layer Mask > Hide All.

4. Select white as your foreground color.

5. Select the Airbrush tool. Use a fairly large brush size. 65 is the setting for this example.

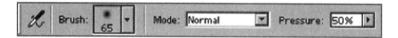

6. Begin painting along the edge you want to 'move'.

   As the white is applied to the layer mask, the blur becomes apparent again, though only along the edge where the Airbrush was applied.

This effect can be enhanced further by duplicating and moving layers so that the image is staggered across the canvas. Try reducing the opacity of the topmost layers so that the original image is not lost in the blur.

Motion Blur and metal textures

Another popular use for the Motion Blur tool is adding realism to metal type and interface effects. Here's how to duplicate this effect the fast and easy way. You may also want to consider saving this as an action (see Chapter 12) so you may duplicate the effect later with a single click of the mouse.

1. Open or create a new image where you want your type.

2. Select the Type tool, and in the tool options bar click on the second button to create a type mask. Now type your text into the image.

3. Select a light gray for your foreground color and a dark gray for the background.

4. Select the Gradient tool and in the tool options bar, set it to a Linear Gradient. Fill your text from the upper left hand corner of the selection to the lower right.

> *The Reflected Gradient works well for this also, but you will want to start your fill from the center of the selection.*

5. Duplicate this layer.

6. Go to Filter > Noise > Add Noise. Set the Amount to 25%, with Gaussian Distribution, uncheck the Monochromatic box and press OK.

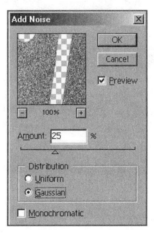

7. Then apply the Motion Blur filter. Set the Angle to 27 and Distance to 20 pixels.

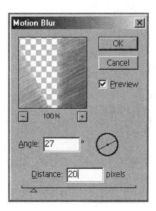

8. We're now going to apply a layer style. Go to Layer > Layer Style > Bevel and Emboss. Set the Style as Inner Bevel with the following settings:

- Technique: Smooth
- Depth: 1000
- Direction: Up
- Size: 9 px
- Soften: 0 px

For shading, use the defaults with the following exceptions: Select the Ring Contour for the Gloss Contour setting by right-clicking on the Gloss Contour box and selecting it. Change the Highlight/Shadow opacities to 100%.

You should have a pretty fair metal effect by now, but to enhance it try applying a curve to the text layer.

9. Go to Image > Adjust > Curves and apply the following settings:

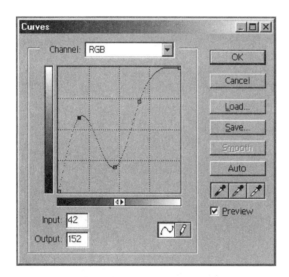

Here's the resulting effect:

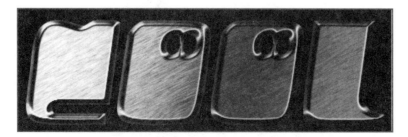

Brush Strokes to Render filter groups

The Brush Strokes, Distort, Noise, Pixelate, Sketch and Render filter groups are wonderful for generating cool images. Artistic filter effects are great, and the variations are limitless. Specific uses are hard to nail down over a large audience; paper required to write that book would wipe out a small forest. Let's go ahead and take a peek at what these groups have to offer, and feel free to experiment at your leisure.

Brush Strokes

The similarity between this filter group and the Artistic filters is striking; in truth they operate on the same precept. The difference here is Brush Strokes pays more attention to edge definition, giving a 'painted' impression.

Accented Edges: This filter sets a trace line around the edges between 2 contrasting colors, either with a glow or darkened line depending on your settings.

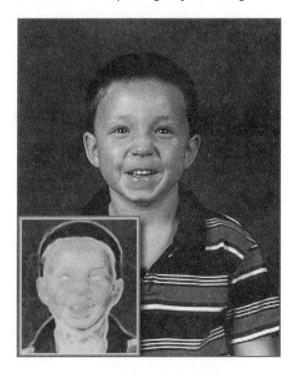

Angled Strokes: This filter recognizes similar colors and blurs them directionally, much like the Motion Blur.

Crosshatch: This filter is similar to Angled Strokes, but blurs in 2 directions simultaneously and overlaps the effect. It tries to emulate a drawing/etching effect called **crosshatching**.

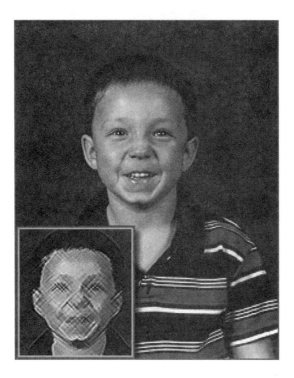

Dark Strokes: Takes the darker areas and increases shading by adding dark diagonal strokes. This filter also adds a blur to the lighter areas.

Dark images will appear black after applying this filter.

Ink Outlines: As the name implies, this filter generates an effect that makes the image appear as though the image was created with pen and ink.

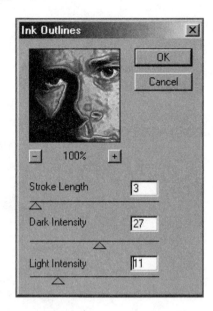

Spatter: Spatter paints your photo on a canvas. This is the only filter in the group that does not accent the edges, or areas between stark color differences in an image. Also, once pixels are grouped together they maintain their original color values.

Sprayed Strokes: Call this one 'Spatter Light with Strokes'.

Sumi-e: This is a more robust version of the Dark Strokes filter. The effect generates dark strokes, but they are thicker than their predecessor.

The remaining sets:

I won't run through the descriptions of the filters here, meaning we can move on to bigger and better things. Here are the lists of what these other filter groups contain. Again, I urge you to try them out at your leisure - experimentation is always (well, almost) encouraged.

Distort Filters:

Diffuse Glow
Displace
Glass
Ocean Ripple
Pinch
Polar Coordinates
Ripple
Shear
Spherize

Twirl
Wave
Zig-Zag

Noise Filters:

Add Noise
Despeckle
Dust & Scratches
Median

Pixilate Filters:

Color Halftone
Crystallize
Facet
Fragment
Mezzotint
Mosaic
Pointillize

Render Filters:

3D Transform
Clouds
Difference Clouds
Lens Flare
Lighting Effects (See Below)
Texture Fill

Sketch Filters:

Bas Relief
Chalk & Charcoal
Charcoal
Chrome
Conte' Crayon
Graphic Pen
Halftone Pattern
Note Paper
Photocopy
Plaster
Reticulation
Stamp
Torn Edges
Water Paper

Sharpening filters

Like the Blur tools, the **Sharpen filters** are some of the more useful in Photoshop. Whilst it is no substitute for having a good image in the first place, they may be used to clean up images that have lost resolution due to poor scans or file size reduction, and can help when trying to draw out contrast in photos for the Web. The first three filters – Sharpen, Sharpen More, and Sharpen Edges – are fine for adjusting images that needn't be precise (as in displaying personal photos on the Web for example), but the illusion of sharpness they create is exactly that: an illusion. These filters do not allow for fine-tuning, and in the case of Sharpen More the change can be quite drastic.

For the reasons stated above, the best tool here at your disposal is the Unsharp Mask tool. We will go into a bit of detail on this great filter, but let's take a look at the other three.

Sharpen/Sharpen More: These filters sample adjacent pixels and adjust the color to give them a bit more contrast, by finding edges and increasing the contrast along them.

Before Sharpen:

After Sharpen:

As you can see, there isn't much difference in the before and after images.

When we get into Sharpen More however, the difference is much more apparent:

After Sharpen More:

That really changes things! Again, the primary reason not to use these filters is there is no way to adjust the amount of change.

Sharpen Edges: Here again, this filter may not be too useful for production work for the same reason as Sharpen and Sharpen More. This filter samples the colors of the image and increases the difference in the edges between the colors of greatest difference.

We can see this effect in action by creating a black/white gradient fill and zooming in.

Before Sharpen Edges:

After Sharpen Edges:

Note that only the pixels next to the areas of greatest contrast are affected. The gradient is still apparent in the lighter shaded area.

Unsharp Mask

This filter is unique in that it creates a second, blurred image that remains unseen by the user. When you apply an Unsharp Mask, Photoshop samples the difference between the 2 images. This invisible mask helps the program distinguish between the areas of greatest difference, smoothing the larger areas of like-colors and darkening/sharpening the edges. In effect you have 2 functions being performed: sharpening and smoothing. The result is an apparently clearer image without an increase in resolution.

Here's an example:

Before Unsharp Mask:

Settings for Unsharp Mask:

After Unsharp Mask:

Unsharp Mask is also **the** tool to clean up those less-than-perfect scans.

Stylize, Texture, Video and Other

As we approach the end of the Photoshop filters menu, we find 4 more sets that, though they can also help create some very interesting effects, can be very specific to particular artists in the Photoshop world as a whole. These filter sets are as follows:

Stylize: These filters offer computer style effects. As such these do not try to duplicate any real world styles:

- Diffuse
- Emboss
- Extrude
- Find edges
- Glowing Edges
- Solarize
- Tiles
- Trace Contour
- Wind

Glowing Edges filter

This is the one filter I use on a semi-regular basis. It is a great tool for turning photos into a reasonable semblance of pencil drawings.

1. Open your image, making sure it is in RGB mode.

2. Go to Image > Adjust > Desaturate

3. Now go to Filter > Stylize > Glowing Edges. If you would like to take out some of the graininess, apply a Smart Blur.

Texture:

This set contains 6 filters, each designed to make an image appear as though it were printed on a rough surface. This filter group is popular for generating backgrounds, applying texture or improving interfaces. The Filters are:

- Craquelure
- Grain
- Mosaic Tiles
- Patchwork
- Stained Glass
- Texturizer

For a quick example of this filter set, take a peek at a photo run through each filter:

Before Texture Filters:

Left to Right, Top to Bottom: Craquelure, Grain, Mosaic Tiles, Patchwork, Stained Glass, Texturizer

Other filters group:

This filter set is designed to allow the user more control over their Photoshop toolbox. With this set you can create your own filters, offset selections, modify masks or make quick color adjustments. Filters in this set are:

- Custom
- DitherBox
- High Pass
- Maximum
- Minimum
- Offset

Creating your own filters

This can be a powerful feature in the right hands, but is probably one of the least used filters in the entire menu.

What this filter does is allow you to set color variations of pixels and those adjacent to them. This principle is based on a set mathematical formula; the process using this formula is called **Convolution**.

With an image open, select
Filter > Other > Custom.

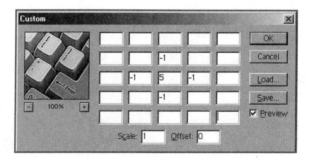

Start entering small number values in the corners, and even try changing the default values in small increments.

Keep an eye on the viewer window to see how the values alter your image.

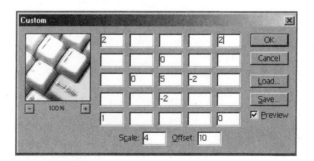

Once you are satisfied, save your filter. These are then saved in a list for you to get at and use in future. Note: Custom Filters have the file extension of .acf.

Video filter set

The primary use for these two filters (De-Interlace and NTSC Colors) is to correct images taken from video for use in other media or to prepare image for video application respectively. Unless you do a bit of video production you'll find little or no use for these filters. If you do video work, however, you will find these fairly useful.

De-Interlace: You have seen the scanlines effect all over the Web. There are actions, tutorials, and .pdf templates on nearly every web site dedicated to Photoshop created for the sole purpose of creating scanlines. Indeed, I use them quite extensively in my work.

Video images are produced by lines shooting across the screen. This causes some horizontal artifacts to be transferred to images taken from a video capture. De-Interlace re-samples the image, trying to compensate for the variations in color caused by the lines.

Due to the limits of print, I'm going to duplicate the effect on a photo using a standard scanlines technique.

For quick scanlines, create a new white image 1 pixel wide by 2 pixels high. Select the pencil tool, and fill the top or bottom half of your image with black. Define the pattern. Now you have a great scanlines pattern to apply to your images!

Image with scanlines:

Oh, if only those pesky scanlines weren't so predominant.

Here's a look at what De-Interlace will do for correcting this problem:

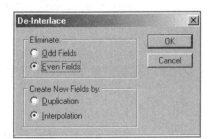

In this case, with the Even Fields selected, our image became significantly brighter. The scanlines are invisible now due to the resampling, but keep in mind that our image only had the illusion of being scanned. True video images may react differently and, in some cases, don't work at all.

Let's take a look at what the Odd Fields will give us:

As expected, this example is significantly darker than the original. The scanlines have been all but done away with, but some additional correction will be needed to make this a quality photo.

All these two options really do is eliminate the odd or even rows, starting from the top of the image.

Duplication: This fills in the deleted row by duplicating the previous scanline. This effect has a tendency of creating a fuzzy or slightly blurred image, so this is not always the best option.

Interpolation: Rather than duplicate already existing lines, this averages the scans before and after the deleted line. The resulting information is then placed in the deleted row. This is by far the best way to retain image integrity and give you a better effect overall.

NTSC Filters: Video operates in a color realm removed from standard imaging, and as a result images that are to be transferred to a video medium need to be converted to a color format the video will recognize. NTSC colors convert the color of individual pixels to the nearest color value a video will recognize. Often the change is indiscernible until placed in your video editing software or viewed on a video monitor.

Third party filters

Adobe Photoshop has created a monster. By this I mean an entire software industry has developed as a result of Photoshop's ability to incorporate plug-ins and filters developed by others. Adobe promotes third party development, providing an in-depth Software Developers Kit on the Adobe web site. This in combination with end user add-on development (actions, brushes, layer styles, patterns, filters, etc.) increases Photoshop's already impressive production values a hundredfold.

A downside to this glut of software is knowing which filters can genuinely help in your work and which are better left to collect dust on the sale rack. This is where organizations such as the National Association of Photoshop Professionals (NAPP) come in. They are the largest trade organization in the world dedicated to Photoshop issues, as well as the publishers of Photoshop User magazine. If you have never visited their web site, I strongly encourage you to do so. Their address is www.photoshopuser.com. This site does charge a yearly membership fee. If you are short of funds you may also visit Planet Photoshop, which is also maintained by NAPP, www.planetphotoshop.com

Other means at your disposal to sorting out which filters to buy are newsgroups, Photoshop related web sites, and online forums devoted to your area of interest. Whether it be image correction, generating online graphics, type effects for print, etc., chances are a general search of Yahoo! or other search engine will turn up several hundred hits.

At this point I want to go through a few of the more popular third party filters available. Sit back and enjoy the show!

Eye Candy 4000

These packages are developed by Alien Skin Software (www.alienskin.com) and are some of the best filter sets available to date. Eye Candy 4000 boasts 23 fantastic effects filters, ranging from Antimatter to Wood. Granted, all of these filters may not be applicable to your work, but those that are definitely compensate for the cost. At the time of writing, a full version of Eye Candy 3 is available for download at www.actionfx.com, and this includes a demo of Eye Candy 4000.

Eye Candy 4000 Filters:

- Antimatter
- Bevel Boss
- Chrome
- Corona
- Drip
- Fire
- Fur
- Glass
- Gradient Glow
- HSB Noise
- Jiggle
- Marble
- Melt
- Motion Trail
- Shadowlab
- Smoke
- Squint
- Star
- Swirl
- Water Drops
- Weave
- Wood

Here's an example created using Eye Candy 4000. The total time to generate this image from scratch was about 2 minutes.

WWW.ALIENSKIN.COM

Auto F/X Software

This company has spent a great deal of time developing quality Photoshop add-ons, and I'd be remiss if I didn't give them a mention here.

Their software bundle (Studio Bundle 2.0) includes Typo/Graphic Edges, Photo/Graphic Patterns, Photo/Graphic Frames, and Ultimate Texture Collections. There is so much in this package you will be hard pressed to get through them all in a moderate amount of time. All of these CDs are professionally done, and the effects can be spectacular.

As I sit here writing this, another software package was delivered to me from this company. It is called **Dream Suite**, and at first glance appears to be yet another powerful package from these fine developers. You may find out more information on all their software at www.autofx.com.

Case Study

Now you have started playing around with filters, you are beginning to see all the amazing things you can do to images. Be careful to avoid the trap of filtering every image to death. There are so many options available but try to use some restraint, so that your images still appear tasteful.

We are going to apply some filters in combination to make our info page a bit more eye grabbing. Let's start with another popular special effect for our final exotic car. It is a technique called "pop dots"; they are a creative way of adding a border to an image. Then we will add a radial blur to give a feeling of motion.

1. Open image of a Mercedes, `info.jpg`.

2. Make a selection well into the border of the image. About an eighth of an inch all round will work fine.

3. We now need to soften the selection, so that it has a gradual edge and not a hard edge. Select > Feather *(ALT+CTRL/CMD+D)* and add a setting of 25 pixels for a nice soft transition.

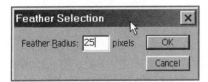

4. The image will have a selection running around it. We will need to invert the selection so that we will be editing the border and not the main image. Select > Inverse or SHIFT+CTRL/CMD+I. Do not deselect the image.

5. Press the Quick Mask button (dotted circle inside square) at the bottom of the toolbox or just press the Q key. You will see the red screen around the image to indicate you are in quick mask mode.

6. To apply our dots pattern: Filter > Sketch > Halftone Pattern... and add the following settings: Size 4, Contrast 0 and leave Pattern Type on Dot.

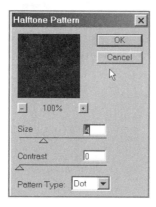

Your image should now look something like this.

7. Press the Standard Mode button in the toolbox or press keyboard again to return to normal mode.

8. Press the DELETE key and the selected areas will be deleted leaving you with your pop dots effect. Deselect your image.

9. We want to lighten the overall image so that we can apply type to it later on: Image > Adjust > Levels (CTRL/CMD+L). Drag the black slider on the very bottom of the Levels box to the right. This will lighten up all the shadows significantly.

10. The next thing we need to do is to resize the image for use as a web page. Set the Width to 760 pixels, using the Image Size box once again. Be sure the resolution is 72 dpi and that Constrain Proportions are checked.

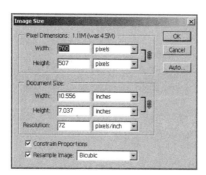

The reason we are setting it to 760 is to try and avoid a horizontal scroll bar appearing on an 800X600 resolution screen, which is the resolution that most monitors are set to. But it really depends on your target audience, if they have their Favorites *window open then the scroll bar will appear anyway! If you are using this case study to prepare your work for presentation on the Web, rather than just a demo, you may want to go back to our splash page and resize that too.*

One thing that really helps type to be more readable with an image in the background is for the picture to be blurred. Since this web page is about cars, let's make the blur look like motion.

11. Filter > Blur > Radial Blur, use Zoom for the Blur Method (leave Quality on Good). Use an Amount of 25%; much higher and you would no longer be able to make out the picture clearly.

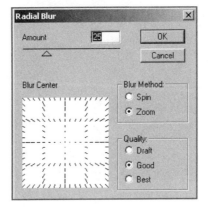

Here is the result of the zoom blur. It's the same effect as a camera lens zooming in on a subject.

info.jpg @ 100% (RGB)

12. Save the image as `info.jpg` at the highest quality.

We have added some nice filtering effects to the image that will be the background for our information page. In the next chapter you're going to learn about advanced layering techniques. We will use these to add the final changes to our images in the next part of the case study, before we finish the case study in Chapter 11 with the final preparations for showing our pages on the Web. I warn you now – the last two sections of the case study are going to be long!

Summary

In this chapter we took a look at the Photoshop 6 filters menu. Perhaps you will not have a need for all, even half, of these filters. Like any good toolbox, it is good to have those extra tools handy, just in case. Adobe is masterful at analyzing all possible uses for their software, and then catering to all those different niches with high performance filters specific to the needs of those designers, whatever their area of expertise.

10 Advanced Layers

What we'll cover in this chapter:

- *Copying layers between documents*

- *Layer masks*

- *Overlaying layers with patterns*

- *Copying layer masks*

- *Combining layer masks and effects*

- *History Brush tool*

- *Layer opacity*

- *Layer blending modes*

- *Layer modes in use*

- *Creative options for layer blending modes*

- *Rendering type*

- *Merging layers*

▶

You are well into your journey and approaching your goals of becoming proficient with the world's most powerful graphics program. This chapter is going to propel you further down the road. Have you ever looked at all those exciting montages and compositions on the Web or in magazines and wondered how they do it? Perhaps this is the reason you are learning Photoshop? These kinds of media are full of incredible pieces of art created in Photoshop. This chapter is going to teach you the secrets of the professionals.

We are going to be learning advanced layers techniques. I am excited to be writing this chapter because I know it's going to have a bigger impact on your design than any other. You will be amazed at the power of layers once they are unleashed and you'll also be amazed at how easy it is. So, let's go spill the beans on those closely guarded secrets...

Copying layers between documents

Before we jump in, let's examine the quickest way to copy layers from one open document to another. All you have to do is open both documents, then copy and paste or drag and drop, using the Move tool, from one document to another (from the source to the target). You can do this with either:

- A background
- A layer
- Multiple layers at once (as long as they are linked)
- Layer styles
- Layer masks

First of all we would open both the target and the source files loaded into Photoshop.

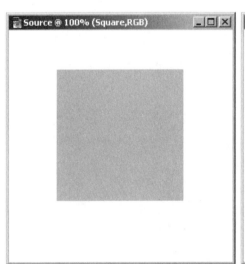

Then drag the layer from the pallet in the source file to the target file.

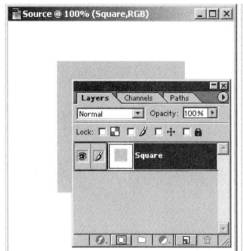 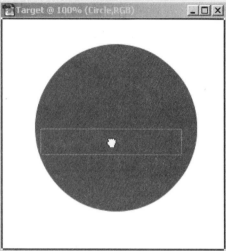

This would leave it on top in the target layer palette.

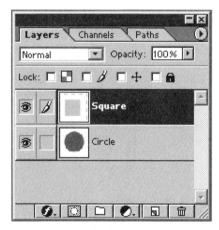

There are some things you need to know when you are copying to a new document:

■ The **Target** document will control the resolution and color space. Because of this the color and size of the layer may change when it is in the new document.

■ To drop the new layer exactly in the center of the target document, hold the SHIFT key while dropping.

You cannot copy an indexed color document into another color space; you have to convert it to RGB first.

When you copy a layer into a new document, sometimes the source file is much larger than the target. Don't panic, it's easily fixed. The solution is to use the **Free Transform** tool to scale the new layer down to the right size.

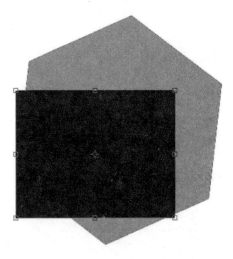

But what if it's so large and you can't see the bounding box? Then you have to zoom out on your image until you can see the bounding box. This is a bit of a pain and it is the one thing I hate about Photoshop 6. In previous versions the bounding box always stayed within the frame. The workaround is to press CTRL/CMD+T for Free Transform (Edit > Free Transform). In the tool options bar there are dimension percentages:

Click on the chain to make sure that the height and width are linked.

Now, in that layer, change them to 50% and the image should now be small enough to see the bounding box, if not, then keep scaling down until you can see the handles. Then you can click and drag to resize like before. Trust me, this tip will come in useful many times.

If you drop the layer into your document and it's too small, you can scale it larger. However you want to try to avoid this as much as possible because when you enlarge an object too much, there won't be enough pixel information to provide a sharp image and the result will be 'the jaggies' (pixelization), unless you are using a vector object.

Layer masks

Since we just covered a little theory, let's stay with the spirit of the book and get you busy before you forget it. Nothing like hands on.

1. Open two documents on your desktop. I've used images of a chessboard and a speedometer. Both these images are 450 x 450 pixels, 72 dpi and RGB. You can use your own images that have some depth of field and are of similar size and DPI, or use the ones on the friends of ED web site. I always like to build in RGB mode, there are several reasons:

   - All the filters will work

   - Smaller file sizes (3 channels rather than 4 for CMYK)

   - Larger color gamut (more colors available)

2. We're going to build a collage with our two images. Drag the source image into the target (in this case I'm dragging Chessboard in to Speedometer), while holding down SHIFT. You will now have 2 documents, the source is unchanged, but the target now has a background and a new layer called Layer 1. Give this layer a suitable name.

3. Close the old document and save the new one under a different name; say speed chess.psd.

4. Now it's time to enter into the really cool stuff; **Layer masks**. This is where we can start to blend different images together really smoothly. With your new layer active, click on the add layer mask button.

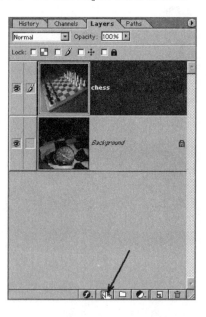

Notice that a mask is displayed next to the layer thumbnail. See the chain? As you are learning, in Photoshop it always means something is linked. In this case the layer mask is linked to the Chess layer.

One more thing to note and this is important; you will see that to the left of the thumbnail, the paintbrush icon is gone and it is replaced with a circle inside a square. This means that when you paint in the image window, you are painting on the mask and not on the layer itself.

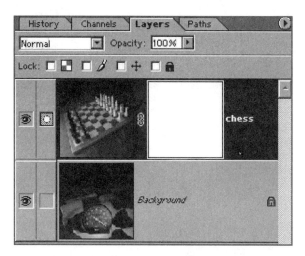

5. Select the Gradient tool. Set it for foreground to background, linear gradient. If necessary, swap the foreground and background colors, so that white is the foreground, and black is the background (press D to switch to the default).

6. Apply your gradient from the top right and drag it about three quarters of the way to the left corner.

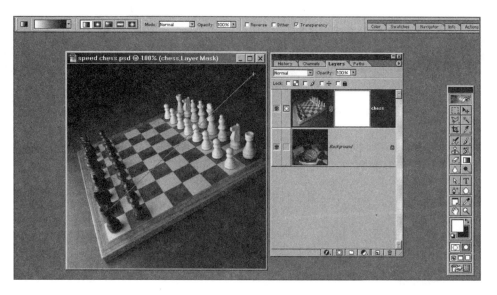

Suddenly we have an instant blend! Wasn't that cool? Go on, hit undo and do it again just for fun. OK, finished playing? Notice that our gradient is now showing in the layer mask.

What just happened? Here is a little more theory, but don't worry, it will be painless.

Imagine that our layer is a really dirty window. So dirty in fact that we can scratch through the dust and make a picture of Doug-the-Dust-Bug with our finger.

Our window has a beautiful criss-cross pattern in the glass. Of course you can't see it because the window is so dirty. If you were to come along with a rag and wipe the top left part clean, you would be able to see the window and Doug would be partly wiped away.

Now the drawback with this is if we wanted to restore Doug, we couldn't, he is gone forever. This is called **destructive editing**. That is the great thing about layer masks. Instead of rubbing away Doug, we can rub away at a mask that represents the positioning of the layer. If we change our mind, we just change the mask. Doug is never touched. This is called **non-destructive editing**.

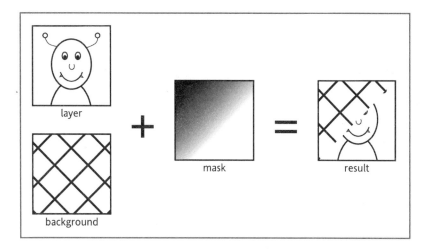

When we add a layer mask to a layer, it reacts with the underlying layers in this way:

- Where we put black on the mask, it erases the layer, and the layers beneath it become visible
- Vice-versa when we paint white into the mask, just like magic we paint our image back in

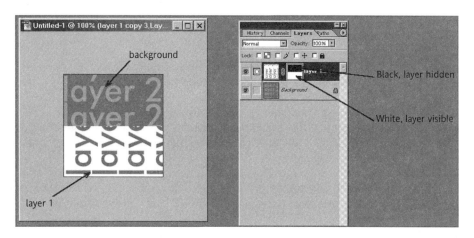

This image demonstrates it even more clearly. See how the mask was filled with black and then I painted in white and it shows the top layer:

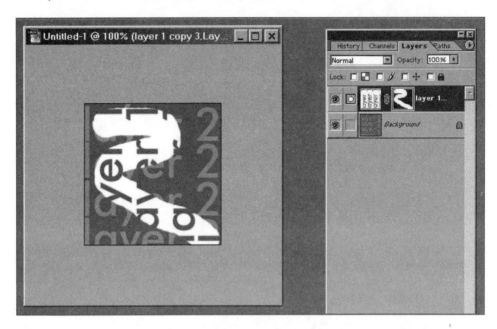

Continuing on our project:

7. Set your foreground color to black, if it's not already (X switches your colors around), and select a 40 pixel hard brush.

8. Paint inside the speedometer. Notice how it appears nice and clear where you paint. Try not to go over edges. (If you want to see what you are doing, reduce the opacity slightly on the layer so you can see what's underneath and work more accurately.)

9. If you wanted you could have used a **circular marquee** and filled it with black. Look at the mask and you will see where the black has been painted around the speedometer.

You can also adjust the opacity of the top layer a bit to help you see what you are doing, then change it back afterwards.

Overlaying a layer with a pattern

A very popular technique in layering and collaging is using patterns to overlay the images. The scan lines and grids are the most popular of the current techniques. Here we are going to walk through the grid technique. First we will make the grid pattern, then we are going to create a layer with the pattern. After that we are going to further explore layer masks with an advanced technique.

1. To make the grid, create a new document. Make it 10x10 pixels, 72dpi and RGB, and be sure to select transparent as the background.

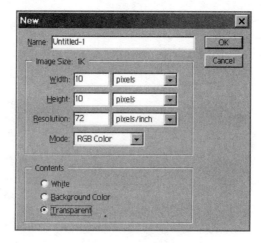

2. Zoom up to 1600% so you can see what you are doing. Select the Single Column Marquee tool.

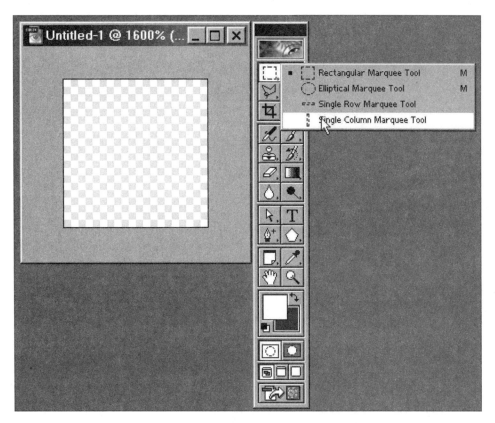

3. Select 1 pixel on the left side and fill with white (Edit > Fill; SHIFT+BACKSPACE). Switch to the Single Row Marquee tool, select the top pixels and fill with white.

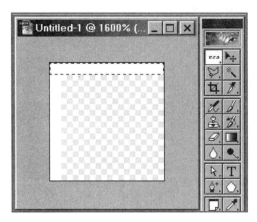

4. All right, you have created the base of the texture. Select the entire document by clicking Select > All and hit Edit > Define Pattern. Name it `grid` and you now have the pattern saved to Photoshop.

5. Back to our collage image: Create a new layer and also call it `grid`. Go to Edit > Fill and then under Contents select Pattern. Find the pattern we created by using the drop-down menu next to Custom Pattern, and select it. Press OK.

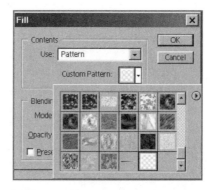

6. We now have a layer filled with a grid pattern.

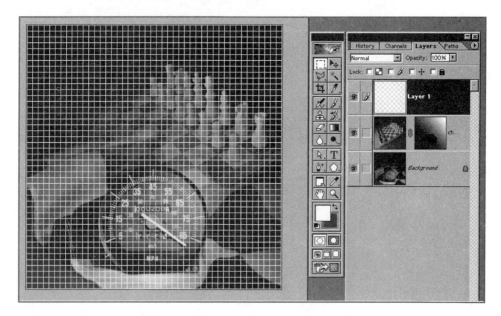

The only problem is that we have the grid covering the entire image. Not too attractive. The trick to great montage is knowing how much is too much of a good thing. The grid covering the entire image is definitely too much.

We already know that the layer mask is an ideal way to hide parts of an image and provide maximum creative freedom. After all, a major part of creativity is experimentation and layer masks provide maximum creativity. Why create a whole new mask, when we can utilize the one we already made on the chess layer!

7. With our Grid layer still active, CTRL/CMD+CLICK on the chess layer mask. You will now see the marching ants to indicate that the mask's selection is active. Do you see that you can load a mask as easy as a layer? The CTRL/CMD CLICK trick is very useful when working with layers and channels.

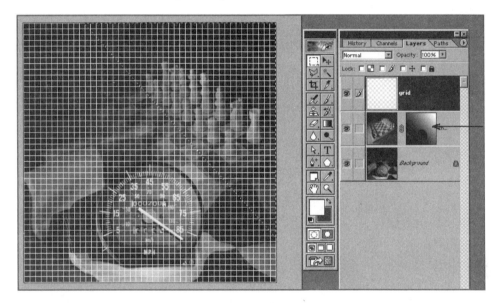

8. Now click on the Add a mask button. Notice that the mask is identical to the chess layer mask? That is how you copy a mask. As long as there is an active selection, the new mask will pick it up. See how the speedometer is visible again? You now have 2 layers with masks. You can create as many layers as you want with masks and they will all interact with each other. However as you add more layers you will find that your file size increases which puts a greater demand on your processor and memory. Save your file.

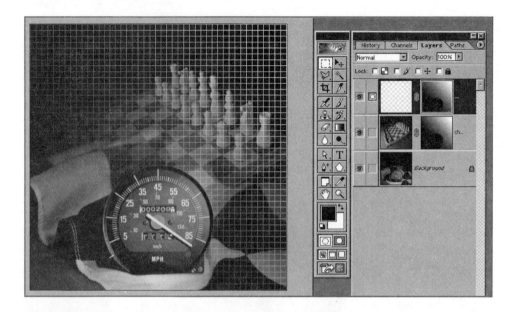

Combining Layer masks and effects

Let's look at another way we can use layer masks to quickly add extra pizzazz to an image. What we are going to do here is apply a filter to just certain parts of an image. Well, at least that's what it will look like. In reality, we will apply the filter to the entire image and then use the layer mask to 'un-apply' the filter to certain parts of the image. We will start with the original image again.

1. Open the original source image (we'll start afresh for this example).

2. The first thing we need to do is duplicate the layer. Do this by dragging the layer into the new layer icon. We now have two identical layers. This allows us to mess up one as much as we want while maintaining a good copy to restore at anytime.

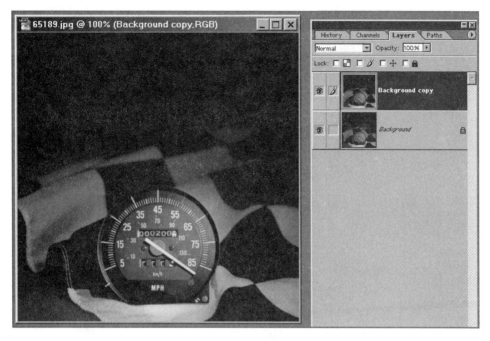

3.   Hide the top layer and select the bottom layer. Let's apply a zoom blur to give the feel of speed and movement. Go to Filter > Blur > Radial blur then select Zoom, give it a setting of 88. Keep the other settings as default. The Best setting is good for the zoom, but to be honest, I don't think the improvement in quality is worth the extra rendering time most of the time. Press OK when you're done.

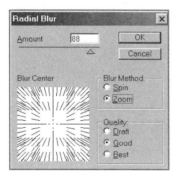

4.   Cool! A totally blurred image.

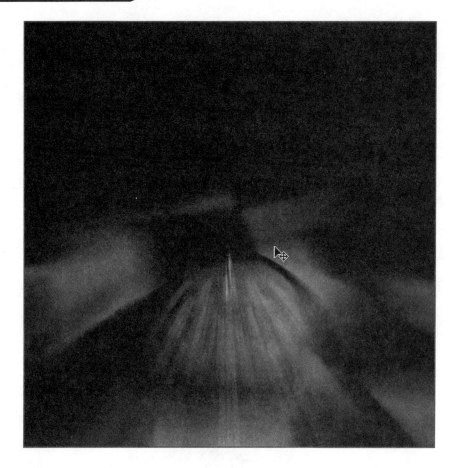

We need to restore the speedometer, otherwise no one will know what the image is supposed to be.

5. Now we'll reveal our top layer by clicking on the eye again.

6. You will see the effect is now hidden because it is on the underlying layer. We'll add a layer mask to the top layer and be sure you are editing on the mask – look for the square with a circle in it.

7. With the Elliptical Marquee tool, make a selection around the speedometer (holding down Shift will keep it a circle, and holding down Alt will start the selection at the center of the circle). If it's not quite centered you can use the arrow keys to nudge it into place.

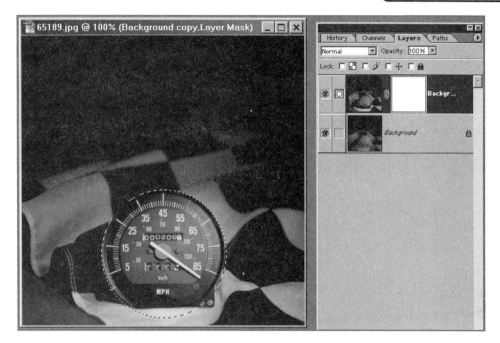

8. Because we want to hide this entire layer *except* for the speedometer, we will need to inverse the selection. Press SHIFT+CTRL/CMD+I or go Select > Inverse. Now fill the selection with black and you will now see your speedometer zooming through space.

9. Looks pretty good! However, I can't resist giving it that little extra something. Did you know that you can apply layer effects to a layer mask? Do this by going to Layer > Layer Style > Blending Options. I added some layer effects just for fun (be sure that the boxes for these options are checked to activate them). The settings are shown here:

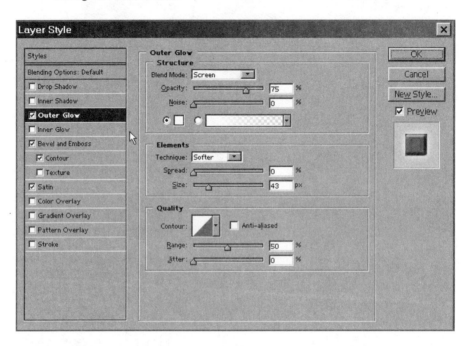

- For Outer Glow, I used the default settings apart from Size, that was pushed up to 43 px.

- For Bevel and Emboss the default settings looked fine.

- For Satin, I dropped the Opacity to 20%, changed the Angle to 27°, Distance to 103 px, Size to 49, and changed Contour to Ring Double.

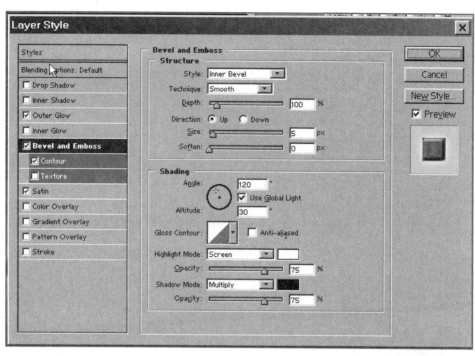

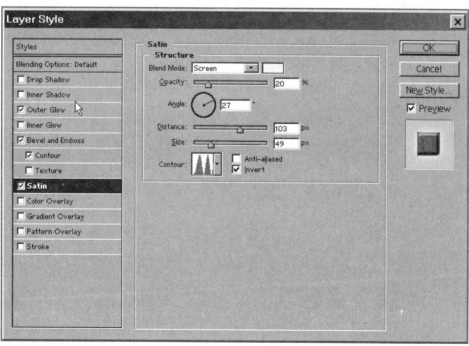

Doesn't that just make the image pop? It's amazing what you can do to an image with layer masks and a little imagination. Save the image as speedo.psd.

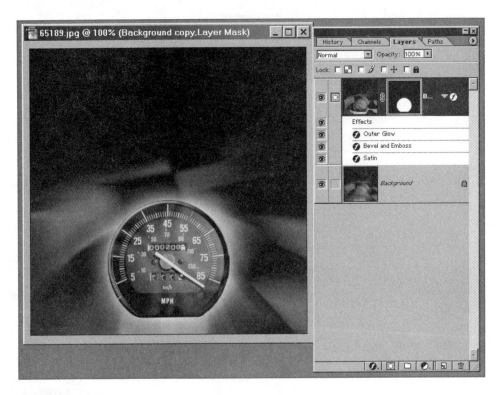

History brush

There is another way to achieve this effect with the use of only one layer and the History brush.

1. Open the image you want to experiment with (I've used the speedometer image again). Also open the History palette.

2. Apply the Radial Blur to the layer. Notice that this new History state is added to the History palette.

The History Brush works just like a regular brush, but it has the ability to go backwards in time. The brush will paint with whatever state you select in the palette. It will begin to paint the image how it was back then, right over the top of the current state.

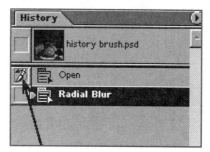

3. Click on the Open state, you will see that your image is now displayed as it was when you first opened it. This is what will be painted by the History Brush.

4. Highlight the Radial Blur state again and select the box just to the left of the Open state.

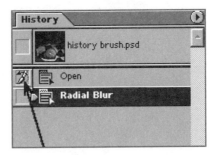

5. Select the History Brush tool and choose a large, soft brush. I chose a soft 30 pixel brush. Now begin to paint onto the speedometer. You will see your old image begin to be restored. Keep painting until you restore the entire part of the image that you want restored.

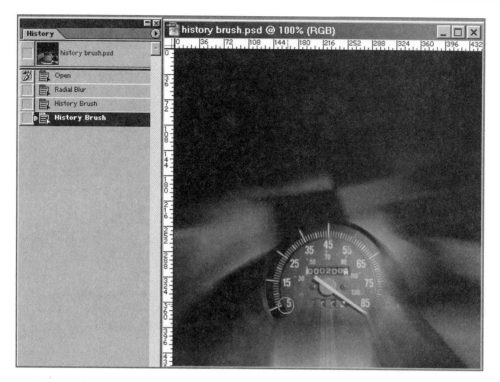

All this on only one layer! This is a very useful trick, with endless creative possibilities. I love to use this trick a lot with photographs. For example, take a picture of a racing car, apply a motion blur to the entire image and then 'history brush' back in the car, this will give a great feeling of movement. Another use of the tool is to desaturate all the color out of an image and then use the History Brush to apply color to only certain areas.

The disadvantage of this is that you can't apply a layer style to the mask because there is no mask. I would also suggest always working like this on a *copy* of your original image, so that you have something to revert to if you mess it all up.

Layer opacity

Returning to our main exercise, let's add the blurred speedometer to the composition we are building.

1. First of all, click on the background in the target document. The reason we do that is because when we drag and drop, the new layer is created right on top of the active layer.

2. Open the image speedo.psd. This will become our source image.

3. In the speedo.psd image, link the two layers in the image so that they will both be moved together.

4. Drag and drop the layers into the speed chess document. Don't forget to hold the SHIFT key while dragging to center them.

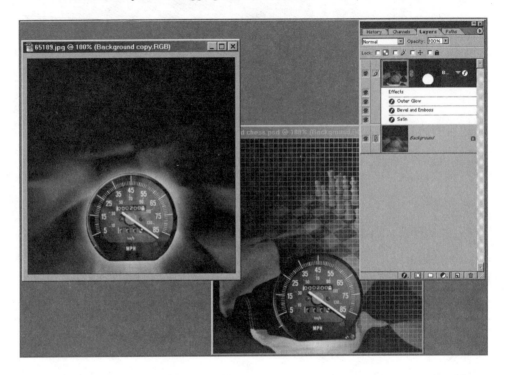

You will see our layers and layer masks are all intact as they are dropped into the new document.

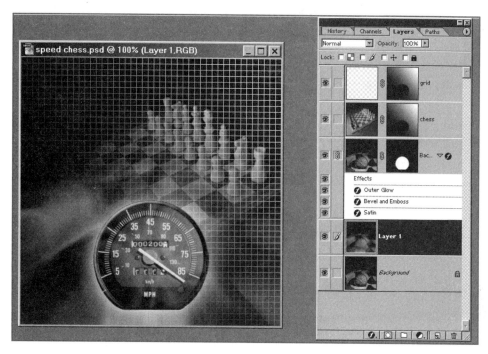

Just a couple of little things to clean up:

Rename Layer 1 as blurred background.

6. I really like the blurred flag, but let's tone it down a bit. Lower the opacity on the blurred layer just enough so we get a nice mix of the blur and the flag underneath.

Double-click on the layer and lower the opacity to 86%.

> *Opacity is just another way of saying transparency. Opaque is the opposite of transparent. As you lessen the opacity you actually make the layer more transparent.*

7. While we are on the subject of transparency, let's lower the opacity to 38% on the grid layer.

That is an integral part of creating montages and collages. You have to be able to have the opacity just right. You can have a terrible looking composition, then tweak the transparency just a bit and turn it into something beautiful.

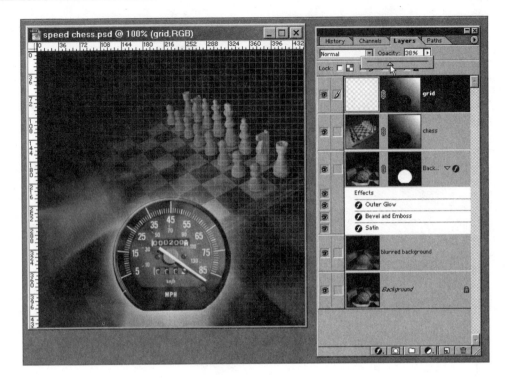

Layer blending modes

Now if you want real interactivity and powerful creative effects, **Layer blending modes** are the way to go.

At the top of the Layers palette is a window where you can select different blending modes. These incredibly useful modes affect the way that layers interact with each other. The best way to really get a feel for these is for you to experiment with them. Find out what works best for the image you are working on. I am going to avoid going into a lengthy, boring explanation of each mode. Instead I will just list them and then show you some ways you can use a couple of them, then it's up to you to experiment! I will explain them as the modes affect the top layer.

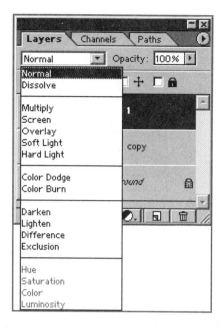

These modes are divided into five types.

Type one

The color and opacity are unaffected.

- **Normal**: This is the standard mode, the opacity affecting the transparency of the layer.

- **Dissolve:** When you lower the opacity the layer dissolves, a bit like bad TV reception, rather than turns transparent.

The dissolve effect can be used to create a nice chalky effect:

Type two

Deals with the screen values of black, white, and gray; the best options for overlaying images and layers.

- **Multiply:** The white areas on the top layer appear transparent. Only the darker areas affect the layer underneath. This is commonly used for drop shadows, allowing the underlying color to bleed through.

- **Screen:** The opposite of multiply. Only the lighter areas will have an effect.

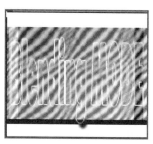

- **Overlay**: Works like multiply mode and screen together the areas with gray value are visible

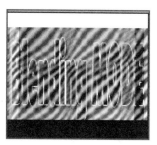

■ **Soft Light**: Very similar to overlay, but with less opacity.

■ **Hard light**: 50% gray disappears and white and black are unaffected.

The Hard Light effect has made the gray shades near 50% transparent, but left them solid at areas of solid black or white.

Type three

Brightens/darkens the base color. Great for highlights and shadows.

- **Color Dodge**: Works a lot like screen, except it lets the colors and underlying texture through. Use this mode to paint highlights onto images.

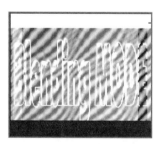

Color Dodge has brought out the lighter areas of the lettering here to enhance their 3D feeling.

- **Color Burn**: The opposite of the dodge mode. Used to paint deeper shadows onto images.

Type four

These are good to get radical and psychedelic effects.

- **Darken**: Where the top layer is darker it becomes dominant. Where it is lighter, the underlying image becomes dominant.

In this image the letter O is in front of the M, but appears behind because it is lighter in that area.

- **Lighten**: The opposite of Darken.

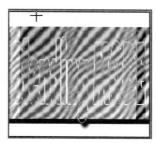

- **Difference**: Inverts the color where the layers overlap. Black is ignored.

- **Exclusion**: Same as difference, but with less intensity.

Type five

Color-based effects; these are more practical modes, which affect certain aspects of the image at a time to change the underlying image.

- **Hue**: This is the way to change the color of an image. When you apply the hue mode, only the color is affected in the underlying image. All the other properties are unaffected.

- **Saturation**: Affects only the **amount** of color in the underlying image. When you overlay with a strong color, the color itself is ignored and only the strength of the color is applied. If the top color is black, white or gray, then the image underneath will appear without color as a grayscale image.

- **Color**: This is like hue and saturation mixed together. This is the best mode for colorizing grayscale pictures.

- **Luminosity**: this is the opposite of the color mode. The color will be preserved, but the grayscale values can be changed.

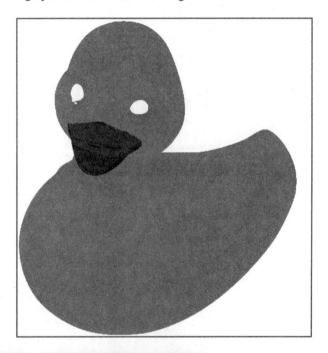

Layer blending modes in use

First let's look at a practical use of the layer blending mode. Then we will explore some creative options. This first example will give you a good idea of the power of layer modes.

We are going to overlay text with an image. By using the blending modes we can hide the paper and keep the text. This is a fairly common effect; a very useful thing to know for working in the real world.

1. Open two documents: a picture document and one of some scanned text. I'm going to use the chessboard image that I used for the main exercises, and an image of a white sheet of paper with black text.

2. We want to overlay the image with the text. Drag the text document into the picture image to create a new layer.

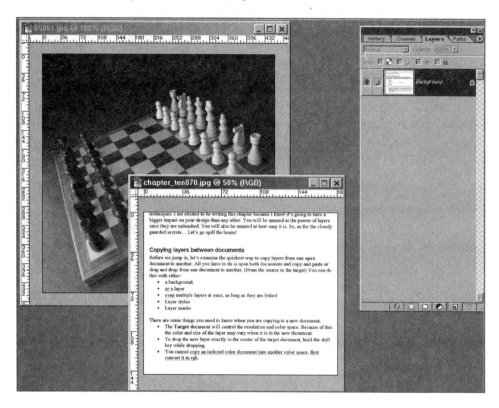

3. You now have the scanned text layer above the picture layer. The problem is that we have all the white paper hiding the image.

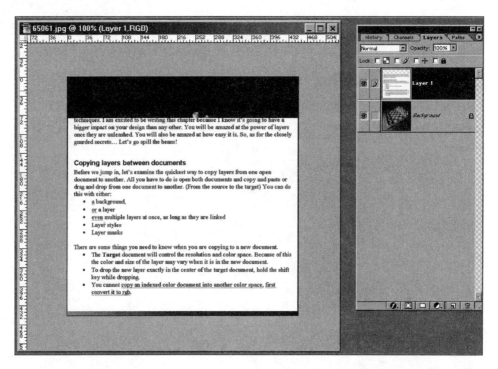

4. We could select all the white and delete it. But there is a better way. On the top layer, change it to Multiply mode. Just like magic all the text is clearly visible and the paper is gone. That's because multiply mode removes white from the top image and keeps the black data. This mode works on the grayscale value and the darker the tone, the more opaque it will be.

5. To show the effect better, I have lightened up the background image by using the Image > Adjust > Levels as shown here. Take the far bottom left slider and move it to the right, the shadows will all be lightened.

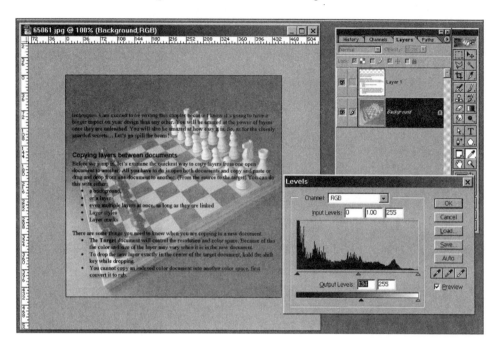

6. Let's try this again, only this time with the opposite problem. We have an image overlaid with reversed text. We have white text with a black background (you can do this to our document by using Image > Adjust > Invert or CTRL+I). This time the goal is to keep the white and hide the black.

techniques. I am excited to be writing this chapter because I know it's going to have a bigger impact on your design than any other. You will be amazed at the power of layers once they are unleashed. You will also be amazed at how easy it is. So, as for the closely guarded secrets... Let's go spill the beans!

Copying layers between documents

Before we jump in, let's examine the quickest way to copy layers from one open document to another. All you have to do is open both documents and copy and paste or drag and drop from one document to another. (From the source to the target) You can do this with either:

- a background,
- or a layer
- even multiple layers at once, as long as they are linked
- Layer styles
- Layer masks

There are some things you need to know when you are copying to a new document.

- The **Target** document will control the resolution and color space. Because of this the color and size of the layer may vary when it is in the new document.
- To drop the new layer exactly in the center of the target document, hold the shift key while dropping.
- You cannot copy an indexed color document into another color space, first convert it to rgb.

7. As it happens, screen mode works the opposite to multiply mode. By changing the mode to Screen, we now have beautiful white type over our image.

techniques. I am excited to be writing this chapter because I know it's going to have a bigger impact on your design than any other. You will be amazed at the power of layers once they are unleashed. You will also be amazed at how easy it is. So, as for the closely guarded secrets... Let's go spill the beans!

Copying layers between documents

Before we jump in, let's examine the quickest way to copy layers from one open document to another. All you have to do is open both documents and copy and paste or drag and drop from one document to another. (From the source to the target) You can do this with either:

- a background,
- or a layer
- even multiple layers at once, as long as they are linked
- Layer styles
- Layer masks

There are some things you need to know when you are copying to a new document.

- The **Target** document will control the resolution and color space. Because of this the color and size of the layer may vary when it is in the new document.
- To drop the new layer exactly in the center of the target document, hold the shift key while dropping.
- You cannot copy an indexed color document into another color space, first convert it to rgb.

Here is a variation of this effect just for fun. I did the split screen effect by selecting the image, moving then to their layers and inverting the layers, then changing the blending mode.

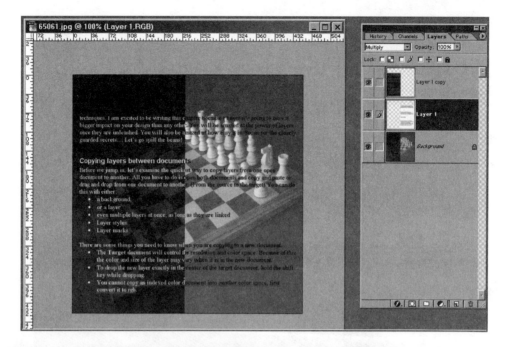

Creative options for layer blending modes

Open up our speed chess image again – it's time to put those lessons to good use.

1. On the top speedometer layer (background copy) Change to Screen mode. See how it lets the white through from the underlying layer? This creates an interesting effect of movement and light. Lower to 49% opacity to increase this effect.

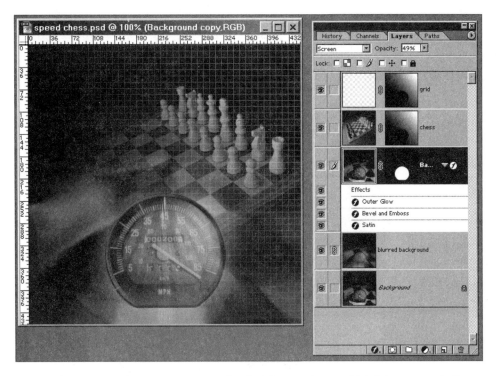

Let me demonstrate how you can use the Overlay mode to add brightness and vibrancy to an image. Almost like shining a soft light on areas of the subject.

2. Create a new layer. Call it overlay and move it to the top. Using the Elliptical Marquee tool draw a large circle, inverse the selection (CTRL/CMD+SHIFT+I) then fill it with white.

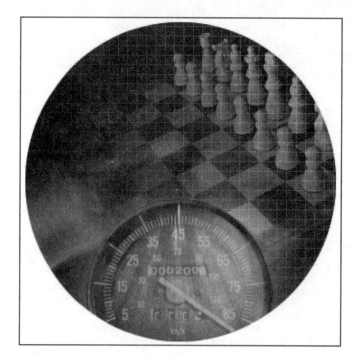

3. Deselect and apply a *Gaussian blur* (Filter > Blur > Gaussian Blur) of about 17 pixels.

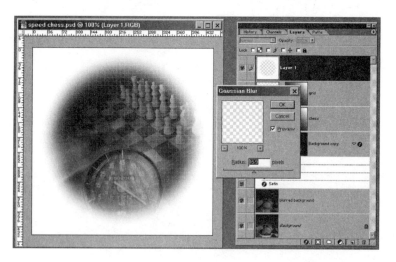

4. Now watch what happens when we apply the overlay mode. With the overlay mode applied, drop the opacity down to 70%.

Doesn't that just strengthen the image? Perhaps subtle, but turn the layer off and see how dull the image looks without it! It is always good to experiment, add layers and try different modes and effects. You could end up with lots of layers that you don't use, but you could always delete them later on or just hide them. A good collage is somewhat like a good music arrangement. The things that make it so good are not really noticed until they are not there. For instance, you don't really notice the rhythm guitar in a band until he or she stops playing, then it sounds like something is missing.

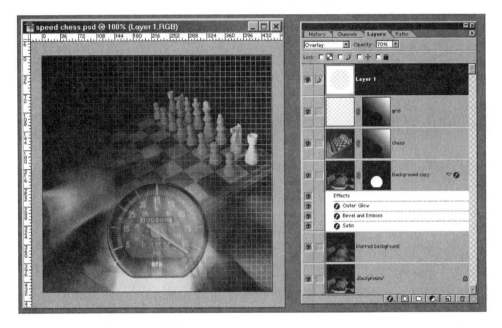

I want to demonstrate this mode again by adding a shaft of light:

5. Create a new layer and call it light. Using the Polygonal Lasso tool, draw the shape of a beam of light (a truncated triangle from top left to right, across the whole image).

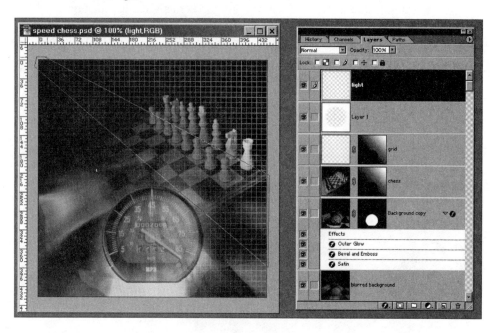

6. Make a feather of 15 pixels to soften the beam. The feather softens the edges of the selection. This will give us a nice blend instead of a hard edge. The larger the feather, the larger the blend and the result is a softer transition. Go to Select > Feather and enter 15 pixels.

7. Now fill with white. What a radical beam of light. We could soften it by lowering the opacity, but the layer modes will be better because it will give a more natural effect in this case because the layer mode changes with the grayscale value whereas the opacity is a 'blanket' effect.

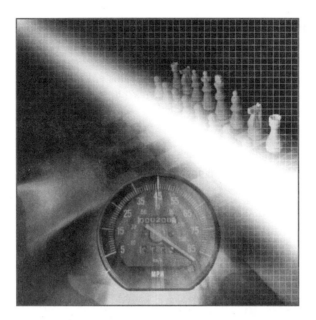

8. Change to Overlay mode and we now have a realistic shaft of light. Notice the change on the white pawns.

Rendering type

As we discussed earlier, type in Photoshop 6 is a vector object. The advantages with that are that it is resolution-independent. That means you can change the size at any time without getting pixelization. Also the type remains editable as long as it's in a type layer. If you want to change the font, color, or your text you can do that even after the document has been saved and re-opened.

When we rasterize type, it changes it from the mathematical vectors into pixels. The type layer changes to a regular layer. Once you have done that, the type is no longer editable as type, but behaves like a regular layer.

"So why would you ever want to rasterize the text?" You ask. Well, there are certain effects you can only apply to rasterized layers. These kinds of effects are the effects that change the pixels. These include the majority of plug-ins, filters and shape transformations.

For the most part, you could get away with using layer styles and keeping your type layers. But there will be times when you will need to break out of the box and rasterize the text to apply these transformations. A good piece of advice I can give you; always rasterize a duplicate of your text layer and always keep the original text layer intact. You can hide the original and work with the copy. You could make a layer set and store all the original text in the folder. Then later if you need to change the text in any way, you will always have the original to go back to. I have learned this one the hard way. "He who learns from his mistakes is smart, he who learns from the mistakes of others is smarter."

Rasterizing type

Let me demonstrate a time where you would need to rasterize the type and how to do it.

1. Enter some text in your document. Here I used 58pt Futura Bold Italic, if you don't have it, use a similar bold-italic sans serif font. I typed the words, "Speed Chess". I moved it to the right, because I want to create a feeling of motion from the left.

2. The way I am going to do this is to duplicate the text layer and blur the copy behind the title. So the first thing to do is duplicate the text layer. I know that in order to blur this layer I will have to rasterize the type layer. There are 2 ways of doing this:

- Apply the filter, you will see a dialog box informing you that you cannot apply this filter to a text layer, and it offers you the choice to rasterize the text. If you click OK the layer will be converted.

- Or, the second method is to RIGHT-CLICK/CMD-CLICK on the text in the Layers palette. A pop-up menu will appear with the option Rasterize layer (on Photoshop 5 and 5.5 the option is "render text").

The second method is the one I prefer, but it doesn't really make any difference. Find what suits your workflow best and stick to that. "Choose wisely Luke and may the force be with you!"

3. Time to add some movement to the type layer. Add a motion blur to the layer (Filters > Blur > Motion blur). Keep it at an angle of 0 degrees. For the blur I chose 88 just to match the speedometer. Press OK and you will see the blur, implying movement and speed.

4. To make it look like our text is zooming across the page, drag the layer beneath the original text layer and move it to the left.

5. Let's add a drop shadow to the type layer to make it pop a bit from the blur (I just used the default settings). As fancy as we get with things, don't forget that clients will want people to be able to read their message.

The finished design. We could use this image as the box front for a chess game or a splash page on a web site.

Merging layers

Once you have created your image you will have several layers. Save your image.

Sometimes you may want to merge some layers. Always save a copy before you flatten it. There are a few reasons to merge: It will reduce the file size so freeing up valuable system resources.

You will need to merge layers for certain multimedia uses and flatten for printing. There are 3 ways of merging layers, accessed from the fly-out menu in the Layers palette, they are:

- Merge Visible: Will merge all the layers that are currently visible.

- Merge Linked: This option will merge all the layers linked to the active layer with the active layer.

- Flatten Image: This will merge the entire document into one background. This will give you the smallest file size, the shortest printing time, and also enable you to attach clipping paths for output in a desktop publishing program.

Output of layers

You can even import your layers into Adobe AfterEffects and Premiere and keep all your layers intact. The layer styles, blending modes, and opacity will remain as you set them in Photoshop.

You can now animate the layers separately and produce some stunning results. To do this, make sure that you save your files at 72 dpi, RGB mode, and as PSD format.

Case Study

You just learned lots of new things about layers. Hopefully, you now have the controls of layer blending modes at your fingertips. These new skills are essential for creating composite images. You're going to have the opportunity to practise these skills now. It's time to take the gloves off and complete our home page, info page and car of the week page. We are going to combine different images together using drag-and-drop and blending modes. We're also going to import a paragraph of text, as well as create some for our pages. So, we have a lot to cover – let's get down to it!

Creating the information page

1. Open info.jpg. Now it's time to add our logo.

2. Open up the logo that we created and saved earlier: logo.psd. In the Layers palette drop-down menu, click on Merge Visible on the logo document. This will merge the logo so that it can be imported as a single layer. When you do this make sure that there is no background color and the checkerboard transparency is showing in the background.

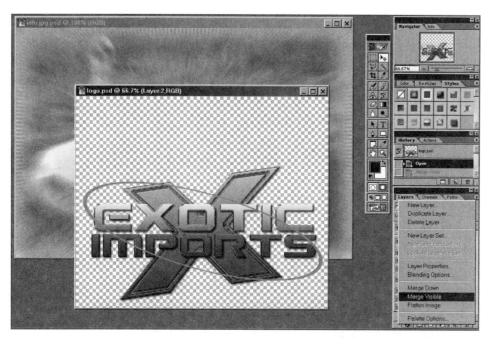

3. Now drag and drop the logo into our info document. Close logo.psd and say Yes when it asks to save the changes. In normal working practice, we would want to keep the logo on separate layers in case we wanted to animate it in Flash or Director for a future project, but it's not necessary here.

4. Using the Free Transform tool, size and reposition the logo to the bottom right hand corner (if you have trouble seeing the bounding box, zoom out).

5. Changing the logo layer to Overlay blending mode allows the image underneath to show through a little bit, giving us a nice blended appearance.

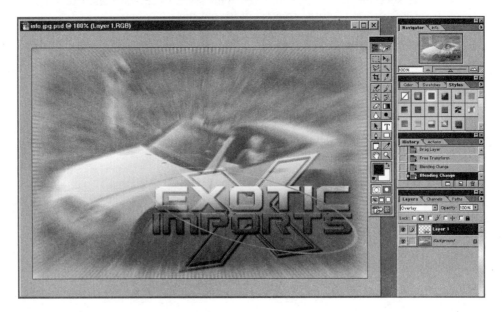

6. Add some text using Arial Narrow Bold set to about 50 pts and black to make the page title "About us". We can use the Move tool to position it where we want.

7. We can also use the Type tool to create a box for a paragraph of text about our product. Select the Type tool and by clicking and dragging, create a text block that can be resized by dragging the handles. This will cause the type inside the box to wrap automatically.

Now type in your information. I used Arial Narrow Regular 18pt, with the leading set to (Auto) in the Character palette. Click the check mark icon in the tool options bar to apply the type.

8. Using the Move tool, reposition the block of text to your liking.

> *You can press the* Ctrl/Cmd *key to do this; it will temporarily switch to the Move tool until you release the key.*

9. Create a new text layer and type the word "Home", I used Arial Narrow Bold Italic and made it 24 pts. This will be our link back to the home page.

10. We are finished with this page for now. Save it as `info.psd`.

Creating the car of the week page

Buckle your seatbelt. We're going to import some text from a PDF document and reverse the color to use it in combination with a dark background and our Lamborghini image.

1. To import our PDF in Photoshop, go to File > Open, and navigate to car of the week.pdf, which can be downloaded from the friends of ED web site.

   A dialog box will come up offering to Rasterize Generic PDF Format, this means that Photoshop wants to convert the PDF into a standard Photoshop layer. The text will be converted to pixels. Change the Resolution to 72 pixels/inch, since this is for online use.

   You could change the dimensions if you wanted, but the document size of 612x792 pixels isn't too big to fit in a web browser window, so it will work fine for our page.

   There are 2 options at the bottom:

   - Anti-aliased is a smoothing technology that smooths jagged and harsh edges. In this case we will turn it OFF because we want the text to be as sharp as possible in order to read it onscreen.

   - Constrain Proportions locks the width and height; this keeps the object from appearing elongated when resizing. Check this box.

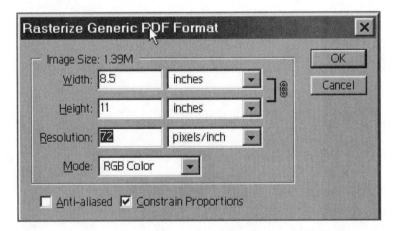

2. Press OK and you now have a new Photoshop document with one layer. Name the layer text.

3. Save the document in the working folder. Call it car of the week.psd.

4. Open the black car.psd image.

   We want to activate the path around the car, so we can copy just the image without the background.

5. Switch to the Paths palette. Notice that path we created is still there. Holding down the CTRL/CMD key, click on the path thumbnail to load it as a selection.

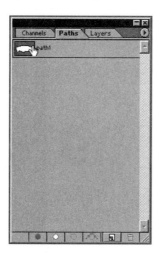

6. Now you can see the selection around the image, we want to copy the car into our other document. With the Move tool, drag the car from the window and drop it into our car of the week document, holding down SHIFT to keep it centered.

We now have a new layer, name it car.

7. The car is too big, so we'll need to resize it. Select Edit > Free Transform (CTRL/CMD+T). In the tool options bar, click the chain icon between W:100% and H:100%. This will constrain the proportions; change the W: (Width) to 40% and the H: (Height) will change to 40% automatically.

Notice that the car fits nicely now? Click the check mark on the right of the tool options bar to apply this effect (or just press the ENTER key).

8. We will need a background for this page, so create a new layer, call it background and drag it to the bottom of the Layers palette.

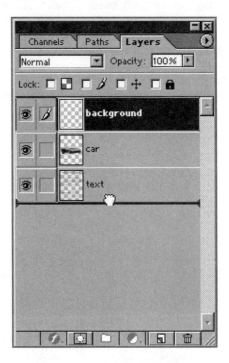

I have zoomed in to 100% for a closer look at what we are doing. Also, at 100%, things display more accurately on the screen.

9. Now fill the background with black. Pressing SHIFT+BACKSPACE, Use:Black will do the job.

10. The type is impossible to read right now, so we will need to lighten it up. The quickest way is to invert it; activate the text layer and press CRTL/CMD+I (Image > Adjust > Invert). There, much better.

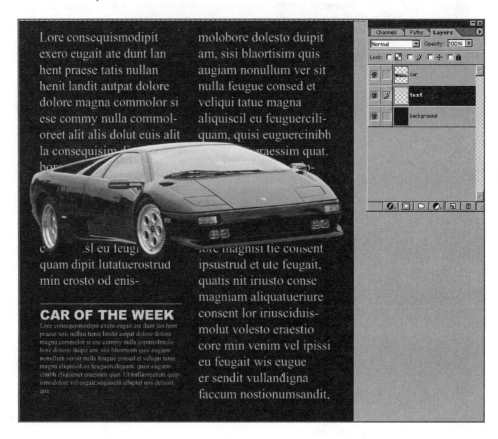

11. Let's put the car behind the text. Drag the car layer under the text layer. Hmm, it's still a bit hard to read, because the tones on the car are 'fighting' with the text.

I think we will darken up the midtones on the car. This will make it blend more with the background, as well as making the text easier to read.

12. With the car layer selected, go to Image > Adjust > Levels (CTRL/CMD+L). Slide the midtone slider (the gray arrow in the middle under the histogram) to the right, until the image is dark enough to blend into the background and the type is clear, then press OK.

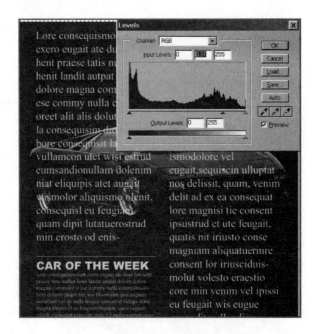

I love this effect, it adds a "mysterious" feel to the design.

13. Save the finished page as `car of the week.psd` (you can replace the old file).

Let's work on the home page now.

Creating the home page

1. Open the home.jpg and yellow car.psd file that we were working on earlier.

2. Resize both documents to 760 pixels wide and then drag and drop the yellow car image into the home document.

We are going to fade-out the back of the yellow car.

3. Add a layer mask to the yellow car layer. Set the foreground and background colors to the default setting (press D). Using a linear gradient and with the layer mask active, add a horizontal gradient; start around the middle of the yellow car and drag left to just past the end of the car. I always drag the gradient past the end of the image when I want it to fade out. The reason I do this is so that the image isn't cut off abruptly, but has a smooth fade to transparent.

This will fade out the back half of the image.

4. Change to Overlay mode, to soften the layer's appearance.

5. Resize and reposition the image to suit your tastes. If you like how it looks right now, feel free to skip this next step.

We are now going to add the logo to the home page.

6. Once again open the logo file and drag and drop the logo into the image. Scale and position the logo as seen here. Rename the layer as logo. Don't change the blending mode here. Since this is the home page, we want the logo strong to reinforce a definite corporate identity.

We now want to change the background from a fixed background to a regular layer, so that we can apply a mask to it. You cannot apply a mask or layer blending mode to a locked background.

7. The best way I know of doing this is to double-click the background in the Layers palette. Once you've done this, the dialog box will ask you for a new name. I used the name mainlayer. The background has now been converted to a regular layer.

8. Create a new layer, fill it with solid black and move it beneath mainlayer. This will become the background for our blend. I chose black rather than white because it produces a stronger contrast against the logo. We really want the logo to stand out.

9. Apply a layer mask to mainlayer and apply a linear gradient from the left to the bottom right, as shown. See how it blends everything so much more smoothly and cleanly?

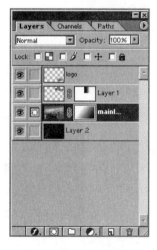

So let's add a glow around it.

10. Select the logo layer and use the Layer Styles to add an Outer Glow. Make the glow color white and use the settings as seen here (I increased the Opacity slightly and increased the Size to 43).

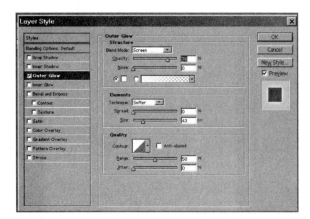

11. Here we have the image so far. Save it in our working folder as home.psd.

All our pieces are now ready. You have produced a collage using layer masks and blending modes. You are definitely going beyond 'basic' Photoshop techniques now. We have all the pages ready to go. In the next chapter we are going to learn about advanced web design, where we will use these in the final part of the case study to add our navigation elements and output our finished web page. So just one (longish) step to go.

Summary

You've just learned a lot of advanced layer techniques, which you can use to produce collages and other effects in your images. As ever with Photoshop, the uses of this tool are limited only by your imagination.

These are the techniques used to create a lot of the multi-layered high tech backgrounds, collages and wallpapers you see around in print, the Web and on TV. I have a lot of people who ask me how to create these at my site www.photoshopcafe.com. Keep adding layers and experimenting with the layer blending modes and after a little experience, you'll be creating some jaw-dropping images.

11 Advanced Web Design

What we'll cover in this chapter:

- Slicing images for the Web

- Using Image Ready to enhance web sites

- Creating animated web elements

- Creating interactive web elements

- Creating image maps

Introduction

Back in Chapter 7, we looked at various factors that go towards making a great web site. As you may recall, we came up with six main areas:

1. Content and Functionality – always keep in mind the ultimate *purpose* of the site

2. Fast download – keep file sizes down wherever possible

3. Information – be sure to adequately *communicate* the purpose of the site

4. Easy navigation – make sure it's obvious how to get around the site

5. Aesthetics – make sure the site is nice to look at

6. The 'Wow!' Factor – impress your visitors, and give them something to remember

The rest of that chapter's discussion focused on image preparation for the Web, and mainly tied in with the second point above. That's probably the easiest part to nail, as it has a nice quantifiable result: quick download = success; slow download = failure. What about the others then?

They're each pretty hard to pin down in terms of 'dos and don'ts', and a great deal has been written about them all. Most of the time they'll boil down to simple common sense decisions based on (a) a clear notion of what the site is trying to achieve and (b) good, accurate feedback from the people who are actually using it. This is really just another way to approach point 1:

What's the site there for, and is it actually working?

Effective communication with users is vital to a good web site, and even if you're not directly involved with providing content like FAQ (Frequently Asked Questions) pages and mail links for user feedback, a well thought-out design can contribute just as much. Consider the following:

- A common theme for each page in a site, helping to establish a sense of unity

- Animated elements that draw attention to a specific element within the page

- Easily recognizable interface elements – buttons that look like real buttons

- Self-explanatory navigation links that change appearance when you move the mouse over them

There's no one-to-one relationship between these techniques and the six points we mentioned earlier: crucially, each technique draws in all six. In the course of this chapter, we're going to see how Photoshop and ImageReady can help us to implement some of these features. We'll use them to create a whole web page, and ensure that all our elements are properly optimized. We'll give ImageReady a proper introduction, and see how we can use it to add some useful and eye-catching features to our pages.

Creating content for simple web pages

Simple HTML pages contain a mixture of text and bitmaps, with hyperlinks allowing the user to jump around to other pages. We can add simple animation using animated GIFs, and additional interactivity using **JavaScript**; this is a scripting language that allows us to capture user events (such as mouse movements and button clicks) and use these to trigger short animations.

So how is Photoshop going to help us do this? Back in Chapter 7, we spent a while looking at Photoshop's Save For Web function, which helped us to optimize how we saved images to disk by showing the effects of various possible compression options along with corresponding stats on the resulting file size and download times. In fact, we barely scratched the surface of this feature; if we use the **Slice** tool to chop up an image in Photoshop, Save For Web can not only save each slice as a separate file, but also generate an HTML file that sticks them together again as required. This has some very important benefits:

- If one part of the image is based on a full color photographic image (and is therefore best saved as a JPEG), while another part is based on two-color line art (and should really be a GIF), we can make them into separate slices and compress each one separately, as best befits it.

- Maybe we want to animate part of the page image. Rather than saving the entire image as an enormous animated GIF file with several (largely identical) frames, we need to save the animated portion in its own GIF file, and the rest of the page in a similarly suitable format. Once again, we can slice up the overall image and save individual slices according to their own particular needs.

- What about this JavaScript business? One of the neatest applications of JavaScript is the **rollover** effect, when an element changes appearance if the mouse is moved over it. This requires us to set some boundaries about the element, and putting it in its own slice does the trick perfectly.

In the following sections, we're going to take a look at using ImageReady to slice up images for use as web pages, and see how it can help us create animations and rollovers.

Slicing and optimization

We'll start by creating a simple web page from a single image. We can add slices that allow us to optimize it for the Web, and then create some more rudimentary pages to allow us to test our navigation.

"Pick Your Game" – a sample page

Perhaps you've just designed a site that uses a lot of Flash content, but still want to cater for folks who don't have the Flash plug-in installed. You therefore recreate as much of the site as possible using plain HTML, and redirect users to the appropriate version of the site.

Now one of the handy things you can do with JavaScript is to detect whether specific plug-ins are installed on the browser. Depending on what it then finds, it redirects to either the simple HTML page or the Flash-based page. The user needn't know anything about the choice – it's all taken care of automatically.

In many cases, this sort of thing is fine – however, I personally prefer to be given the choice, and never use this automatic method myself. Most of the time I'll want to see the Flash-based site, but occasionally I'll want the faster loading and stripped down HTML site. I remember one occasion when I was in panic mode wondering what time I was due to speak at a conference. I was in a desperate hurry, and just wanted to see the timetable of events. While my computer was quite capable of showing me the Flash site, I didn't *want* it!

For precisely this reason, I always add a manual selection screen. Here's one such screen I have used in the past:

You'll find this image saved as start_screen.psd in the support download for this chapter. There are a couple of important things to notice here:

- Unlike print-based graphics, this image has been designed with optimization in mind. It has many areas of solid color, and was designed specifically with the GIF format in mind.

- The page provides just as much information as is necessary; everything is functional rather than flowery.

- The image has had all extraneous border areas cut. Again, we want only the essential part of the image, so we have cropped all but the core graphic.

In short, there's a totally new mindset at work. While the number of people with 'broadband' access to the Web is steadily rising, a large proportion of users are still viewing sites via 56K dial-up connections, and our sites must reflect this. Even if the user *does* have a broadband site, they expect the extra content to be rich media, not pretty (but enormous) bitmaps...

Where should we slice the image?

OK, on with the show. The next thing we need to do is split our image into slices. In doing so, we are looking for three main types of section:

- **Buttons** provide navigation support. The user can click on them to jump to another page. We need to separate out the areas we wish to use as buttons, and assign URL addresses to each of them.

- **Static graphic areas** do nothing more than look nice. We need to identify each main area of graphics, and establish the most efficient format (file type, compression ratio, number of colors) in which to save it.

- **Spacers** are blank areas that don't require any images.

Normally, you'd start by planning out your page and using Photoshop to create a full image of it from scratch. In this case let's run with what we already have and load start_screen.psd.

How do we slice the image?

Now, although we can define our slices in Photoshop, I find it's better to do it all from within ImageReady, which is designed specifically for web manipulations, and therefore has a better-suited interface. You should recognize a lot of the functionality, as many are taken straight from the familiar Photoshop environment, and we encountered many of its web-oriented features when we used Photoshop's Save For Web back in Chapter 7. Don't let this fool you though – ImageReady is a powerful (and very useful) tool in its own right, as we're going to see.

To jump across to ImageReady, simply click on the icon ![icon] at the bottom of the toolbox.

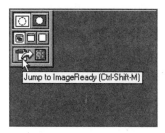

Note that this actually gives us a whole lot more than a quick way to jump between Photoshop and ImageReady: it lets us work on the same image from either application, and automatically updates the working image when we jump from one to the other. (We'd otherwise have to save the working file, close it down, and open it up again in the other application.)

Obviously, this saves time if we want to jump to and fro between the two applications while working on a single file; but why should we need to do this? Here's one example:

- We're optimizing slices in ImageReady, but we notice that this would be a whole lot easier with a minor alteration to the original image.

- We jump across to Photoshop and make this alteration.

- We then jump back into ImageReady and carry on optimizing our slices.

Slicing large images and optimizing by hand before this sort of magic was fiddly, monotonous, and prone to mistakes of the 'go back and start again' variety. Then the client would stipulate a couple of 'minor' changes and you'd have to do it all again! It was something you wouldn't wish on your worst enemy.

The first time you jump across, ImageReady may take a little while to load up, but subsequent jumps to and fro should be much faster.

Slicing Our Image

1. Select the slice tool icon 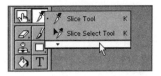 in the toolbar, and click-hold it until you see a small menu present both Slice Tool and Slice Select Tool options. We're going to be using both of these options quite a lot in the following steps, and will therefore want to switch easily between the two. Let's get a head start by making them both easily available.

2. Select the small down arrow at the bottom of the menu, and the menu should be replaced with a window containing icons for both tools. This should help speed things up considerably.

Slicing our buttons

Now we're ready to create some slices. We'll start by marking out our navigation buttons: the two circled line drawings on the left of the image.

3. With the Slice tool still selected, drag out a rectangle that includes the two elements that we're going to use as buttons – as shown below. We want to be sure to include the left edge, so it is probably best to switch to full screen and start dragging from outside and to the left the image.

This part of the image (the area you just selected) has now become a slice. You should see a number in the top left corner, signifying the slice number – this is our first slice, so it will be 01. The text has a blue background, which signifies that it is a **user slice** (that is, created by you). You'll see that the right half of the image is grayed out (to signify that it's currently deselected) and has been labeled 02. In this case, the label background is also light gray, which indicates an **auto slice**, so-called because ImageReady created it automatically.

Our user slice must now be split into three areas, for two buttons and a spacer at the top:

4. Select Slices > Divide Slice… and the Divide Slice window should appear:

5. We now want to divide our slice into three sections, stacked vertically, one on top of another. Counter-intuitive as it may seem, we need to check the Divide Horizontally Into checkbox, and then set the slices down, evenly spaced radio button. Enter 3 in the textbox, and make sure the Divide Vertically into checkbox is unchecked.

Well, we now have three slices, but they are all the wrong height.

6. Use the Select Slice tool to drag the bounding boxes so that the slices end up as shown below. You may want to zoom in a little so that you can place them accurately.

Our button slices are now complete, so we can turn our attention to the currently grayed out right hand side. First, click over it with the Slice Select tool to make it the current selection. Before we can edit an auto slice, we must convert it into a user slice, which we can do in one of two ways:

- Select Slices > Promote to User-Slice from the menu bar.

- Right/CTRL-click on the slice and select Promote to User-slice from the context menu that pops up.

Either way, slice 02 will now have a blue box in the top left hand corner, signifying that it's now a user slice; more to the point, we can now edit it.

Slicing out blank space

There's rather a lot of blank space in this slice, and there's no point in saving huge solid areas of black as images when we can simply specify 'black' as a background color for that region on the page. We can therefore cut down our total page size a lot by creating as many empty slices as possible.

1. Since we have three blocks of text with a huge space separating two of them, let's start off by 'dividing horizontally' into four slices, in much the same way as the last set of slices we created.

2. Now edit the slices (using the Slice Select tool) so that they look like the picture below:

Of course, we could have left slice 02 and slice 04 as a single slice. However, bear in mind that larger slices will take longer to load, leaving more noticeable pauses between the appearance of each slice. Using smaller slices helps ensure that the user will see as much of the page as possible as soon as possible (though the page as a whole always takes the same time to load).

Well, we have now finished our slicing – the next stage is optimization.

Setting up empty slices

As you can see, slices 01 and 05 are completely blank, so we can safely delete them.

1. Select each slice in turn, and hit the DELETE key to get rid of them.

They will now revert to grayed-out auto slices. If we leave them like this, the final web page will display them in whatever color you've set as the background color for the page as a whole. As long as this is black, we should be fine – just in case we need to change this in the future though, it's a good idea to set a background color for each of the missing slices individually.

2. We can do this via the Slice palette, which you've probably seen lurking round the bottom of the screen since we started up ImageReady – assuming you have slice 01 selected, it will look like this:

If you can't see it anywhere, make sure you've got one of the Slice tools selected, and hit the Slice Palette... button on the Slice tool palette at the top of the main window:

We must now do the following to each of the empty slices:

3. Change Type: to No Image

4. Change BG: to black – either click on the drop down arrow (and pick the bottom right swatch entry) or click on the list entry (which initially says None) and select it from a color picker. This is the background color for this slice, which will become an empty table cell in the final HTML.

The Slice palette should look like this when you are done:

We can use the **Text** field to specify any text or HTML that we want to put in that cell in the table. If you're familiar with HTML, you might want to use this to:

- Insert some formatted text, which is far more bandwidth-friendly than a bitmap containing text – this is almost always preferable unless you're after a very specific effect or happen to be using a non-standard font.

- Insert some HTML that embeds something else, such as a Flash animation or even streaming video. You'd need to make sure that this content was no bigger than the cell space, or the slices would be pushed apart.

If you need to add a lot of HTML, you can use a text or HTML editor by right/CTRL-clicking on the empty slices, selecting Jump to, and picking the editor of your choice. If you try adding plain text, you won't see anything, since the text and background will both be black. However, you might like to select slice 06 and try out the following line of HTML:

```
<font color=white face=Arial>You can put your
➥HTML in here</font>
```

5. You won't see any change on the sliced image, since we're only adding content to the HTML that will be generated when we ultimately save the page. However, we can easily preview our page: we just need to press the Preview button. Okay, I'm assuming that you're also using Internet Explorer here; of course, this will look different if you use another browser. You can also preview the page by hitting CTRL+ALT+P/COMMAND+OPTION+P. Here's how it looks:

6. If you scroll down a little, you can take a look at all the HTML we've generated so far – and all without getting our hands dirty! For the purposes of this example, we don't really need anything extra in these cells, so let's backtrack a little, and leave the Text boxes blank for now. Don't worry though, as this experience won't go to waste!

Optimizing non-empty slices

1. We still need to optimize our remaining slices, so select slice 02 and configure the Optimize palette as shown below:

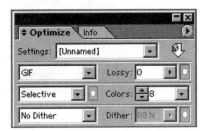

2. Since we have a black and white image, we can safely drop the Colors count right down to 8 without losing the smooth edges of the white text (and therefore keeping it readable). Note that as you change the number of colors, the file size calculated for that slice (displayed at the bottom of the slice palette) changes accordingly.

> *Remember that you can select the **2-Up** tab from the top of the Image window, to compare appearances and download times (in whole seconds) for the image as it is both before and after optimization.*

You'll see that I have not selected Web for the colors, and have instead gone for selective, which chooses the best colors, irrespective of whether they are web-safe. This is because most computers nowadays can display a sufficient range of colors to make web-safe palettes all but obsolete – consequently, I tend not to use them.

I've also selected No Dither, since my design uses solid colors and doesn't really need to be dithered.

3. Settings for the other text slices (slices 04 and 07) are just the same as this one's, so let's copy our optimization settings for slice 02 over to the others. We can do this by dragging the small arrow in the top right corner of the Optimize palette and dropping it on each of the other slices in turn.

4. Our two buttons feature no text at all, so they can make do with even fewer colors. Let's give slice 03 the same settings as above, but this time with only four colors. Finally, copy the settings over to slice 06.

5. We have now optimized our entire image for a good fast download. We can check out the full download time as follows:

● Select the 2-Up tab

● Use Select > All Slices or CTRL/CMD+A to select all the slices

● Look at the figures shown at the bottom left of the screen.

These are telling us that the whole page is 8.204 kilobytes in size and will take 2 seconds to load via a 56K modem – pretty good going! The user shouldn't have to wait too long at all! You can check out timings for various other connection speeds by clicking the arrow by 56.6K... and selecting another entry from the drop-down list.

> *Of course, you can still make changes to the optimize settings you've assigned to each slice (or even rearrange the slices completely if you want) to see how this affects the appearance and download time of the individual slices and the page as a whole.*

6. We have now optimized our page for fast download, so let's save our source file as start_screen_optimized.psd. We can now start thinking about adding a few usability features into the mix.

Usability

When most browsers load up images, they start out showing a series of boxes that show where the bitmaps will go. HTML lets you assign text to each of your image elements – referred to as **alt** (or 'alternative') text – which is displayed in the boxes until the bitmaps have been loaded. The purpose of this text is to describe what each bitmap shows, and this can serve a number of uses:

● Users can get a good idea of the overall content of the page long before it's finished loading. This might even be enough to persuade them to stick around for the lengthy download to run its course.

● Some people set their browser to view text only, which means that no bitmaps will be loaded at all. The browser stops at the bounding boxes, but will also show the alt text; so once again, the user can still see what the bitmaps are all about.

■ Web readers for visually impaired people use the alt text to tell users what the bitmaps are showing. If you don't add any text, the web page will be totally inaccessible to them.

Obviously, this final point is far and away the most important, as it has the potential to make or break your site for a massive group of potential users. What's more, aside from issues of losing traffic and simple fair play, there are also potential legal considerations to be aware of.

> *In the US, the 'Americans with Disabilities' Act already stipulates requirements to make the life of people with disabilities easier, and this is likely to be applied to web access soon. Designers will have to make the web as accessible as far as is reasonably practical, and for HTML, this includes adding descriptive alt text to allow visually impaired people to use the Web. Even if it doesn't become law soon, I'm sure you'll agree that we, as designers, have a moral imperative to make the small changes necessary*

Message text is just like the tool-tips that appear when you leave the cursor over an icon in most applications; leave it long enough and a small help box appears telling you what will happen when you click the icon. In HTML, we can specify message text to similarly describe the purpose of our navigation buttons.

Adding usability features

1. Now, make sure you have start_screen_optimized.psd open in ImageReady. To add either type of text we must expand the Slice palette to show some additional fields. Either select Show options from that palette's fly-out menu or double-click on the Slice tab.

   Additional fields will appear as shown below:

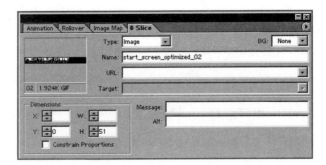

2. Now you can see the Message and Alt text fields, it's simply a case of selecting each non-empty slice and adding some appropriate text. Note that all these slices will require alt text, but only the buttons need message text. I have given my slices the following text fields:

Slice	Message Text	Alt Text
02		Pick your game
04		Flash site
07		HTML site
03	Take me to the Flash site...	Click here for Flash site
06	Take me to the HTML site...	Click here for HTML site

3. Only buttons can have message text, so the browser will now assume that slices 03 and 06 *are* buttons. If you now preview the web page, you should see text appearing as you mouse around the bitmap. You should also see a 'hand' icon when you rollover the button slices, and may hear a clicking noise when you press a button (assuming your browser is set up to do so).

Our simple page now displays in a browser, can download at a fairly speedy rate, and comes complete with quite a user-friendly interface; but it still doesn't actually *do* anything – in many respects, it might just as well be a simple bitmap. It's about time we started changing that.

Adding and testing navigation

So far, we haven't defined any actions for our buttons, so it's hardly surprising that they won't do anything – rather like an unwired light switch. Well, it's now time for us to do a little wiring! When we were adding the alt and message text for our slices, you may have noticed a couple of other fields that we haven't mentioned so far.

One of these was the URL field, in which we can name a web page for our buttons to link to. If we were linking to a different site, we'd need to use a full address (www.friendsofed.com, for example) but since this will be a local page on the same machine, we can just refer to the file name. So, for the top button, put flash.html in the URL field, and in the bottom one put html.html.

We are almost ready to save the HTML and sliced GIFs. First though, we need to tell ImageReady how to save it all.

1. Select File > Output settings > HTML... from the menu bar.

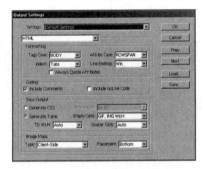

These are the HTML settings that ImageReady will use to create our web page. We don't need to change anything, but if you know your HTML, you may like to explore the available options, so that the final page is coded just the way you want it.

2. Click Next to get to the next set of options in the Output Settings dialog, which looks at our web page's background. We can add an image here if we want, but for now let's just change the background color to black (just as we did for the background color of the two auto slices).

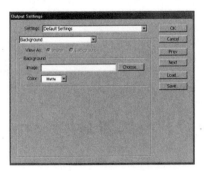

3. Hit Next to see the remaining two Output Settings windows. Again, you don't need to change anything, as they just specify how ImageReady will name each of the elements in the web page; unless you have a particular reason to change them, the defaults should be just fine.

Adding web page information

1. In a similar fashion, we can give our web page a title and add some copyright information. Just select File > Image info to call up the Image Info dialog, and enter some appropriate text as shown below:

2. Whatever you enter against Page Title will appear in the title bar of the browser window for that page. Anything in the Copyright box will be embedded as a comment within the HTML. Of course, a copyright notice is legally meaningless unless it's dated, so put that in if nothing else, along with your name.

    When you enter a URL for a web site, you can get away with entering just the location of the directory that the web page is in, such as www.friendsofed.com. In fact, the full URL of the first page of any site usually takes the form www.friendsofed.com/index.htm, which also names a specific file.

3. By default, ImageReady names the HTML file after the image file (you might have noticed this from the last two Output Settings screens), so let's resave our image as index.psd.

4. We can now use File > Save Optimized As to export our complete web page – save the HTML file as index.html in a folder called myWebPage. Take a look in here, and you'll find that a subfolder called images has also been created, containing image files index_02.gif, index_04.gif, index_06.gif, and index_07.gif from all the slices we defined earlier. You will also see a file called spacer.gif, which is used to make sure that any gaps arising between the elements in our page are filled with the page background color.

5. A browser requires every one of these files to show the page correctly, so to upload this page to the Internet, you can simply FTP everything contained in the myWebPage folder, rather than running the risk that you'll miss a crucial file. If you now double-click index.html, your web page should appear as depicted on the next page:

You should find that the browser shows the page title as Pick Your Game, and that the alt and message text pop-ups all work properly. Unfortunately, clicking on either button causes a page cannot be displayed message, since we don't yet have the pages flash.html or html.html (as we specified earlier on).

6. Let's quickly create a couple of placeholders to take the place of our Flash and HTML sites, so that we can check that our buttons work properly. Call up a text editor and enter the following lines of code:

```
<HTML>
 <HEAD>
  <TITLE>Flash Placeholder</TITLE>
 </HEAD>
 <BODY BGCOLOR=#00FFFF>
  Placeholder for Flash site
 </BODY>
</HTML>
```

Save this file as flash.html in the same directory as index.html, but don't close the text editor just yet.

7. Now change this code to read:

```
<HTML>
 <HEAD>
  <TITLE>HTML Placeholder</TITLE>
 </HEAD>
 <BODY BGCOLOR=#FFFF00>
  Place holder for HTML site
 </BODY>
</HTML>
```

8. Save this file as `html.html` in the same directory.

9. Each of these two very simple pages displays text in the browser window indicating which version of the site we've linked through to. Call up `index.html` again, and try clicking on each of the buttons – you should find that they both successfully link to the appropriate placeholder. Remember you can navigate back to `index.html` by hitting the browser's Back button.

Note that the links on `index.html` still won't work if you're previewing the page in ImageReady; the pages we have specified in our links are relative to where `index.html` is. Put another way, the buttons will only look for the two placeholder pages in the same directory that `index.html` is in. ImageReady's preview files use your operating system's temporary folder, and will therefore not find these placeholders.

You could use absolute URLs, which would include the full path to the placeholders (such as c:/.../flash.html), but you would have to change these all to web addresses (such as http://www.../flash.html) for it to work on the Web. By using relative addresses you can run the site from anywhere at all, since all addresses are relative to `index.html`.

> *The only place where you have to use absolute addresses is if you are linking to a web address that is not part of your site (such as http://www.friendsofed.com).*

Although the page we have created so far is very basic, this is how web pages tend to be designed. You start out with a set of very basic pages that mostly consist of content free placeholders. After checking that the navigation works between pages (by adding simple buttons), you can go on to slowly replace the placeholders with the final pages. In our example, we would replace `html.html` with the first page of our HTML-based web page, which would in turn link to the rest of the HTML site.

Hand-coding vs. WYSIWYG

Although some developers now use programs like Dreamweaver and Front Page (What You See Is What You Get editors) to automate some of the HTML creation, you will find that you will always be dipping in to hand code bits of HTML.

Until very recently, the majority of web design houses never used advanced HTML editors like the ones mentioned. Although some modern editors get close (Dreamweaver is particularly good, but Microsoft HTML editors are really awful at optimizing), there is really only one way to produce lean optimized HTML: hand coding. If you take the plunge and try it, you may well soon be writing code faster than someone working with a big fat application that is more complicated than HTML anyway!

The only thing that traditionally takes ages when producing HTML web pages is creating the image slices, optimizing them, and putting them into a table. This is what ImageReady and Photoshop concentrate on doing for us, and this is all a professional web designer for moderately sized sites actually needs, so Adobe have got it dead right!

The only time you won't want to hand code is for particularly complex sites that use a large amount of client or server side scripting, in which case you need an environment to test and debug your code.

There are a few things we can add to our page so we will look at those next. We will then end with a case study of a complete site that was created within Photoshop and Image Ready.

Image maps

When you move your mouse around the buttons, you will notice that the active area includes the whole slice. Surely it would be more appropriate if it just included the actual button areas? We can do this via an *image map*. This is a map that sits above the bitmap and acts like an invisible button. The advantages of using maps are:

- Using rectangular slices as buttons areas doesn't allow you to make buttons that are circular (as are many buttons) or if you are using images as buttons – such as a small car image to use as a button to that particular models page. By using an image map you can define the car outline as the button area.

- You can have as many image maps as you want per slice, which means that you can have as many buttons as you want per slice.

- Image maps don't have to be just for buttons. You could for example, have loads of image maps over a roadmap, each of which brings up a message text telling you what area the cursor is over.

Adding image maps

1. Load `index.psd` back into Photoshop and jump across into ImageReady (you could also just start in ImageReady, but in a normal workflow you would be jumping to Photoshop to make minor corrections, it's a good idea to get into the habit of viewing both applications as part of the same thing.

2. Delete the URL and Message text for both buttons. This has turned our two buttons back to static text, and you can check this by looking at the page in the default browser.

3. Select the Circle Image Map tool and then drag out a circle that is roughly the same size as the top button. You don't have to be exact in either position or size because we will fine-tune it in a moment. Once you have created the circle, you can position it via the X and Y values in the Image Map tab of the Slice palette (or you can use the arrow keys, which is perhaps quicker), and vary the R value so it just fits over the inside radius of the button as shown below.

4. Enter flash.html in the URL field and Take me to the Flash site... as the alt text.

5. Do likewise for the lower button, adding html.html for the URL, and Take me to the HTML site... for the alt text. We could now actually save the two buttons as one slice now, via the Slice Select tool. To do this you would click on one of the buttons and then SHIFT-select the other. You'd then choose Slices > Combine Slices to merge slice 03 and 06 into one. We're actually going to leave the buttons as two slices because:

   ■ It allows us to create *rollovers* for each button – more on this soon.

   ■ It gives more information to the folks relying on the alt text to read the site. When combining slices be aware that you may be making your site less accessible to some people who rely on the alt text to read your site.

6. Save the file index.psd with File > Save and then select File > Save Optimized to create a new HTML file that includes the image maps. Make sure you have Save as Type set to HTML Only, because we have not changed the GIFs. Save to the same place as the original index.html.

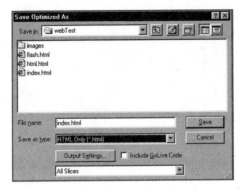

7. You will see a Replace Files dialog pop up when you hit Save. This allows you to choose which files to update if you know that only some need updating.

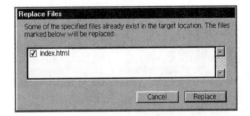

8. While we could have used File > Save Optimized, it is usually more prudent to use Save As; since you'll often be overwriting several files, and it is well worth going through all the prompts so that you are aware of exactly what will be overwritten. If you now double-click on the new `index.html` file, you will see that the buttons are now circular rather than the previous rather messy rectangles.

Rollovers

Rollovers allow us to change the appearance of a button (or static images) depending on whether the mouse is over it or not. They even allow us to add further changes based on whether the mouse has been clicked on the button, or rolled back out – for now though, we're only interested in the rollover state.

To add a rollover state we need two button images:

■ The normal state

■ The rollover state

We're going to create a new layer that includes our rollover button states, and need to select all the buttons on the page.

You may find the following steps a little fiddly, so you might want to have a look at the end result via `index.psd` in the download for this chapter if you get stuck.

Adding rollovers

1. Use the Slice Select tool to select all the slices and choose Select > Create selection from slices to select the whole image.

2. Now select Edit > Copy (or CTRL+C) to copy the contents of the selection, followed by Edit > Paste to paste it into a new layer. Repeat to create another copy.

3. Use the Layer Options palette to rename these layers as OverState1 and OverState2.

Now we can create our 'mouse over' state graphics.

4. Pick the OverState1 layer, and use the Paint Bucket tool to fill the inner background of the *top* button with a light gray. This is how the button will look when the user's mouse pointer is over it:

5. Now do the same for the second button in layer OverState2, as shown on the next page:

We now have to tell ImageReady which layer should be used for which state.

6. Select slice 06, and pick the Rollover tab from the Slice palette.

You'll see a single thumbnail labeled Normal, representing how we want the slice to look when the cursor is not over the image map. Of course, there are no other images defined here at the moment, so it will currently look like this even when the pointer is bang on top of it. Let's do something about that.

7. Using the Layers palette, make both OverState layers invisible as shown below:

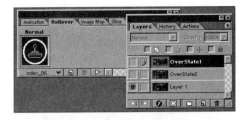

8. Click on the New Rollover State icon at the bottom of the Rollover palette. A new rollover state called Over will now appear with a small arrow to the left of its title.

If you click on this title, a pop-up menu will appear that shows the various different states for which you can define separate images. We're not going to do anything with these, but you might like to investigate for yourself what effect each one has.

9. We must now specify what the Over state should look like. Make the Overstate1 layer visible (and, if necessary, make the other layers invisible). You should end up with a pair of states that look like the image on the next page:

10. Now work through the same process for the other button, using the layer OverState2 to provide the rollover image:

Updating the color palette

1. Since we have changed the colors in two of our slices, the optimized color palette for each one is now incorrect, and ImageReady will signify this by placing a little yellow warning triangle in the corner of the Color Table palette. Don't worry too much about this though – just click on the triangle and ImageReady will calculate a new palette for you.

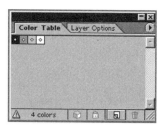

2. Save the image as index.psd, and Save Optimized to generate and save the new HTML (which will now include JavaScript to animate the rollovers and update the GIF slices). Only two of the slices actually need re-optimizing, so you may like to specify just slices 03 and 06 in the Replace Files window we saw earlier. Even if you don't, the other slices will be saved in just the same way as they were before, so in this case, it doesn't really matter whether you do or not.

3. If you now preview the page (remembering that the links will not work), you will see that the buttons now become highlighted when the mouse pointer is moved over them. You'll also see that the page's file size has gone up slightly. Each of

the rollovers requires two GIFs: one for the normal state and one for over. Obviously, it's best to keep rollover slices small, since they effectively double the size of the slice in memory.

> *You can actually make changes in slices other than the button slices themselves as part of your rollover state. For example, we might make the text in the slices to the left of the buttons glow on the over state. Keep an eye on file sizes when you do this sort of thing though; gimmicky effects quickly push up download time for relatively little entertainment value.*

4. By using File > Save Optimized As and overwriting our test site, you can see the full effect so far when you double-click `index.html`.

Rollover animation is a simple **event-driven** effect; the animation occurs when the user *does* something. We can also create animations that run all the time, and this is what we'll look at next.

GIF animations

As we described in Chapter 7, GIF animations consist of a number of images in a single file, which are shown in quick succession to create the effect of animated graphics. For the same reasons mentioned above, GIF animations can become very bandwidth heavy unless you:

- Keep the animated slice small. You are generating a new slice for every frame, and this can quickly mount up.

- Keep the number of frames low. Stick to 5 large, unsubtle animation steps rather than a 30 frame smooth animation.

Everyone who has been on the Net will have seen more than a few sites that become sluggish because the designer couldn't resist putting a pointless GIF animation in there somewhere. Such an animation may be cute the first time, but it can try patience if the user has to come back to the site several times and wait 15 seconds for the same old animation every time.

Even folks designing banner ads have come to realize this, and usually limit the total file size of a banner to about 12K. If your animations come in any bigger than that, you'll probably not get many repeat visitors, and you certainly won't be able to sell your skills creating web banners!

Now that we've set the scene for all the pitfalls associated with animated GIFs, let's take a look at how we can create a simple animation.

Animation with ImageReady

In ImageReady we can create, edit, and rearrange frames quickly, creating an animated sequence rather like we did with the rollovers. The two palettes we will be concerned with here are the Animation palette and the Layers palette. Each alteration to the image will be placed in its own layer, and the layers will ultimately become the frames of our animation.

Let's put something eye-catching in the top left corner of the 'Pick Your Game' page. We have a slice ready and waiting, which is 115 pixels wide and 38 pixels high. First, let's switch back to Photoshop, where we can make ourselves a new image to base the animation on.

1. Create a new RGB image called Bars with the dimensions shown above, and give it a black background to match the rest of the page.

2. Create a new layer called Bar1, and use the Rectangular Marquee tool to select a rectangular area along the bottom of the image – make it about 6 pixels high, and leave one or two pixels' clearance at either end. Fill it with orange, and it should look something like this:

3. Now create another new layer, and call it Bar2. Drag the marquee up by about 8 pixels, and flood fill once again:

4. Repeat this process until you have five bars and your image looks like this:

5. Now select the Bar1 layer, and double-click on its entry in the Layers palette. We're going to apply a couple of layer effects.

6. In the Layer Styles dialog, double-click Bevel and Emboss, set the shading angles for this effect to 90 degrees and 70 degrees, and hit OK. The first of the bars should now look shiny.

7. Select Layer > Layer Style > Copy Layer Style, link all the other layers, and then select Layer > Layer Style > Paste Layer Style to Linked. Now we've applied the layer style to all of the bars, the image should look like this:

8. Now we can switch back into ImageReady, and start animating our image. Make sure you have both Animation and Layers palettes handy. Initially, the Animation palette will show you a single frame, reflecting the current appearance of the image:

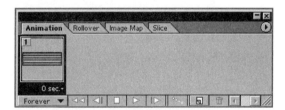

9. If we now make all our layers invisible, you'll see this reflected in the frame:

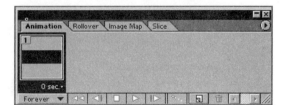

10. If you now make a new frame (by clicking on the 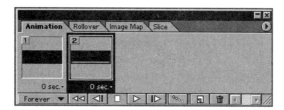 icon), and make the Bar1 layer visible again, you'll notice that it's only the currently selected frame that gets updated to look like the current image – frame 1 still shows no bars at all.

11. Try hitting the play button  and you'll see the image appear in a separate window, with a single bar flashing on and off. Well it's animated, but it's not that interesting. Let's add some more frames, with a new bar appearing in each one:

Not bad, but if you take a look at the animation, you'll see that the sudden jump from frame 6 back to frame 1 (each time the animation loops round) looks rather ugly. What can we do to fix this? We could always set the animation to play just once, using the drop-down menu from the bottom left corner of the palette. On the other hand, we could add some more frames to make the transition a little smoother. So far our GIF file is weighing in at only 945 bytes, so we can certainly afford to add a few more.

12. There are plenty of ways we could tackle the transition back to frame 1 – we might just make them disappear in the reverse order to that in which they appeared (like the equalizer on the front of a sound system); or we might fade them out by changing the opacity of the layers. Here's how I've done it:

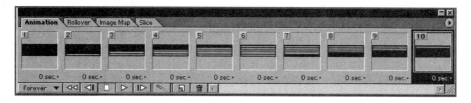

The bars start appearing from the bottom, and they start disappearing from the bottom. The overall effect is as if something was moving upwards through the frame. This works out a lot easier on the eye.

13. One more feature we should consider is the ability to set a delay between frames. It's very simple do this: just click the small arrow next to the delay indicator on the bottom of the frame. By default, this reads 0 sec. – you really can't miss it. When the drop-down menu opens, pick a delay from the list.

14. Let's add a slight pause after frame 1 appears, so that the bars appear (and disappear) smoothly but intermittently. Select the drop-down menu from frame 1, and pick 1.0. Play the animation back again, and you'll spot a distinct one-second pause between bursts of moving orange bars.

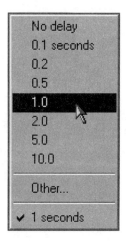

15. Now let's save the animation by selecting File > Save Optimized As from the menu bar. Save it in the myWebPage/Images folder, as bars.gif. We can now add it into the page.

16. Call up index.psd and select slice 01, which is where we want to put the animation. At the moment, this is set to No Image, so ImageReady takes care of filling it for us when the HTML is generated. Let's change this, so that it'll show up in the code as a file called index_01.gif.

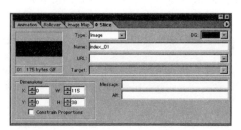

17. Save the page (File > Save Optimized As again) and take a look in the images sub-folder. We don't need the existing `index_01.gif`, so delete this and replace it with our animation, by renaming `bars.gif` as `index_01.gif`. Note that because we've tweaked the page outside of Photoshop/ImageReady, there's a risk that we'll overwrite our handiwork when the page is next saved – so if you do save again, be sure to tell ImageReady *not* to replace that particular GIF. Likewise, if you make any changes to the animation, be sure to save your updates to `images/index_01.gif`.

Case Study

This is where it all comes together. The moment you have been waiting for... where we take all the pieces we have produced so far and turn them into a functional web site. It's worth noting here that we are going to produce the entire site in Photoshop and ImageReady just to show you what these applications are capable of. I would suggest, in the 'real world', using a combination of Photoshop and an HTML editor like Macromedia Dreamweaver or Adobe GoLive, because they offer much more powerful HTML options. Photoshop will produce stunning images and the navigation you need. However, it is recommended to produce your text in HTML, because of faster downloading of text than graphics, also it's much easier to update your content in HTML. Look at Chapter 13 for more information on using Photoshop with programs like Dreamweaver.

This is a long one, but there's a lot of good stuff jammed in here. We are now going to produce all our navigational elements. You're going to practice creating rollovers, image maps, slices and optimizing images. Then we are going to export our finished web site.

Creating type for different states

1. Open our image `home.psd`.

2. Using the Type tool add some menu items. We are just doing a small web site here to demonstrate the abilities of Photoshop and ImageReady, so we just added two areas and an email link. I used Arial Narrow Bold Italic, mainly because everyone has this font or one that resembles it. I used black and 24 pt.

We want to make a rollover that will change when the mouse moves over the type.

3. Duplicate the type layer by dragging it into the New Layer icon.

4. Hide the top type layer: This will be the 'normal state'. We're going to attach a Layer Style to the lower type layer to create our 'rollover state'. Click on the 'f' icon at the bottom of the Layers palette. I used a yellow Color Overlay (R: 250, G: 250, B: 0) and a dark blue Outer Glow (R: 0, G: 0, B: 150). Following the settings here will give a nice contrast to the normal state.

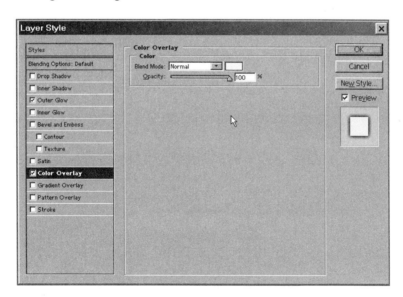

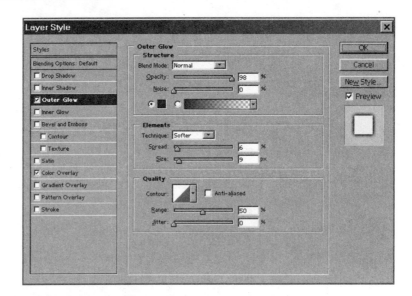

Slicing up our image

1. Now save `home.psd` and launch ImageReady. Press the bottom button in the toolbox.

    Now we are in ImageReady. It's time to slice and serve our images.

2. Click on the Optimize tab (in the well next to Info); set it for JPEG and 42, to keep the file size small.

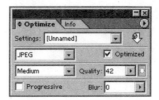

3. Select the text layer that we just applied the effects to (which should still be the active layer; mine is called ABOUT US) and click on Layer > New Layer Based Slice.

This gives us a good starting place to begin our slices.

4. Using the Slice tool, draw a box around the words CAR OF THE WEEK.

It should look something like this when the new slice has been added.

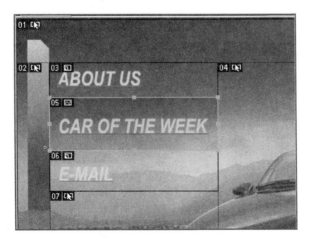

5. Because several small slices will usually load faster than one large image, divide the large image area with another slice. Most browsers will allow several images to download simultaneously, so you can have several slices appearing at once.

6. Change to the Slice Select tool. This way we can select our slices to work with them.

Select our original layer based slice. This is the one around our entire menu: slice 03. We cannot resize this manually until we promote it to a user slice. Then we can resize it to our tastes. Go to Slices > Promote to User-slice.

Still with the Slice Select tool, pull the bounding box up until the slice is just around the words ABOUT US and fits nice and snugly against the slice around CAR OF THE WEEK.

7. With the Slice tool, draw a new slice around E-MAIL.

We've now finished creating our slices. It's time to apply properties to them.

Attaching links to the slices

1. With the Slice Select tool, click on slice 03, ABOUT US. In the Slice palette under URL, assign `info.html` as the link for this slice.

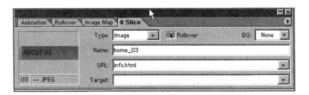

2. For CAR OF THE WEEK assign `car-of-the-week.html`. (Note the hyphens are essential, ImageReady will automatically assign them to spaces on the HTML documents you create.)

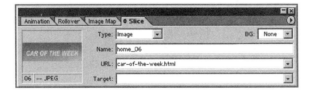

3. For the E-MAIL slice, add: mailto:webmaster@xoticimports1.com. The mailto: is HTML code that will launch the user's email program and insert our address into the To line.

All the links are now set up. All that remains is to set up the rollover effects. We need to do two things here:

- Put the rollover text above the regular text, so that it will be seen when the mouse rolls over.

- Separate the different lines of text for the rollover, so only the word we roll over will be highlighted and not the entire menu.

Creating the rollovers

1. In order to separate the text, we must change it to a regular layer. Click on the rollover text (ABOUT US layer with Effects), right-click on the layer name and choose Render Layer.

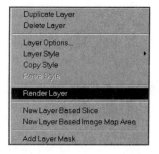

2. To separate the text, draw a selection around the top two menu items. Press SHIFT+ CTRL/CMD+J (Layer > New > Layer via Cut is a bit long-winded!). This will move the selection to a new layer.

3. Now select the new layer. Draw a selection around the top menu item and press CTRL/CMD+SHIFT+J again. You now have each of the three menu items' rollover effects on their own layers.

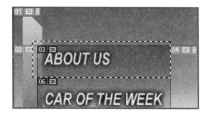

4. This is what you should see in the Layers palette. Name each one after the text contained in that layer by double-clicking on the layer, and add 'over' to indicate that it'll be the rollover state. (You can check what the text is by clicking on the eye icon next to that layer and the text will disappear.)

   Hide the rollover layers and show the plain text layer.

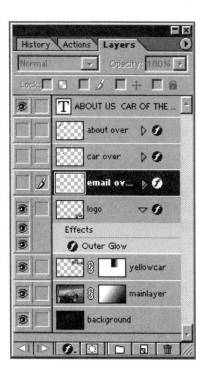

5. If you try to make a rollover now, you will notice that the yellow for the rollover state doesn't show; this is because the original layer is hiding it. To solve this problem, move the text layer under the three rollover layers.

Let's add the rollover effects. Remember how a rollover works in ImageReady? In each 'state' whatever is visible on the main screen will be what the viewer sees.

6. Select the E-MAIL slice and open the Rollover palette. Press Creates new rollover state icon at the bottom of the palette. Select the Over state in the palette and show the email over layer in the Layers palette.

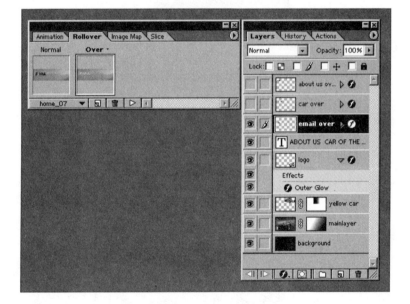

7. Do the same thing for the CAR OF THE WEEK link. Select the slice, press the new state icon, then on the OVER state in the rollover palette, show the car over layer.

8. Once again, repeat the steps for the ABOUT US link.

9. That's it! The rollovers are programmed and ready to test. Seems almost too easy, huh? Save your file in the Final folder as home.psd. Press the Preview in Default Browser button.

Test your rollovers in the web browser. We are only concerned with the rollovers working correctly at this stage (each turning yellow when the mouse is over them). If they don't work, go back and check that everything is done correctly.

Once you are satisfied with your rollovers, it's time to export your whole document as a working web page.

10. Go to File>Save Optimized As and choose the same directory that you saved the earlier page index.html in. Save as home.html for Save as type choose HTML and Images.

Perfect! You have now created your home page. Let's finish off the info page.

This is the page where you would put all the information about your company and products.

Adding more to the info page

1. Open info.psd in ImageReady.

What we are going to do is attach a link to the word Home, so that we will be returned to the home page when we click on it. We're going to be using a different technique this time, called an **image map.**

2. Select the Rectangle Image Map tool.

With this tool, draw around the word Home, then click on the Image Map palette. Attach the link to the URL line by typing home.html into the box.

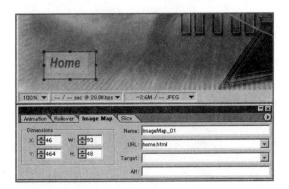

3. Click on the Optimize palette, select JPEG and go for a Quality of about 42.

4. If you want you can slice the image. I haven't done it here for simplicity's sake. In a real-world situation I would slice the image into about 4-6 pieces, so that it would load more quickly. With photographic images use JPEGs, but with 'flat' images GIFs are the best option.

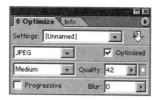

4. File > Save Optimized As.... Once again save to the web directory and name your file info.html.

5. We only have one page left to work on. Here we're going to add a home page link with an image map. We will then break the page into three slices and optimise them differently. We will do all of these tasks in ImageReady.

Outputting the car of the week page

1. Launch ImageReady. In the Working folder open the car of the week.psd document. Let's add some text for the home page link.

2. Select the Type tool and then in the top tool bar select Arial Narrow Bold Italic at 18 px or something similar. For color select a yellow (FFFF00 or R: 255, G: 255, B: 0).

Click on the bottom left and type the word "Home".

We will add an Image Map do this in exactly the same way we did with the info page.

3. Select the Rectangular Image Map tool and draw a box around our word "Home".

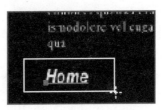

In the Image Map dialog box set the link to home.html. Also in the Alt box enter home. This will cause the mouse pointer to show the label home when it is stationary on the link.

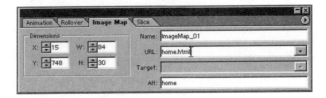

We're going to slice the page into three slices to help it load faster. The second reason is so we will be able to optimize each section with the picture separate from the text, the reason will be explained soon.

4. Choose the Slice tool and create three slices on the page. Starting at the top left drag down and to the right. Stop just above the picture of the car. Drag a second one from the far left just below the car, to the bottom right. (One for the car will automatically be created.)

    You should now see the page sliced into three.

5. Change to the Slice Select tool and select the top slice. In the Optimize palette, choose the GIF format and reduce the Colors to 32.

    You could go as low as 2, but the edges of the type would look a bit rough. Even though you only see 2, there are some transition colors that soften things a bit. You could probably go as low as 8 colors on this image and it would still look OK.

    The reason I chose the GIF format for this slice is two-fold:

- Large areas of smooth color, repeating patterns and line art reduce much better than photos in the GIF format, resulting in a smaller file size.

- Text and solid color tend to look sharper in GIF than JPEG.

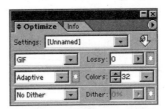

6. Select the bottom slice and repeat the same settings that we used for the top slice.

7. Select the middle slice, the one with the car image on it. For this slice we used the JPEG format and set it at 42. JPEG works best for photos: It supports more colors and produces a smaller file size than a GIF for photographs.

Now we've optimized the slices it's time to export the web page.

8. File > Save Optimized As…. Under our web folder, save as car of the week.html. ImageReady will now save your images and build your HTML page.

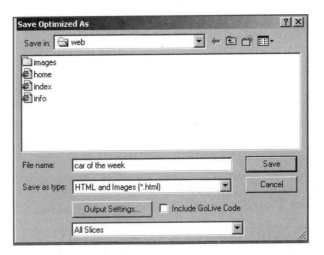

9. Resave and close your PSD document, in case you want to play around more in the future...

Congratulations! You have now finished building your web site. To launch it, navigate to your directory and launch the `index.html` page and click your way around your new creation. Have fun with it and show it off to your friends. Think of how far you have come from when you first opened this book: You have learned a whole host of skills.

This ends our case study project, but it doesn't end your learning experience. Take a coffee break and look at your new web site, you have earned it. When you are ready, continue your journey. We still have two more chapters – a chapter on actions; how you can automate your Photoshop functions, and after that, you will learn about outputting your pages and using Photoshop with other programs. Then check out all the resources that we've listed in the Appendices. Bon voyage!

Summary

In this chapter, we've seen how we can use Photoshop along with ImageReady to help us build whole web pages, and create useful and eye-catching elements for those pages.

We started out by looking at the mechanics of slicing an image up, so that it can be used as the basis of a web page. We identified areas that were blank, and those that were to be used as part of the interface, and saw how we can optimize the page as a whole by optimizing the individual slices that make it up.

We looked briefly at some basic issues of usability, adding tooltips and alt text to each of the relevant images on the page, and got some navigation links up and running. We then rounded things off with a look at ImageReady's support for creating image maps, rollover effects, and animated GIFs.

12 Actions and Automation

What we'll cover in this chapter:

- *Actions*

- *Workflow tips*

- *Automation*

- *Notes and annotation*

- *Online resources*

OK, so you've worked your way through the book and you can do some amazing things with your images. It's been great fun but, just occasionally, doing the same thing over and over again can seem a little repetitive, possibly even a shade dull. Not to worry though, the good people at Adobe have thought of even that.

In this chapter we'll meet Actions, Photoshop's answer to repetitive tasks. We'll also take a look at the various other techniques to speed up your work and collaborate with others to complete large projects efficiently. So let's get going...

Actions

Actions are, in reality, files that tell Photoshop to do certain things in a certain order (like macros in Word). They are pre-recorded commands that, when played back via the Photoshop Actions palette, will reproduce the effect or shortcut recorded into them on a new image, an open image, or even a whole batch of images.

Actions hold a place close to my heart, as I cut my teeth learning Photoshop in the early stages by attempting to duplicate the effects that were on sale as third party actions. They taught me the application of filters, introduced me to channels, and ultimately increased my production time in ways I never thought possible. When a person becomes 'Action Savvy', they can alter existing actions to fit their specific needs on a project, and even develop their own shortcuts where none existed before. For dynamic typography and interface design, Layer Styles have adopted many of the steps that had to be included in actions previously, but Layer Styles will only take you so far. For that reason actions still deserve the recognition that sometimes eludes them.

People use actions for different tasks. Some use them to generate cool type. Some use them to create frames for images. Some people even use their knowledge of actions as a business, hiring themselves out to corporations and showing them how to increase production time on large graphic design projects.

In fact, I could talk about what a good idea these little scripts are all day, but instead we'd better get on with finding out how they work.

What can be recorded in actions?

Though not everything can be recorded, most tools and commands may be recorded in actions. Some other items, such as paths, require specific steps for inclusion.

Here's a breakdown of Action friendly tools and commands:

- Tools (except Paint tools, Dodge, Burn, Sponge, the Sharpen and Blur tools and Background Eraser tool)

- Functions performed in the Layers palette:

    - Filters
    - Selections
    - Resizing
    - Copy/Paste
    - Transform
    - Image Adjustments

- Functions performed in Channels

- Functions performed in Paths (as long as they are pre-named paths)

- History palette functions

- Actions palette functions (called 'nesting': including an action within an action)

Paths are special in that a path drawn while the action is recording cannot be recorded. Paths can be included if they are pre-saved and named in the Paths palette. You can then select the name of the path you wish to use and choose Insert Path from the Actions menu. Now this path can be used on other files, as well as for other commands in the same action.

Brushes are unique also. If the same set is loaded on your computer with the same hierarchy or position, the action will allow you to use the same brush. The action doesn't care about the brush name, but rather its position in the Brushes palette. If you have a different brush set chosen (and therefore a different brush in the position the action uses), you may have very different results when the action is played.

If you work with these scripts for a while, you may find other non-recordable items. For this reason you should always test your action to ensure it runs through to completion. If you find an item that doesn't record properly, you can use an Insert Stop command to allow you to do some manual work midway through an action.

The Actions palette

By default, the Actions palette is tucked behind the History palette. You can bring it to the front using the menus (View > Show Actions) or the keyboard shortcut F9.

When you bring up the Actions palette it will be in one of two modes:

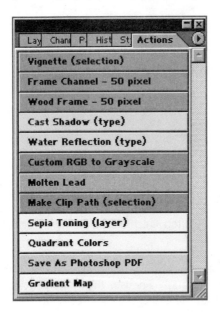 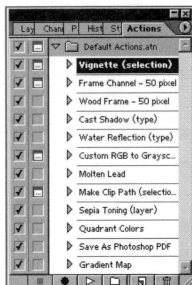

- ■ **Button Mode** (on the left) Displays the actions as a button. Pressing the button activates the action. You may not edit or record when in Button Mode.

- ■ **Edit Mode** (on the right) In this mode the actions are displayed as a list of commands. In Edit Mode you can record, edit, re-arrange commands and so forth. You may also play the action by clicking the Play icon located at the bottom of the palette.

You can switch between the two modes using the Actions palette menu and checking or unchecking the Button Mode option (at the bottom).

The Actions menu

Actions were created to manage and increase a person's workflow when using Photoshop. They can be invaluable time savers, especially when managing and altering multiple images.

Several action sets are shipped with Adobe Photoshop 6. To access them, click the small arrow in the upper right corner of the Actions palette.

When the Actions menu opens, click on Load Actions. You will find them in the folder Photoshop 6 > Presets > Photoshop Actions.

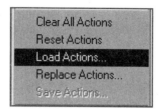

Before you start manipulating actions, let's take a look at what we are dealing with. Though much of the Actions palette menu may seem self explanatory, it would still behoove us to give it a look over.

The top of the menu has 5 options:

■ New Action allows us to begin recording a new action in the selected Action Set. In this window you may name the action you are about to record, select the set in which the action will be placed and later saved, assign the action a shortcut key combination (more on this later) as well as color code the action for easy categorizing when in Button Mode. Clicking on record starts the process so that anything done in Photoshop from then on will be recorded, until you press stop.

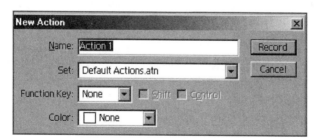

- New Set, a set is a group of actions, typically placed together as they are similar in function or are grouped to perform a series of commands for a specific job. For instance, if there is a folder of images that require a sepia tone, an unsharp mask, a resolution change, etc., with identical settings applied to each image, then those actions might be grouped together in the same set. Actions may only be saved inside Sets (a bit like folders). If you create a single action and want to save it, it still needs to be saved in a set.

- Duplicate will duplicate whatever is selected in the Actions palette. You may duplicate a set, an action, or a command within an action. This function is only available in Edit Mode.

- Delete deletes the Set, Action, or Command selected.

- Play begins playing the selected action.

The next section of the menu concerns itself with recording options.

- Start Recording begins the recording process.

- Record Again allows the user to select an action and re-record the steps with new settings.

- Insert Menu Item allows the user to include non-recordable steps into the action. Painting and toning tools, view and window commands, and tool settings cannot be recorded. This is where Insert Menu Item comes in handy!

- Insert Stop allows the user to inject vital information into an action in the form of pop-up messages. The action ceases to play until the user injects the requested step or reads the information and presses continue or the play button again.

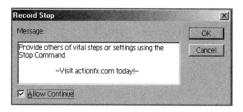

● Insert Path allows complex paths to be included in the action.

The third section of the Actions palette menu allows us to set some action attributes and playback options:

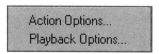

● Action Options allows us to again change the color-coding of the button, change the action's name or assign shortcuts. In all there are 60 combinations of shortcuts we can create for actions.

● Playback Options allow us to set the pace at which the commands in an action are reproduced. Accelerated allows the action to run unimpeded. Step by Step will allow for a short pause during the action playback, and with the Pause For option we can actually set the amount of seconds between commands that the action will delay for. Lastly we can stop the action to inject Audio Annotation. We will talk more about this later in the chapter.

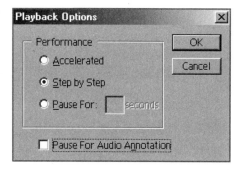

Be warned, even a 1 second delay will slow down the action immensely.

The last two portions we are concerned with deal with what actions are found in the palette, loading and saving them, and finally the mode of the palette:

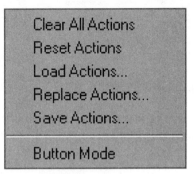

- Clear All Actions removes all actions from the palette.

- Reset Actions restores the default actions to the palette.

- Load Actions allows the user to load new actions for playback. The actions already in the palette will remain present.

- Replace Actions will replace the actions loaded with new ones. The old actions will be removed from the palette.

- Save Actions allows the user to save a new or adjusted action. Remember, though, that it saves a whole set at a time.

- Button Mode toggles the palette between Button and Edit modes.

The rest of the menu (if there is anything there at all) is a storehouse of previously loaded actions. If you wiped out the palette but need to find an action you were just working with, check this portion of the menu before you lose any hair... chances are it is hiding in this list.

Playing Actions in Button Mode

Button Mode displays the actions in the loaded set as color-coded beveled buttons. The button displays an action's name and any shortcut key combinations assigned to the action.

Oil Pastel	Shft+F5

The Oil Pastel action is one of the Image Effect actions sent with the program, but you could use another if you like. I've altered it here by assigning a shortcut key combination to the action. Again, this is done from the Actions palette menu when in Edit Mode by opening the Action Options and assigning key combinations.

1. Let's run this on a photo. Open a picture for a practice run, or download and open `barrel.psd` from the friends of ED web site.

2. We now have the choice to either run the action by pressing the button or using the assigned shortcut keys. Go ahead and press play.

3. Er... that's it. Photoshop will perform a series of commands on your image, altering it as per the Action Designer's specifications.

Some of the actions only work on selections (marked in brackets). Try selecting the barrel and using the Vignette (selection) action from the Default Actions set. There really isn't much to learn from Button Mode, it is fairly self-explanatory. We can't record, edit, or change the playback options, so let's jump over to where the meat of these little scripts reside - in Edit Mode.

Actions in Edit Mode

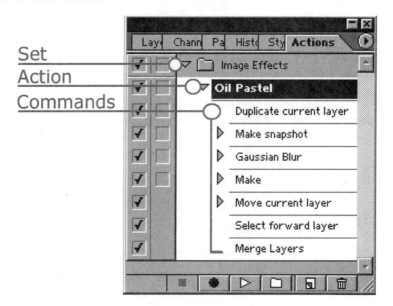

The appearance of the Actions palette in Edit Mode is quite different from Button Mode, and may be a bit daunting at first. Let's have a little look at what is going on here.

There are several actions in the default section. Click on the arrow to the left of Oil Pastel to reveal its steps (you might need to do the same thing with the set first).

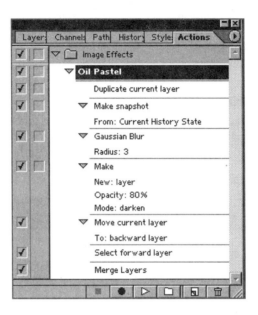

The check boxes along the extreme left hand side allow us to toggle that item or command in the palette on or off. Generally these are all checked. If you want to test how the deletion of a step will affect the action, click the checkbox so that it is empty, and run the action. That step will be bypassed. This is helpful when troubleshooting difficult commands.

The second column allows us to toggle on/off the **modal controls** for commands in the actions. Not all steps have modal controls available. The modal control pauses the action so that you may insert your own values for that step: for instance, if you were to insert a modal control next to the Gaussian Blur command, you could change the setting of 3 to something more suited to your work, either increasing or decreasing the value.

When we get to the actual commands list, this is broken down into 3 main levels:

- **The Action Set** contains either one or many actions. By saving multiple actions to a set, we can categorize actions that pertain to a specific job. For instance, in a set named 'Web Adjustments', you could have actions that apply an Unsharp Mask, reduce the size, apply the Save For Web command, all in separate actions. Remember that actions may only be saved in sets.

- **The Action** is a series of Photoshop commands, recorded in advance, to be applied to an image or batch of images.

- **The Commands** are the individual steps applied to an image during the course of an action.

Clicking the arrow to the left of a list item either collapses or expands the hierarchy for that item. For instance, if I click the arrow next to the set name, I will either see only the set in the palette (collapsed) or I will be able to view all the actions in that set (expanded). We can extend our view by expanding the commands within the action as well.

Editing command settings

If a command in an action has a toggle dialog on/off checkbox next to it, then changing the settings of a command is simple. A pop-up will appear when that step is reached. Not all commands have this option, so in order to change the settings for those commands we would have to do so manually inside the action. You can alter the options, such as button color, for the whole action by double-clicking on its entry in the palette. If you want to keep the new settings, resave the set.

Using drag and drop we can change the order of action commands, drag actions to new sets, duplicate and delete commands and actions.

> *Remember, if you deleted anything from the set that you want to retrieve later, save the set under a new name.*

The record/play controls

If you have a tape player or any software that has a playback option, then you should immediately recognize some of the controls found at the bottom of the Actions palette in Edit Mode.

From left to right, the icons function as follows:

- Stop stops both recording and playback

- Record, when depressed, records every step into the action until the stop button is pressed.

- Play plays (runs) the selected action

- Create New Set creates a new Action Set, useful as actions must be saved as part of a set.

- Create New Action creates a new action within the selected set.

- Trash/Delete – no prizes for anticipating this button's function.

Increasing productivity and saving time

So how can actions increase productivity? I'm sure you have an idea already. If we can record all the steps needed for image correction, button creation, watermark insertion and so forth, and save those recordings for playback later, we can save loads of time by not having to repeat step-by-step image correction over and over again. We simply load the action that performs the required steps, and play it back on the new images. Now a process that could take a half hour freehand can be duplicated EXACTLY within a matter of seconds.

Creating an action

Now that we have some of the basics out of the way, let's get right into these little scripts and see firsthand what they can do!

For the first example, let's work on an existing photograph. You can download this image, `london.jpg`, from the friends of ED web site.

This would be a great photo, but there seems to be a bit too much red. Also, the image is a bit dark. Now if I had several photos with similar problems, I would want to create an action to correct the lot of them, rather than do so manually one at a time.

1. On the bottom of the palette, click the New Set icon.

2. Give the set a name like Take the Red Out, or whatever you prefer.

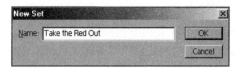

3. Click the New Action icon.

4. In the pop-up, we can name our action even though it has yet to be recorded. You can also do this later by going to the Actions palette menu and select Action Options. We can also choose the set where the action will be saved, assign our shortcut, and color-code the action.

5. Click Record. Everything performed in Photoshop will now also appear as a step in the action, including the exact settings for that step or command.

6. Begin your image correction. Tips on this can be found in Chapter 8, but remember that you won't be able to do anything using the paint tools.

7. When you are satisfied with the result, hit the Stop icon. If you want to change a setting, double-click the command name in the Actions palette and edit the setting in the pop-up.

Why stop there? Once you have your set created, you may want to have more than one action included. Though you could save all of your commands in one action, you might want to separate the functions into separate actions.

Say the color appeared correct on an image but you still wanted to apply a Smart Blur and size reduction. You could turn off the color correction command within the action by unchecking the box to the left of the command in the Actions palette. Alternatively you could copy the action (Duplicate on the Actions palette menu) and delete the command from the duplicate.

Development

Here's a little trick that I use actions for extensively. As you may be aware, Photoshop allows us to create custom brushes, gradients, styles, etc. for later use within the program. Say I want to 'paint' with a leaf. I can define a picture of a leaf as a brush, save it, and later paint with the leaf on whatever image I so choose.

Likewise I can define an image as a pattern, save the pattern set and then re-use that pattern in a layer style at a later date.

What does all this have to do with actions? Say you don't want to keep all your great add-ons to yourself, but want to share them with the world. Then let's say you are like me and develop a web site with the sole purpose of sharing your creations. The web site picks up traffic, your visitors begin to demand more updates and new downloads, you struggle to keep up with demand while your spouse threatens to pack up the kids if you don't shut the computer off occasionally. Oh, if only there were a way to automate the process! Your visitors would be happy and your family would remain intact. Bonus!

You see where this is going. Of course actions can help speed up the process.

1.   Open several images you would like to define as patterns.

2.   Create a new set, and give it a name.

3.   Click the New Action icon, name it and set up a color/shortcut if you like, and click record.

4.   Define one of your open images as a pattern.

5.   Close the image.

6.   Stop recording.

The action should look like this:

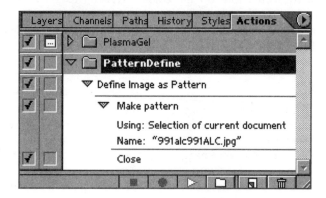

When this action is run on an open image, the image will be defined as a pattern and then closed without altering the image.

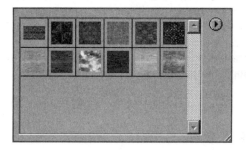

A quick note on patterns

Any image can be defined as a pattern, but not all images make good patterns. When you look for images to use as patterns, try to stick with those that are seamless. There are endless supplies of seamless patterns online: try performing a search for 'seamless backgrounds'.

Another consideration is to stay away from dark images, as they are harder to pull detail out of. If you happen to like a particular design in a dark image, there is a way to pull out the design, if not the color: Apply the pattern to the layer, then apply a white Color Overlay set to Difference mode (remember, double-click on the layer in the Layers palette to change its style). I love that trick – it massively increases the number of effects you can create from a single pattern.

From my experience, light metallic and wooden textures garner the best effects, but that may merely be personal taste. As always, the word of the day is experiment!

Quick scan lines

Actions can help create frequently used special effects to dress up designs. Here's a quick action you can make to reproduce the popular scan lines effect.

1. Open the image you would like to apply scan lines to.

2. Create a new set. Call it Special effects.

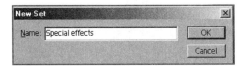

3. Click the New Action icon. Name the action simple scan lines. Click Record.

4. Switch to the Channels palette. Create a new channel.

5. Select the Single Row Marquee tool. Click in the channel to bring up a single row selection, as near to the top of the image as possible.

6. Fill the selection with white.

7. Expand the selection by 1 pixel (Select > Expand).

8. Go to Edit > Define Pattern.

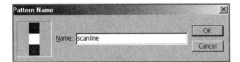

9. Deselect the area using Select > Deselect or COMMAND/CTRL-D.

10. Using the Layers palette, create a new layer, and fill it with the scan lines pattern.

11. Set the layer mode to Overlay, and reduce the opacity of the scan lines layer to 50%.

12. Stop recording and save the action set.

Printing Actions

This is one of the best features regarding the Actions palette, and for some strange reason there was no documentation regarding printing actions included in the Adobe materials or help files. In Photoshop there is a way to save an action set, including every command, setting, adjustment and so on, which you may print and learn from. It is often difficult to follow along while an action is playing, even in Step-By-Step mode, and actually understand the settings being applied and their effect on the image.

To save an action as a text file: Highlight the action set in the Actions palette. Click and hold COMMAND+OPTION/CTRL+ALT on the keyboard, open the Actions palette menu and go to Save Actions. Instead of an .atn file (the normal file extension for actions), Photoshop adds a .txt extension. You can now save the action as text for viewing/printing in your notepad, Simple Text, Word, or your favorite writing program.

Workflow

Let's think about the term workflow for a minute. Work implies a series of functions or tasks that must be completed in order for a desired/contracted result to be achieved. Most often work results in compensation (monetary or otherwise) for the successful completion of those tasks. If a person is unable to achieve the desired result in a timely manner, 'Work' could change to 'Out of Work' in short order.

That's where 'Flow' comes in. This indicates a smooth, continual process of production. When things run smoothly it is much easier to meet those desired deadlines with a product suitable for the particular need. This is a learned process that comes with experience and knowing the best tools, techniques, and shortcuts that apply for the work at hand. Nobody, and I mean nobody, knows all the best routes to all destinations. Once you travel to the same place a few times, you can figure out better ways to get there. Why? Because you are familiar with that particular part of town.

Photoshop is the same. Once you go through a process a few times, you may find easier ways to perform a task or reach your destination. You may even catch on to creating action sets for multiple processes applied to images in the same project.

This section isn't really about teaching you anything specific, as it would be presumptuous to think a few words could manage your business for you. What it can do is make you aware of the options available inside the Photoshop environment that can help to make your work flow.

Know your software

Anyone can own a toolbox, but it doesn't help when your car breaks down if the tools are still wrapped in plastic. Get into the software, work with it, play with it, get down, get funky... you may stumble on that killer shortcut the world has been dying to discover! You will increase your familiarity and knowledge of what Photoshop is capable of as well.

Know your keyboard

Keyboard shortcuts are excellent for increasing production time. Nearly every command in Photoshop has a shortcut attached, and the help files that shipped with Photoshop categorize and list these shortcuts extensively. If you find yourself using the menus a lot, check for the shortcut. These are written next to many of the common menu options.

Know your project

Are you working on web images? Production photos? The project will determine the best way to set up Photoshop. If you are designing a web site with many similar elements (buttons, text, frames for images), creating layer styles for application on various elements in the page will definitely save time. If you are correcting photos, then actions may be the answer. If you have a hundred pictures requiring the same edits, then actions working with the Batch command could possibly shave hours off the project.

Know your resources

If you have a specific need that you just can't figure out, chances are that someone in this big old world has come to the same hurdle and found a way over. Aside from books, there are some valuable online resources to find information: check the newsgroups, do a web search, sign up for mailing lists. There are some great people out there just itching to share their knowledge, so utilize them!

Automation

If you go to File > Automate, you will see several additional ways to automate image processing in Photoshop.

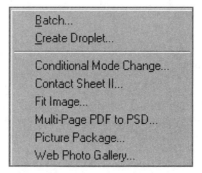

The two items of primary interest in the Automate menu are the Batch command and Create Droplet. We will come back to these shortly. The other items in the lower portion of the list do have their usefulness also.

Conditional Mode Change

The Conditional Mode Change command allows you to convert the color mode of an image during batch processing.

What's the benefit here? When you insert this command into an action, you can run the action on images with different color modes. If this command were not present, whenever the action reached an image that was in a different color mode from the original recording, an error message would pop up. This command helps alleviate that problem.

Contact Sheet II

This command processes a folder of images, creating sheets of thumbnail images. Each image is opened, a thumbnail image created, and the thumbnail is then positioned on a contact sheet with other thumbnails from the folder. Adobe had the right idea when creating this function, but some users find an action better serves for creating mass thumbnails.

In the Contact Sheet II dialog box you can specify the source folder, whether or not to include subfolders, contact sheet dimensions and color mode, thumbnail number and placement (across first, down first), Columns, Rows, and choose font attributes for labeling the thumbnails on the Contact Sheet.

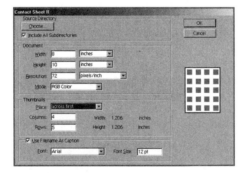

Fit Image

This command allows you to set an image's dimensions without altering the proportions of the image. True, this can be done with the Resize command to a degree. Resize, however, adjusts the size of the image itself, whereas Fit Image tells Photoshop what size image the photo can 'Fit' into. The image will be scaled to fit the area, leaving blank areas if necessary (in much the same way as movies are sometimes 'letterboxed' to fit on a TV screen).

Fit Image will always choose the 'smaller' setting: if the height setting would produce a smaller image, this would be used. If width produces a smaller image, then this is the one selected.

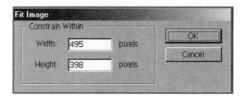

When this command is performed, the image resolution does not change, and the file size will increase or decrease accordingly.

Multi-Page PDF to PSD

Do you have a PDF file that you would like to convert to an image? This is the command for you. This will convert all or part of a PDF file to PSD format.

> *Be sure to back up the PDF file prior to running this command! Once converted, it is an image. You can no longer edit it and the output will be at a lower resolution than the original PDF file.*

Any images that were included in the PDF file will need to be opened after the conversion. The dimensions of the new image file are founded in the original PDF page size.

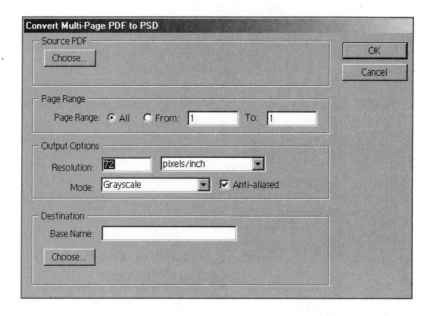

Picture Package

Have you ever had portraits done? When I was a kid we dreaded the yearly photo shoot. Now that I'm a parent I relish putting my children through the rigors of sitting still for endless photo sessions. After paying a small fortune, my wife and I eagerly anticipate opening the package containing the pictures. That's when the reality of those school photo-shoots rushes back to haunt us. Invariably one of the kids has either blinked, frowned, or stuck out their tongue in nearly every pose. Usually there is just one good picture that we can torment all our relatives and friends with. That sheet of salvageable image is then diced up and shipped to every grandparent, aunt, cousin, passing acquaintance...

The Picture Package function was designed with those photo sheets in mind. With it you can place several copies of a photo in varying sizes outside of the photo sheet document. The photo is then resized and placed in the photo sheet.

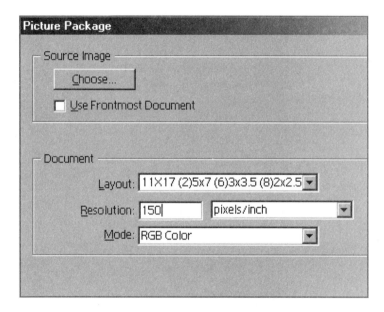

Batch Processing

This function runs in conjunction with the Actions palette, and for those who process multiple images as a course of their work this command is invaluable in the automation process. With an action you can process an image with the settings defined by the action. With batch processing, you can process hundreds of images, each conforming to the specification of the action attached to the batch. When you have a series of images that need to share the same attributes, this command is invaluable.

1. Open an image. Create your action using this image as a model, or load the action you want to run in the Actions palette.

2. Create two folders. Place the images you want to run the action on in the first folder. This will be your source folder. The second will be the destination folder where the updated images will be saved.

3. Go to File > Automate > Batch. In the Play section of the dialog box, choose the action set, and action that you wish to run. Choose the Source of your images. You have three options:

- Folder
- Import
- Open Files

For this example we will be choosing Folder.

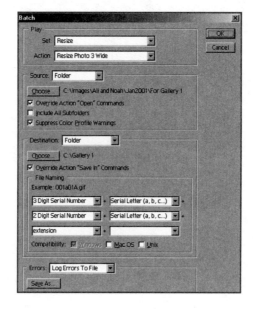

4. In the Source field, choose the folder that contains the unaltered images.

5. Select Override Action "Open" Commands, uncheck Include All Subfolders, and check Suppress Color Profile Warnings.

6. Choose your Destination. Here again, there are three choices:

- None
- Save and Close
- Folder

We will be saving to the folder we created.

7. Check Override Action "Save In" Commands.

8. This next portion is very cool. We can tell Photoshop to automatically name the processed files using combinations of file names, numbers, letters, dates and file extensions. Do so now.

9. Select system compatibility.

> You may either choose to have Photoshop stop for errors, or have the error messages logged to a file. The latter option is preferred if you plan to process large quantities of images while you are away from the computer.

Batch processing has a wide range of uses for people in all areas of image processing. Corrections to color, alterations to image size, embedding of watermarks and creating thumbnail previews are just a few examples. Images may even be imported directly from external hardware such as digital cameras and scanners for Batch Processing.

Running multiple actions in one batch

This is a popular request in the Photoshop forums. There is a way to run multiple actions in a single batch process: Include a batch command within the action! In other words, record a new action that includes batch processing attached to other actions. It can be confusing, but it can also be very powerful and an immense time saver.

Droplets

A Droplet is similar to Batch Processing, but with one very unique difference. Where a **Batch** is a function of Photoshop, a **Droplet** is its own little program designed to reside on your desktop or a folder on your computer. You set these up the same as a Batch and they work in a similar fashion. After you create a Droplet, you can place its icon on your desktop, drag and drop image files directly over the icon, and they are then processed in Photoshop.

Photoshop need not be open to activate the Droplet. The Droplet will open Photoshop for you and begin running the corresponding action on the image or folder of images.

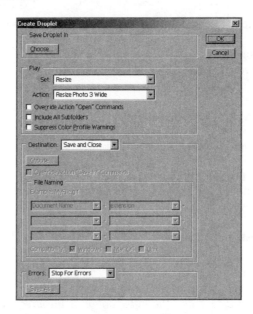

What this option is doing is allowing you to save a Batch command as a file for re-use. Not only can you save the settings of a Batch this way, but this also gives you yet another cool tool which you can distribute to your friends or co-workers. Droplets can be saved to disk, stored on a CD, sent via email and even distributed on a web site.

Annotations

Photoshop offers two more unique tools for streamlining workflow. These are the Notes tool and the Audio Annotation tool.

Notes tool

This is a nifty way to paste a note right onto an image. Though not as fancy as some of the other tools, this is very helpful in delivering thoughts to other designers who will be viewing the image or injecting notes to yourself when you have to leave a project. These can help remind you where you were when you stopped work the last time.

Audio Annotation tool

If you have a microphone and a sound card, you can make use of this feature. Similar to the Notes tool, this allows you to inject brief audio messages into an image.

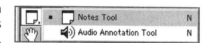

This tool may not be the best option for everyone, as the inclusion of audio messages in a production environment has very little useful application. The audio files will increase the file size immensely, which on a multi-layer PSD file can only hinder its manageability. Play with this one on personal photos, but use the Notes tool for messaging in a busy environment.

Summary

Automation isn't a cure-all for every situation. Some processes will still need to be hammered out by hand, but being familiar with your automation options will definitely help you shave some time off those pressing projects. As always, getting into the program and working with it both during production and in free time is the best way to learn.

Online action resources

There are several helpful sites on the Internet where you can download, upload, or learn about actions from others who share an interest in these little scripts.

The Action Xchange:
http://www.actionxchange.com
This site has recently been acquired by Adobe, but is still the best on the Web for downloading actions, as well as allowing you to contribute your own. Not only can you download thousands of Photoshop Actions, but GoLive actions are offered as well.

Action Fx Photoshop resources
http://actionfx.com
My own web site. Download dozens of Actions, Layer Style sets, and Brushes for Photoshop in the free area. There are also several tutorials to get you working with Actions. If you like what you see you can buy a membership for access to over 3000 additional Photoshop add-ons created by me.

Elated
http://www.elated.com
Download several helpful Action Kits from this great resource! This site also has some great tutorials with the Graphics-minded Web Designer in mind.

WebTekNique
http://www.webteknique.com
Yet another great site for Actions. Very well done. Also offering tutorials to get you started.

Deep Space Web
http://www.deepspaceweb.com
A great site devoted to my favorite topic: Photoshop. Downloads, tutorials, forum, plug-ins, brushes... not to mention the webmaster is a really nice guy. Check this one out!

Action Addiction
http://www.actionaddiction.com
A long running site, with plenty of actions to keep you busy!

There are many more online. Performing a simple search for 'Photoshop Actions' should garner you a very large list. Thanks to all the helpful designers out there willing to share their work!

13 Printing and Output

What we'll cover in this chapter:

- *PDF; what it is and how it helps your workflow*

- *Extracting PDF images in Photoshop*

- *Getting creative with PDF*

- *Print options*

- *Proofing and printing workflow*

- *CMYK profiles*

- *Clipping paths in Photoshop with a page layout program the pro way*

- *Photoshop and Illustrator*

- *Photoshop and Flash*

- *Photoshop and Dreamweaver*

▶

In this chapter we are going to look at different ways of outputting Photoshop documents and also look at combining Photoshop with some other software.

PDF

Ever since the Web has been around, people have been searching for ways to:

- Save documents in a cross-platform format

- Find ways to display layouts on the Web without losing their formatting

- E-mail documents with layouts intact

Adobe came to the plate with Acrobat, now at version 5. This has pretty much become the standard around the world for creating and viewing PDF files. PDF is the abbreviation for Portable Document Format. Using Adobe's technology we are now able to build your documents easily, directly from your page layout program. If you have Distiller installed, you can set it as a 'printer' and producing a PDF document is as simple as printing from any program on your computer.

Even better, Adobe has built the ability to generate PDF documents from its products like Illustrator, InDesign, PageMaker and of course Photoshop. These documents can be viewed by millions of people who have installed the free Acrobat reader software available from www.adobe.com/products/acrobat/readstep.html.

In this chapter we're looking at how Photoshop can open and generate files in PDF. The full version of Acrobat can embed hyperlinks, animations, forms, sound and even video clips. In short, we dare not scratch the surface lest we need another 500 pages!

One of the great things I love about PDF is the ability to e-mail layout proofs to clients. They receive them instantly and can add annotations. It will come back with a red line through a chapter and a sticky note attached saying, "What were you thinking Colin, this doesn't go here!" I then make the change and zip it off again, all done in an hour. Much better than making a color proof, waiting for it to be collected and delivered, waiting for it to be returned, making the change etc.. Of course you still have to do color proofs at some stage, but PDFs save a lot of time and money.

The other great thing about PDF, is the ability to output the same document in either a high-res or low-res format. The low-res will email quickly, and all the fonts will be sharp because they are embedded. I can also go from Mac to PC and back without anything being changed, even the fonts will look identical.

At high resolution, PDF is good enough to send to the printers, and many designers and publishers use this method today because it solves the nightmare font issues.

The picture below shows a document I threw together using InDesign, Adobe's premium page layout software.

From InDesign, I exported the image as a PDF. As you can see here, the document is now in Acrobat and it is exactly the same. Except now it is portable. I could print it, e-mail it, put it on a disk, even post it on the Web and people wouldn't need InDesign or my fonts to view it exactly as it looks here. Now I think Adobe deserves a handclap for that one!

Extracting PDF images in Photoshop

You just had a brief introduction to PDF. We are now going to look at some of the more advanced options available, and a neat trick that I am sure you will enjoy!

We can actually take the pictures out of a PDF, (depending on the security settings) and open them as separate documents in Photoshop. Once they are in Photoshop they become flattened, native PSDs and we can apply filters, add layers, save as any format and treat them like any Photoshop document.

Want to know how? Of course you do.

Viewing PDF images in Photoshop

1. In Photoshop go to File > Import > PDF Image....

2. Open the PDF file pdf template.pdf from the friends of ED site (This will work with any PDF that contains images).

3. The PDF Image Import dialog box will open and you will notice at the bottom it gives you a count of the images in the document. Here, it says we have two. Image one is displayed in the window. We can press the arrow key and view image 2 if we wish. Pressing Go to image imports just that image. Let's press Import all images so we import both.

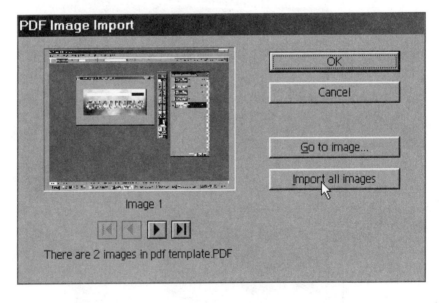

4. Now we have both images open as documents in Photoshop. Go to Image > Image Size and set the desired resolution, 72dpi for screen or 300dpi for print. We need to do this because the resolution will have been changed from the standard if it has been resized during layout.

Getting creative with PDF

What if you told me you wanted to take the page I created in Acrobat, and add a colored background, with all the text and images intact, using Photoshop? A few years ago I would have told you, "You're crazy."

We already know how to bring the pictures into Photoshop, but we can also bring the entire document into Photoshop. Now we're going to import a PDF document in Photoshop, then we're going to apply it to a colored background, and save it as an image file.

Altering the PDF in Photoshop

1. This time instead of going to the Import menu, click on File > Open. Change Files of type to All Formats or Photoshop PDF. Find our PDF document (pdf template.pdf) and click on Open.

2. A new dialog box will pop up asking to rasterize the PDF document. Let's keep the original size and set the resolution to 300dpi so that it will be high enough resolution for printing. If you're short on memory, you could use a lower resolution, that will be processed more quickly and use less RAM.

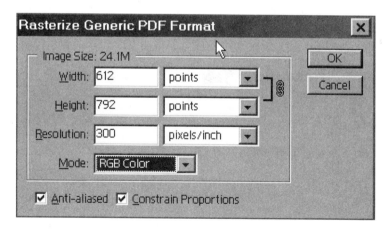

3.   After a few seconds of computing (depending on the power of your machine), the document will appear in all its glory in Photoshop. It is treated just like other imports of vector images, (e.g. Illustrator or Freehand files) and rasterized, fonts and all. You will no longer be able to edit the text, so I hope you already did your proof reading.

> *Watch out though; rasterized text prints very badly as it is half-toned (treated like an image) which leads to fuzzy edges.*

4.   Notice here that there is a checkerboard pattern in the background, showing that there is transparency in the document. That is because I used transparent text boxes in InDesign. You could do the same in Quark or PageMaker.

It's called Layer 1 in the Layers palette (the page is flattened).

5.   Now take any image, here I dug up good old Photoshop Pete from Chapter 5. Drag and drop it into the document as outlined in Chapter 10.

6.   We can then resize to fit our page and drag the layer underneath Layer 1 (our rasterized PDF).

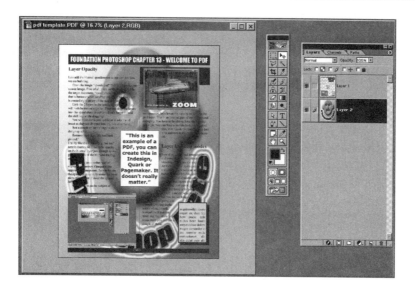

7. As we have already done in the course of this book several times, use the levels to lighten the background. I prefer this method over dropping the opacity because it only lightens the shadows and doesn't affect the lighter tones. Using the Image > Adjust > Levels, slide the bottom left hand arrow to the right as shown here. This will lighten up the image sufficiently for the type to be readable, and not cause too much distraction from the foreground elements and page layout.

A background is not the focus of the page and as such should not draw the focus of the eyes away from the content. This is a common mistake of novice designers, in both print and web design; getting so carried away with new tricks that you lose the message and the audience.

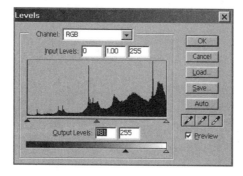

8. Zoom up to 100% and you will notice that the text is still readable although it has lost some of its sharpness. You could save this image as a TIFF and print it on your inkjet printer, resample it down and embed it into your web page as a graphic or export it as a PDF. This method works well for comp layouts and prints reasonably well on an inkjet, but it is not really appropriate for high quality output.

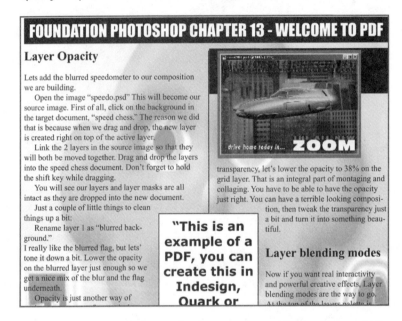

Here's a little trick that I sometimes employ, to save time while working on high resolution projects, like magazine ads or articles. Using the method above, I import the PDF to act as a template showing me the positioning of the text. I can then design my background in Photoshop with a good idea of how it will look when placed in the final page.

When I am finished, I delete the PDF layer and save the background as a flattened TIFF. I then place the TIFF image beneath the text in my layout software and it fits perfectly! No more guessing or tedious measuring.

Print options

One of the parts of Photoshop to have a facelift for version 6.0 was the printing options. Let's take a look the enhanced features under File > Print Options…

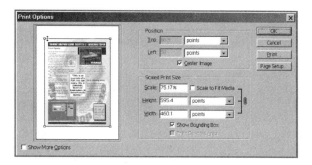

A really nice feature is the Scale to Fit Media. If you have ever printed anything on an inkjet printer you will notice it has a tendency to cut things off around the edges. This is called gripper space. The printer is unable to print right up to the edges, and as a result there can be some clipping of your images. The scale to fit option will slightly reduce your print size so it will all fit. Of course whatever size your image is, it will be reduced so you can print it. If you have a 33-inch wide document, it will fit on a letter-sized sheet. You have the option to reduce or enlarge by size or percentage.

Another nice feature is the preview. You can see how your document will look on the printed media.

When the Show Bounding Box option is enabled (but the Scale to Fit Media is not), you can drag to resize with your mouse in the preview window.

When you click on Show More Options, you will see some advanced options available to you for use in proofing and prepress (below).

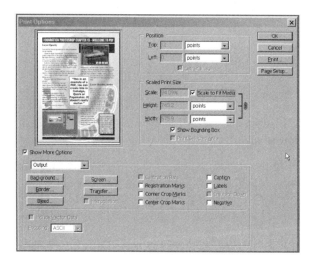

Proofing and printing workflow

Proofing is a term used for any color print that you can use to preview what the final printed piece will look like. OK, buckle up and get ready for 100 pages of theory all jammed into just a couple!

The typical workflow for a commercial project goes something like this:

- Work order – the client/art director's requests and needs

- Hand sketch – your layout concept, can be really rough

- Comp – produce a rough or marker mock up of the layout

- Color proof from ink jet printer

- Approval from client/art director

- Produce full resolution work

- Second color proof from inkjet or fiery

- Second approval from client/art director

- Send to film - image setter/service bureau. This process is called 'flashing' or 'ripping' to film

- Proof Blueline for layout and typesetting

- Check match-print/color-key for color accuracy

- Press-check for correct setup

- Finished piece

Depending on your setup and office/clients, you might have a slightly different approach, but this is the general idea.

When your work is printed, typically a piece of film is made for each channel that is printed. Generally for 4-color work you will have four pieces of film: cyan, magenta, yellow and black. If there are any added spot colors, these pieces of film will also be included. The film is a sheet of plastic with black dots in a very fine pattern.

The current way of producing film is called digital output; this is film produced from your digital file. You may also hear the term 'camera ready' used. This is really a throwback from the old-school ways, when a piece of art would be mounted on an art-board and photographed with a special camera for producing print film.

The film is then used to burn plates, which in turn will be used on the printing press to produce your final printed piece. In some of the newer printing processes called CTP (Computer to plate) the film step is bypassed altogether. Which makes proofing all the more important.

Let's look at a typical color proof and explain some important features.

There are 2 types of proofs:

- **Initial proof** could be a color laser or inkjet. Shows the layout and gives an idea of the color.

- **Color key** or **match print** are produced from the actual film and are very accurate. What you see is more or less what will be printed. You will always lose a small amount of vibrancy in the colors because of dot gain (ink spreading on the paper). The color key is generally 4 sheets of transparent plastic, each printed in its respective CMYK color. When stacked together they will show how the final piece will look. The other type is the Kodak match print. This is a high quality color print on a sheet of photographic paper. This type of proof resembles a photograph.

The main advanced printing options:

- **Crop marks** indicate the trim size of the page

- **Registration Marks** are used to ensure that the plates are correctly lined up with each other

- **Color bar** is printed outside the crop marks and used to help calibrate the color and tones

- **Caption** will print out any text entered into the file info box

- **Labels** will print the title of the document on top

- **Negative** will output the image as a negative

- **Background** allows you to set a color to be printed outside the image area

- **Border** prints a black border to run around the image, you can specify its size

- **Bleed** prints the crop marks on the inside of the image area, so when the page is cropped ink goes right up to the edges

Line screen

Print is measured in lpi (Lines per inch), known as the **line screen**. Typically a newspaper or other low quality print will be 85lpi. A magazine is 133lpi-150lpi. A high quality brochure would run either 150lpi, 175pli or even 200lpi. Other terms to look out for are:

- **Emulsion** is a term that refers to which side of the film the black is printed on. "E-Down means that the black is printed on the bottom of the sheet. This is standard for the US.

- **Positive/Negative** refers to the film. While in Europe positive film is widely used, it is pretty much standard practice to use 'negatives' in the US.

CMYK profiles

When you are working on a four-color job it is always a good idea to request a CMYK profile from your printer. Generally they will send you an ICC file which you can load into Photoshop. This is done using Edit > Color Settings then, under CMYK option, select Load. Then you can load the .icc file the printer provided.

This will ensure that when you convert your images to CMYK that the settings are the best match for the printer's set-up.

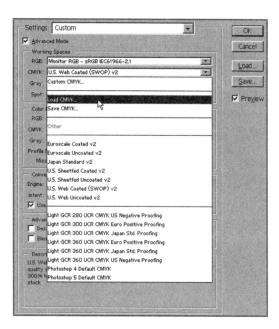

If the printer doesn't send the file, but rather gives you the settings another way, they can be added to Photoshop by going to Edit > Color Settings under CMYK option, select Custom CMYK. Enter your settings into the boxes.

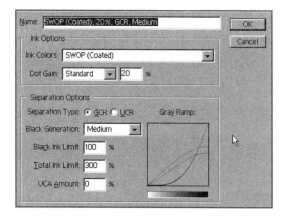

I hope you now have some kind of an idea what happens to your file now when you send it to the printers.

Let's wrap up this chapter and the book with some ways you can use Photoshop with other programs...

Clipping paths in Photoshop with a page layout program

As we heard earlier in the book, clipping paths are a method of defining which area of the image your layout software prints. What we are going to do is take this image (a guitar) and separate it from its background, to use it for print in a page layout program.

Importing an image into a page layout program

1. The first thing that we need to do is draw a path around the object with the Pen tool (P). You will see the working path in the Paths palette; from the drop-down menu choose Save Path.

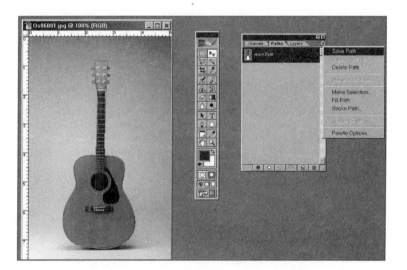

2. The default name Path 1 will work just fine for our purposes.

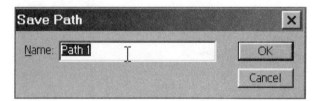

3. Still working in the Paths palette, select the Clipping Path option.

4 This dialog box will appear and in the drop-down menu select our defined path: Path 1. Our path is now set as the clipping path in Photoshop. Just leave the flatness as the default setting.

5. Save the document. Choose EPS (Encapsulated Postscript) or DCS (Desktop Color Separation) 1.0. Either format will work for our purpose since they both support clipping paths. I chose DCS. The DCS 2 option is only used for outputting spot color channels.

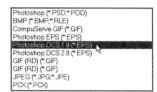

Under the preview I chose 8-bit TIFF, so that I will get a color preview of my picture when I import it to my layout software. The other option is a 2-bit TIFF. But this will only display a dithered black and white representation of our image.

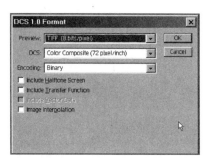

6. Now I am using InDesign, but the principle is exactly the same for Quark Xpress or PageMaker etc. This next part is meant to give you an idea of what you could do using InDesign, since this is a Photoshop book, we won't look at it in great detail (A 60-day tryout version an be downloaded from www.adobe.com/products/tryadobe/main.html#InDesign).

7. First of all we open our InDesign or Quark document with text that we want to wrap around our image, `Pdf template.idd`.

8. Let's import the image: File > Place, I selected my EPS image and clicked OK.

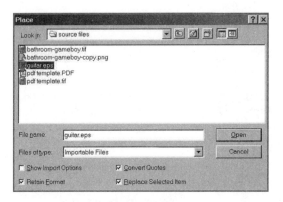

9. Click anywhere with the cursor and you can see that our guitar has been successfully imported minus the background.

10. The next thing we need to do is tell our layout software that we have a clipping path. With InDesign that is Object > Clipping path.

11. Under Type, select Photoshop Path.

12. Now InDesign knows where the path is. Notice that the type still doesn't wrap, that is because we still have to set the text wrap options. In the Text Wrap palette click on the Wrap Around Object Shape button. Generally the default settings should work well for the spacing.

13. Now see how the text wraps around the guitar image. Notice how the document background can show through nice and clean. This is the same method that magazine and brochure designers use all the time.

14. Double-click the scale option and enter 70%. There, the size looks much better.

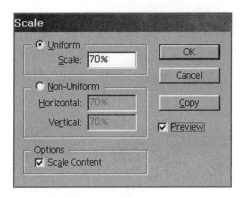

15. Drag the image into position and notice how the path moves with it. That is because the clipping path is attached to the image frame.

Pick up any magazine and have a look through it and see how many clipping paths you can notice. Now you can look and say: "I know how they did that!"

Photoshop and vector programs like Illustrator

There are a number of ways to use Photoshop and Illustrator together. We already know we can export paths from Photoshop to Illustrator, but we can also export entire images into Illustrator, or other vector programs like Freehand, or Corel Draw. This is in much the same way that we can open these vector images in Photoshop. Many illustrators draw the basic outlines in Illustrator and then paint the color in Photoshop.

Improving an Illustrator image in Photoshop

Getting really deep into painting techniques is beyond the scope of this book, in fact entire books have been written on the subject. So I just want to demonstrate what is possible in Photoshop and Illustrator together and give you a brief overview.

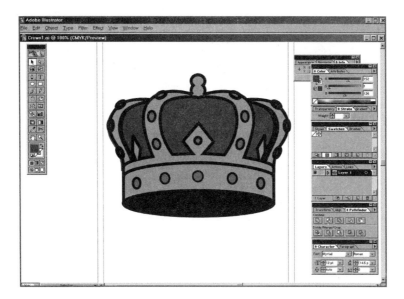

Here I have a piece of clipart I found on the Corel Draw CD; I could have modified it in Corel Draw or Freehand, but I chose Illustrator just to stick with Adobe for now (again, a trial can be downloaded from the Adobe site). I'll show you what I did with Illustrator but you can load a similar image, crown.eps, from the friends of ED site for use with the later steps.

■ I separated the 2 parts of the image (by ungrouping the objects and dragging the purple 'velvet' area away) before exporting them from Illustrator, so that I could work on them as layers.

■ In Illustrator I saved this image as an Illustrator EPS, this seems to be the format that imports into Photoshop most successfully.

1. We can open Illustrator images in Photoshop by clicking on Open, (crown.eps from the support files) selecting EPS and importing the image. Let's rasterize at 150 dpi and RGB color. That's good enough for an inkjet printer. Once you click OK, the image will be converted to bitmap.

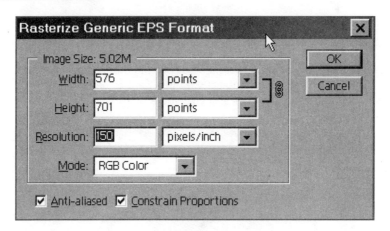

2. Here is my image in Photoshop; until it was imported it was a vector image, which could be resized without any jagged edges occurring, but as soon as we applied the rasterization, it changed into a bitmap image.

3. Now we can separate the elements into two layers and align the 'velvet' background under the metal part of the crown. Do this by selecting one of the areas and RIGHT-CLICKING (COMMAND-CLICKING on a Mac) inside the selection. Chose Layer via Cut from the pop-up menu.

4. Now it's time to play around with the image using the techniques you have learnt. I used the Airbrush tool to make the image appear to have more depth. I did this by lightly painting shadows and highlights. Then I applied drop shadows to the metal part of the crown and the image as a whole. I also applied a slight bevel to the gold part of the crown I added white highlights to the jewels with the Airbrush tool to make then look more shiny. After all the painting, I rotated the entire image.

   As you can see this is an easy way to jazz up boring clipart. This also shows the superior painting power of Photoshop over the vector formats. Both types have their strengths and weaknesses but as far as realism goes, Photoshop shines.

Photoshop and Flash

I am sure this question is going to occur to you sometime, so I will answer it here. "How do you get a Photoshop image into Flash, without the background?" You can use this same method for Macromedia Director too.

Importing an image with a transparent background into Flash

1. Put your image on a separate layer with a transparent background.

2. Go to File > Save for Web and select either a PNG or a GIF. I chose PNG24 because the image quality is higher, though the trade off is that not all browsers recognize it, unlike the ubiquitous GIF. We want to do our compression in Flash for two reasons; we don't want to do it twice, and Flash does a better job of compressing files.

3. Check Transparent and make sure Matte is set to None. If you are going to be using the image with the same colored background all the time then you could select a matching matte option and save it to your disk.

4. Launch Flash and click File > Import

5. The only options we need are the ones that will get us our image so check Include Images **and select** Flatten Image.

6. Now we have the image in Flash.

7. Open the Library (CTRL/CMD+L) and select our object. In the Library palette, click on Options > Properties. Here is the information about our imported image. We want to optimize its size now because the image is still huge.

8. Uncheck the box that says Use document default quality.

9. Compression set to JPEG is great for our purposes. Change the quality to a lower level – I would go for 35, which will give us a small file size, but you may find the quality trade off too strong.

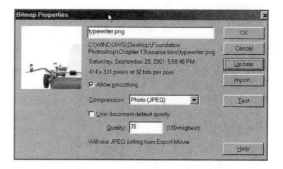

10. Let's have a look and see what has happened to our image... To see the results of our compression: Press Test and you will see the details in the dialog box. Notice that the file size is now 13.7kb, that's a long way from its original 548.1 kb. Click and drag on the preview to scroll around, and see the effect it has had on our image quality.

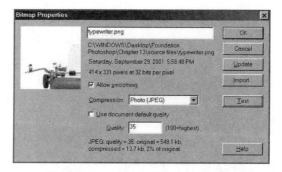

11. Let's just change one thing to make the image more flexible and manageable in Flash. With the image selected: Press F8 *or* Insert > Convert to Symbol to convert our image to a symbol. Name it Typewriter (or something appropriate) and click the Graphic radio button.

12. You could add all kinds of motion and interactivity to your image now, then finish your composition, and publish your Flash movie complete with a Photoshop image.

An interesting thing to note about Photoshop and Flash: Did you know that you can export your animated GIFs from ImageReady right into Flash? Flash will assign them frames and reproduce the animation for you.

■ Create your animated GIF in ImageReady and save it as a GIF.

■ Create a blank movie clip first, that way it will be easier to resize and reposition the animation on the stage.

■ Import the GIF the same way we imported the previous image. A dialog box will ask us if we want to import the entire sequence. Click Yes.

■ The animation will not show until you go to Test movie. Also be sure that your animation has no tweened transparency because Flash will not maintain any Photoshop opacity settings.

Photoshop and Dreamweaver

No good Photoshop book is complete without mentioning Dreamweaver or GoLive. I want to quickly show you my design workflow for my web site. The first thing I did is create the entire site in Photoshop, including rollover images. It is a very common practice among designers to create the layout in Photoshop first, and then slice up the images and build the site in GoLive, Dreamweaver, FrontPage, ColdFusion or another WYSIWYG HTML editor.

ImageReady makes it so easy to apply advanced features like rollover images, image maps, slicing images and animations. It also does an outstanding job of optimizing the images for a small file size and fast download. There are many things that ImageReady cannot do, like handling body text in HTML, tables and frames, and integrating with Flash and sound. The solution is to use the two programs together to produce professional web sites.

Weaving your dream

1. Once you have finished your design in Photoshop use the Jump to ImageReady button at the bottom of the toolbox.

2. ImageReady is the place I like to do all my rollovers and slices. At the time of writing, these tools are more powerful and easy to use in ImageReady. Then I optimize and export the whole shooting match to HTML. These techniques have been covered in Chapter 11 and in the case study.

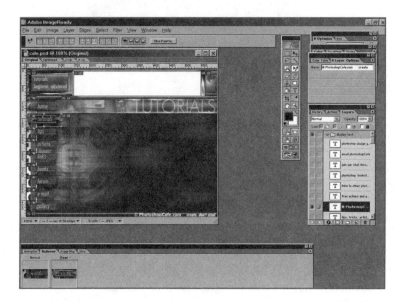

3. Here we have the document in Dreamweaver. It's time to add your content.

A little thing I like to do is, delete the image in the main body of the document, and set it as the background image in the table. That way I get to build my main design in tables, which I prefer over layers because layers are so unpredictable when the viewer changes browsers, screen resolution or font size. Don't flame me if you disagree, it's just my opinion. Everyone needs to find what works best for them and work with their own system. Check your target audience before you begin to design a web site. This will give you an idea of the screen resolution they are using, and browsers etc. For example, if you are designing for designers, you know the majority of them will be using reasonably current systems, and a high-resolution display. For a mainstream site you should expect users to have older machines with smaller resolutions; believe it or not many people simply aren't interested in, or cannot afford to, upgrade their machines every couple of years.

4.   The place where we can run into some trouble here is when we try to modify one of the rollovers. In Dreamweaver, the behavior is called a custom script and can't be modified without going into code level... or can it?

Well I'm glad you asked. If you go to www.macromedia.com and pop into the Dreamweaver exchange, you will find a little plug-in behavior called "Insert ImageReady HTML". This little behavior created by Massimo Foti for Lynda.com converts the ImageReady code into native Dreamweaver code! That's one of the reasons why Dreamweaver remains the most popular WYSIWYG (What You See Is What You Get) HTML editor. If you have a version of Dreamweaver older than version 4, you will need to download the free extension manager as well.

5.   Once you have converted the code to Dreamweaver you can treat it like a native Dreamweaver document. Once I have created the basic page, I will save it to file and then use it as a template to build all the other pages in my web site. You can still place Photoshop images into Dreamweaver. I will make unique page titles for each page.

When you have built the basic framework for your web site, then it's just a matter of plugging in all your content and extra images, movies, and sound clips. Soon you will have all your new Photoshop images up on your web site for the whole world to view and enjoy.

Game over

Now you are familiar with the tools and interface of Photoshop. You understand the painting and selection tools. You've worked with paths, layers, channels, and color. You have designed work for print and the Web. And you've used actions, filters, layer styles and corrected images.

Congratulations! You have successfully finished an intensive instruction in Photoshop. You are no longer a 'newbie'; you are now officially a Photoshopper! Our goal has been more than just showing you a few cool tricks. We have endeavored to train you to become a thinking designer. Apply what you have learned now and there is no limit to what you can achieve.

Where to now? Experimentation is key to mastering any program. You won't be just clicking blindly anymore, but you have an understanding of what is happening. Check out some of the resources in the appendix and keep on having fun. Look at other people's work and learn from them. Remember; there is never a traffic jam on the extra mile!

For further inspiration, I recommend the New Masters Of Photoshop book also by friends of ED. This book will inspire you and give you an idea of the type of things you will be eventually creating with Photoshop.

Thanks for reading this book; we enjoyed investing this time with you. Happy Photoshopping!

A   Sourcing Artwork

Here is a list of useful web sites:

Photoshop sites

Adobe	http://www.adobe.com
National Association of Photoshop Professionals	http://www.photoshopuser.com
Planet Photoshop	http://www.planetphotoshop.com
Photoshop CAFE	http://www.photoshopcafe.com
Action FX	http://www.actionfx.com
Neofrog	http://www.neofrog.com
Anders Qvicker	http://www.aqa-d.se
GFX	http://user.fundy.net/morris
Photoshop gurus handbook	http://gurus.onlinedesignschool.com
PS workshop	http://www.psworkshop.net
Phong	http://www.phong.com
Eyeball design	http://www.eyeballdesign.com
JLS websource	http://www.jlswebsource.com
thinkdan.com	http://www.thinkdan.com
Designs by Mark	http://www.designsbymark.com
Stewart Studios	http://www.stewartstudio.com
myjanees	http://www.myjanee.com

Drawing

PolyKarbon	http://www.polykarbon.com
Psionic	http://www.psionic.pwp.blueyonder.co.uk

Plug-ins

Alienskin	http://www.alienskin.com
auto fx	http://www.autofx.com
Extensis	http://www.extensis.com
Andromeda	http://www.andromeda.com
Corel	http://www.corel.com
Procreate	http://www.procreate.com

Fonts

1001freefonts.com	http://www.1001freefonts.com
fontsource	http://fontsource.jlswebsource.com

DTP

CreativePro	http://www.creativepro.com
Desktop publishing.com	http://desktoppublishing.com
Deezin	http://www.deezin.com
coolgraphics	http://www.coolgraphics.com

Stock Photos

Comstock	http://www.comstock.com
Photospin	http://www.photospin.com
photodisc	http://www.photodisc.com
geddyone.com	http://www.gettyone.com
corbis	http://www.corbis.com
Hemera studios	http://www.hemerastudio.com

Magazines

Design Graphics	http://www.designgraphics.com.au
Computer Arts	http://www.computerarts.co.uk
Macdesign	http://www.macdesignonline.com
Photoshop User	http://www.photoshopuser.com
Inside Photoshop	http://www.elementkjournals.com/ips
Dynamic Graphics	http://www.dgusa.com
PEI	http://www.peimag.com

Copyrighting images

US Copyright office   http://lcweb.loc.gov/copyright
Digital watermarking   http://www.digimarc.com

Freelancing gigs

Guru   http://www.guru.com

Scanning tips

If you ever scan anything that has been process printed like a magazine or postcard, you will find that there is a pattern of dots in the scan. This is called a **moiré pattern** (pronounced more-ay). The pattern comes about by the scanner seeing the dots in the printing. If your scanner has a DESCREEN option, turn this on to fix the problem. Otherwise scan at an angle.

Make as many tonal corrections as possible on the scanning software before you scan the image. The better the quality before Photoshop, the better the result.

If you are scanning an image of 15cm (6 inches) and you want to blow it up to 30cm (12 inches) at 300dpi, scan at 100% and 600 dpi. Resize the image in Photoshop later.

Always scan in the center of your scanner, there is usually a 'sweet spot' in the center and the quality near the edges could be bad because of light leakage.

DV Tips

Get a FireWire card if you can for the fastest uploading speed. If you want to make a still capture, copy 3 or 4 frames to Photoshop and experiment with layer blending modes to get the sharpest image.

B Image File Types

- **Photoshop PSD** This is the primary format for use in Photoshop. This format allows you to save your image with multiple layers (and their styles) intact. PSD also allows for saving of channels, selections, unrendered text and any color index/palette. These files must be converted to another format before use, but .psd is ideal for a work in progress.

- **BMP** The .bmp file extension indicates the Bitmap format. This format is primarily used for Windows-based imaging, as with Windows Paint image editing software. Bitmaps consist of an array of **scanline** rows, each array indicating a series of byte values. Bitmaps come in monochrome, 16 colors, 256 colors, and 16.7 million colors.

- **CompuServe GIF (GIF87a, GIF89a)** This format has a maximum of 256 colors. GIF stands for **Graphics Interchange Format**. Due to the 256 color limit and process of compression, GIF files are (or have been) the format of choice for Internet graphics. Due to this same restrictive limit, it is best to use this format only when dealing with solid colors. Photographs and images with multiple colors are better served in other formats, such as JPEG. The GIF format was designed for online transmission and interchange of raster images independent of hardware or display concerns. **GIF89a** is an update to **GIF87a**, allowing for transparent pixels. This format is popular for web design, as it allows the background image to be seen around odd shaped images such as buttons. When using GIF, it is worth noting that animated .gif support is different than regular .gif support.

- **Photoshop EPS** EPS stands for 'Encapsulated Post-Script'. EPS is used to transfer Postscript art between applications, and is supported by most illustration, graphic and page-layout software. Though EPS does not support layers (see Photoshop PSD), EPS does support Lab, CMYK, Indexed Color, RGB, Bitmap, Duotone, and Grayscale. When saving in EPS format, vector images are first rasterized and the information stored in pixels.

- **DCS (Desktop Color Separations)** A version of EPS that allows for saving color separations of CMYK images. Primarily used to export images containing spot channels. DCS requires a PostScript printing device.

- **JPEG** Stands for 'Joint Photographic Expert Group'. Designed primarily for displaying photographs on the Web. Supports CMYK, RGB, and Grayscale. JPEG retains color information in RGB format. This format is best used on tone-sensitive images. File compression is a result of selectively discarding information from an image.

> *Higher levels of compression result in lower quality images. This information, once discarded, cannot be retrieved.*

- **PCX** Similar to the Bitmap file format, this image type is primarily used on PC based platforms. PCX does not support custom color palettes. However, PCX does support RGB, Grayscale, and Bitmap color modes.

- **Photoshop PDF** Allows creation of images and page layouts viewable with Adobe Acrobat. This allows users without Photoshop to view the document with any version of Acrobat or Acrobat Reader, and on any platform.

> *Although Photoshop can open and recognize both Photoshop PDF and Generic PDF files, you may only save files as Photoshop PDF. When Photoshop opens a Generic PDF file, the file is automatically rasterized and loses editing ability in Acrobat. It supports all standard Photoshop color modes, JPEG and Zip compression, but does not support Bitmaps.*

- **PICT File** Commonly used to transfer images between applications on Mac operating systems. Sometimes used in print, though should not be considered for high-resolution output. PICT Supports RGB images with single alpha channels, Bitmap, Grayscale, and Indexed Color.

- **PICT Resource** This is **Mac only** - a PICT file used by onscreen images: Splash screens and the Scrapbook are common examples of PICT Resource files. You may specify compression and bit depth when saving in PICT Resource format.

- **PIXAR** Designed specifically for use on high-end PIXAR workstations and software, such as those used in Disney Computer Animations. This allows Photoshop to open PIXAR developed 2D/3D images. It supports RGB and Grayscale with single alpha channels.

- **PNG** 'Portable Network Graphics' was developed as a patent-free alternative to GIF. Though they have limited support from browsers, these are fast becoming an alternative of choice for web designers. It supports 24 bit images, offers lossless compression, and offers better transparencies than GIF in that the 'jaggies' are significantly reduced. PNG supports RGB, Grayscale, Indexed Color, and Bitmap-mode images without alpha channels. It also preserves transparencies of RGB and Grayscale images.

- **RAW** This is used for transferring image files between platforms and applications. RAW files are actually lines of code that describe the color information in the image. RAW files support RGB, CMYK, and Grayscale images with single alpha channels. Colors are represented in numbers from 0 to 255, with black=0 & white=255.

- **Scitex CT (Continuous Tone)** Developed for use on high-end Scitex Scanners and computers. It supports CMYK, RGB, and Grayscale, but does not support alpha channels.

- **TARGA** This was designed for systems using TrueVision, Radius, and Media 100 video boards. It's also commonly supported by MS-DOS color applications and supports 16-bit RGB, 32-bit RGB, Grayscale, and Indexed Color Images. However it does not support alpha channels. When saving in RGB, TARGA allows the user to choose pixel depth.

- **TIFF** 'Tagged Image File Format' is the primary format for outputting to film or print. TIFF is a flexible Bitmap image format used or supported by nearly all image-editing, paint, and page layout applications. Most scanners may produce TIFF images. TIFF supports RGB, CMYK, Lab, Indexed Color, and Grayscale images with alpha channels, and Bitmap images without alpha channels. TIFF also supports layers, which will be retained if opened in Photoshop. TIFF files are fully compatible on both Mac and PC formats, and are the file type of choice for print output.

Photoshop Specific File Types

The versatility of Photoshop to create and save presets for later use on other images and projects, has created numerous file types with extensions that may be unfamiliar to new users. Here's a quick list that will hopefully shed light on these mysterious extensions:

.abr	- Brush Set
.aco	- Color Swatch
.act	- Optimized Colors
.acv	- Curve
.ado	- Duotones, Quadtones, Tritones
.asl	- Layer Style Set
.atn	- Action Set
.csh	- Custom Shapes
.grd	- Gradient Set
.iros	- Optimized Output Settings
.irs	- Optimized Settings
.pat	- Pattern Set
.sch	- Contours

C Monitor Calibration

Before we can make changes to any images, we need to be sure that the image on our monitor is a good representation of the scanned content. An uncalibrated monitor is fatal during image correction because the image we are trying to correct may bear no resemblance to the final printed image. Luckily, Adobe has included *Adobe Gamma*, which allows us to calibrate our monitor. It is installed as part of the typical PhotoShop install.

If you are using an LCD flat panel monitor, you should **not** use Adobe Gamma, which is designed for Cathode Ray Tube (CRT) based monitors. Most LCD monitors are less prone to displaying misleading colors in any case (although you need to make sure you are looking straight at the LCD at all times during editing because they do tend to lose contrast if you view them from a large angle).

Some design houses use a hardware-based color correction, in which case you would not use Adobe Gamma because it will be less accurate.

Adobe Gamma will only give you the best possible output for your monitor, (and this may still not be adequate) if your artwork is destined for commercial color printing... one to muse on if you advance on to professional print-based graphic design. A cheap monitor may seem cost effective, but may lead to expensive re-prints in the long run, not to mention irate clients!

Gamma is a separate application and cannot be accessed from Photoshop directly. To access Gamma you need to:

- For a Mac - From the Apple menu, select Control Panels > Adobe Gamma.

- For a PC - Select (starting from the start icon on the taskbar) Start > Settings > Control Panel > Adobe Gamma or (starting from the My Computer icon on the desktop) My Computer > Control Panel > Adobe Gamma. Don't go any further until you have read the information on the next page.

> *A well-calibrated monitor isn't your only problem if accurate reproduction is a concern; the image scanner in a professional commercial print environment is also crucial. For cheaper image scanners that cannot be calibrated, you have no guarantee that the scanned image will have the same color variations as the original printed image. Assuming you have a properly calibrated monitor, you should compare the original printed image against the monitor display and make color/brightness/contrast corrections using the Image > Adjust menu items and not via the monitor brightness/contrast controls (which will take your monitor out of calibration).*

Start the application; making sure that the lighting in your room is at its normal setting. If, like me, you are prone to working all day and all night to meet deadlines, you may want to run Gamma twice; once for natural daylight, and once for artificial lighting. As you will see later, you can also use Gamma to see what a web page will look like on both a PC and Mac irrespective of which one you are actually using, so you might also want to consider creating profiles such as 'Mac Gamma' if you are using a PC, and vice versa.

You will see the following window appear;

Some monitors have digital brightness/contrast controls, and they are changed via a little pop-up window that opens in the center of the screen, which unfortunately is exactly the same place as the Gamma window appears! If your monitor has such a pop-up, move the Gamma window away from the center, because you will be varying contrast/brightness whilst looking at the Gamma window.

Selecting the Step By Step option is probably the easiest version to go for if you are using Gamma for the first time. Select the version and hit Next. Gamma will now prompt you for a profile to start with. Some standard monitors have a default profile, and if you press Load you might be able to recognize your particular monitor, otherwise just hit Next.

Gamma will now ask you to adjust the monitor brightness and contrast controls. The set of squares you will see in the window have been enlarged and exaggerated below right. The calibration is carried out as follows:

1. Set the contrast to maximum (or near maximum if your monitor starts to give an overly washed out picture at the maximum)

2. Adjust the brightness control so that the center gray square is as dark as possible, whilst still being visible from the black frame around it. You must also end up with an outer frame that is still white

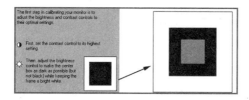

3. Next, Gamma will ask you to select the monitor phosphor type. Some manufacturers specify the monitor phosphor type in the product documentation, but most don't bother unless the monitor is from their 'Pro' range. If you can't locate the required data, accept Gamma's guess.

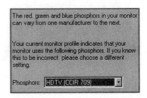

4. The next step will look at how your monitor displays mid tones. The first thing is to find the current gamma value.

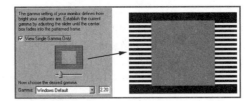

The slider alters the color of the central square. The object is to increase the slider value until the lines just become the same color as the square, at which point the box will appear to fade into the lines. The blown up image above right is not quite there yet; the square is still darker than the lines. Some monitors tend to tint everything (usually towards magenta or cyan), and if this is the case, you can work on the red, blue and green components separately by unchecking View Single Gamma Only. The diagram below shows three sets of square/sliders, and although they look like different shades of gray in the book, they are actually the single gray square (above) but with a strong red, green and blue tint.

5. Once you have done this successfully, you can then select a desired Gamma, which will be either Windows Default or Mac Default.

The final thing you need to do is set the white point of your monitor. To create white requires the monitor to force the phosphor dots affected to display their maximum values of red, green and blue. Usually though, the monitor is slightly out, giving you a tinted white. The default, 6500K is a bright white corresponding to a very bright white that would be seen if, for example you looked at a piece of paper on a bright day.

6. To check whether the default is correct, hit Measure.

> For best results, eliminate all ambient light before proceeding.
>
> Your screen will go black and you will be presented with 3 squares.
>
> Choose the most neutral gray square on the screen. Clicking on the left or the right square will reset the squares to be cooler or warmer.
>
> Clicking on the center square or pressing the Enter key will commit your choice.
>
> Use the Esc key to cancel the operation and return to this step.

You will see the instructions given above. Eliminate all ambient light means close the curtains if you are in daylight, or turn off the lighting if it is dark.

7. You will then be presented with a black screen with three squares, two of which will be slightly tinted (usually towards cyan or magenta), and one which will be a neutral (or uncolored) gray. In modern monitors, the white point is fairly accurate, and you should see very slight tinting, which is why the program asks you to get rid of ambient lighting. If the neutral gray is not the center square, the white point is not neutral white, and you need to click on the square that is most neutral. This will continue until the square you select is the central one.

8. Finally, Gamma allows you to save your profile. This is recommended because it will give you a good starting point for the next time you calibrate. Adobe recommend that you perform calibration once a month because your monitor display tends to age and change over time, but you may prefer to do it only when you are creating content that is intended for print.

Index

The index is arranged hierarchically, in alphabetical order, with symbols preceding the letter A. Many second-level entries also occur as first-level entries. This is to ensure that users will find the information they require however they choose to search for it.

DESIGNER TO DESIGNER™

The New Masters Series – Advanced – *Showing it*

Where can you find out what inspires the top designers? Where can you learn the secrets of their design techniques? New Masters is the ultimate showcase for graphics pioneers from around the world, where they write about what influences their design and teach the cutting-edge effects that have made them famous.

The Studio Series – Intermediate – *Doing it*

The essence of the studio is the collective – a gathering of independent designers who try out ideas and explore techniques in finer detail. Each book in the studio series assumes that the reader has learned the fundamentals of the topic area. They want to grow their skills with particular tools to a higher level, while at the same time absorbing the hard-won creative experience of a group of design experts.

The Foundation Series – Starting out – *Learning it*

Every web designer benefits from a strong foundation to firmly establish their understanding of a new technology or tool. The friends of ED foundation series deconstructs a subject into step by step lessons – stand alone design recipes that build together into a complete model project. Practical, intuitive – a must-have resource.

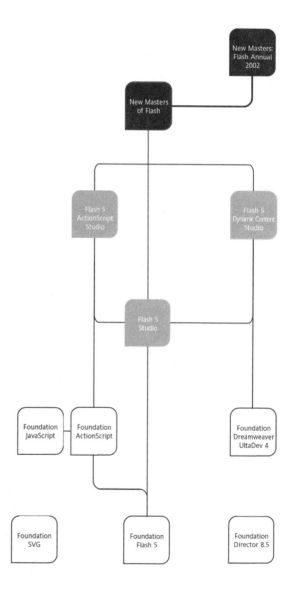

freshfroot
motion web mindfood

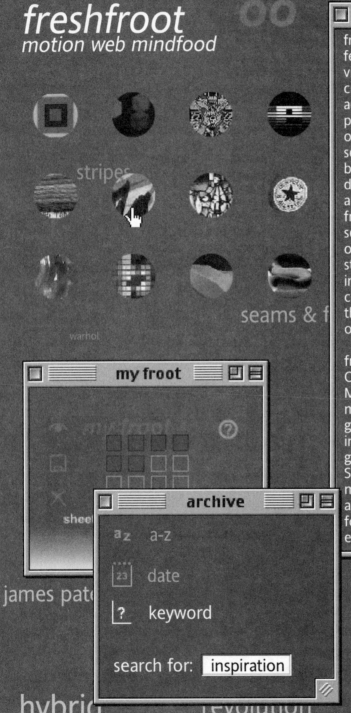

stripes

seams & f

warhol

seven day itch

freshfroot is where friends of ED fertilise the designer mind. It's a visual search engine, a daily creative resource and a hard-to-kick addiction. Everyday the froot pickers, along with a select band of celebrity guest editors, search through the web's good, bad and ugly to bring you the diamonds – categorised, critiqued and instantly searchable. freshfroot rejects the usual search engine criteria in favour of daily themes that pull together stylistically similar works and images to provide the rock solid creative resource to complement the technical resource on offer in our books.

freshfroot is the place where Mike Cina, James Paterson, Golan Levin, Mumbleboy, Brendan Dawes and many other new and future masters go to share their inspirations and be inspired. It's the place everyone goes when they need fresh ideas fast. Submit your own found or created masterpieces, spout your opinions and share ideas in the discussion forum. Get involved, be inspired and escape the mediocre.

my froot

my froot

sheet

archive

a-z   a-z

23   date

?   keyword

search for: **inspiration**

james pate

forward

urban

playground

hybrid   revolution   brendan dawes

freshfroot.com
daily

Be inspired.

freshfroot#1 created by ross mawds
simian superstar, new master, friend and froot editor. we love you

friendsof

DESIGNER TO DESIGNER™

NEW MASTERS